THE OFFICIAL
MATCHDAY PROGRAMME BOOK

THE OFFICIAL
MATCHDAY PROGRAMME BOOK

Good **afternoon** and welcome to **Goodison** for today's game...

THE OFFICIAL
MATCHDAY PROGRAMME BOOK

Copyright © Everton Football Club

Written & Compiled by James Cleary
Cover by Michael Perry

Published by Trinity Mirror Sport Media
Managing Director: Ken Rogers
Senior Editor: Steve Hanrahan
Editor: Paul Dove
Senior Art Editor: Rick Cooke

Senior Sub-editor: Roy Gilfoyle
Sub-editor: Alan Jewell
Design: Colin Harrison
Senior Marketing Executive: Claire Brown
Senior Book Sales Executive: Karen Cadman

Published in hardback in Great Britain in 2013.
Published and produced by: Trinity Mirror Sport Media,
PO Box 48, Old Hall Street, Liverpool L69 3EB.
Images: Trinity Mirror, PA pictures, Gavin Buckland

ISBN: 9781908695567

Printed and bound by CPI Group (UK) Ltd, Croydon, CR0 4YY

Everton

THE OFFICIAL MATCHDAY PROGRAMME BOOK

CONTENTS

INTRODUCTION...8

1878-1960........10

1960-1970........28

1970-1980........62

1980-1990........114

1990-2000.....166

2000-2013......210

STOP PRESS
248-255

"THE VALUE OF EVERTON PROGRAMMES CANNOT BE MEASURED IN MONEY. THEY ARE PRICELESS, TANGIBLE REMINDERS OF MOMENTS IN TIME"

Football has gone through a series of transformational changes during 125 years as the most popular competitive sport in England. However, throughout the generations, a few traditions have endured.

One of them is the match programme. The modern, slick, glossy product is unrecognisable from the single-page sheets distributed at the end of the 19th century, but it is firmly rooted in the past.

They remain part of the matchday ritual and highly collectable, even though we now live in a 24-hour, multi-media digital age, which provides instant access to an incalculable, constantly updating morass of reports, rumour, features, facts, opinion and statistics.

This book is a fascinating insight into the evolution of the Everton programme, and acts as a social as well as sporting history lesson. For many fans, they form part of an alliterative trio of essentials that complete their going-to-the-game routine: a pie, a pint and a programme.

Once hoarded at home, they become treasured souvenirs of memorable matches and, as the seasons go by, collections can grow from the tens to the hundreds and, for some, even into the thousands.

You don't have to be an obsessive to love programmes, though. No matter how humdrum the game may appear, certain examples can have a special meaning – your first match, a childhood birthday treat, or a match attended with a now departed relative.

As this publication will demonstrate, it's easy to be drawn in while flicking through programmes, where heroes of yesteryear remain eternally young and the adverts and fashions provide a flavour of the time.

You are reminded of long-forgotten facts among the entertaining profiles, random features and characters that helped make up the programme. They also provide an insight into the issues of the time and how football was perceived nationally.

The shared interest in Everton meant pen-pals could be established via the letters page, a forum that was an early example of social media in action. Programmes grew in popularity from the 1950s and '60s as clubs produced more original content and gradually realised the value to them of what was then the only means of communicating directly with their supporters.

Before formal pre-match press conferences, which are reported breathlessly and instantly in the Premier League era, this was the only outlet where you could be sure of hearing directly from the manager, as well as reading about the home lives, interests, likes and dislikes of your favourite players.

In decades past the adverts would generally feature local businesses, promoting ales and car sales, while now they are more likely to promote multi-national corporations.

As well as providing sentimental meaning, programmes can also be big business, with rare editions or those from historical occasions changing hands for significant sums.

Typing 'football programmes' into the search function of eBay on the day this piece was written threw up 299,545 results. Narrowing the search to 'Everton football programmes' still led to 8,737 hits. The most expensive item was a complete collection of Everton programmes covering 40 years. Bids started at £2,000. An edition from a friendly against a Cork Select XI in May 1948 had a reserve price of £299.99. The programme for a home fixture with West Brom in 1911/12 (which also doubled as a publication for Liverpool Reserves v Bury) could be purchased for £159.

Ultimately, though, for most, the value of Everton programmes cannot be measured in money. They are priceless, tangible reminders of moments in time, viewed through the prism of the boys in blue.

Alan Jewell,
Everton programme co-editor 2006-2009

A programme can be a reminder of a golden moment of your match-going days

Early Days

Early programmes were basic publications
that developed as the club developed,
and where adverts could be just as
entertaining as the articles

The early incarnation of the match 'magazine' was a simple affair,
shared with neighbours Liverpool from the early years of the 20th
century. Eventually known as the 'Everton & Liverpool Official Football
Programme', the glorified pamphlet was mainly utilised to advertise
the wares of businesses in the city.

Everton would not have their own official club programme until the
1935/36 season, the clubs going their separate ways to fulfil the needs
of their own fans.

One of the club directors was tasked with producing the publication, with
the first inside page, 'Evertonia', updating fans on recent results and
general goings on around the club.

The opposition were covered by a couple of pages, latter editions even
giving rise to a team photograph. Regular match photography would not
be used until the late 1960s.

One other notable feature would be the centre spread team listings,
the 'formations' being surrounded by advertising. The back page would
usually include local advertising, plus a fixture list.

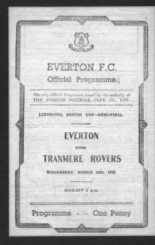

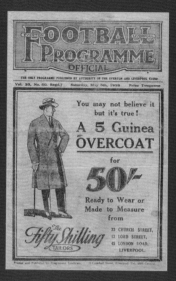

MUNRO & FORD, 69, GREAT CHARLOTTE STREET.

Price 1d.

EVERTON
v.
CHURCH,

ON EVERTON GROUND, ANFIELD.

KICK OFF, 4 P.M.

ON SATURDAY, APRIL 30th, 1887.

EVERTON TEAM.

Umpire.—Mr. J. RICHARDS.

Referee.—

Goal:
Jolliffe.

Right Back: Left Back:

MATTHEWS'
FOOTBALL BOOTS

Sole Agent—
FRANK BRETELL,
SANDON HOTEL.

Cheapest and most durable Boots in the district. Lined with Leather throughout. Extra strong Toe, with wide Waist. Worn by Members of the Everton and Stanley.

Price, 8/6; Boys' Size, 6/11.

Selected covers from up to 1960. Clockwise from above: v Church, 1886/87; v Arsenal, 1927/28; v Tottenham Hotspur (FA Cup), 1949/50; v Fulham, 1952/53; v Portsmouth, 1955/56; v Aston Villa (FA Cup), 1958/59; v Leeds United, 1959/60; v Luton Town, 1956/57; v Red Star Belgrade (friendly), 1957/58; v Aston Villa, 1947/48; v Grimsby Town, 1945/46; programme topper, 1904/05; v Blackpool, 1938/39

The Everton and Liverpool Official Football Programme.

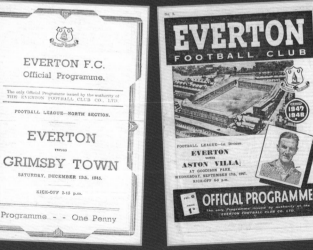

EVERTON F.C.
Official Programme.

The only Official Programme issued by the authority of THE EVERTON FOOTBALL CLUB CO., LTD.

FOOTBALL LEAGUE—NORTH SECTION.

EVERTON
versus
GRIMSBY TOWN

SATURDAY, DECEMBER 15th, 1945.

KICK-OFF 2-15 p.m.

Programme - - One Penny

EVERTON
FOOTBALL CLUB

FOOTBALL LEAGUE—1st Division

EVERTON
versus
ASTON VILLA
AT GOODISON PARK.
WEDNESDAY, SEPTEMBER 17th, 1947.
KICK-OFF 6-0 p.m.

OFFICIAL PROGRAMME
The only Programme issued by authority of the EVERTON FOOTBALL CLUB CO. LTD.

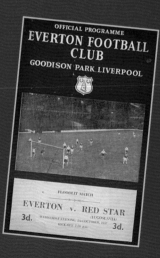

OFFICIAL PROGRAMME
EVERTON FOOTBALL CLUB
GOODISON PARK, LIVERPOOL

FLOODLIT MATCH

EVERTON v. RED STAR
(JUGOSLAVIA)
WEDNESDAY EVENING, 23rd OCTOBER, 1957
KICK-OFF 7.30 p.m.

3d.   3d.

Make your next HOLIDAY FIXTURE
a trip to

HOLIDAY ISLAND

Where promenades are full of fun and gaiety, but there are also miles of unspoiled rocky coast and sandy bays. Where there is every facility for golfing, fishing, boating, motoring, cycling, swimming, theatres, dancing—everything to make your holiday complete — and only a few hours by rail/sea or air.

ISLE ⊕F MAN

FREE GUIDE sent on request for 2½d. postage—
S. R. BOND, Tourist Board, Isle of Man.

FIXTURES—1956.

FOOTBALL LEAGUE

1956

Jan. 7—Bristol City (3rd Round) Home
  ,, 14—Charlton Athletic ....Home
  ,, 21—Tottenham Hotspur ....Away
  ,, 28—

Feb. 4—Portsmouth ....Home
  ,, 11—Newcastle United ....Home
  ,, 18—Arsenal ....Away
  ,, 25—Bolton Wanderers ....Home

Mar. 3—Manchester City ....Away
  ,, 10—Sunderland ....Home
  ,, 17—Huddersfield Town ....Away
  ,, 24—Cardiff City ....Home
  ,, 30—Sheffield United ....Home
  ,, 31—Aston Villa ....Away

Apr. 2—Sheffield United ....Away
  ,, 7—Wolverhampton W. ....Home
  ,, 14—Chelsea ....Away
  ,, 21—Blackpool ....Home

CENTRAL LEAGUE

1956

Jan. 7—
  ,, 14—Bury ....Away
  ,, 21—Barnsley ....Home
  ,, 28—

Feb. 4—Liverpool ....Away
  ,, 11—West Bromwich Alb. .....Away
  ,, 18—Stoke City ....Home
  ,, 25—Aston Villa ....Away

Mar. 3—Wolverhampton W. .....Home
  ,, 10—Manchester City ....Away
  ,, 17—Sheffield Wednesday .....Home
  ,, 24—Huddersfield Town ....Away
  ,, 30—Sheffield United ....Away
  ,, 31—Blackburn Rovers ....Home

Apr. 2—Sheffield United ....Home
  ,, 7—Blackpool ....Away
  ,, 14—Bolton Wanderers ....Home
  ,, 21—Chesterfield ....Away
  ,, 28—Manchester United ....Away

W. Jones & Co. Ltd., 7-11 Hunter Street, Liverpool, 3.

v Charlton Athletic, 1955/56 – Includes Isle of Man 'Holiday Fixture'

NEXT MATCH HERE.

FOOTBALL LEAGUE.

Everton v. Blackburn Rov.

SATURDAY, JAN. 4th, 1947.   Kick-off 2-30 p.m.

Usual Admission Prices.

THE ATHLETIC EVENT OF THE SEASON

WHIT MONDAY, MAY 26th, 1947, 1—9 p.m.
at the
SPORTS STADIUM, ELLESMERE
(On Main Crewe to Oswestry G.W.R. Line)
Athletics under M.C.A.A. Permit and Rules.   Cycling under N.C.U. Permit and
Rules.   Open Horse Jumping Competition under B.S.J.A. Rules.   Mounted
Gymkhana.   Sensational and continuous Variety Arena Programme.   Fun Fair, and
many Side Attractions.

There is only one place where you can possibly go on Whit Monday.
Hon. Secretary: E. W. ATKINS, The Savings Bank Buildings, Ellesmere. (Tel. 138).

EVERTONIA (continued).

COUPONS.
We are indebted to Harry Stott, N. S. Campbell, L. J. Westhead, James
Briggs, and many others who do not desire their names mentioned, for their
great help. For the time being we must respect their desires, and put aside
our Motto in favour of theirs. They like the idea of our latest, which suggests
that by any subscription, "You can keep the kit fit."

AUTOGRAPH.
The irrepressible "Wally." Signed from West Bromwich Albion in
1938/39 Season, and played in many games that year when we won the League
Championship. Together with "Stevie" were known as the Goodison Twins.

DOROTHY'S CAFE   ::   ::   6, COUNTY ROAD

Near the Ground

For "local" meals, before and after the game.

Above, left to right: v Aston Villa, 1946/47; v Aston Villa, FA Cup, 1958/59

EVERTON
(Blue Jerseys)
Right   DUNLOP (1)   Left
PARKER (2)   JONES (3)
GABRIEL (4)   LABONE (5)   MEAGAN (6)
LILL (7)   COLLINS (8)   VERNON (10)   RING (11)
HARRIS, J. (9)

Referee:
Mr. C. H. Sant
(Crewe)

Linesmen:
Messrs. H. Osliffe (Yellow Flag)
and I. Sleddon (Red Flag)

McCOLE (9)
MEEK (11)   CAMERON (10)   REVIE (8)   FRANCIS (7)
GOODWIN (6)   CHARLTON (5)   GIBSON (4)
CALDWELL (3)   ASHALL (2)
BURGIN (1)
Left   (Blue and Gold Jerseys)   Right
LEEDS UTD.

Centre spread v Leeds United, 1959/60

Dorothy's Cafe :—: 6 County Road

Near the Ground

For " local " meals, before and after the game.

1946-50

Prominent post-War programme advertising included supporters being enticed to consume 'local' meals at Dorothy's Cafe on nearby County Road; would punters be tempted by a potential after-match visit to Princess Super Cinema in Kirkdale? Barker & Dobson's latest sweet sensations, cameo chocolates regal fruit drops; there was Afrikander tobacco, for the older crowd ('It's cheaper to smoke a pipe!' – the enticing tagline); an October 1946 fixture against Albion Rovers ('at present heading the Scottish League Division "B"'); Roger's Taxis 'for home and away games'; Mayfair on Lime Street ('You'll be served quickly and courteously with delicious food in very pleasant surroundings').

AFTER THE MATCH VISIT THE
PRINCESS
SUPER CINEMA, KIRKDALE.   Tel.: Bootle 1032

Matinee Daily at 2-15.   Evening continuous from 6-15
Sunday continuous from 5 p.m.

ST. EDWARDS' (BOYS) SILVER PRIZE BAND.
Conductor: A. Polet.

HE SAVED THE GAME
WHAT COULD BE GRANDER
THAN VICTORS CROWN
OF
AFRIKANDER

**BARKER & DOBSON'S
CAMEO CHOCOLATES
REGAL FRUIT DROPS**

FOOTBALL NEWS and FORECASTS by a WINNING TEAM
in
SPORTING RECORD
Every Wednesday   Price 3d.

MUSICAL SELECTIONS BY
ST. EDWARDS' (BOYS) SILVER PRIZE BAND.
Conductor: A. Polet.

THE WINNER!

pipeful of
3/4½ PER OZ **AFRIKANDER**
IT'S CHEAPER TO SMOKE A PIPE!

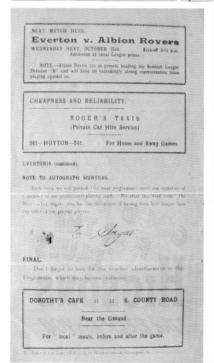

NEXT MATCH HERE.
Everton v. Albion Rovers
WEDNESDAY NEXT, OCTOBER 23rd.   Kick-off 3-15 p.m.
Admission at usual League prices.

NOTE — Albion Rovers are at present heading the Scottish League Division "B" and will have an exceedingly strong representative team playing against us.

CHEAPNESS AND RELIABILITY.

ROGER'S TAXIS
(Private Car Hire Service)

541—HUYTON—541.   For Home and Away Games.

EVERTONIA (continued).

NOTE TO AUTOGRAPH HUNTERS.

FINAL.

DOROTHY'S CAFE :: :: 6, COUNTY ROAD

Near the Ground

For " local " meals, before and after the game.

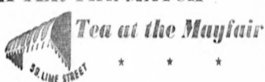

AFTER THE MATCH
Tea at the Mayfair
59 LIME STREET
*   *   *

Before the match, of course, Lunch at the Mayfair
You'll be served quickly and courteously with
delicious food in very pleasant surroundings.

MAYFAIR

59 LIME STREET · LIVERPOOL

A CITY CATERERS RESTAURANT

All refreshment bars on this ground are run by
THE LIVERPOOL CITY CATERERS LIMITED · 4-12, MARYBONE · LIVERPOOL 3

When
the final
whistle blows...

you'll be ready for that high tea at the MAYFAIR Restaurant, 59 Lime Street. (Why not have lunch there before the match?) In the meantime there are 17 Refreshment Bars on this ground where you can get snacks and a cuppa or a soft drink. All are run by the

CITY CATERERS

THE LIVERPOOL CITY CATERERS LTD · MARYBONE · LIVERPOOL

"And set his heart upon the goal, not on the prize"
(version)

·SHOUT·
YOURSELF
HOARSE

if you wish — and you will quickly recover at one of the 17 refreshment bars on this ground, where you can get a cuppa or a soft drink and a snack provided by the

CITY CATERERS
who run all the refreshment bars here.
THE LIVERPOOL CITY CATERERS LTD., MARYBONE, LIVERPOOL

You can't beat BENT'S! The FAVOURITE ALE!

Another SURE winner is BENTS STONE STOUT

BENTS · BREWERS · LIVERPOOL & STONE

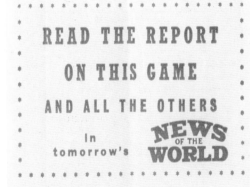

READ THE REPORT
ON THIS GAME
AND ALL THE OTHERS
in tomorrow's NEWS OF THE WORLD

Hand rollers...
you can't
beat it...

STILL THE
BEST VALUE!

RINGER'S A1 LIGHT TOBACCO

DART IN for a —

Higson's Brown Ale

Double Top

1950-60

The 1950s brought a more modern era for advertising. Clockwise from top: City Caterers/Mayfair Restaurant rebranding; City Caterers again - why not rest your vocal chords at a refreshment bar in the ground?; Bent's - The Favourite Ale, shirt-sponsored goalkeeper benefiting from said product; Ringer's A1 Light Tobacco - Still the best value!; Higson's Double Top, complete with mysterious face; News Of The World, match reports as standard; Higson's Double Top, with a goalkeeper more interested in boozing than playing!

both premier honours, tripped up badly since Everton wrested the lead during the sequence of cup tie tussles in which the Yorkshire team were concerned, and as can readily be imagined it was too much to expect, that so hard worked a side could continue on a successful career. Their two defeats during the week placed the championship safely in Everton's grasp but to both organisations every credit is due for the gallant manner on which they have acquitted themselves during strenuous times.

If ever there was a Football Season that brought " ups and downs " for clubs, the present stands pre-eminent. If one looks back just a few months, the prospects for the championship were extremely bright. In fact the championship stakes seemed a possibility for them. Then just about Easter, the gloom over the club was such, that fears for their ultimate safety were being freely expressed. They changed into joy—exuberant joy—

when points were gained at the expense of the great and brilliant Yorkshire side, and fears were once again allayed. All was considered plain and safe sailing to the end. Yet we all know how desperately in earnest all the clubs in the lower section of the table have been, and how last Saturday, the crowd turned out at Anfield with the fore-knowledge that the locals had to make their supreme effort.

"Tis strange. Last season the Blues were struggling and striving against perverse fate which seemed to have marked them as doomed. They just escaped at the eleventh hour and Liverpool have now passed through such another anxious experience. To them sincere congratulations are offered. They overcame all difficulties by a supreme endeavour which was recognised as that of men who refused to surrender. They kept the flag flying and next season will still have the opportunity of appearing in the best class.

EVERTON FOOTBALL CLUB COMPANY LTD.

SEASON 1927-28

Directors:

W. C. CUFF, Esq. (Chairman), E. GREEN, Esq. (Vice-Chairman),
A. R. WADE, Esq.   H. BANKS, Esq.   JOHN SHARP, Esq.,
A. COFFEY, Esq.   W. C. GIBBONS, Esq.   Dr. CECIL S. BAXTER.
                        W. J. SAWYER, Esq.

Secretary - THOS. H. McINTOSH.

EDITOR'S NOTE BOOK.

TWELVE months ago, Everton were in the depths, and now, we hail them as the proud leaders of the Premier League, the most exciting competition in the realms of football. When we come to consider in detail the performances of the team this season, we cannot but admit to a feeling of astonishment mingled with admiration at their notable success. With three exceptions, the team is the same that last campaign, and in addition, the recovery from the dreary January and February record must be taken into account. Beaten at Leicester on March 17th by the only goal scored, the Goodison players have kept their record intact and have annexed fourteen points out of a possible sixteen since that date, Derby County and Bury checking the run in drawn games at Goodison. Consistency has been the characteristic. Dean has, of course, been a grand leader among forwards that have been brilliant at times and erratic at others, but taking the team all through, they have not only proved themselves an entertaining, but an ideal League Championship side. Huddersfield Town, who not so long ago were greatly fancied for

Programme editorial and 'Blue Jottings' v Arsenal, 1927/28 – (Above) Everton, worthy leaders of the 'Premier League, the most exciting competition in the realms of football'. Note no reference to the possibilty of Dixie Dean overhauling the goalscoring feats of George Camsell for the highest number of goals scored in a season in the top four English leagues; opposite page – Observations from the previous game at Burnley, Dean's goalscoring exploits, plus the tour to Switzerland

THE EDINBURGH

LORD STREET
'Phone Bank 4706

LUNCHEONS	- - - - - - -	1/-, 1/6, 2/6
TEAS	- - - - - - -	1/-, 1/3, 2/6
DINNERS	- - - - - - -	from 3/6

Also Service a la Carte.
J. W. SMART'S ORCHESTRA plays daily . . . .
12-30 to 2 p.m.; 4-15 to 7-15 p.m.; 8-15 to 9-45 p.m.
DANCE TEAS 1/6.   EVENING DANCES 1/6 (Saturday 2/6).

EVERTON—CENTRAL LEAGUE FIXTURES.

Date 1927.	Name of Club	Where Played	F	A	Pts.	Date 1928.	Name of Club	Where Played	F	A	Pts.
Aug. 27.—	Sheffield W.	A	1	3	0	Jan. 2.—	Blackpool	H	2	2	1
Sept. 3.—	Birmingham	H	4	2	2	,, 3.—	Bolton W.	A	1	3	0
,, 5.—	Blackpool	A	0	4	0	,, 7.—	Birmingham	A	0	2	0
,, 10.—	Stoke City	A	1	6	0	,, 21.—	Stoke City	H	2	2	1
,, 17.—	West Brom. A.	H	4	1	2	,, 28.—	West Brom. A.	A	1	2	0
,, 24.—	Huddersfield T.	A	3	1	2	Feb. 4.—	Huddersfield T.	H	2	4	0
Oct. 1.—	Oldham Ath.	H	7	3	2	,, 18.—	Manchester U.	H	2	2	1
,, 8.—	Manchester U.	A	1	2	0	,, 21.—	Oldham A.	A	4	3	2
,, 15.—						,, 29.—	Bradford City	A	2	2	1
,, 22.—	Preston N.E.	A	2	4	0	Mar. 3.—	Preston N.E.	H	3	1	2
,, 29.—	Burnley	H	11	0	2	,, 10.—	Burnley	A	0	0	1
Nov. 5.—	Bury	A	1	1	1	,, 14.—	Liverpool	H	6	2	2
,, 12.—	Sheffield U.	H	4	1	2	,, 17.—	Bury	H	0	0	1
,, 19.—	Aston Villa	A	2	4	0	,, 24.—	Sheffield U.	A	3	3	1
,, 26.—	W'hampton W.	H	1	4	0	,, 31.—	Aston Villa	H	2	3	0
Dec. 3.—	Derby C.	A	3	0	2	Apr. 6.—	Blackburn R.	A	6	0	2
,, 10.—	Leeds U.	H	3	2	2	,, 7.—	W'hampton W.	A	1	2	0
,, 24.—	Manchester C.	H	4	5	0	,, 9.—	Blackburn R.	H	4	4	1
,, 26.—						,, 14.—	Derby C.	H	3	1	2
,, 27.—	Bolton W.	H	1	2	0	,, 21.—	Leeds U.	A	2	2	1
,, 31.—	Sheffield W.	H	2	0	2	,, 23.—	Liverpool	A	2	1	2
						,, 28.—	Bradford C.	H	5	1	2
						May 5.—	Manchester C.	A			

EVERTON JOTTINGS.
By "BLUE MANTLE."

The Blues wound up a brilliant series of away victories by defeating Burnley at Turf Moor, this being their third consecutive success on their opponents' territory. Seeing that the home team were anxious to improve their position, the triumph of our players was all the more meritorious. There was no suggestion of end of the season football in this game and the occasion served for Dean to bring his toll of goals to within two of Camsell's Second Division record of last season. Again our club has garnered more points from away matches than any other organisation in their class. Twenty-three points from twenty-one away games is a highly meritorious performance, a feat equalled only by Leeds United who will be on view again at Goodison Park next season. After the contest to-day the team will make ready for their tour in Switzerland, where it goes without saying, they will have a great reception. Games will be played at Basle (May 12th), Berne (13th), Geneva (17th), and Zurich (20th). Dean will take part in representative games against France in Paris (17th), and against Belgium in Antwerp (19th), the players returning from their tour on May 23rd.

CHARLTON ATHLETIC F.C. — 1956

OUR VISITORS.

The Arsenal provide the attraction in the closing game of the season at Goodison Park and as Everton know their position there is bound to be a stern tussle for points. Since the Londoners were re-elected to the premier division immediately following upon the war period, they have fared uncommonly well from their visits to Walton. In the season of 1919-20 they won by the odd goal in live and on their next visit prevailed by four goals to two. Their next appearance resulted in a division of honours, but in the two following seasons results ran favourably to Everton by 1-0 and 3-1. Then came two successes by the Arsenal with scores of 1-2, to be defeated last season by 3-1. Thus the High-bury club have obtained nine points out of the last sixteen at stake on to-day's enclosure; on the other hand Everton have enjoyed a better record at Highbury than at home.

The clubs have a season in London in Le warfare, and the Blue the narrow margin of seal this campaign somewhat mixed exper opened strongly after do first game at home again for quite a lengthy peri a position among the first in the chart. A series of January and February club in the lower half, t terly they have specialise drawn games. The clu cured the double event a pense of Liverpool and Bu have won at Portsmouth, have divided the points at Birmingham, West Ham, Cardiff, Middlesbrough and castle. The Arsenal sha points with Wednesday at H during the week, but can s hope to further improve their p this afternoon.

Aston Villa Pen P

NIGEL SIMS (Goalkeeper).—Born in Derbyshire stones, but is agile and quick to grasp a situation. His part in Villa's F.A. Cup success in 1957. Sims learned Soccer, and understudied Bert Williams of Wolves befor March, 1956. A safe handler of the ball, Sims has a pa

STAN LYNN (Right-back).—A part-time professiona before going to Villa Park in 1950, Lynn has improved s one of the soundest backs playing. Good positioning and a hard man to beat, and he is also a fine kicker of a dead b king".

PETE ALDIS (Left-back).—A product of local juni Birmingham-born player, and has been at Villa Park since chance two years later, but took some time to establish a because of injury. Good on either flank, he has developed defender, and his partnership with Lynn is well-founded and

JOHNNY DIXON (Inside-forward).—Popular Johnny p since 1944 and gained reward for his loyalty when he received the Queen in May 1957. He was at inside-left then and the bra line. He also excels in the role of deep-lying centre-forward, constructive ability Dixon has a sharp eye for a goal and the abili Was Villa's top scorer for several seasons.

JIMMY DUGDALE (Centre-half).—Liverpool-born Dugdale Cup-winner's medals, one gained with West Bromwich Albion in with Villa in 1957. Villa paid a five-figure fee for him in February the club and Dugdale have every cause to feel satisfied.

VIC CROWE (Right-half).—A Welshman who has lived in the his boyhood days. He joined Villa in 1952. Made many appearances Team either as a right- or left-half before he eventually made the right his own half-way through last Season.

WILLIAM MYERSCOUGH (Outside or Inside-forward).— Bolton-born, went to Villa from Walsall in 1955, and played at centre Wembley in the Cup-winning side of 1957. Bill is a clever and cool c forward with a penchant for centering a particularly good ball, and he can well, be it with either foot or head.

JACK SEWELL (Inside-right or Centre-forward).—Sheffield Wednes a record fee of £34,500 to Notts. County for Sewell in 1951, and four years went to Villa Park. A hard-working inside-forward who learned much a craft from Tommy Lawton when with Notts. County, Sewell possesses a ha and often acts as a "double spearhead" in the attack.

GERRY HITCHENS (Inside or Centre-forward).—Gerry made a great tion in Midland Junior football before joining Cardiff City for whom he played fine games before joining Aston Villa in December 1957. He is a fast and brain player and is a dangerous man whenever in the vicinity of the opposing goal, fo has a great shot in either boot and usually knows where to place the ball.

RON WYLIE (Inside-forward).—A scheming and elusive inside-forward who County. Joined Villa last November from No. makes opportunities for his comrades. Though of slight build, this young Scot is s the tough variety and good to watch.

PETER McPARLAND (Outside-left).—This Irish international winger, whom Villa secured from Dundalk in 1952 was the key opportunist of their Cup attack in Season 1956-57, and it was fitting that he should score their two goals in the Final. Tall and speedy, McParland is hard to hold when in full cry down his wing, and he is adept at stealing into the middle to meet centres from the opposite flank. He is particularly adept at scoring with his head and also possesses a good shot.

LESLIE SMITH (Outside-right).—Not to be confused with Villa's well known Outside-left of the same name. Leslie went to Villa Park from Wolverhampton Wanderers in February 1956 and has given yeoman service to the Club as its regular right winger ever since. He is a fast and clever player who knows the quickest way to goal and has a goodly number of goals to his credit.

EVERTON FOOTBALL CLUB CO. LTD

Chairman: F. MICKLESFIELD
Vice-Chairman: J. C. SHARP
N. W. COFFEY C. E. BALMFORTH
R. E. SEARLE J. TAYLOR R. A. JOYNSON E. HOLLAND HUGHES J. MOORES
Secretary: W. DICKINSON
Manager: J. J. CAREY

EVERTONIA

Very few people would have thought at the beginning of the season that last home league game would mean so much in the winning or losing to both U United, our visitors to-day, or ourselves. It is really looking as though the va problems at the foot of the Division I table may not be sorted out until almo last gasp of the season in a melodramatic finale. There are so many clubs in this season and the final fixtures are so tangled and there are so many ifs and that it would be a brave man who would predict, with any certainty, who goes or stays up.

When one thinks of Leeds United, the name of John Charles is autom coupled with the Yorkshire club. It was with United that he is to-day. First as a centre ha his star matured into the top class performer that earned him the nickname of 'the gentle giant' (on few press-inspired names which fits his bearer) and later as a centre forward spread everywhere he travelled in Great Britain. United, relegated in 1946-4 in company with Brentford, would have found the promotion hurdle vas difficult, if not completely impossible without the valuable goals (30) scored b from centre forward. That was in 1955-56 season, and the following term he on his scoring performances by banging in 38 goals, and being the inspir very creditable performance by Leeds United in finishing eighth in the Firs table.

It is rather surprising to note that United club (the present organisati is no more than 40 years old. Formed in 1920 and elected almost immedia Second Division of the Football League, the new body took the place at B of the old Leeds City club which was eventually forced to give up the existence in 1919. Leeds at that time was very much a rugby-minded cit clubs of repute playing the game. United did very well to finish fourteenth that first trial season. They have been something of a shuttlecock of a s first early days, particularly between the years 1920 and 1938. We foll some pen pictures of the Leeds United players from which the side w today:

LEEDS UNITED PEN PICTURES

E. BURGIN (Goalkeeper).—Transferred from Doncaster Rovers, March, 1958. Formerly with Sheffield United. England 'B' International.

R. WOOD (Goalkeeper).—Transferred from Clitheroe, May 6th, 1952. Born Wallasey.

J. ASHALL (Right-back).—Born Temple Norman-ton, Derbyshire, and graduated through the Northern Intermediate, Yorkshire and Central Leagues.

T. CALDWELL (Left-back).—Transferred from Huddersfield Town, Is a Youth International.

E. GOODWIN (Wing-half).—Transferred from Manchester United in March this year. Has been down well with the United's first team and has settled in a regular in United's first team.

J. CHARLTON (Centre-half).—Born Ashington. Signed Professional forms May, 1952, after graduating through the Junior teams.

A. GIBSON (Wing-half).—Born in Girvan and secured in 1951 from Coylston Juniors. Graduated through the Junior teams.

G. FRANCIS (Outside-right).—Signed Professional forms in July, 1957. Born Johannesburg. Played with City and Suburban, Johannesburg. Played at Goodison last Saturday for Utd. Reserves.

W. BREMNER (Inside- or Outs Professional forms on 11th Secured from Gowanhill Junio through our Juniors. Scottish tional. Born Stirling, Scotland

R. CAMERON (Inside-right). Queens Park Rangers, July Schoolboy and Juvenile Inter Greenock, Scotland.

J. McCOLE (Inside-right). Bradford C. in September 17th Falkirk. Scottish Juvenile.

D. REVIE (Inside-right). Sunderland November 1956 Manchester City, Hull Cit S'k England International C Runners-up medals. C 1955-56. Born at Middlesb

W. CUSH (Inside-forward ferred from Glenavon Nov Lurgan. Irish Internatio Team, 1958.

G. MEEK (Outside-left International, and othe Academicals in 1952. during his National Servi

OPPOSITION NOTES...

Considering the small pagination of the matchday programme, the opposition were given their fair share of space. 'Evertonia' on P2 usually made reference to the exploits of the Goodison visitors, while Pen Pictures would often take up another one or two pages.

As shown by the Charlton Athletic team picture opposite, supporters were often given more pictorial guides to the visitors than the home side, presumably as home fans would have few opportunities to put names to faces, with blanket football TV coverage still generations away.

Blackburn Pen Pictures

H. LEYLAND (Goalkeeper).—Signed from Everton for start of 1956-57 season, and has proved a real bargain buy. Liverpool-born. Specialist at cross-shots, and a believer in starting attacks with the thrown clearance.

K. TAYLOR (Right-back).—A North-Easterner who joined the Rovers straight from school and had to wait five years for his chance. When he got it he made the grade straight away, and only injury has kept him out for two seasons. Small, but very quick, and a deadly tackler.

D. WHELAN (Left-back).—A product of Wigan Boys' Club, developed into a strong and reliable player through our junior teams, and is now considered a regular first team player.

R. CLAYTON (Right-half).—At 23, the Rovers' captain and England's inevitable choice for right-half, Clayton is one of the strongest, most dynamic players in the game. An attacking wing-half, who switches the play by skilful use of the long ball.

M. WOODS (Centre-half).—The powerful—over 6-ft. and 12 stone—Woods is kingpin of the Rovers' defence, one of the best in the Football League. Woods was a bargain buy from Everton 20 months ago. A brainy type of centre-half, who uses the ball in the clearance.

M. McGRATH (Left-half).—Quiet-spoken Dubliner, from manager John Carey's first club, Home Farm. Only 21, in his first full season as a Rovers senior player, he has already won Eire "B" honours and is a strong fancy for full honours before long. Tackles like a terrier and is strong on constructive play, too.

B. DOUGLAS (Outside-right).—Blackburn's pride and joy is the diminutive Douglas, local-born and a Rovers' player since he left school. A personality in the Matthews-Finney class because of his ability as a ball player. An immediate riot when he took over on England's right wing, he could become one of the all-time greats.

P. DOBING (Centre-forward).—Joined the Rovers straight from school at Crewe. His father played Rugby League football. Dobing, at 19, is a great prospect. Powerfully-built and fast, he is a splendid header of the ball and has a shot in both feet. Is doing his National Service in the East Lancashire Regiment.

A. D. DOUGAN (Centre-forward).—Secured from Portsmouth late last season, is now a firm favourite at Ewood Park, height 6 feet 1 inch; weight, 12 stone.

A. M. McEVOY (Inside-forward).—Signed from Bray Wanderers as a junior, made progress through our junior teams, is a crafty player with good ball control. Height, 5 feet 9 inches; weight, 11 stone 3 lbs.

A. MacLEOD (Outside-left).—Tall, rangy Scot, signed from St. Mirren in August, 1956. Fast and direct and a consistent scorer.

B. ECKERSLEY (Left-back).—Former Southport lorry driver, who has been with the Rovers, his only senior club, for 11 years. Ex-England player, and still very much in the international class. Vastly experienced, a beautiful clean kicker and a believer in attacking play.

CUP TIE TICKETS

::::::::

As the seating accommodation at Port Vale is extremely limited, seats can only be provided for Shareholders. This will be an all ticket match with prices as follows:- Stands 7/6 and 6/-, Paddock 4/-, Enclosure 2/6, Ground 2/-.

Shareholders will be entitled to one seat or two paddock tickets, and season ticket holders will be entitled to one paddock ticket each. These should be applied for by post before Saturday, 21st January, enclosing the 4th round voucher from the season ticket book, which will be stamped and returned for use in case of a replay, correct remittance and stamped addressed envelope. The outside of the envelope must be marked "*Shareholder*" or "*Season Ticket Holder*" as the case may be.

The balance of paddock and enclosure and ground tickets will be sold to supporters on a fixed selling date which will be announced in the local press as soon as this has been agreed.

No postal applications from the general public for these tickets will be considered.

LEAGUE TABLES

(Up to and inclduing Saturday, 7th January, 1956).

LEAGUE—DIVISION 1.

	P	W	D	L	F	A	Pts
Manchester U.	26	14	6	6	53	38	34
Blackpool	25	12	6	7	51	48	30
Luton Town	25	12	5	8	48	34	29
Burnley	25	11	7	7	39	31	29
Charlton A.	26	12	4	10	56	51	28
Sunderland	25	11	6	8	54	58	28
Wolves	25	11	5	9	56	43	27
Everton	26	10	7	9	39	41	27
Portsmouth	25	11	5	9	50	55	27
Chelsea	25	10	7	8	36	41	27
Bolton W.	25	11	4	10	47	35	26
Newcastle U.	26	12	2	12	60	46	26
Manchester C.	25	9	8	8	47	44	26
West Brom. A.	26	11	4	11	35	36	26
Preston N.E.	26	10	5	11	47	41	25
Birmingham C.	26	9	6	11	49	43	24
Arsenal	25	8	8	9	34	41	24
Cardiff C.	25	9	4	12	32	49	22
Tottenham H.	25	8	3	14	32	42	19
Aston Villa	26	5	9	12	31	45	19
Sheffield U.	25	7	4	14	34	46	18
Huddersfield T.	25	6	5	14	32	62	17

CENTRAL LEAGUE

	P	W	D	L	F	A	Pts
Manchester U.	25	20	3	2	80	19	43
Liverpool	25	16	6	3	53	34	38
Everton	26	15	6	5	54	33	36
Sheffield W.	25	12	5	8	49	37	29
West Brom. A.	25	12	5	8	50	40	29
Blackpool	25	11	6	8	52	38	28
Wolves	25	13	1	11	62	46	27
Sheffield U.	26	10	6	10	28	30	26
Manchester C.	25	11	3	11	52	51	25
Burnley	24	9	6	9	46	49	24
Bury	24	11	2	11	46	57	24
Preston N.E.	25	9	6	10	30	46	24
Newcastle U.	25	8	7	10	46	49	23
Aston Villa	24	7	9	8	40	37	23
Blackburn R.	25	9	4	12	36	44	22
Bolton W.	23	8	5	10	24	27	21
Stoke City	25	9	5	11	26	52	19
Leeds United	25	8	2	15	41	49	18
Derby County	24	6	6	12	23	43	18
Chesterfield	25	6	5	14	30	39	17
Huddersfield T.	26	5	7	13	37	57	17
Barnsley	25	5	5	15	28	64	15

TEAM RESULTS, TEAMS AND SCORERS

WEDNESDAY, APRIL 13th, 1960

Reserves (2) v. West Brom. Res. (1) (Away)
Griffiths; R. Parnell, Bramwell; Gabriel, Billington, G. Sharples; Boner, Tyrer, Wignall, Harland, Shackleton.
Scorer: Harland (2).

SATURDAY, APRIL 16th, 1960

Reserves (1) v. Leeds U. Res. (1) (Home)
Griffiths; R. Parnell, J. Bramwell; A. Jarvis, D. Gorrie, Peat; Boner, Shepherd, Wignall, Harland, Laverick.
Scorer: Boner.

Everton 'B' (5) v. Blackburn R. 'B' (0) (Away)
W. Mailey; Watson, Griffiths; Gannon, J. Atherton, O'Brien; P. Maddocks, G. Morton, Bentley, Edwards, Godfrey.
Scorers: Bentley (3), Godfrey (2).

Everton 'C' (0) v. Preston N.E. 'C' (1) (Away)
P. Dunne; R. Burgan, C. Bridge; B. Coupe, K. Edwards, A. Bermingham; C. Davidson, F. Stewart, D. Chesters, R. Evans, D. Griffiths.

MONDAY, APRIL 18th, 1960

Reserves (1) v. Huddersfield T. Res (1) (Home)
O'Neill; Tansey, Bramwell; A. Jarvis, Billington, King; Boner, Tyrer, Shackleton, Wignall, Laverick.
Scorer: Shakleton.

Everton 'C' (5) v. Burnley 'C' (0) (Home)
P. Dunne; R. Burgan, C. Bridge; B. Coupe, K. Edwards, F. Stewart; C. Davidson, A. Alexander, D. Chesters, R. Evans, D. Griffiths.
Scorers: Chesters (4), Alexander.

TUESDAY, APRIL 19th, 1960

Reserves (0) v. Huddersfield T. Res. (0) (Away)
O'Neill; Parkes, Tansey; King, Billington, Rea; Godfrey, Shepherd, Shackleton, Harland, Laverick.

LEAGUE TABLES

Up to and including matches played 18/4/60

FOOTBALL LEAGUE—DIVISION I

	P.	W.	D.	L.	F.	A.	Pts.
Wolves	39	23	5	11	100	63	51
Tottenham	40	19	11	10	79	48	49
Burnley	38	22	5	11	81	59	49
Sheffield W.	40	19	10	11	77	54	48
West Brom. A.	39	18	10	11	80	54	46
Newcastle U.	40	18	8	14	82	74	44
Bolton W.	40	18	8	14	55	50	44
Manchester U.	40	18	7	15	95	75	43
Preston N.E.	39	15	12	12	75	72	42
Fulham	40	16	9	15	71	79	41
Blackpool	40	15	9	16	57	66	39
West Ham	40	16	5	19	73	87	37
Chelsea	40	14	9	17	75	84	37
Leicester	40	12	13	15	64	73	37
Arsenal	40	14	9	17	63	77	37
Everton	40	12	11	17	72	73	35
Blackburn	39	15	5	19	57	66	35
Manchester C.	39	15	3	21	74	81	33
Nottingham F.	39	12	8	19	47	73	32
Birmingham	38	11	9	18	57	76	31
Leeds U.	38	10	10	18	60	87	30
Luton T.	40	8	12	20	47	70	28

FOOTBALL LEAGUE—DIVISION II

	P.	W.	D.	L.	F.	A.	Pts.
Aston Villa	40	24	9	7	86	40	57
Cardiff	39	23	10	6	87	58	56
Middlesbrough	39	19	8	12	86	59	46
Huddersfield	40	18	9	13	69	50	45
Liverpool	39	18	9	12	84	64	45
Sheffield U.	39	17	11	11	64	50	45
Rotherham	39	17	11	11	58	54	45
Charlton	40	16	13	11	84	82	45
Ipswich T.	40	19	6	15	78	65	44
Bristol R.	40	17	10	13	68	76	44
Leyton O.	40	14	13	13	71	58	41
Lincoln C.	40	15	7	18	72	74	37
Swansea T.	39	14	9	16	74	79	37
Scunthorpe	40	13	10	17	55	67	36
Sunderland	40	12	11	17	51	61	35
Brighton	40	11	12	17	62	73	34
Stoke C.	40	13	7	20	63	80	33
Portsmouth	40	10	11	19	57	70	31
Derby C.	40	12	7	21	55	75	31
Plymouth	39	11	9	19	57	87	31
Bristol C.	39	11	5	23	57	86	27
Hull C.	40	9	9	22	45	75	27

CENTRAL LEAGUE

	P.	W.	D.	L.	F.	A.	Pts.
Manchester U.	40	25	8	7	108	62	58
Liverpool	40	20	12	8	96	55	52
Newcastle U.	41	18	12	11	94	55	48
Wolves	38	20	8	10	84	51	48
Stoke C.	39	20	8	11	71	46	48
Sheffield U.	38	19	10	9	70	56	48
Blackburn R.	39	18	9	12	75	62	45
Sheffield W.	38	19	7	12	64	55	45
Derby C.	40	16	9	15	78	69	41
Burnley	39	17	6	16	60	63	40
Preston N.E.	39	13	13	13	62	68	39
Everton	36	13	12	11	66	57	38
Aston Villa	40	14	9	17	80	64	37
West Brom. A.	38	16	5	17	78	64	37
Bury	40	12	13	15	61	64	37
Manchester C.	40	15	7	18	77	85	37
Huddersfield T.	40	11	13	16	50	73	35
Blackpool	40	12	7	21	79	86	31
Bolton W.	40	8	11	21	51	96	27
Chesterfield	39	8	11	20	44	92	27
Barnsley	38	9	4	25	41	108	22
Leeds U.	38	6	8	24	44	102	20

"WE HOPE 'THE ROAR' WILL SHAKE, IF NOT BREAK, A FEW SPOTS IN THE POTTERIES"

THE CUP.

By our 3—1 victory over Bristol City last Saturday, the first hurdle·on the Wembley road was taken satisfactorily. It was an enjoyable game, especially to our supporters, as some very entertaining football was played by both teams. It was in the early part of the second half that the City team had their best spell and showed the form which has taken them to a challenging position for promotion in their Division of the League.

When Cyril Lello received his injury midway through the second half, it looked as though Dame Fortune had switched her favours towards the City team but, from then onwards, the game swung in our favour and two more goals came our way. The final score justified our first half superiority.

To those who listened in last Monday to the Cup Draw, it was an agonising wait to learn which team was to be our opponents in the next round. We were left in the last three in the bag. When it did come it was to Port Vale away.

While most teams are always hoping for a HOME draw, it cannot go on indefinitely. It could have been a much tougher proposition—on paper—and it could have been much more inconvenient for travelling arrangements for our supporters. We hope 'The Roar' will shake, if not break, a few spots in the Potteries on the 28th January.

In among the opposition references, advertising and centre-spread team sheets, previous match reports were noted almost in the manner of a Parish noticeboard.

The cutting (above), refers to the previous weekend's FA Cup third-round home clash with Bristol City in January 1956. The 3-1 victory, 'the first hurdle on the Wembley road was taken satisfactorily'. 'Dame Fortune' appeared to favour the away side when Cyril Lello picked up an injury – with substitutes still a decade away from being permitted – 'but from then onwards, the game swung in our favour and two more goals came our way'.

Note was also made of the draw pairing Everton with Port Vale away. 'It could have been a much tougher proposition – on paper – and it could have been much more inconvenient for travelling arrangements for our supporters.'

'Evertonia' (right), from the 1959/60 programme against Blackburn Rovers, trumpeted the sale of 'pre-match reserved tickets', for 'always one of our most popular fixtures'. Rovers had enjoyed an impressive start to the campaign, while ex-Evertonians Matt Woods and Harry Leyland were in their ranks. Blues boss Johnny Carey had joined Everton from Blackburn, 'and will have the interesting task of plotting his old club's downfall'. One other opposition player of note to Evertonians would be 'Royston Vernon, Welsh international inside-forward, who has recently been involved in a spot of domestic bother with his club.'

A brief history of Rovers concludes the piece, with nine of the club's legends listed, 'nine men worth a king's ransom at present-day prices and whose names and deeds are mentioned almost with bated breath wherever football is talked about.'

EVERTON FOOTBALL CLUB CO. LTD.

Chairman: F. MICKLESFIELD
Vice-Chairman: J. C. SHARP

R. E. SEARLE   N. W. COFFEY
C. E. BALMFORTH   C. H. ASKHAM
J. TAYLOR   R. A. JOYNSON
E. HOLLAND HUGHES

Manager: J. J. CAREY
Secretary: W. DICKINSON

EVERTONIA

BLACKBURN ROVERS

A visit from Blackburn Rovers is always one of our most popular fixtures as our sales of pre-match reserved tickets show and the game this evening has proved no exception to the rule. Apart from the fact that since Rovers came back to Division I, good, entertaining football has flowed from the side, the team has included several players of the crowd pulling and pleasing variety; we make no apologies for picking out Ron Clayton, who has been tipped to succeed Billy Wright for the England captaincy; Bryan Douglas, who looked to have the whole International field before him but has suffered much recently from troublesome injuries; Royston Vernon, Welsh International inside-forward, who has recently been involved in a spot of domestic bother with his club; and of course, the two ex-Evertonians who are doing so well at Ewood Park, Matt Woods and Harry Leyland. A strong dose of added flavour to an already piquant dish is the fact that present Everton Manager, J. Carey, came to Goodison from Blackburn and will have the interesting task of plotting his old club's downfall.

These notes were written before the results of last Saturday's games were known and it is possible that Blackburn have been toppled from their proud perch as league leaders. Their record so far this season is outstanding and it shows that of the three games played at Ewood Park up to Friday last, Rovers won all three, scoring eight goals to one against and that of two away fixtures, one has been drawn and one won. Overall goal average 13-3, points scored, nine out of a possible ten. Some record!

Blackburn Rovers have been a great club in the truest sense of the word, ever since the start of football as we know it in its organised form. To mention the word 'cup' is to think of Newcastle United, Villa and Blackburn. Six times winners, including a straight hat trick of victories, Rovers at one stage in the early days, were such a powerful club that practically nothing could stand up against them and they steamrollered to cup victories in 1884, 1885 and 1886 with some of the greatest names in English football. Get hold of an old timer and say the names of Bob Crompton (who held a record number of English caps for many years), Jockey Simpson, Joe Clennell and Sam Wolstenholme to him and see the reaction. Follow up with those of Syd Puddeyfoot, 'Ossie' Campbell, Jock Hutton, Ronnie Sewell and Arthur Rigby and there you have nine men worth a king's ransome at present day prices and whose names and deeds are mentioned almost with bated breath wherever football is talked about. It was these great players that were primarily responsible for Rover's magnificent spell when, within a period of only nine years, the club took home the Cup on five occasions. Changing to league aspects, Blackburn Rovers enjoyed an unbroken spell of First Division Football stretching from 1878, the date of the founding of the Football League, right through to 1936 season when relegation overtook Blackburn —but for two years only.

A.N.OTHER ON THE SCORESHEET!

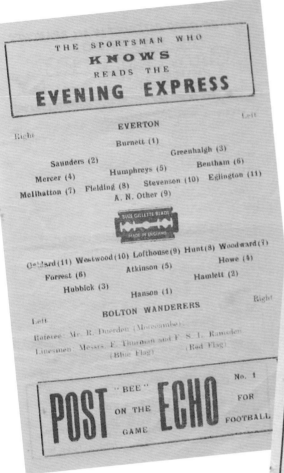

Bolton listings, 1946/47

The team sheet included in the match programme included the then 'traditional' 2-3-5 formation for the Trotters, while Everton went 'experimental' with a 2-3-4-1 line-up. The main note for the Everton XI is the listing of the mysterious 'A.N. Other' as No.9, a name always ignored when Everton's greatest centre-forwards are mentioned. It turned out that Billy Higgins played in that position, being on target in the 2-1 victory.

Advertising included local newspapers the Evening Express, the Post and the Echo, plus note of Blue Gillette Blade - 'Made In England'.

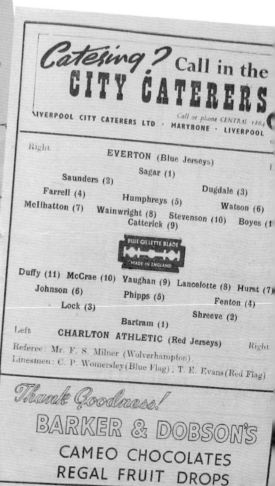

Addicks line-up, 1946/47

'A.N. Other' had been replaced by Harry Catterick by the time Charlton Athletic visited Goodison towards the end of the campaign.

Advertising again included Gillette, with 'City Caterers' given prominent billing as well as Barker & Dobson's cameo chocolates and regal fruit drops.

EVERTON FOOTBALL CLUB CO. LTD.

Chairman: R. E. SEARLE

Vice-Chairman: F. MICKLESFIELD

J. C. SHARP N. W. COFFEY
C. E. BALMFORTH C. H. ASKHAM
J. TAYLOR R. A. JOYNSON
E. HOLLAND HUGHES

Manager: J. J. CAREY

Secretary: W. DICKINSON

EVERTONIA

ASTON VILLA

Out of all the outstanding newsworthy things that Villa have done since the club was first formed in 1874, two things seem to strike the writer when idly glancing through some facts and figures concerning the famous Midland club. The first item is a widely known one that Villa have won the cup more times than any other club, the win over Manchester United at Wembley in May 1957 representing the seventh occasion upon which the cup has gone back in triumph to Villa Park. It is truly a great achievement and particularly so when one also knows that Villa have been beaten finalists twice (1892 and 1924) and have been semi-finalists on no less than fifteen occasions; this latter figure is also a record, held jointly with Blackburn Rovers. The cup final dates are of interest and are hereby detailed:— 1887, 1895, 1897, 1905, 1913, 1920, 1957. A significant fact is that four of the wins came in the first thirteen years between 1887 and 1905: two in the next fifteen years up to 1920; and one only between 1920 and 1958, a period of 38 years. Our old friend Joe Mercer, now Villa Park boss after a brief sojourn with Sheffield United, may have some ideas about improving the last figures quoted!

The second item which may be much less widely known is that the Midlands club also jointly holds the record of the number of goals scored in one season in League matches. It was in season 1930-31 that Villa finished the full programme of League games with the massive total of 128 goals for; 78 against. This works out to an average of over three goals per game. This equals the league record and the First Division record absolutely.

Villa have had some wonderful players in their claret and light blue over the years, and the years between the wars showed particularly clearly just how rich Villa were in talent. There were the following whose value would be just incalculable today who helped to put Villa on top: Barson, Broome, Ducat, Hardy, Houghton, Moss, Smart, Starling, Walker and Waring. Ten players out of a list of no less than twenty-one who played for England between 1920 and 1939. In addition, there were a number of equally famous men who appeared for Wales and Scotland within that period. There were names like Blair, Cummings, Gibson and Massie who donned the blue of Scotland many times and Astley, Griffiths and Phillips who represented Wales. It was in 1936 that the Villa, struggling late on in the season to avoid the

dreaded drop into Division II, went into the transfer market and spent something like £35,000 in a bid to avert the threatening disaster of relegation. Despite the expensive importations, Villa still went down but within two years the new blood showed its worth and Villa came back at the end of 1937-38 season.

SOCCER STORY

A happy sequel to our projected trip to Spain to play a match in Madrid has been brought to our notice which we think may be of interest to many of our supporters. The match, which was to have been played on January 14th, unfortunately had to be cancelled owing to difficulties raised by both the English and Spanish Football Associations. However, a match was in fact played and one of the fair sex, a Lady Carmen Polo de Franco, was the guiding light behind the whole idea. This lady is in charge of the relief work amongst the injured and homeless victims of the terrible tragedy of Ribadelago. This was the small village which was completely wiped out except for the local church, when a huge dam, built high over the village, burst its banks and flooded the entire valley below—and the village of Ribadelago. It was suggested that a game should be played to raise funds for the distressed, and upon being approached, the Czech Manager of Atletico Madrid, Senor Daucik and his opposite number with Real, Senor Luis Carnaglia, readily agreed to form a team. Fortuna Dusseldorf, from the same West German League as Schalke 04 and Borussia Dortmund, made up the opposition and the match was played under floodlights at the Bernabeau Stadium in Madrid.

The standard of opposition which we would have had to face can be judged almost by the great players who were unable to find a place amidst this galaxy of stars. No spot could be found for Real's goalkeeper, Hernandez or for that great inside-forward Ferenc Puskas. The combined Spanish team included Kopa of France, Vava of Brazil and Di Stefano of Argentina and Spain as that great up the inside forward trio. In addition, Santamaria of Uruguay and Spain was at centre-half.

We are indebted for this interesting soccer story to Mr. H. J. Rock, Manager of G. K. Tyre Services of Liverpool who had the clipping sent to him and thought it might be of interest to our club and its supporters. We are always pleased to hear of any yarns or anecdotes of an interesting nature about soccer and should anyone think they have something which deserves a wider audience, they are invited to send it along to the club for consideration for inclusion in future programme issues, letters, which should be sent to the club offices at Goodison Park, should be marked 'programme' on the front.

F.A. CUP 5th ROUND REPLAY

Should a replay be necessary in our cup-tie v. Aston Villa this will be played at Villa Park on Wednesday next, 18th February, kick-off 7.15 p.m.

A limited number of tickets will be available for reserved seats at 8/6 and 6/- each. These will be available only for Shareholders and some Stand Season Ticket Holders. Shareholders will be entitled to 1 Ticket each in exchange for the spare coupon No. 48 from the "SELF" season ticket.

For Stand Season Ticket holders, each spare coupon No. 48 bears a serial number and if the LAST number is a 3, 5, or 7 application may be made for one ticket in exchange for this coupon.

All the above tickets will be on sale after the match on Saturday, February 14th, at 5.15 p.m., from Gwladys Street.

There will be no tickets available for the general public and admission to the ground and enclosure will be by payment of cash at the turnstiles on the day of the match.

The records used in our Musical Programmes have been supplied and can be obtained from ROBERT CREASES MUSIC STORES, 14 County Road, Walton (H.M.V. Record Agent — 5 minutes from Goodison Park).

Villa notes, 1958/59

An FA Cup fifth-round visit of Aston Villa on Valentine's Day 1959 failed to break the tone of the 'Evertonia' section, with Villa's cup credentials given top billing. Star names from years gone were hailed, their 'value would be just incalculable today', while the list of international talent to have represented the club was also recognised.

While potential replay information was included – unfortunately a 4-1 home defeat put paid to the Blues' cup ambitions – 'Soccer Story' included curious details of a charity match in Spain, which Everton had been unable to play in, apparently 'owing to difficulties raised by both the English and Spanish Football Associations'.

Season tickets, 1959/60

The final home game of the 1959/60 season, against Leeds, included season ticket selling details for the following campaign.

Ground tickets were cheapest at £2.5.0, with prime spots in the old Main Stand and Bullens Road selling for £7.7.0. All home league matches and reserve games were covered by the ticket, as well as offering priority for home cup-ties and floodlit matches, still a novelty which often attracted huge crowds in the era.

Season Tickets for Season 1960-61

Prices of Season Tickets for next season are as follows:

GROUND	... ...	£2 5 0
PADDOCK	... ...	£3 5 0
Goodison Road Stand		
Block 'D'	... ...	£6 6 0
Block 'F'	... ...	£7 7 0
Bullens Road		
Centre Stand 'A' and 'B' (Centre)	... ...	£7 7 0
Centre Stand 'A' and 'B' (Sides)	... ...	£6 6 0

In addition to entitling the holder to admission to all League and Central League Matches, the season tickets will contain vouchers giving priority for home Cup ties and special Floodlit Matches when tickets are booked for the appropriate section for which they hold season tickets.

Renewal forms will be sent out to all present Season Ticket holders in due course, and applications for renewal should not be sent in before these are received.

If renewal forms are not received by May 14th application for renewal can be made by letter enclosing renewal vouchers and correct remittance.

The application form below may be used for NEW applications for Season Tickets which must be accompanied by the correct remittance but as the available tickets are limited all applications will be dealt with in strict rotation. The tickets available are in the Bullens Road Stand at £7.7.0 and £6.6.0 each.

To the EVERTON FOOTBALL CLUB CO. LTD.

Season Tickets at £..............

I desire to purchase.............. in the following names

each and enclose remittance value £..............

Tickets to be sent to:

Name..............

1960-1970

The Mersey Millionaires, a new era and success-starved Everton fans were finally rewarded...the programme also got its first official editor

In the Sixties the match programme continued to be considered little more than an opportunity to publicise the team sheet. There were few pictures, news was scarce and advertising remained the dominant factor, publicising club information, employment opportunities or a variety of ale and cigarette products.

The cover changed little. From a brief flirtation with a generic Everton player kicking the 'o' in the club name, the more stylish cover featuring Goodison Park remained a fixture until the end of the decade.

The appointment of the programme's first official editor, Mike Beddow, in 1969 (director Fred Micklesfield had looked after the publication previously) was the start of a change into producing something that was more appealing to fans. David Exall was recruited as the club's first promotions manager to look at ways of maximising income – with the matchday programme one of his first priorities. The subsequent appointment of Beddow also came at a time when the programme was taken up by the majority of the match-going crowd.

One other addition which appealed to fans was the 'Football League Review', which was an additional pull-out. Introduced in 1967/68, the club took on the extra cost, with the 6d cover price remaining unchanged.

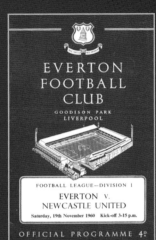

EVERTON
FOOTBALL
CLUB

GOODISON PARK
LIVERPOOL

FOOTBALL LEAGUE—DIVISION I

EVERTON v.
NEWCASTLE UNITED

Saturday, 19th November 1960   Kick-off 3-15 p.m.

OFFICIAL PROGRAMME 4D

EVERTON

EVERTON FOOTBALL CLUB
OFFICIAL
PROGRAMME 4D
FOOTBALL LEAGUE - DIVISION I

EVERTON
v
NOTTINGHAM
FOREST
Saturday 7th October, 1961
Kick-off 3-15 p.m.

GOODISON PARK · LIVERPOOL

EVERTON

EVERTON FOOTBALL CLUB
OFFICIAL PROGRAMME 6D
FOOTBALL LEAGUE—DIVISION I

EVERTON
v
LIVERPOOL
Saturday, 22nd September 1962
Kick-off 3 p.m.

GOODISON PARK · LIVERPOOL

EVERTON
FOOTBALL
CLUB

GOODISON PARK
LIVERPOOL

FOOTBALL LEAGUE DIVISION I

EVERTON v.
WEST BROMWICH ALBION
GOOD FRIDAY, 27th MARCH, 1964
Kick-off 3-0 p.m.   Price 6D

OFFICIAL PROGRAMME

EVERTON
FOOTBALL
CLUB

GOODISON PARK
LIVERPOOL

FOOTBALL LEAGUE — DIVISION

EVERTON v.
CHELSEA
SATURDAY, 26th FEBRUARY, 1966
Kick-off 3 p.m.   Price 6D

OFFICIAL PROGRAMME

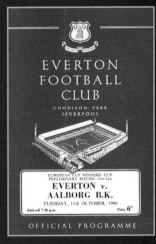

EVERTON
FOOTBALL
CLUB

GOODISON PARK
LIVERPOOL

EUROPEAN CUP WINNERS' CUP
PRELIMINARY ROUND—2ND LEG

EVERTON v.
AALBORG B.K.
TUESDAY, 11th OCTOBER, 1966
Kick-off 7.30 p.m.   Price 6D

OFFICIAL PROGRAMME

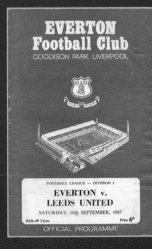

EVERTON
Football Club
GOODISON PARK · LIVERPOOL

FOOTBALL LEAGUE — DIVISION I

EVERTON v.
LEEDS UNITED
SATURDAY, 16th SEPTEMBER, 1967
Kick-off 3 p.m.   Price 6D

OFFICIAL PROGRAMME

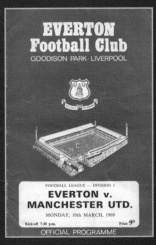

EVERTON
Football Club
GOODISON PARK · LIVERPOOL

FOOTBALL LEAGUE - DIVISION I

EVERTON v.
MANCHESTER UTD.
MONDAY, 10th MARCH, 1969
Kick-off 7.30 p.m.   Price 9D

OFFICIAL PROGRAMME

Everton
MATCHDAY MAGAZINE 1s

MANCHESTER CITY
Football League - Division 1   SATURDAY, 29th AUGUST, 1970   Kick-off 3.0 p.m.

GOODISON PARK · LIVERPOOL

Selected covers, clockwise from above: v Bangu (friendly), 1960/61; v Blackpool, 1962/63; v Aston Villa, 1962/63; v Manchester United, 1967/68; v West Bromwich Albion, 1969/70; v Arsenal (League Cup), 1969/70; v Sheffield United, 1964/65

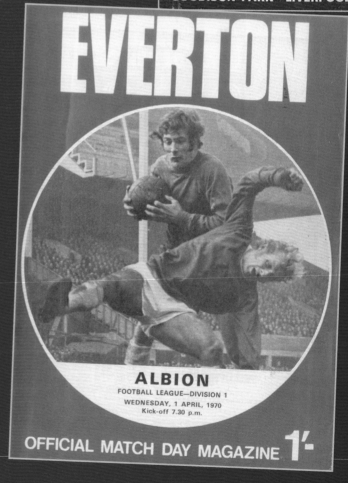

EVERTON
Football Club
GOODISON PARK · LIVERPOOL

NIL SATIS · NISI OPTIMUM

FOOTBALL LEAGUE — DIVISION I

EVERTON v.
MANCHESTER UNITED

SATURDAY, 19th AUGUST, 1967

Kick-off 3 p.m.   Price 6ᴰ

OFFICIAL PROGRAMME

TODAY'S LINE-UP

JACK SHARP
SPORTS
LIVERPOOL

EVERTON
(Royal Blue Shirts, White Shorts)
1   Gordon West
2   Tommy Wright
3   Sandy BROWN
4   Howard KENDALL
5   Brian LABONE
6   Tommy JACKSON
7   Alan WHITTLE
8   Alan BALL
9   Joe ROYLE
10   John HURST
11   Johnny MORRISSEY
12

MANCHESTER CITY
(Red and Black Stripes, Black Shorts)
1   Joe CORRIGAN
2   Tony BOOK
3   Glyn PARDOE
4   Mike DOYLE
5   Tommy BOOTH
6   Alan OAKES
7   Mike SUMMERBEE
8   David CONNOR
9   Francis LEE
10   Neil YOUNG
11   Ian BOWYER
12

Referee:
        K. Howley
        (Teesside)

Kevin Howley has refereed over 100 internationals or European competitive matches plus the 1960 F.A. Cup Final. He has been a League referee since 1954. Married, with two sons, Mr. Howley is employed by I.C.I. at Teesside.

Linesmen:
   P. Cogan (Red Flag)
   I. T. Smith (Yellow Flag)

Printed by Liverpool Litho Limited, Member of the Seel House Press, Seel Street, Liverpool L1 4AY.

v Manchester City, 1969/70 - the first season of back-page team line-ups...

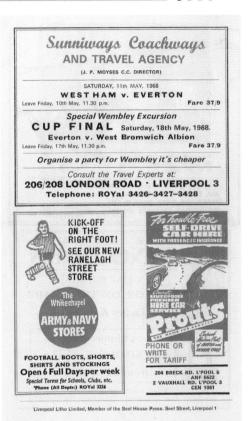

v Fulham, 1962/63; (right) v Stoke City, 1967/68

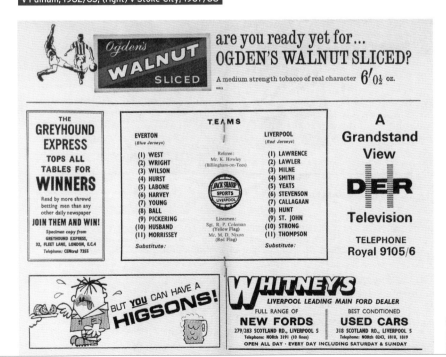

v Liverpool, FA Cup, 1966/67 – centre spread

Everton Football Club Co. Ltd.

(Founded 1878)

Chairman : JOHN MOORES

Directors :

R. E. SEARLE	J. C. SHARP	N. W. COFFEY
C E. BALMFORTH	F. MICKLESFIELD	J. TAYLOR
R. A. JOYNSON	E. HOLLAND HUGHES	

Manager : H. CATTERICK   *Secretary :* W. DICKINSON

EVERTONIA

In view of the serious injury position which has arisen so early in the season, Manager Harry Catterick was invited to contribute a few notes to this programme and below will be found a few views of his on the situation.

" The season is less than a fortnight old yet already the great feeling of optimism shared by all our supporters has been somewhat dampened by the unhappy start which we have made.

To return pointless from West Bromwich and Fulham was bad enough but to be deprived of the services of such players as Bobby Collins, Alex Young, and Alec Parker, through injuries sustained in the West Brom game, was indeed a cruel blow. With Frank Wignall not yet having recovered from the foot injury he received in America, our Reserve strength has been sorely taxed and when one considers that many of our younger players are still very inexperienced I have been confronted with a problem which has no easy solution.

Naturally, the risk of injury to key players is always there and must be faced but, as yet, we are not fully equipped to withstand such a weakening of our playing strength. Indeed, few clubs would be able to. However, that is little consolation when we had such high hopes of getting off to a good start.

Nevertheless there is still every reason to hope that the results will come, particularly when we are free of the injury bug which has struck at such a vital time.

My main concern is for the team to play not only attractively, but effectively. Already indications are that teams will be playing harder than ever before and, if we are to enjoy a high position, then determination, as well as ability, must be displayed in every game.

Our efforts will be directed to this end and I am hoping that the results achieved will bring pleasure to all Evertonians."

HARRY CATTERICK,

Manager.

3

"MY MAIN CONCERN IS FOR THE TEAM TO PLAY NOT ONLY ATTRACTIVELY, BUT EFFECTIVELY..."

H arry Catterick was a man who liked to keep his cards close to his chest – and with the official match programme not incorporating a regular managerial feature until Billy Bingham's appointment in 1973, there are few examples of his words in these pages.

However, one such instance is noted opposite. Invited to speak ahead of the home game against his previous club Sheffield Wednesday in September 1961, he reflected on an inconsistent start, as well as injury problems that had robbed the side of three of their best players.

"Naturally the risk of injury to key players is always there and must be faced but, as yet, we are not fully equipped to withstand such a weakening of our playing strength."

Despite the problems, he vowed that results would come, and "that the results achieved will bring pleasure to all Evertonians".

The improvement would prove to be long-term, as a subsequent 4-0 home defeat to the Owls would be the start of a sequence of three successive losses without scoring. The Blues eventually recovered to finish fourth in Catterick's first full season as boss – and go on to land the league championship the following campaign.

"IT WAS NOT THE BAIT OF MEXICO WHICH MADE ME CHANGE MY MIND"

One of the popular early features introduced in 1969, the 'Players Profile' featured heroes of the day in action, or in the case of skipper Brian Labone, opposite, relaxing on holiday in Malta with wife Pat.

The captain's insistence that his loyalty lay first with Everton and not England's prospective defence of the World Cup in Mexico the following summer would have been welcome news for Evertonians, particularly in light of Brian's initial decision to retire – a decision later reversed.

The short life-span of a players' career was also indicated by Brian's thoughts about the end of his contract. "In two years time I shall be 31, which is old by modern standards."

The revelation of Johnny Morrissey's Liverpool allegiance may not have gone down well with some Evertonians – although 'only "blue" blood runs in Johnny's veins now'. Two goals in four games at the start of the 1969/70 had seen the winger enjoy "a bit of glamour treatment from the crowd," while he came close to his vow to hit double figures - finishing with nine.

As you can read on page 10, the South American trip was no holiday.

Holiday place in the sun for skipper Brian Labone and his wife Pat was Malta.

Brian Labone

BRIAN LABONE

I'm still playing...for Everton NOT Mexico

For sustained consistency over eleven years, there are very few players to match BRIAN LABONE, the Everton skipper and centre-half, who today reaches a milestone—HIS 400TH LEAGUE APPEARANCE FOR THE BLUES.

Since making his League debut, at 18, against Birmingham City at St. Andrew's, Labone has starred as a member of the League Championship side, of a winning F.A. Cup team, and, now, as England's centre-half.

So the lad, who took some persuading to forgo a possible University education when he was at Liverpool Collegiate, can look back with no regrets.

Yet the pressures of modern soccer put Brian on the verge of quitting soccer to join his father's central heating firm some two years ago.

"It was NOT the bait of Mexico which made me change my mind," says Brian, "I DECIDED TO CONTINUE PLAYING BECAUSE EVERTON ASKED ME TO STAY ON FOR A LITTLE WHILE LONGER— IT WAS AS SIMPLE AS THAT.

"I have signed on for a further two years from the start of this season with an option for another two years. In two years time I shall be 31, which is old by modern standards."

Brian's career highlight? The Cup victory over Sheffield Wednesday.

"I didn't get such a thrill when we won the Championship," he says. "But the Cup is sudden death—and the way we won it was fantastic. When we went two behind, I honestly thought we had had it. THEN CAME THOSE THREE GREAT GOALS. IT WAS WONDERFUL."

players profile

No. 12:
KEITH NEWTON

Full name: Keith Robert Newton.
Born: Manchester.
Signed: December 15, 1969.
Debut: v. Derby County, December 20, 1969.
League Appearances for Everton: 12.

*   *   *

Honours: F.A. Youth Cup winners medal with Blackburn, four Under-23 appearances, 16 England Caps, five Football League appearances.

*   *   *

Schoolboy hero: I usually watched my soccer, as a lad, at Maine Road and my idol was Bert Trautmann. Then, when I was older and went to Blackburn, I thought Bryan Douglas, on his day, was incredible. I have seen him play some bewildering games. His type of player isn't around nowadays, for there is a tendency for stronger, faster players.

*   *   *

Choose any player (from another club) to play alongside you: Bobby Charlton—he has always impressed me. He is the ideal type, has a perfect temperament and loads of ability. I usually share a room with him when we're away with England and we've done a lot of talking about the game together. What has impressed me is the way he has broken out of his poorish spell to be playing as well as ever. Every player dreads hitting a bad patch, because the more you try, the more you seem to get worse. It's a terrible feeling, I can tell you.

*   *   *

Best player in your position: The two full backs I like are Tommy Wright and Terry Cooper. I hadn't seen a lot of Tommy before I came to Goodison, but his strength and ability has impressed me, while Cooper's attacking game

make him a fine player, too. The ideal full back was really Ray Wilson.

*   *   *

Favourite ground: Old Trafford, I think. It's very much like Goodison with its big stands, big crowd and great atmosphere.

*   *   *

Match you remember most: The first time I played at Hampden Park. It was my third game for England and we beat them 4-3. Incidentally, Ray Wilson was injured—that's how I got my chance that day. It was a bit frightening, playing before 120,000 people. And that Hampden roar is quite something, though they didn't have much to roar about that day—not until near the end anyway.

*   *   *

Who was your choice for Footballer of the Year?: Like the writers I named Billy Bremner . . . but what about little "Bally"?

*   *   *

What countries have you played in?: U.S.A., Canada, Mexico, Brazil, Uruguay, Sweden, Germany, France, Austria, Belgium, Holland, Hungary, Rumania, Italy, Spain, Turkey, Israel, Yugoslavia.

*   *   *

What do you want to do when you finish playing?: This is something I have not given much thought to, because when you join a new club, you're obviously looking forward to spending quite a spell in the team. But I have a tendency not to want to stop in the game. I think it's a hard life for a manager.

*   *   *

Hobbies: Golf, tinkering with the car, bit of gardening.

*   *   *

Pet Hate: People who talk behind your back—people who whisper in your company.

*   *   *

Musical Taste: General pop and light (very) classical.

Keith Newton

The 1969/70 Players Profile series evolved into a more in-depth Q&A format, with defender Newton being the subject here, and fans being encouraged to 'cut out and collect this intimate record of the Goodison stars'.

Newton has positive things to say about Bobby Charlton and former Everton full-back Ray Wilson ("the ideal full-back"), while also admitting to being surprised by the ability of Tommy Wright, Newton having only recently joined the club.

He is insistent he hasn't thought too much about life beyond playing, although "I think it's a hard life for a manager".

"Tinkering with the car" is deemed a hobby, while "light (very) classical music" is among his tastes. However, "people who whisper in your company" are not to his liking...

Heads...Dixie gets my vote!

WHERE'S TED SAGAR NOWADAYS? The answer: he's the landlord of the Blue Anchor Hotel at Aintree

WE'RE LOOKING FOR YOU!

Dixie Dean . . . Joe Mercer . . . Dave Hickson. These are just a few of the famous Goodison Park names who will be featured during our search into the exciting history of Everton.

Many others are also lined up to be included in this intriguing study of the club's ups-and-downs. But, equally, there are many old players we WANT to feature . . . and CAN'T because we've lost contact.

Promotions Manager David Exall would be pleased to hear the current whereabouts of all old Everton stars. Why not drop him a line at Goodison Park, Liverpool 4, if you know of a likely candidate for the series?

"But every goalkeeper should attempt to establish an understanding with his co-defenders", insists Ted. "In my opinion, the greatest centre half I played with was T. G. Jones. What an artist he was. Cool and dominating, he had a habit of casually back-heading centres to me. This was a feature of the understanding we had".

"Mind you, we did come unstuck once and then the ball whistled past me off T.G.'s head from six yards range. But he was a supreme centre half. To my mind, only John Charles proved T.G.'s equal".

But it was not the Everton defence which hogged the headlines back in the early '30's — it was an attack which hammered home 121 goals in 1930-31 and 116 the following season. Top of the scorers' list was, of course, the great Dixie Dean.

Where are the individuals?

"YOU DON'T NEED ME TO TELL YOU THAT DIXIE WAS THE GREATEST HEADER OF THE BALL I EVER SAW", says Ted.

"One move in particular brought Dixie plenty of goals. T. C. F. Johnson, one of the best long passers of the ball in his day, used to switch the attack by flinging over a crossfield pass to right winger Critchley, who could really move. The centre would come over and there was Dean to thump it home".

It's no great shock to discover that Ted is not over-enthusiastic about the way the modern game is played. "They are killing off the individualist", he says.

"We went out and played our natural game and attacking football resulted. Now the emphasis is on team work. Granted, the tackling is harder and faster, but where are the individuals?

"Mention Alan Ball, Bobby Charlton and George Best and that's that. But pre-war every side had three or four men in the side who could be classed as characters".

● In the programme for next Tuesday's game against Manchester United, Ted talks about his save to remember, and names his all-time Everton XI . . .

22

An extract from an interview with Ted Sagar, 1969/70 - an advocate of W.R. Dean

"OVER 100 YARDS AWAY IN THE EVERTON GOAL GORDON WEST SHOWED THE KOP WHAT HE THOUGHT OF ALAN WHITTLE'S SUCCESS"

12

THE 'BLUES' FOR THE REDS!

REVENGE IS SWEET . . . AND NEVER MORE SO THAN WHEN WINNING AT ANFIELD !

The 2-0 success over the Reds neatly avenged our 3-0 upset at Goodison in December and was our third away win in succession at a vital time in the race for the Championship. The goal that snapped the Derby Day tension came from Joe Royle . . . a happy 21st of the season for our centre-forward!

On the left, Joe gets up to beat Ron Yeats and Ray Clemence and head over the two Liverpool defenders after 11 minutes.

Goal No. 2 came in the second half from Alan Whittle to give the blond bombshell his eighth goal in 11 League games this season.

Below left, Alan peers round Geoff Strong to watch his shot fly past the stranded Clemence, and, on the right, he turns away to meet the jubilant Colin Harvey.

Over a hundred yards away, in the Everton goal, Gordon West (right) showed the Kop what he thought about Alan's success.

Pictures:
GARY TALBOT

Match action reflecting on a crucial derby victory in the West Bromwich Albion programme of the 1969/70 season

PUTTING YOU IN THE PICTURE

Big Joe Royle never shirks the hard work up front and here we see the First Division's leading goal-scorer fighting hard for reward against opposition from West Ham defenders Stephenson and Lampard at Upton Park.

Joe Royle's goalscoring exploits were captured in pictures in 1969/70 programmes for the games against Manchester City (above) and West Bromwich Albion (right)

JOE'S JOY

Joe Royle's 20th League goal of the season (top) clinched the 3-2 victory over Spurs and left nothing but dejection (bottom) for England, Bond, Want, Beal and Morgan.

1961-63

An array of alcoholic delights were aimed at Evertonians in the early 1960s with the staple ales of Threlfall's and Higsons blending in with the more exotic choice of Martini.

Local car dealers Allison Bros. Ltd offered some of their wares in the Birmingham City programme of 1961/62, with the description for the 'NEW NSU Prinz 4 Saloon' catching the eye: '...only two grease points and just about the nippiest little car on four wheels'.

The People newspaper also enjoyed utilising 'The School Of Science' Everton link in their advertising to the home faithful...

1964-67

STOP PRESS! proclaims the below ad, taken from the Inter-Cities Fairs Cup programme against Manchester United of 1964/65. The reason? The Austin 1800 is now available – in Moorfields. The Sporting Chronicle also used the match programme to trumpet their 'accurate forecasts'.

Liverpool Fire Brigade were recruiting in 1967, utilising the FA Cup derby to target Liverpool's three teams: 'Everton, Liverpool and the Auxiliary Fire Service.'

1967-70

'Thirst division champions' Threlfall's had been taken over by Whitbread by the late 1960s, the Poacher Brown Ale celebrating by lining up for a 'team photo'. Meanwhile, there was a thumbs-up for Ford, recruiting in Halewood.

BILLY BINGHAM

Congratulations once again to Billy Bingham on his selection to play for Ireland against England at Wembley next Wednesday.

Since his first selection in 1952, Billy has never been dropped by his country. The few games that he has missed have been caused either by injury or his Club unable to release him.

Ireland realise the worth of this grand player ; one wonders how long it will be before Scotland realises that there are some grand Scottish players in the Everton team.

INTERNATIONAL HONOURS

Congratulations to two of our Scots players on their selection for the national team. Alex Scott gains his first cap since he came to Everton on Scotland's right wing. Jimmy Gabriel is named as a reserve to travel. This is the twelfth time that Alex Scott has been selected to play for Scotland—all his other caps being awarded during his spell with Rangers. The last time he played for his country was against Wales two years ago. Jimmy Gabriel has one full cap for Scotland dating from his first season with Everton when he turned out against Wales three years ago. Scotland must be in a very strong position to be able to go without his services for so long. Everton fans would add that the solutions to some of Scotland's problem positions are to be found at Goodison Park.

EVERTON V. WEST BROMWICH ALBION

Despite the absence of Bobby Collins and Alex Young, the blues secured a splendid victory against West Brom. last Wednesday, by 3 goals to 1. It was not only the win which pleased, but also the manner in which it was obtained, for every player gave his utmost in endeavour and skill. The goals were scored by Micky Lill, Roy Vernon (penalty) and Billy Bingham. An unusual incident occurred in the second half, when Referee Mr. R. H. Windle was knocked out by the ball hitting him and had to retire, with one of his linesmen taking over the whistle.

PUBLIC ADDRESS SYSTEM

For the next few matches, patrons may notice changes in the Public Address System. Experiments are being tried with a view to obtaining the most suitable one for our requirements.

WITH THE JUNIORS

Everton " A " 2, Blackburn Rovers " A " 2. Played at Bellefield, 26/8/1961. This was a very even game, which Everton were somewhat unfortunate to lose. A little slackness in defence allowed the Rovers to score twice in the closing minutes.

Everton :—A. Rankin, R. Burgan, D. McKenzie, B. Rees, B. Coupe, D. Preston, G. Humphreys, Chris Green, W. Bennett, T. Wright, T. McDonald.

Everton " B " 1, Blackburn Rovers " B " 2. Played at Bellefield, 28/6/61. This was a poor game, which neither side deserved to win.

Everton :—Baker, Harcombe, Coxon, Morris, Griffiths, Johnson, Jill, Harvey, Oldham, Bradley and Williams.

CATERING

Like the Public Address System, the catering on the ground last season came in for a certain amount of criticism. Alterations have now been made in these arrangements and a bigger selection of snacks and beverages may be obtained at any of the 18 refreshment bars in all parts of the ground.

Top to bottom: Billy Bingham's international call-up warrants a mention (v Blackburn Rovers, 1961/62) - as does that of Scottish duo Alex Scott and Jimmy Gabriel (v Blackburn Rovers, 1963/64); match news - 'referee Mr R. H. Windle was knocked out', '...a poor game which neither side deserved to win' in among the PA system 'experiments' info and catering criticism (v Sheffield Wednesday, 1961/62)

EVERTON FOOTBALL CLUB *(Founded 1878)*

Chairman: J. C. SHARP

Directors: N. W. COFFEY
C. E. BALMFORTH
JOHN MOORES
G. A. WATTS
J. P. HACKING
T. H. W. SCOTT

Manager: H. CATTERICK

Secretary: W. DICKINSON

Today, we have the pleasure of launching the first issue of our new match-day magazine.

And we emphasise the word *magazine*. Entertainment, information and value for money are all factors which go to swell the new interest in high-quality programmes.

Whilst with my previous club—Birmingham City, I was proud to be associated with a magazine that was named as best in the Second Division for the last two seasons. Now, surrounded by the immense potential of Goodison Park, I am aiming for an even higher level publication in order to carry off the First Division "title".

You will find that this issue is divided into six sections:

1. **Club comment and opinion.**
2. **Detailed analysis of the opposition.**
3. **Club gossip and features on the players.**
4. **General features, with articles from top-name writers.**
5. **Statistics, ranging from fixtures to a comprehensive record section as the season grows.**
6. **History, with old players delving into Everton's famous past.**

Other features, including action pictures from previous matches and Supporters' news and travel arrangements, will be added.

We hope you enjoy the new style—please let us know!

DAVID EXALL

"WE ARE SORRY THAT OUR POPULAR SKIPPER BRIAN LABONE HAS NOTIFIED THE CLUB HE INTENDS GIVING UP FOOTBALL"

LET'S GET IT RIGHT

Every Evertonian is sorry that our skipper popular Brian Labone has notified the Club that he intends giving up football at the expiration of his current contract with the Club to go into business. It was characteristic of Brian that he should give the Club good notice of his intentions, and it was appreciated. We feel this is an opportune moment to put things right so far as Brian is concerned. It has been going on for months, and, in fact, was referred to again in one of the week-end papers that Labone finished with football at the end of this season. That is wrong. Brian, we are delighted to point out will be playing NEXT season for the simple reason that he intends fulfilling his contract, and that does not expire until June 30th, 1969. As a matter of fact if Brian decided to have one more season he could be on that World Cup trip to Mexico.

Top: Promotions manager David Exall shouts about the launch of the new match programme (v Crystal Palace, 1969/70)
Above: The club confirm the news that captain Brian Labone plans to retire at the end of the 1968/69 season (v Tranmere Rovers, FA Cup, 1967/68)

EVERTON FOOT

Back Row: Brown A. D., Bennett H., Rankin A., Barnett G., W
Coach/Trainer, T. G. Watson Asst. Coach/Trainer, Pickering F.
Ball A. J., Royle J., A. Proudler, Asst. Coach/Trainer. Second Ro
Harvey C., Wright T., Trebilcock M.   Front Row: Labone B. L

CLUB 1967–68

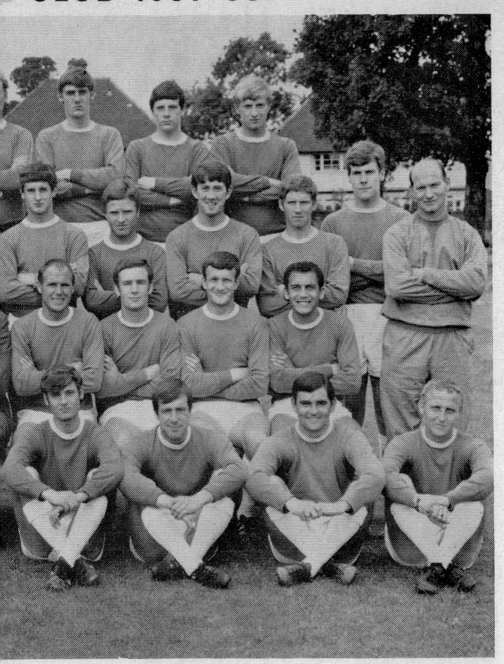

enyon R., Thornton F., Owen T. *Third Row:* T. Eggleston, Senior
F., Smith D. L., Hurst J., Husband J., Brindle W., Kendall H.,
le D. W., Scott A. S., Morrissey J., Mr. H. Catterick, Wilson R.,
A., Turner D., Wallace A., Styles A., Glover G., Humphreys G.,

Back Row: H. Bennet, J. Royle, G. West, G. Barnett, A. Clar
Middle Row: W. Dixon (Senior Trainer/Coach), T. Hughes, M. Lyons, F. Darcy, J. Hurst, B. Labone, R.
Front Row: W. Brindle, G. Humphreys, J. Husband, T. Jackson, T. Wright, A. Ball, C. Harve

...n, B. Jones, D. Johnson, T. Casey (Assistant Trainer/Coach).

...Jones, A. Styles, M. Westburgh, B. Turner, S. Seargeant, T. Darracott, A. Proudler (Asst Trainer/Coach).

...atterick (manager), A. Brown, A. Whittle, J. Morrissey, T. Owen, H. Kendall, W. Kenny.

Everton squad shot taken at Bellefield, 1969/70, published in the Crystal Palace programme

SHEFFIELD WEDNESDAY PEN PICTURES

RON SPRINGETT (goalkeeper). Winning his spurs in League football with Queen's Park Rangers, he was signed by Wednesday on 13th March, 1958, at a five-figure fee. Two days later he made his Wednesday debut and proved to be the man the club had needed to solve a long-standing problem. His reputation grew so rapidly that within 18 months he had gained representative honours and for the last two seasons has been England's goalkeeper. Ron has also played for the Football League. A Londoner.

PETER JOHNSON (right back). A native of Rotherham, Peter first played as professional for Rotherham United, sometimes as a back, sometimes as centre-forward. Signed by Wednesday on Christmas Eve, 1957, Peter has played successfully in both positions for Wednesday, too, but until Ron Staniforth became player-manager of Barrow in season 1959-60, Peter became first choice as right back and last season was an ever-present.

DON MEGSON (left back). Signed as an amateur outside left in October, 1952, Don had trial spells in various positions—inside left, left half, centre-half, outside left—before he finally settled down as a left back. He became a professional in June, 1953, but it was not until 14th November, 1959, that he made his League debut against Burnley. Don never missed a match to the end of the season. Last season saw him steadily enhance his reputation and gain representative honours. Born at Sale, Cheshire.

TOM McANEARNEY (right half back). Played well enough last season to command the attention of Scottish international selectors. Tom came under Wednesday's wing as a youngster from Dundee and, turning professional in October, 1951, when 17, he has now made close on 250 League appearances. He made his League debut against Liverpool in September, 1952.

PETER SWAN (centre half back). And still England's centre-half despite the double fracture of his left shoulder in the motor coach crash on the Great North Road last Boxing Day night (1960). Born at South Elmsall, Peter came to Hillsborough straight after leaving school. He had been outstanding in Doncaster Schoolboys' football and he became a professional in November, 1953, and an amateur on 31st May, 1952, he became a professional on 5th November, 1956. A six-footer, he made the debut against Barnsley in 1957-58 had established himself in the ... by the end of season 1957-58 and also accorded England Under-23 honours ... representational and then accorded ... the season before last and also gained Football ...

TONY KAY (left half-back). Sheffield-born and the captain of Wednesday. Tony is a Hillsborough product for he came here straight from school. That was nine years ago. Becoming a professional in May, 1954, he made his first League appearance against Bolton Wanderers in April, 1955. For the past three years he has been a power at left half and in the last two years has had several England Under-23 honours. He has also gained Football League honours. A prodigious worker and craftsman.

DEREK WILKINSON (outside left, or right). Signed for Wednesday from Stalybridge as a professional in 1953. A year later, almost to the day, he made his League debut against Cardiff City. Derek has made close on 150 League appearances. Has scored 36 League goals. Fast and direct, he can be very tenacious. Has had Football League honours.

BOBBY CRAIG (inside right). A Scot transferred to Wednesday from Third Lanark in November, 1959. He may be short of inches, but he's stocky and has cunning ... as craft. Can use both feet well and has been a very capable successor to the ... Redfern Froggatt.

... (centre-forward). Sheffield-born, Ellis joined the club from a ... He was an amateur with Wednesday for a couple of ... In April, 1955, in which year he made his League ... formidable man for opposing defences to ... especially dangerous with his heading.

... player and son of a ... John signed ... Quixall ...

Hand rollers... you can't beat it..

RINGER'S **A1** LIGHT TOBACCO RINGER'S A1

STILL THE BEST VALUE!

A.1. 52

MANCHESTER UNITED F.C.

5

FOLLOWING IN REAL MADRID'S FOOTSTEPS

That is Leeds' ambition

The smallest thing Don Revie ever did for Leeds United was to discard their old strip of blue and gold.

But now Leeds stand at the top of English football and await their challenge for the European Champions' Cup, that change in the days of Second Division depression carries extra meaning.

All-white, the new Leeds' colours, also happen to be the symbol of Real Madrid, the greatest post-war club side in Europe.

Another set of "Lilywhites"—in the shape of Revie's fiercely ambitious Leeds—could be about to embark on full rule of the European soccer community.

Revie makes no secret that he chose white because it reminded him of Madrid. "I think small and you stay small", I thought. "So I thought big and followed Real ...

Yes, just a small item ... something which could have been an empty gesture. But it HAS taken significance because of Revie, because of former Chairman Harry Reynolds (the man who gave Revie his first ...

chance as manager), and because of Revie's superbly efficient Elland Road set-up.

Leeds have had to buy their success. The £165,000 he paid for Allan Clarke in fact equalled their previous pay-out for the team—and that was on only three player's: Giles, O'Grady and Jones.

With Clarke added to their record-breaking Championship side, Leeds can face the European Cup with confidence that they can emulate Celtic and Manchester United.

No side can have entered this top competition with more Continental experience. Since 1965 they have played no fewer than FORTY ONE individual matches in the Fairs Cup ... winning trophy once in two Final appearances. Only four clubs, Real Zaragossa, Bologna, Dinamo Zagreb and Ujpest Dozsa, defeated them in this period.

During these four seasons, Leeds played a remarkable number of 241 games in Europe and England. A wonderful example of ... **PRACTICE MAKES PERFECT!**

How the Champions win their honours

One could fill all 24 pages of this magazine with tales of how Leeds United's great rise to power in the 'Sixties'. But we'll just flip through some of the most important personalities and facts.

Every top side needs a top COACHING SYSTEM. Leeds have that by way of **Syd Owen**, the former Luton centre half who is chief coach, and trainer **Les Cocker**, who has been in charge of England's Under-23 team.

Every top side needs a DOMINATING SKIPPER. Leeds have him in Scottish international **Billy Bremner** whose pet hate is people who say Leeds have no skill. "It makes me sick when people talk as if we are a bunch of cloggers," asserts Billy.

Every top side also needs a MIDFIELD GENERAL. Leeds found theirs at Old Trafford when they paid only £36,000 for Eire international **Johnny Giles**, the other half of the Bremner-Giles combination that has prompted Leeds to great things.

One need only remark that both players captain their countries. But, though they have shared all Leeds honours, Giles is one up on Billy ... he owns a 1963 F.A. Cup medal from his Manchester United days!

Every top side needs STRONG RESERVES. Leeds are lucky here to have **Paul Madeley**, a one-man "reserve team" on his own!

Paul, so highly rated that he played for Sir Alf Ramsey's England XI in the Expo Tournament in Montreal, still can't win a regular place for himself. Last season the Leeds-born star flitted around the side as deputy for Cooper, Charlton,

Lorimer, Jones and Giles.

But Leeds also have other top-quality reserve men. Players like Rod Belfitt, a more than useful striker, and forward Michael Bates. And, since Allan Clarke's arrival, Leeds started this season with only one place open to either Lorimer or Mike O'Grady, an England winger last season.

GARY SPRAKE . . . Wales and Leeds goalkeeper

Every top side also needs a TOP GROUND. Leeds, who had gates of only 9,000 when Revie started ... to re-build, can, and do, cater for 50,000 with the help of a new double-decker stand behind one goal.

But, above all, every top side needs a **GREAT MANAGER.** D ... Revie is surely this.

LEEDS UNITED, 1969-70. Left to Right: Back: Don Revie, Paul Reaney, Norman Hunter, Rod Belfitt, Eddie Gray, Mike O'Grady, Jack Charlton, Gary Sprake, David Harvey, Mick Jones, Paul Madeley. Front: Allan Clarke, Terry Cooper, Terry Hibbitt, Billy Bremner, Johnny Giles, Peter Lorimer.

4

LIVERPOOL PEN PICTURES

JAMES FURNELL (Goalkeeper). Born Manchester. Signed from Burnley February 1962. Played thirteen games in our first team last season.

GERALD BYRNE (Right-back).—Born Liverpool. Joined this club from school and was signed as a professional in August 1955. He has played for England in an 'Under 23' International match. Made thirty-three first team appearances last season.

RONALD MORAN (Left-back).—Born Liverpool. Joined this club straight from school in 1952, turning professional at seventeen. Has played for the Football League team. Made thirteen first team appearances last season.

GORDON MILNE (Right-half).—Born Preston. Signed from Preston North End in August 1960. Son of Preston N.E. manager. Made forty-two first team appearances last season.

RONALD YEATS (Centre-half).—Born Aberdeen. Secured from Dundee United in July 1961. A tall and powerful player who has played for Scotland in Youth International matches and has been reserve for 'Under 23' and full Scottish teams.

THOMAS LEISHMAN (Left-half).—Born Stenhousemuir. Signed from St. Mirren in November 1959. Gained a Scottish Cup Winners' medal in 1958. Made forty-one first team appearances last season.

HIGSONS BREWERY

BREWERS OF

Double Top

PEN PICTURES—*continued*

KEVIN LEWIS (Outside-right).—Born Ellesmere Port. Joined Sheffield United as a professional and came to Liverpool in June 1960. A former England Youth International, he is a fast and clever player with a terrific shot.

ROGER HUNT (Inside-right).—Born Golborne. Signed by Liverpool as an Amateur from Stockton Heath in May 1958 becoming a professional on completion of his National Service. Played for the Football League team last season and was reserve for the World Cup party in Chile. Made forty-one appearances in our first team last season.

IAN ST. JOHN (Centre-forward).—Born Motherwell. Joined Motherwell when he was seventeen and transferred to Liverpool in May 1961. Has played for Scotland on quite a number of occasions. A clever ball player with an amazing turn of speed.

JAMES MELIA (Inside-left).—Born Liverpool. Joined Liverpool as a Ground Staff boy straight from school, becoming a professional at the age of seventeen. Has represented England in both Schoolboy and Youth International matches.

ALAN A'COURT (Outside-left).—Born Prescot. Joined Liverpool as an Amateur to become a professional in 1952, making his League debut in 1953. He has been capped for England, playing in the World Cup games in Sweden, also toured the Far East with the F.A. team in 1961.

IAN CALLAGHAN (Outside-right).—Born Liverpool. Former Liverpool schoolboy. Came through our Junior teams, turning professional in April 1960. Made twenty-three appearances in the first team last season.

OPPOSITION NOTES...

The opposition Pen Pictures continued to dominate the pages until the programme relaunch in 1969. Often 'topped and tailed' by advertising for supporters' staples – booze and fags – prominent sign-off comments about players, who were often given their full Christian names like Ronald Yeats and Gerald Byrne, included:

Ron Springett - He is a Londoner.
Tony Kay - A prodigious worker and craftsman.
Kevin Lewis - A fast and clever player with a terrific shot.
Ian St John - A clever ball player with an amazing turn of speed.

A bigger, redesigned programme allowed more space for content to breathe in 1969/70, with more pictures and features, as well as lengthier player write-ups. Despite this, the sign-offs often remained succinct - as these Manchester City notes (right) highlight:

Colin Bell - Rates with the best for creative skill and punch.
Francis Lee - If it comes to a penalty, then Lee is a power-packed menace.
Neil Young - A local.
Ian Bowyer - A masterly header of the ball.

A PICTURE THAT TELLS A STORY

Picture by 'Manchester Evening News'

A picture that records two seasons of historic achievement by Manchester City. The trophies, all actually received by City within 12 months, are (from left): The F.A. Charity Shield, the League Championship Trophy and the F.A. Cup. The players . . . Back (from left): Heslop, Oakes, Doyle, Mulhearn, Booth, Dowd, Bowles, Coleman (now Sheff Wed.), Mann, Pardoe. Front: Connor, Owen, Bell, Book, Lee, Summerbee, Young. Inset: Bowyer, Corrigan.

MERCER'S MEN ON PARADE TONIGH

JOE CORRIGAN (Goal): Older City fans are already regarding this young local as *"the new Swift"*—a fine successor to Frank, who, from 1934, became the most-popular goalkeeper in the world, and who died at Munich in 1958. Joe only came in for four games last season, but is now firmly-established as one of the brightest prospects. Under-23 cap in October.

TONY BOOK (Right-back): Club skipper who is the joint holder of 'The Footballer of the Year' title. Bath City and Plymouth Argyle enjoyed Book's skill before he joined City in 1966. At well over 30, he has led them to League and F.A. Cup triumphs.

GLYN PARDOE (Left-back): Known as 'The Bear'. Glyn has the distinction of being City's youngest-ever debutant. Just 15 and 314 days when making his debut. Hails from Winsford and was a Schoolboy International. Also capped by Under-23's.

MIKE DOYLE (Right-half): Known as 'Tommy' in the dressing-room, so avoiding confusion with Summerbee. Doyle was signed from Stockport Schoolboys, and has been full-time since 1964.

TOMMY BOOTH (Centre-half): No doubt you'll recall that Tommy scored the goal in the Cup Semi-final last term. It was his first-ever goal too! Also a local, and a full-timer for two years.

ALAN OAKES (Left-half): Alan, another from Winsford, has a keen urge to play for England, and, on current form, Sir Alfred might do a lot worse. Has been selected for the Football League team.

MIKE SUMMERBEE (Outside-right): Back in his native county after spells in the West Country with Cheltenham and Swindon Town whom he left for City in August 1965. Can lead an attack. England International.

COLIN BELL (Inside-right): Already an established English star, Bell is a North-Easterner discovered and developed by Bury but who has really "made it" with City. Rates with the best for creative skill and punch.

FRANCIS LEE (Centre-forward): Originally a winger with Bolton Wanderers, 'Franny' is a priority for the World Cup. A strike from any attacking spot and, if it comes to a penalty, then Lee is a power-packed menace.

NEIL YOUNG (Inside-left): His renowned left-foot won the Cup last May. Originally played on the wing and still exploits a long, raking stride inside. A local.

IAN BOWYER (Outside-left): Like his Manager, comes from Ellesmere Port. A graduate of the junior teams, Ian made his debut last season, but has reached maturity this. A masterly header of the ball.

DAVID CONNOR (Midfield): We were poised to sign David last season, but he decided against the move, and, ironically remained to become Alan Ball's "shadow" in the Semi-final.

PALE ALE

FINAL LEAGUE TABLES 1966-67

LEAGUE—DIVISION I	P.	W.	D.	L.	F.	A.	Pts
Manchester U. ...42	42	24	12	6	84	45	60
Nottingham F. ...42	42	23	10	9	64	41	56
Tottenham H. ...42	42	24	8	10	71	48	56
Leeds U. 42	42	22	11	9	62	42	55
Liverpool 42	42	19	13	10	64	47	51
EVERTON 42	**42**	**19**	**10**	**13**	**65**	**46**	**48**
Arsenal 42	42	16	14	12	58	47	46
Leicester C. 42	42	18	8	16	78	71	44
Chelsea 42	42	15	14	13	67	62	44
Sheffield U. 42	42	16	10	16	52	59	42
Sheffield W. 42	42	14	13	15	56	47	41
Stoke C. 42	42	17	7	18	63	58	41
West Brom. A. ...42	42	16	7	19	77	73	39
Burnley 42	42	15	9	18	66	76	39
Manchester C. ...42	42	12	15	15	43	52	39
West Ham U. ...42	42	14	8	20	80	84	36
Sunderland 42	42	14	8	20	58	72	36
Fulham 42	42	11	12	19	71	83	34
Southampton ...42	42	14	6	22	74	92	34
Newcastle U. ...42	42	12	9	21	39	81	33
Aston Villa 42	42	11	7	24	54	85	39
Blackpool 42	42	6	9	27	41	76	21

CENTRAL LEAGUE	P.	W.	D.	L.	F.	A.	Pts
Blackburn R. ...42	42	27	8	7	93	43	62
EVERTON 42	**42**	**26**	**7**	**9**	**100**	**50**	**59**
Wolves. 42	42	25	8	9	102	46	58
Liverpool 42	42	23	8	11	83	37	54
Newcastle U. ...42	42	22	7	13	87	61	51
West Brom. A....42	42	21	8	13	87	64	50
Huddersfield T.	42	19	11	12	69	55	49
Manchester U....42	42	19	8	15	76	50	46
Sheffield U. 42	42	19	4	19	60	66	42
Manchester C. ...42	42	20	2	20	75	87	42
Stoke C. 42	42	18	5	19	65	71	41
Leeds U. 42	42	16	8	18	65	63	40
Burnley 42	42	13	14	15	60	60	40
Blackpool 42	42	13	10	19	64	78	36
Preston N.E.......42	42	14	8	20	50	70	36
Bolton W. 42	42	15	5	22	55	69	35
Bury 42	42	13	8	21	67	92	34
Sheffield W. 42	42	11	10	21	50	80	32
Barnsley 42	42	12	8	22	46	77	32
Aston Villa 42	42	12	7	23	54	79	31
Derby County ...42	42	8	13	21	42	93	29
Chesterfield 42	42	9	7	26	38	97	25

EVERTON FOOTBALL CLUB FIXTURES — SEASON 1967-68

1967		Last Season		This Season		Aggregate Gain or Loss	
		Res.	Attend.	Res.	Attend.	Pts.	Attend.
Aug. 19 Manchester U. ......H		1–2	60,657				
„ 23 Tottenham H..........A		0–2	—				
„ 26 Sunderland ....A		2–0	—				
„ 29 Tottenham H. ....H		0–1	50,108				
Sept. 2 †Wolverhampton W ...H		3–1	36,619				
„ 5 West Ham U. ....H		4–0	42,504				
„ 9 Fulham ....A		1–0	—				
„ 16 Leeds U. ....H		2–0	48,738				
„ 23 Liverpool ....A		0–0	—				
„ 30 Leicester C. ....A		2–2	—				
Oct. 7 Southampton ....H		0–1	44,997				
„ 14 Chelsea ....A		1–1	—				
„ 24 West Bromwich A. ...H		5–4	45,165				
„ 28 Newcastle U. ....A		3–0	—				
Nov. 4 Manchester C..........H		1–1	33,239				
„ 11 Arsenal ....A		1–3	—				
„ 18 Sheffield U. ....H		4–1	36,722				
„ 25 †Coventry C. ....A		1–0	—				
Dec. 2 Nottingham F..........H		0–1	34,084				
„ 9 (1) Stoke C. ....A		1–2	—				
„ 16 Manchester U..........A		0–3	—				
„ 23 Sunderland ....H		4–1	30,943				
„ 26 Burnley ....H		1–1	44,063				
„ 30 Burnley ....A		1–1	—				
1968							
Jan. 6 †(2)Wolverhampton W.A		4–2	—				
„ 13 Fulham ....H		3–2	31,496				
„ 20 Leeds U. ....A		1–1	—				
„ 27 (3)							
Feb. 3 Liverpool ....H		3–1	64,318				
„ 10 Leicester C. ....H		2–0	47,267				
„ 17 (4)							
„ 24 Southampton ....A		3–1	—				
Mar. 2 †Coventry C. ....H		0–1	38,127				
„ 9 (5)							
„ 16 West Bromwich A. ...A		0–1	—				
„ 23 Newcastle U. ....H		1–1	38,364				
„ 30 (6) Manchester C. ...A		0–1	—				
April 6 Arsenal ....H		0–0	45,745				
„ 13 Sheffield U. ....A		0–0	—				
„ 15 Sheffield W. ....H		2–1	38,355				
„ 16 Sheffield W. ....A		2–1	—				
„ 20 Chelsea ....H		3–1	39,316				
„ 27 (SF) Nottingham F....A		2–3	—				
May 4 Stoke C. ....H		0–1	44,005				
„ 11 West Ham U. ....A		3–2	—				
„ 18 (Final)							

†For points and attendance comparisons substitute Wolverhampton Wanderers and Coventry City for the relegated Aston Villa and Blackpool respectively.

ST. JOHN AMBULANCE BRIGADE

The First Aid Services on this Ground are provided by No. 5 Area of the St. John Ambulance Brigade, whose members work entirely voluntarily. New Recruits, Men, Nurses, Boy and Girl Cadets from 11 years, are very welcome.

Apply in the first instance to:
THE AREA SECRETARY, 31 Renville Road, Liverpool, 14

WHO PLAYED? WHEN & WHERE...

Date	Fixture	Att.	Result	Total Points	Position	West	Wright	Brown	Kendall	Labone	Harvey	Husband	Jackson	Royle	Hurst	Morrissey	Ball	Kenyon	Darcy	Whittle	Brindle	Bennett	Humphreys G.	Newton
Aug. 9	Arsenal	44,364	1-0	2	—	1	2	3	4	5	6	7	8	9	10^1	11		12						
" 13	Man. U.	60,151	2-0	4	—	1	2	3		5	6	7	4	9	10^1	11	8^1	12						
" 16	C. PALACE	50,700	2-1	6	1	1	2	3		5	6	7	4	9^1	10	11^1	8			12				
" 19	MAN. U.	53,185	3-0	8	1	1	2	3		5	6	7	4	9^1	10	11^1	8^1			12				
" 23	Man. C.	43,676	1-1	9	1	1	2	3		5	6	7	4	9	10	11^1	8			12				
" 26	SHEFF. W.	46,480	2-1	11	1	1	2	3		5	6	7	4	9	10	11^1	8^1							
" 30	LEEDS U.	53,253	3-2	13	2	1	2	3	4	5	6	7		9^2	10	11	8^1							
Sept. 3	Darlington (LC)	13,860	1-0	—	—	1	2	3	4	5	6	7		9	10	11	8^1							
" 6	Derby C.	37,728	1-2	13	3	1	2	3	4^1	5	6	7		9	10	11	8							
" 13	WEST HAM U.	49,052	2-0	15	3	1	2	3	4	5	6	7		9^1	10	11	8^1							
" 17	Newcastle U.	36,360	2-1	17	1	1	2	3	4	5	6	7^1		9	10	11	8^1							
" 20	Ipswich T.	23,251	3-0	19	1	1	2	3	4	5	6	7^1		9^1	10	11	8^1							
" 24	Arsenal (LC)	36,119	0-0	—	—	1	2	3	4	5	6			9	10	11	8	12	7					
" 27	SOUTHAMPT'N	46,942	4-2	21	1	1	2	3	4	5	6			9^2	10^1	11^1	8		7					
Oct. 1	ARSENAL (LC)	41,140	1-0	—	—	1	2	3	4^1	5	6			9	10	11	8		7					
" 4	Wolves	40,348	3-2	23	1	1	2	3	4	5	6^1			9^1	10	11^1	8		7					
" 8	C. Palace	33,967	0-0	24	1	1	2	3	4	5	6	7		9	10	11	8							
" 11	SUNDERLAND	47,271	3-1	26	1	1	2	3	4^1	5	6	7		9^1	10	11^1	8							
" 15	Man. C. (LC)	45,643	0-2	—	—	1	2	3	4	5				9	6					7	8	10	11	
" 18	STOKE C.	48,684	6-2	28	1	1	2	3	4	5	6	7^1		9^2	10	11^2	8^1							
" 25	Coventry C.	37,862	1-0	30	1	1	2	3	4	5	6	7		9^1	10	11	8							
Nov. 1	NOTTM. F.	49,610	1-0	32	1	1	2^1	3	4	5	6	7		9	10	11	8							
" 8	Albion	34,922	0-2	32	1	1	2	3	4	5	6	7		9	10	11	8							
" 15	Chelsea	49,895	1-1	33	1	1	2	3	4	5	6	7^1		9	10	11	8							
" 22	BURNLEY	46,530	2-1	35	1	1	2	3	4	5	6	7		9^1	10	11	8^1			12				
Dec. 6	LIVERPOOL	57,026	0-3	35	1	1	2	3	4	5	6			9	10	11	8	12		7				
" 13	West Ham U.	26,670	1-0	37	1	1	2	3	4	5	6			9	10	11	8	12		7^1				
" 20	DERBY C.	44,914	1-0	39	1	1	2		4	5	6	7		9	10	11	8^1	12						3
" 23	MAN. C.	51,864	1-0	41	1	1	2		4	5	6	7		9	10		8	12					11	3
" 27	Leeds U.	46,770	1-2	41	1	1	2		4	5	6			9	10	11	8^1			7				3
Jan. 3	Sheff. U. (FAC. 3)	29,116	1-2	—	—	1	2		4		6			9	10	11	8^1	12		7				3
" 10	IPSWICH T.	42,510	3-0	43	1	1	2		4^1		6			9^2	10	11	8			7				3
" 17	Southampton	27,516	1-2	43	2	1	2		4	5	6	7		9		11^1	8	12		10				3
" 24	NEWCASTLE U.	42,845	0-0	44	2	1	2		4	5	6	7		9	10	11	8	12						3
" 31	WOLVES	45,681	1-0	46	2	1	2		4	5	6	7		9^1	10	11		12		8				3
Feb. 14	ARSENAL	48,566	2-2	47	2	1	2		4	5	6	7		9	10	11				8^2				3
" 21	COVENTRY C.	45,934	0-0	48	2	1	2		4	5	6	7		9	10	11	8							3
" 28	Nottm. F.	29,174	1-1	49	2	1	2		4	5	6	7		9^1	10	11	8							3
Mar. 7	Burnley	21,114	2-1	51	2	1	2		4	5	6			9	10^1	11	8^1			7				3
" 11	Tottenham H.	27,764	1-0	53	1	1	2		4		6			9	10	11	8^1	12		7				3
" 14	TOTTENHAM H	51,533	3-2	55	1	1	2	3	4		6			9^1	10	11	8^1	5		7^1				
" 21	Liverpool	54,496	2-0	57	1	1	2	3	4		6			9^1	10	11	8^1	5		7^1				
" 28	CHELSEA																							
" 30	Stoke C.																							
April 1	ALBION																							
" 4	Sheffield W.																							
" 8	Sunderland																							

Home Fixtures In CAPITALS.   Everton's score first.   Figure in italics indicates player substituted.   Superior figure indicates goals scored.

1st DIVISION searchlight

EVERTON APPEARANCES 1969-70

	Best	Average			Home					Away					
				P.	W.	D.	L.	F.	A.	W.	D.	L.	F.	A.	Pts.
	57,026	48,556	EVERTON	37	15	3	1	39	17	10	4	4	24	15	57
	46,770	35,591	Leeds U.	36	14	4	0	46	12	6	10	2	29	21	54
	61,479	40,301	Chelsea	36	11	7	1	33	17	7	6	4	28	20	49
	41,826	35,781	Derby C.	37	13	3	3	39	13	6	4	8	16	21	45
	54,496	44,219	Liverpool	37	9	7	4	31	20	8	4	5	28	19	45
	55,420	37,319	Newcastle U.	37	12	2	4	33	14	3	9	7	12	16	41
	43,648	32,901	Coventry C	35	8	5	5	30	24	8	4	5	17	14	41
	50,783	31,722	Wolves	37	8	8	3	30	21	4	7	7	23	27	39
	60,514	53,187	Manchester U	35	7	7	3	26	22	5	8	5	25	26	39
	38,740	24,415	Stoke C.	36	8	7	2	25	17	4	7	8	21	28	38
	59,484	35,825	Arsenal	37	5	9	4	23	20	5	8	6	21	23	37
	63,013	34,153	Manchester C.	35	8	6	5	25	20	5	4	7	23	22	36
	42,075	26,268	Nottingham F.	37	7	8	2	23	20	2	9	8	21	35	35
	50,474	35,070	Tottenham	36	8	2	8	20	19	5	6	7	25	32	34
	28,000	16,712	Burnley	37	6	6	7	29	27	4	7	7	20	29	33
	45,488	28,679	Albion	36	8	5	5	31	23	4	3	11	17	29	32
	41,643	30,625	West Ham U.	38	6	7	5	22	19	4	4	12	22	37	31
	31,044	22,911	Southampton	37	3	10	6	23	26	2	5	11	19	33	25
	30,076	20,605	Ipswich	37	6	5	7	16	17	1	5	13	16	41	24
	45,086	25,140	Sheffield W.	37	6	5	7	22	23	2	3	14	14	40	24
	49,498	30,142	Crystal Palace	38	4	5	10	18	35	1	9	9	14	27	24
	36,504	19,119	Sunderland	37	4	8	5	15	21	1	3	16	12	44	21

(Leagues games only)   (Up to and including Wednesday, March 25)

	League App. Gls.		F.A. Cup and F.L.C. App. Gls.		Everton Career Records (League) Aps. Gls.	
Ball ...	32	9	4	2	147	60
Bennett ...	0	0	1	0	2	0
Brindle ...	0	0	1	0	1	0
Brown ...	26	0	4	0	164	8
Harvey ...	30	2	3	0	216	8
Humphreys G.	1	0	1	0	12	2
Hurst ...	37	5	4	0	161	21
Husband ...	29	6	2	0	108	36
Jackson ...	14	0	2	0	29	0
Kendall ...	31	3	5	1	101	10
Kenyon ...	3	0			13	0
Labone ...	34	0	5	0	431	2
Morrissey ...	36	8	4	0	203	23
Newton ...	12	0	1	0	12	0
Royle ...	37	21	5	0	118	62
West ...	37	0	5	0	272	0
Whittle ...	11	8	3	0	12	8
Wright ...	37	1	5	0	215	2

LEADING GOAL SCORERS

DIVISION ONE

Osgood (Chelsea)	27
Astle (Albion)	26
Clarke (Leeds U.)	22
Best (Manchester U.)	21
Royle (Everton)	21
Curran (Wolves)	21
Hutchinson (Chelsea)	19
Hurst (West Ham U.)	18
Channon (Southampton)	17
Robson (Newcastle U.)	16
Hector (Derby C.)	16
Jones (Leeds U.)	16
Kidd (Manchester U.)	16
Bell (Manchester C.)	15
Clarke (Ipswich)	15
Giles (Leeds U.)	15
Graham (Liverpool)	15
Kindon (Burnley)	15
Lee (Manchester C.)	15
Lorimer (Leeds)	15
O'Hare (Derby)	15
Burrows (Stoke C.)	14

Suggett (Albion)	14
Durban (Derby C.)	13
Greaves (West Ham)	13

DIVISION TWO

Bridges (Q.P.R.)	23
Byrom (Bolton W.)	23
Hickton (Middlesbrough)	23
Marsh (Q.P.R.)	20
Horsfield (Swindon T.)	19
Toshack (Cardiff C.)	18
Woodward (Sheffield U.)	18
Chilton (Hull)	17
Clark (Cardiff C.)	17
Worthington (Huddersfield)	17
Hiron (Portsmouth)	16
Noble (Swindon T.)	16
Wagstaff (Hull)	16
Fern (Leicester C.)	15
Hatton (Carlisle)	15
Balderstone (Carlisle)	14
Endean (Watford)	14

Martin (Blackburn R.)	14
Pickering (Blackpool)	14
Possee (Millwall)	14
Reece (Sheffield U.)	14
Bolland (Millwall)	13

DIVISION THREE

Macdonald (Luton T.)	22
Jones (Bury)	22
Macdougall (Bournemouth)	22
Earle (Fulham)	21
Conway (Fulham)	19
Andrews (Shrewsbury)	18
Chappell (Reading)	18
Ham (Bradford C.)	18
Kerr (Bury)	18
Bell (Reading)	17
Stubbs (Bristol R.)	17
Evans (Barnsley)	16
Gilliver (Brighton)	16
Yardley (Tranmere R.)	16
Bickle (Plymouth)	16
Buck (Rochdale)	15

Bullock (Orient)	15
Jenkins (Rochdale)	15
Rudge (Torquay U.)	15
Graydon (Bristol Rov.)	14
Harkin (Shrewsbury)	14
Smith (Tranmere R.)	14

DIVISION FOUR

Cassidy (Scunthorpe U.)	21
Howarth (Aldershot)	21
Kinsey (Wrexham)	20
Brace (Grimsby)	19
Brown (Aldershot)	19
Gwyther (Swansea T.)	18
Masson (Notts C.)	18
Price (Peterborough U.)	18
Hall (Peterborough U.)	17
Fletcher (Lincoln C.)	16
Fairbrother (Northampton)	16
James (Port Vale)	16
Smith (Wrexham)	16
Williams H. (Swansea)	16
Barker (Notts C.)	15

League, F.A. Cup, and League Cup games—up to and including Wednesday, March 25.

"I CAN ASSURE YOU THAT YOUR ENTHUSIASM IS A BIG HELP TO THE PLAYERS"

C oncerns over the distribution of FA Cup final vouchers prompted the club to issue an announcement early in the 1961/62 season.

A perennial problem still debated today, Everton decided to offer vouchers in the club programme to potential buyers after season-ticket holders and shareholders had obtained their tickets. In light of some complaints over the difficulty of purchasing a programme, the club insisted there were sellers outside the ground - or 'from one of the 18 Refreshment Kiosks in all parts of the ground'. The piece ended on a slighly sinister note:

'This is the last time this announcement will be published. It is felt that all our supporters will now be fully conversant with the arrangement.'

To the club shop next (right) - or the club secretary - as photographs, ties and lapel badges were on offer in the 1961/62 season.

Mischievous youngsters continued to wreak havoc during reserve games, prompting the club to issue this statement (right) in the 1963/64 Blackburn Rovers programme. Pitch encroachment concerns were also raised, a rule some Evertonians often have trouble remembering...

IMPORTANT ANNOUNCEMENT—CUP FINAL TICKETS

Each year, 92 Football League Clubs commence a new Season each hoping that it will be their good fortune to appear at Wembley in the Final of the F.A. Cup. Should this happen the fortunate Club's administrators are faced with the tremendous problem of trying to deal fairly with their supporters in the disposal of the allocation of Cup Final Tickets, the supply of which does not nearly equal the demand.

In the case of Everton, as with all other clubs should they be successful in reaching the Final, first priorities must go to the Shareholders and Season Ticket holders. The comparitively few tickets left for distribution amongst the thousands who would like tickets provides a problem that would take the wisdom of a Solomon, if all are to be satisfied.

In an effort to try and find an answer, the Everton Board have decided to include on Page 3 a Cup Final Voucher. If, and only if, Everton reach the Final, after the Shareholders and Season Ticket holders priorities have been dealt with, the next priority will be given to Supporters who hold a full set of programme vouchers. Obviously, even then, this does not guarantee a ticket, for this will depend on the number of applicants with Vouchers. But, at least, the holders will have the opportunity of purchasing a ticket before those who do not hold vouchers. Should the demand of the holders of a full set of vouchers not reach the number of tickets available, those holders of vouchers with the next higher total will then come into consideration. Therefore, in your own interest, save your Programme Vouchers.

Last Season, complaints were received that Spectators were unable to obtain programmes.

It is best to obtain these from the sellers outside the ground. If, however, you fail to obtain one there, arrangements have been made for supplies to be obtained at any of the 18 Refreshment Kiosks in all parts of the ground.

This is the last time this announcement will be published. It is felt that all our supporters will now be fully conversant with the arrangement.

IN THE SHOP WINDOW

Post Card Size Photographs Everton F.C. 1961/2 Price 1/- Post Free
Everton F.C. Ties ...   .   „ 11/6 „
Everton F.C. Lapel Badges   ...   .   „ 2/6 „
Address your applications to Secretary, Everton F.C., Goodison Park, Liverpool, 4.

5

CHILDREN AT CENTRAL LEAGUE GAMES

Despite repeated warnings about the misbehaviour of children in the Stands at Central League games, there has been no improvement and considerable damage is being caused to the seats in all Stands. As nearly all these children gain admission by Season Tickets, the Directors have been reluctantly compelled to withdraw Stand privileges for children using Stand Season Tickets at Central League games in future, unless accompanied by an adult, and then they will only be admitted to the Ground through the Ground Season Ticket turnstile.

It must also be emphasised that it is against the rules of the Football Association for anyone to encroach onto the pitch, either before, during, or at the conclusion of a match.

BRIAN HARRIS

Heartiest congratulations to Brian Harris and his Bride who signed up for life on Monday 11th December.

This is probably the longest contract he will ever sign, and we extend our best wishes to them both for a very happy future.

Back to December 1961, and a hearty congratulations to Brian Harris and his Bride, as announced in the pages of the Fulham programme, 'probably the longest contract he will ever sign'.

Chairman Jack Sharp addressed the fans in the new-look 1969/70 programme, beginning with a progress report on the new Goodison Road Stand. Work was set to continue throughout the season, 'and we apologise for any inconvenience these alterations may cause'.

There was word for the pitch, with problematic drainage issues hopefully a thing of the past.

On-field progress, and better luck with injuries, was the wish for the side, while 'we must never forget the great part played by Mr Catterick'.

The big talking point remained the club's failure to overturn a ruling on the Inter-Cities Fairs Cup one city, one team rule.

Everton's Talking Point Colum

Platform

SETTING THE GOODISON SCENE

—with The Chairman

Once again it is my pleasure to extend a welcome to our Supporters at the beginning of a new season.

The first thing you will see is that one-third of the Goodison Road Stand has been demolished and the new portion is under construction. We have had to seat existing ticket holders, temporarily, in the Stanley Park Goal Stand, but we hope to complete the new seating and re-allocation by the end of September.

Work will continue throughout the season on the interior of the stand and we apologise for any inconvenience these alterations may cause.

During the close season, the pitch has been re-surfaced by the addition of sand and this, we hope will, considerably improve the drainage problems which we have had for sometime.

Last season, our players once again showed great ability, a fact recognised by the International Selectors in picking Labone, Ball, West, Wright and Harvey for England and Jackson for Ireland and additionally, Hurst, Kendall and Royle, for the England Under-23's.

It is a record of which all Evertonians must be proud and on which we must congratulate the players.

In the F.A. Cup, we reached the Semi-Final for the third time in four years, a fine record, but, unfortunately, we suffered defeat, Manchester City winning 1—0 a few minutes from time.

We improved our position in the League, being third as against fifth in the previous season, and this, despite losing the services of Howard Kendall from 1st February and also suffering from injuries to Colin Harvey. Injuries have a great bearing on a team's success. Let us hope that we keep clear of them this season and, if we do, then we must look forward with optimism.

Whatever success the team achieves, we must never forget the great part played by Mr. Catterick.

ONCE AGAIN WE WILL NOT BE IN EUROPE.

J.C. Sharp.

I attended the General Assembly of the European Fairs Cup at Budapest in June and made the proposal that the rule which precludes two teams from the one City competing, be rescinded, but the proposal was narrowly defeated.

It was a great disappointment, a it means that Newcastle and Southampton, in 8th and 9th position in the League respectively, will be competing in the Fairs Cup next year.

We have recently appointed a Promotions Manager in the person of Mr. David Exall and his duties will be to organise fund-raising schemes and edit the programme. This has been entirely re-designed and I feel sure you will find the new layout a great improvement.

In conclusion, I would like to thank our spectators for the wonderful support the club received last year and express the hope that it will continue.

I can assure you that your enthusiasm is a great help to the players in their efforts to put the Everton Football Club on top of the football world, which, I am sure, is the fervent wish of us all.

OPEN 7 DAY

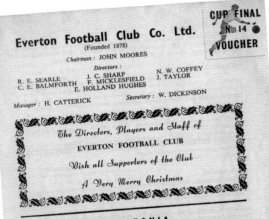

Everton Football Club Co. Ltd.
(Founded 1878)

CUP FINAL
No. 14
VOUCHER

Chairman : JOHN MOORES

Directors :
R. E. SEARLE   J. C. SHARP   N. W. COFFEY
C. E. BALMFORTH   F. MICKLESFIELD   J. TAYLOR
                  E. HOLLAND HUGHES

Manager : H. CATTERICK   Secretary : W. DICKINSON

The Directors, Players and Staff of
EVERTON FOOTBALL CLUB
Wish all Supporters of the Club
A Very Merry Christmas

EVERTONIA

Our Visitors

Today we welcome Fulham on their third visit to Goodison Park since gaining promotion to Division 1 in 1959. Last season they were defeated 1-0 and the previous season the game finished in a 0-0 draw.

Their home is Craven Cottage, which was acquired in 1886. It had been the home of Bulwer Lytton, and it was there that "The Last Days of Pompeii" was written. Ever since, the club in possession there has been known as the "Cottagers".

Like many other clubs Fulham started as a Church organization, St. Andrew's F.C. in the middle eighties. By 1885 it was playing at Putney in the West London League and became the leading junior club in the district, going through the London League undefeated and, as Fulham, gaining entrance to Division 2 of the Football League at its first application with twenty-eight votes.

This success was in no small measure due to the club's financial strength and its playing facilities, as well as to the fact of its having won the Dewar Shield in 1905 and the Championship of the Southern League in 1907.

Fulham stayed in Division 2 until 1928, when they were relegated to the Southern Section. It took them four seasons to get out, but in 1933 they were back in Division 2 and reached third place that year. Promotion to Division 1 came in 1949, but for three seasons only, and from 1952 they remained in Division 2 until achieving promotion in 1959.

In the F.A. Cup, the "Cottagers" made their first real mark in 1903 when they met and lost to Arsenal. Next season it took Reading three attempts before winning. In 1905 the second round was first reached, but the football world was surprised in 1907-8 when Fulham got to the semi-final by beating Luton, Norwich, Manchester City and Manchester United before losing to Newcastle. It was not until 1935-6 that similar success was achieved, when in turn, Brighton, Chelsea, (a great day that) and Derby Co. were defeated, only to find Sheffield United the better side at Molyneux ground. Since the last war the sixth round proper was twice reached before another semi-final appearance in 1958 when the "Cottagers" lost to Manchester United in a replay.

3

Xmas wishes, 1961/62

'A Very Merry Christmas' to Everton supporters, proclaimed page two of the Fulham programme in December 1961.

'Evertonia' then retained much of its usual theme, focusing on the opposition and the Cottagers' history - the only comment of real note being the cup victory over local rivals Chelsea in 1935/36 ('a great day that').

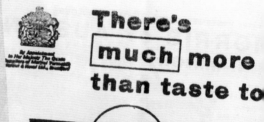

There's
much more
than taste to
MARTINI
Sweet, Dry and Bianco

See the champions, 1962/63

Suggestions that too much of the advertised product would encourage fans to sign up are uncertain, although Martini's programme placement does seem a little curious.

Still, season tickets would likely have been an easier sell than in most campaigns, the final game Fulham programme showing a small rise from the start of the decade.

Top price was £9 for central areas in the Goodison Road stand, Bullens Road and Paddock - with terrace tickets £3.5.0-£4.5.0.

SEASON TICKET PRICES 1963-64

Prices of season tickets for next season are as follows:—

	£	s	d
Goodison Road, Block "F"	9	0	0
Goodison Road, Block "D"	8	0	0
Bullens Road Centre Stand "A"			
Seat Nos. from 1 to 45	9	0	0
Seat Nos. from 48 to 85	8	0	0
Bullens Road Centre Stand "B"			
Seat Nos. from 1 to 17	8	0	0
Seat Nos. from 20 to 64	9	0	0
Bullens Road South End	8	0	0
New Paddock Seats (Centre)	9	0	0
New Paddock Seats (Sides of Centre)	8	0	0
Terraces Ground	3	5	0
Paddock	4	5	0

In addition to entitling the holder to admission to all League and Central League Matches, the Season Ticket will contain vouchers giving priority for home Cup-ties and special matches when tickets are booked for the appropriate section.

Renewal forms will be sent out to all present Stand Season Ticket Holders shortly and applications for renewal should not be sent in until these are received. If a renewal form has not been received before May 11th, application can be made by letter enclosing renewal vouchers and correct remittance before June 10th.

For new applicants it is unlikely that season tickets will be available other than for Bullens Road (South End) and the new Paddock Seating. Applications should be sent by post enclosing remittance to the Everton Football Club, Goodison Park, Liverpool 4.

13

Everton Football Club Co. Ltd.

(Founded 1878)

Chairman: J. C. SHARP

Directors:

N. W. COFFEY   C. E. BALMFORTH   F. MICKLESFIELD
J. TAYLOR   JOHN MOORES   G. A. WATTS
Manager: H. CATTERICK   *Secretary:* W. DICKINSON

CUP FINAL No. 1 VOUCHER 1967-68

A MESSAGE FROM THE CHAIRMAN

Mr. J. C. Sharp

In extending a welcome to you may I introduce myself as your new Chairman.

I have strong family connections with the Club as my father, the late Jack Sharp, was a player from 1900-1910 and was a Director from 1920 until his death in 1938.

I was elected to the Board in 1946 and have served under many Chairmen and this experience should stand me in good stead.

Last year the playing season was perhaps not as successful as we had hoped but nevertheless it cannot be said that there was any real reason for dissatisfaction. Our players by good team work and endeavour reached the Quarter Finals of the F.A. Cup, and those who were fortunate enough to see the game against Nottingham Forest will know that the game could so easily have gone the other way. Although not qualifying for a European competition next season, the experience gained during the past five years must be of help when next we are in Europe, which we hope will be in the near future, having failed this year by only one place.

And now to the prospects for the coming season. We have in Mr. Catterick a Manager of proved ability in whom we have every confidence, also a first class training staff and I feel we must view the future with a considerable amount of optimism with the great number of talented players we have on our books. One of the biggest hazards, especially at the commencement of the season, is injuries to players in key positions and it is my fervent hope that we steer clear of them so that success will not be jeopardised by the injury bug.

The beginning of the season is always approached with a sense of excitement but what could be more exciting than our match today with Manchester United, the League Champions. Such opposition will provide a stern test and a victory could undoubtedly instil in our players a feeling of confidence in the future and I am sure they will be helped in their endeavours by the enthusiastic vocal support of the Everton Spectators.

We have constantly in mind improvements to the Stands and Terraces in order to provide better facilities for our spectators and also the playing pitch to help our players. With this in mind we have removed the soil warming wires and installed a new system of drainage on the herring bone system from which we hope to reap the benefit of a level well drained pitch.

During the World Cup there was criticism that the wall around the ground was too low and dangerous to players running off the pitch and so we have increased the height to obviate any danger.

In conclusion I would like to thank you for your support which is second to none and if you should in your enthusiasm criticise the Directors and Staff please remember we all, including yourselves, share the same aim—the success and prosperity of the Everton Football Club.

Chairman's message, 1967/68

New chairman Jack Sharp introduced himself to fans in the opening-day Manchester United programme, outlining his credentials for the post through his father's Everton links and his own place on the board for the previous 21 years.

The previous season's sixth-placed finish and subsequent failure to qualify for Europe was deemed something of a setback, although 'the experience gained during the past five years must be of help when next we are in Europe'.

Harry Catterick was given firm backing and there was excitement at welcoming the league champions to Goodison. Sharp also promised further ground improvements to stands and pitch, as well as the low wall around the ground.

As a final note, he reminded supporters to 'please remember we all, including ourselves, share the same aim – the success and prosperity of the Everton Football Club.'

1970-1980

With colourful characters and a transitional spell on the pitch, that was reflected in a more colourful and frequently changing programme for the fans to read off it

A barren decade on the field, in the wake of the record-breaking title success of 1970, off the field the programme began to engage fans.

From basic club news and ticket information, player features began to become the norm. Fans also began to see more 'exclusive' shots of players in non-match action poses – while interview fact-files made fans more aware of a player's personality. Stock answers to 'favourite food' and 'favourite singer' can best be summed up by the title of 1970s Notts County player David McVay's 2003 memoir *Steak...Diana Ross*.

Covers varied throughout the period, with colour more apparent as the decade progressed. The mid-1970s cover (opposite page), for the late August clash with Derby County, was clearly an experiment deemed too expensive as it was rarely used until 1978/79. Other 'seasonal cover patterns' included the opposition team line-up in 1971/72, and topical quotes from home and away players in 1973/74.

One other note was the departure of editor Mike Beddow in 1976. A news story had appeared in the *Liverpool Echo* related to the match with Sheffield United in August 1971 noting:

Despite a price increase, Everton's programme sale on Saturday was the highest percentage sale in their history. Four out of every five spectators bought a programme, giving an 80 per cent return, compared with the previous best of about 60 per cent.

However, on Beddow's departure, he commented in the match programme that 'I could not sign off without thanking you, the readers – sadly a diminishing number.'

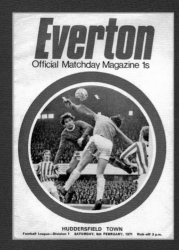

Everton

Official Matchday Magazine 1s

HUDDERSFIELD TOWN

Football League—Division 1   SATURDAY, 6th FEBRUARY, 1971   Kick-off 3 p.m.

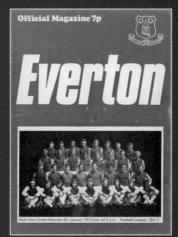

Official Magazine 7p

Everton

West Ham United Saturday 8th January 1972 kick-off 3 p.m.   Football League - Div. 1

Everton

Coventry City Saturday 7th April 1973 kick-off 3 p.m.   Football League Div. 1

official magazine 8p

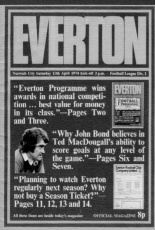

EVERTON

Norwich City Saturday 13th April 1974 kick-off 3 p.m. - Football League Div. 1

"Everton Programme wins awards in national competition ... best value for money in its class."—Pages Two and Three.

"Why John Bond believes in Ted MacDougall's ability to score goals at any level of the game."—Pages Six and Seven.

"Planning to watch Everton regularly next season? Why not buy a Season Ticket?"— Pages 11, 12, 13 and 14.

All these items are inside today's magazine   OFFICIAL MAGAZINE 8p

EVERTON

MAN ABOUT THE WORLD ... DAVE CLEMENTS SHOWS OFF A COLLECTION OF INTERNATIONAL JERSEYS. SEE 'GOODISON GALLERY' INSIDE

EVERTON v DERBY COUNTY
FOOTBALL LEAGUE DIVISION ONE, SATURDAY 30th AUGUST, 1975
OFFICIAL MATCHDAY MAGAZINE 15p

EVERTON

LEAGUE DIVISION ONE   MONDAY 3rd JANUARY 1977   PROGRAMME 15p

EVERTON v TOTTENHAM H.

EVERTON

DIVISION ONE   v CHELSEA   29th APRIL 1978   PROGRAMME 15p

Today's match is sponsored by

JAKA FOODS GROUP LIMITED
Finest Quality
DANISH
Cooked Meats

EVERTON

LIVERPOOL

Saturday 20th October 1979   Kick-off 3 p.m.   Football League
Official Match Day Magazine   Price 20p   Division One

Today's match is sponsored by

JAKA FOODS GROUP LIMITED
Finest Quality
DANISH
Cooked Meats

EVERTON

Today's match sponsored by
Glass Glover Group

Official magazine 10p
Everton v Panathinaikos
European Champions Cup
Quarter Final—first leg
Tuesday 9th March '71

Everton
IN EUROPE

Everton
official matchday magazine 15

Newcastle
United

Official Magazine 7p

Everton

December 1971 kick-off 3 p.m.   Football League - Div. 1

Selected covers, clockwise from above:
v Panathinaikos (European Cup), 1970/71;
v Newcastle United, 1970/71; v Huddersfield
Town, 1971/72; v Chelsea, 1973/74; v Liverpool,
1974/75; v Leeds United, 1974/75; (centre
programme) v Ipswich Town, 1972/73

Opposite page covers, clockwise from left:
v Arsenal (League Cup), 1975/76; v AC Milan
(UEFA Cup), 1975/76; v Carlisle United (League
Cup), 1975/76; v Aston Villa (FA Cup), 1977/78;
v Norwich City, 1979/80; v Bristol City, 1978/79;
v Manchester City, 1978/79; v Bolton Wanderers
(League Cup), 1976/77; (centre programme)
v Leicester City, 1976/77

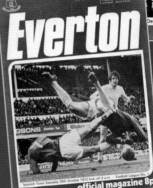

Everton

Ipswich Town Saturday 28th October 1972 kick-off 3 p.m.   Football League Div. 1
official magazine 8p

EVERTON

"There have been many players who have had their careers
cut short more tragically than
me: and without having tasted
the success that came my way with
Everton."—Tommy Wright

"Soccer Inflation... the story
of how the British record
transfer fee trebled between
Alan Ball's move to Everton
and the arrival of Bob Latchford seven
and a half years later."—Page 17.

OFFICIAL MAGAZINE 8p

SATURDAY 16th NOVEMBER 1974 KICK-OFF 3 p.m.   LEAGUE DIV. ONE

EVERTON

LEEDS U. SATURDAY 28 SEPT. 1974 KICK-OFF 3 p.m.   FOOTBALL LEAGUE DIV. 1

WELCOME
TO THE
LEAGUE
CHAMPIONS

OFFICIAL
MAGAZINE
10p

EVERTON
LIVERPOOL

OFFICIAL
MAGAZINE
10p

ENGLAND'S TOP SOCCER CITY
See inside for the facts
of the Merseyside power

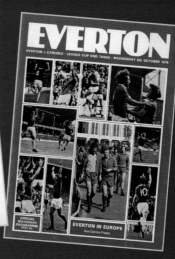

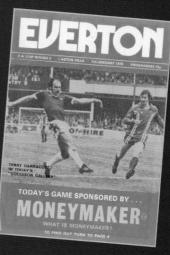

TEAMCHECK

EVERTON
(Royal Blue Shirts, White Shorts)

1 Dai DAVIES
2 Mike BERNARD
3 Steve SEARGEANT
4 Mike LYONS
5 Roger KENYON
6 Mick BUCKLEY
7 Bill KENNY
8 Martin DOBSON
9 Jim PEARSON
10 Bob LATCHFORD
11 Dave CLEMENTS
12

LEEDS UNITED
(White Shirts and Shorts)

1 David HARVEY
2 Paul REANEY
3 Trevor CHERRY
4 Terry YORATH
5 Gordon McQUEEN
6 Norman HUNTER
7 Peter LORIMER
8 Allan CLARKE
9 Joe JORDAN
10 Johnny GILES
11 Paul MADELEY
12

Referee: R. B. Kirkpatrick (Leicester)
Roger Kirkpatrick, the managing director of a hosiery company, has been on the League list since 1966. Married with two sons, he enjoys playing squash, golf and five-a-side football. He is president of the Leicestershire Saturday Teens League.

Linesmen:
W. D. Cashmore, Stoke-on-Trent
(Red Flag)
C. Tracey, Blackpool (Orange Flag)

match number
6

JACK SHARP
SPORTS
LIVERPOOL

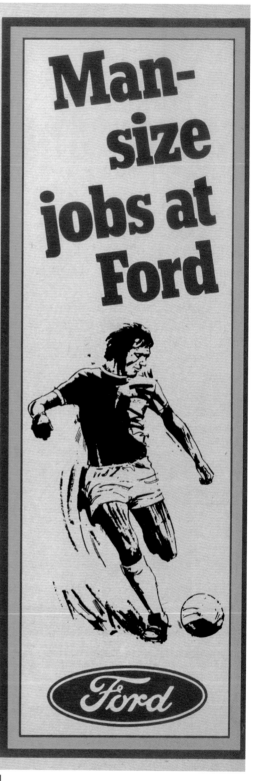

Man-size jobs at Ford

Ford

v Leeds United, 1974/75 – Ford recruitment drive in full effect...

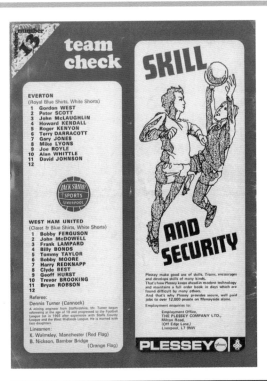

team check

number 13

EVERTON
(Royal Blue Shirts, White Shorts)
1 Gordon WEST
2 Peter SCOTT
3 John McLAUGHLIN
4 Howard KENDALL
5 Roger KENYON
6 Terry DARRACOTT
7 Gary JONES
8 Mike LYONS
9 Joe ROYLE
10 Alan WHITTLE
11 David JOHNSON
12

WEST HAM UNITED
(Claret & Blue Shirts, White Shorts)
1 Bobby FERGUSON
2 John McDOWELL
3 Frank LAMPARD
4 Billy BONDS
5 Tommy TAYLOR
6 Bobby MOORE
7 Harry REDKNAPP
8 Clyde BEST
9 Geoff HURST
10 Trevor BROOKING
11 Bryan ROBSON
12

Referee:
Dennis Turner (Cannock)
A winning engineer from Staffordshire, Mr. Turner began refereeing at the age of 13 and progressed to the Football League list in 1960 after experience with Staffs. County League and the West Midlands League. He is married with two daughters.

Linesmen:
K. Walmsley, Manchester (Red Flag)
B. Nickson, Bamber Bridge
(Orange Flag)

SKILL AND SECURITY

Plessey make good use of skills. Trains, encourages and develop skills of many kinds.
That's how Plessey keeps ahead in modern technology and maintains a full order book in days which are found difficult by many others.
And that's why Plessey provides secure, well paid jobs to over 12,000 people on Merseyside alone.

Employment enquiries to:
Employment Office,
THE PLESSEY COMPANY LTD.,
Milton Road,
(Off Edge Lane),
Liverpool, L7 9NW

PLESSEY

TEAMCHECK

EVERTON
(Royal Blue Shirts, White Shorts)
1 David LAWSON
2 Mike BERNARD
3 Steve SEARGEANT
4 John HURST
5 Roger KENYON
6 Dave CLEMENTS
7 Colin HARVEY
8 Mick BUCKLEY
9 Bob LATCHFORD
10 Mick LYONS
11 John CONNOLLY
12

NORWICH CITY
(Yellow Shirts, Green Shorts)
1 Kevin KEELAN
2 Mel MACHIN
3 Colin PROPHETT
4 Dave STRINGER
5 Duncan FORBES
6 Steve GRAPES
7 Trevor HOWARD
8 Ted MACDOUGALL
9 Colin SUGGETT
10 Phil BOYER
11 John SISSONS
12

Referee: H. G. New (Bristol)
Harry New, a chartered electrical engineer who is married with a son and a daughter, has handled more than 100 First Division games since being appointed to the League list in 1960. He began refereeing in Hampshire and progressed through the Football Combination. Took charge of the FA Charity Shield (1968), FA Amateur Cup Final (1973) and England v Young England (1968).

Linesmen: N. Hayes, Atherton (Red Flag)
P. Green, Birmingham (Orange Flag)

voucher number 24

PLESSEY

ANOTHER GREAT TEAM

League leaders in telecommunications, Plessey grow from strength to strength. Internationally respected for their technological advances, Plessey are also one of Merseyside's largest employers. Study their form. They're worth watching.

PLESSEY TELECOMMUNICATIONS LTD.
Milton Road, (off Edge Lane)
Liverpool L7 9NW.

PLESSEY

Clockwise from above: v West Ham United, 1971/72; v Norwich City, 1973/74; v Arsenal, 1978/79; v Chelsea, 1977/78 – the potential for employment switches from Plessey to Ford

THE TEAMS

EVERTON
Royal Blue Shirts, White Shorts
1 GEORGE WOOD
2 NEIL ROBINSON
3 DAVID JONES
4 MIKE LYONS
5 BILLY WRIGHT
6 JIM PEARSON
7 ANDY KING
8 MARTIN DOBSON
9 BOB LATCHFORD
10 GEORGE TELFER
11 DAVE THOMAS
12

CHELSEA
Yellow Shirts and Shorts
1 PETER BONETTI
2 GARY LOCKE
3 GRAHAM WILKINS
4 IAN BRITTON
5 MICKEY DROY
6 STEVE WICKS
7 STEVE FINNIESTON
8 RAY WILKINS
9 TOMMY LANGLEY
10 KEN SWAIN
11 BILL GARNER
12

E24

REFEREE: P. N. WILLIS, MEADOWFIELD, CO. DURHAM.
Peter Willis, a Schools Road Safety Officer in Co. Durham Police Force, began refereeing in 1963 and then progressed via the Northern League. Played football for a Northumberland County side and was a P.E. Instructor in the Royal Horse Guards.

LINESMEN: J. A. WEST, SHEFFIELD (Red Flag)
G. BOOTHMAN, BURNLEY (Yellow Flag)

Man-size jobs at Ford

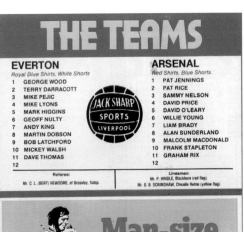

THE TEAMS

EVERTON
Royal Blue Shirts, White Shorts
1 GEORGE WOOD
2 TERRY DARRACOTT
3 MIKE PEJIC
4 MIKE LYONS
5 MARK HIGGINS
6 GEOFF NULTY
7 ANDY KING
8 MARTIN DOBSON
9 BOB LATCHFORD
10 MICKEY WALSH
11 DAVE THOMAS
12

ARSENAL
Red Shirts, Blue Shorts.
1 PAT JENNINGS
2 PAT RICE
3 SAMMY NELSON
4 DAVID PRICE
5 DAVID O'LEARY
6 WILLIE YOUNG
7 LIAM BRADY
8 ALAN SUNDERLAND
9 MALCOLM MACDONALD
10 FRANK STAPLETON
11 GRAHAM RIX
12

Referee:
Mr. C. L. (BERT) NEWSOME, of Broseley, Salop.

Linesmen:
Mr. P. HINDLE, Blackburn (red flag);
Mr. D. B. SCRIMSHAW, Cheadle Hulme (yellow flag).

Man-size jobs at Ford

GORDON LEE

This season we have done well in the League whereas last season our best form was reserved for the Cup competitions. Basically, I feel we will benefit more from success in the First Division because we are going into Europe next season and that will be nice for the supporters as well as for the development of the side.

I think we have tried hard to be the best, and if we were not quite good enough to win the title, whether we finish second or third, we have made a lot of progress. This time last year if the results had altered the other way, we could have been in the Second Division. I'm thinking in particular of the games against Bristol City and Stoke City, which, if they had been lost, could have had us looking at this season from a completely different angle.

This year we have been in there pitching and whilst we fell just short of the Championship, we must regard it as a good season. We have worked hard and have tried to be positive, but maybe we have been too positive, if you can look at it in that way. We have sometimes attacked too quickly, all helter-skelter, and conceded things in the process.

Because we haven't won the title, it probably means that we haven't defended enough. You only have to look at the records at the top, where Coventry and ourselves have scored most goals, to realise that we must have conceded too many.

However, we build our hopes on goals and the season has been a success from that point of view. Looking at the defensive record, it's true to say that we may have had more injuries in this area of the team. I'm thinking of Roger Kenyon, Mark Higgins and Terry Darracott, although George Wood and Mike Lyons have joined Andy King in keeping ever-present records.

Still, we have a lot to build on for next season and, whatever the pressures, I know it's better to be going for the Championship than trying to keep out of the bottom three. That, for me, is the yardstick to measure our progress compared with last season.

Now we're in Europe, let's hope we stay there and develop a constant pattern of competing at this level. It's a new experience for me and it will be nice for the supporters to see Continental teams. We have had a lot of experience of big matches and, so far, we have just failed on the big games – the League Cup Final, the FA Cup semi-final, and the disappointment against Liverpool at Goodison this season. Europe will help us get used to such big matches and I hope that we can then start producing our best on the big occasions.

If I could pick out one match from the season, it would be the one against Coventry. That was the dream match to win 6-0. It all happened and it was wonderful entertainment for the fans. Not only that, it's nice to look back on good days when we get to the last day of the season!

To be entirely constructive, however, I would say we played very well until Christmas, then had one or two injuries and the understanding went, leading to a few indifferent results – the 6-2 defeat by Manchester United and going out of two cups in quick succession. We became a little bit inconsistent and simply haven't played well enough since Christmas.

We beat Derby and Ipswich when the points were important and last Saturday at Middlesbrough, we got something without playing well. This is a sign of a side working hard when not at its best and such results account for our high placing.

I would like to congratulate Nottingham Forest on winning the Championship and hope that we can be there next season. But we still have plenty to be happy about. Bob Latchford has got into the England team, Andy King is in the Under-21 side, Mike Lyons has been a good captain, and it's to be hoped that George Wood and Trevor Ross can break through for Scotland next season. The Reserves have also done well and that is another good sign for the future.

Above all, I want to thank you, the supporters. You have been right behind us and played your part. On the other hand, we may have given some of our better performances away from home, but we'll try for a few more like Coventry to make next season even more exciting at Goodison.

GORDON LEE

EVERTON FOOTBALL CLUB, FOUNDED IN 1878, GENERAL ENQUIRIES 051-521 2020

CHAIRMAN T. H. W. SCOTT,   VICE-CHAIRMAN P. D. CARTER

Directors J. C. SHARP, G. A. WATTS, A. W. WATERWORTH JP, K. M. TAMLIN, J. SEARCH

Manager **GORDON LEE**,   Secretary **J. GREENWOOD**,   Promotions manager R. WILLIAMS

Above: v Chelsea, 1977/78 – the final match of the campaign, with Latchford on the verge of his 30-goal milestone

"IF ANYONE TRIES TO TAKE ADVANTAGE OF ME THEY FIND OUT - QUICKLY - THERE IS A HARD SIDE TOO"

H arry Catterick's 12-year tenure was brought to a close in 1973, the Cat being invited to 'move upstairs' as performances, results and his dealings in the transfer market became more miss than hit - while his health was also beginning to suffer, having suffered a heart attack in January 1972.

Former title winner Billy Bingham stepped into the breach after moves for names such as Revie and Clough came to nothing. His first column, in August 1973, touched on the decision to fine players on the club's pre-season tour ("I am a reasonably affable person but if anyone tries to take advantage of me they find out - quickly - that there is a hard side too").

Bingham led the Blues back into Europe and came close to landing the title in 1974/75, and after a brief caretaker spell in charge by Steve Burtenshaw, Gordon Lee was appointed in early 1977.

Lee came close in both cup competitions that year, failing at the third hurdle in the League Cup final before being denied in an FA Cup semi-final replay to Liverpool after seeing a late winner chalked off in the first game. The former Newcastle boss did at least deliver a repeat dose of European football - and some frank manager's notes...

CLUB TALK

We arrive at today's match having picked up nine points from our last five fixtures, in the course of which we have also become the First Division leaders.

We know we are there to be aimed at and that as long as we are in this position – and we hope we are still there at the end of April – teams will be pulling out that little bit extra to beat us.

This most certainly applies to Carlisle, our visitors today, for, in their first-ever season in this division, they are striving hard for every point and I am sure they will provide us with stern opposition.

The result which took us to the poll position was achieved last Saturday at Derby and, unhappily, we appear to have become involved in controversy once again and have, in fact, been described as "robots" by their assistant manager, Mr. Des Anderson.

I know what my reaction would be, as manager, if Stewart Imlach was to make such comments about the opposition after a match. What Mr. Anderson says or does, however, is Dave Mackay's immediate concern, and not mine, and, in any event, his comments sound very much like sour grapes because his team lost.

The pitch at the Baseball Ground was in a very poor condition and it contributed to the fact that the game was not much of a spectacle and also to some of the physical incidents which occurred. People who talk about cultured football should try playing on a pitch like that. It was better suited to horses than footballers.

I do not condone physical football and at half time on Saturday I told the players to "cool it", to forget personal vendettas and to calm down. I did this because I knew the best way we could win was to keep cool clear heads on our shoulders.

WE ADAPTED OURSELVES TO A BAD PITCH BETTER THAN DERBY AND DESERVED TO WIN.

I noticed a quote by Dave Mackay in which he pointed out that no Derby player was booked, while three of our players had their names taken. I trust he was not trying to make out that his players were whiter than white, because, for the life of me, I could not understand why two or three of the Derby players were not cautioned as well.

I was delighted that Bob Latchford's goal earned us both points and equally as pleased that it wasn't a penalty – otherwise Des Anderson might have protested to the Football League.

Only a few hours after assuming the leadership, we were paired with Altrincham in the third round of the F.A. Cup. I can assure them of a sincere welcome to Goodison Park and hope that the tie attracts a big gate and provides the spectators with a full afternoon's entertainment.

It has long been my contention that this season's League Championship will go to the club that has strength in depth in its first-team squad and the ability to string together a consistent run of results.

What has been particularly pleasing to me has been the way we have been able to overcome some serious injuries and the manner in which the players who have been brought into the side have responded with flair and spirit.

You must consider that at various times we have had players like Roger Kenyon, Bob Latchford – and, in fact, still have Martin Dobson and Mick Buckley – absent from action through injury, but the team have still managed to go 15 matches without defeat. It speaks volumes for the way all the lads have got down to it.

Finally, on behalf of all of the staff and players, I would like to wish you all a very happy day next Wednesday and hope that 1975 will again prove to be a notable one for all Evertonians.

BILLY BINGHAM

Billy Bingham uses his programme column to dismiss the likelihood of a player scoring 30 league goals...
(v Arsenal, League Cup, 1975/76)

"IT IS JUST A PITY NEITHER GOODISON PARK NOR ANFIELD CAN SATISFY THE DEMAND FOR TICKETS"

GORDON LEE

EVERTON v Liverpool..... What CAN you say about it? It's always the big one as far as Merseyside is concerned but this season, because of the situation in the league, it has to be everyones choice of Match of the Day, regardless of where they come from.

What more can you ask? Here are two great clubs occupying the top two positions in the league and both having successful seasons and contesting for the points in front of a full house. You could not get a more appetising prospect, it is just a pity that neither Goodison Park nor Anfield can hold sufficient numbers to satisfy the demand for tickets.

We have played well this season and I am very pleased with what we have done. But I am sure that Bob Paisley is equally as pleased with the form his side has shown so far with the only blemish being the European Cup defeat by Nottingham Forest.

We have played completely differently on our last three matches — at Ipswich and QPR in the league and against Dukla in the UEFA cup. At Portman Road we played very well after the interval: at Loftus Road we turned on some great football for the first 45 minutes and in between we put our game together for the entire 90 minutes against Dukla.

It is a pity that we will not be going to Prague next week with a lead of 2 clear goals and their late goal here, one which I though was somewhat freakish, has put a completely new complexion on the 2nd leg because of the away goals rule.

Possibly our biggest failing this season has been that we have not converted as many opportunities as we should have, especially when one considers the unquestioned calibre of the players on the staff. At Ipswich we hit the woodwork a number of times' against QPR we should have had the game completely sewn up by half time; and against Dukla we had by far the better of the game without really pressing home our territorial superiority.

Without doubt a very big factor in QPR being able to get back into the game was the injury to Mike Lyons. In my view Mike is a symbol of Everton and is a great driving force on the field.

Unfortunately, it looks as if we shall be without him today because of injury and it is also doubtful whether he will have recovered in time for next Wednesday.

As I see it Mike is to Everton what Bob Paisley is to Liverpool. They both have a genuine desire to win something, not only for themselves but for everyone — their team-mates, the Club and supporters — and they are able to transmit this will to win to all those around them.

Success is never an individual thing. It is achieved by a lot of people playing their part at every level with everyone pulling in the same direction for the good of the Club.

It could be said that we have our hands full with Liverpool today and Dukla next Wednesday. But just take a look at our next two fixtures. They are both against Nottingham Forest, the first on Saturday in the league on their ground and 3 days later in the league cup here at Goodison.

That is some programme. But if you wish to be successful you have to cope with periods such as this. It will demand a lot from the players but I know we are all genuinely looking forward to the Challenge. Exciting times are ahead and we will do our best to enjoy them.

Gordon Lee relishing the derby battle, ahead of the 1978/79 Liverpool fixture

I'M PROUD TO BE CAPTAIN OF EVERTON SAYS ALAN BALL

Club Talk

I am proud and very gratified at being appointed club captain of Everton. This is a great club and for the Manager, Mr. Harry Catterick, to show his faith in me by making me skipper has given me a tremendous thrill. If I can make half as good a job of it as Brian Labone has done then I'm sure everyone will be more than happy.

In a way I have been fortunate in that throughout my career I have played alongside captains who are widely respected by professionals all over the country. As a lad with Blackpool, Jimmy Armfield was my skipper. Then came those two stalwarts for club and country Bobby Moore and Brian Labone.

Armfield was the perfect man for a young lad to get to know when he first enters this game – especially a lad like myself who used to get carried away a little at times. Jimmy was the complete Skipper. A word here, a bit of advice there, and it seemed he spared extra time for the younger members of the side – Jimmy made life seem easy on the pitch.

Always willing to help anyone – and it seemed he spared extra time for the younger members of the side – Jimmy made life seem easy on the pitch. He was a man who could inspire confidence and his conduct was a tremendous example to the entire side.

Then, when I moved and began to play for England I came into close contact with Moore and Labone, two very similar men in their outlooks. Both are gentlemen who lead by example and both are extremely good readers of the game.

Moore – what can I say about him that players and critics the world over have not? – is not a great talker on the field. He calmly gets on with the game and I can tell you there's no more reassuring sight when things aren't going too well than to see Bobby setting things up from the back as if we were 10 in front.

Brian Labone too, is a man who won the respect of his colleagues by the high level of his own game.

I know that many people are expecting great things from me as Brian's successor. As always I shall do my utmost not to let them or the club down. And a final thank you to those of you who have written to me wishing me well.

ALAN BALL

[Everton Football Club crest and listing:]

erton
otball
ub

[Founded 1878]

...rman
Watts

...Chairman
Hacking

...ectors
...Sharp
...W Coffey
...hn Moores
...H W Scott
...W Waterworth JP

...lanager
...arry Catterick

...ecretary
...W Dickinson

...Promotions Manager
D H Exall

Alan Ball, 1970

With Brian Labone stepping down ahead of his retirement at the end of the season as captain, midfield star Alan Ball took on the responsibility ahead of the Blues' championship defence of 1970/71.

Noting the biggest captaincy influences in his career – Armfield, Moore and Labone himself – Ball vowed that "I shall do my utmost not to let them [the people] or the club down."

Mike Lyons, 1979

Ahead of the final home game of the 1978/79 campaign against West Brom, Lyons reflected on a number of subjects:

A season of improvement for certain players; an upcoming end-of-season trip to Egypt; the hospitality at Finn Harps, the backing from the travelling Evertonians - plus home fans' frustrations; and the publicity surrounding West Brom's 'Three Degrees' - Regis, Cunningham and Batson.

CAPTAIN'S PAGE

ALTHOUGH the season is not finishing quite as we would have liked from the team's point of view, there's no doubt that several individuals have advanced their claims for international recognition during the past nine months.

If I were to pick out just one player, then I would say Billy Wright has had a tremendous first season. He got into the England Under-21 team after only a handful of League appearances and showed his versatility by playing for his country at right back when he had been playing at centre half for Everton. In my book, Billy has established himself as a real contender to be our Player of the Year.

When Billy went into the England squad, it was unfortunate that Mark Higgins was out of our first team at that time. Had he been in regular First Division action, I'm sure that he and Billy would have played alongside each other for England.

Bob Latchford has won most caps by playing in all of England's full internationals this season. Although he hasn't reached last year's peak of 30 League goals, he has collected his fair share. He's the type of player who will always score goals and no matter how much people criticise him, he won't let you down in the art of snapping up chances. His form for England is the perfect example. More popular players in the eyes of the media have struggled to score at international level, but Bob has netted four times in his three full appearances against Denmark, Eire and Northern Ireland.

George Wood has yet to play for Scotland but I'm sure he would have done had the game against Belgium not been postponed because of the bad weather in February. George has proved himself to be one of the three or four best goalkeepers in the First Division and his reward should be a cap at the end of the season.

Andy King had a very good first half of the season – as they keep reminding us with that shot of his goal against Liverpool on

Match of the Day! – but he has struggled recently because of a niggling knee injury.

We'll be going off to play a couple of matches in Egypt this month. We've had quite a bit of flying – playing games in Holland, Northern Ireland and Libya, as well as a training break in Majorca – but we didn't do as much travelling as we hoped for in the UEFA Cup. I thought the trip to Finn Harps was the most enjoyable. The food was good, the people were very friendly, and the country was beautiful.

We had excellent support in our games in Europe and I also think our away following is the best in the League. At home, the fans have got on to us at times, possibly because they feel a little bit cheated after the good start, but in some other matches they have really tried to get behind us. We would like more of that next season. Winning honours is something that we have to do together – we need you to keep us going when we're not playing well.

Finally, I'd like to stress how important it is for us to chase both points tonight – both from a point of view of personal pride and also for getting that qualification for Europe.

West Bromwich Albion will be a tough side to beat. They can be very exciting at times, but I wonder whether the Press have got it right in heaping so much of the praise on to their younger players. The most valuable men to the team are possibly the experienced defenders, John Wile and Alistair Robertson. They are both well rated within the game, and with the side having done so well, they might have got more recognition by now.

Obviously, a lot of publicity centres on Cyrille Regis, Laurie Cunningham and Brendon Batson. Too much is made of their colour and I don't see why this should be mentioned as often as their ability. They are natural athletes and it's worth remembering that the world's best player of recent times is coloured – the one and only Pele.

LIFE WITH LYONS

Hello again! It's nice to have the chance of again bringing you news from behind the scenes at Goodison Park.

Perhaps the best way to start the first column is to have a look back at one or two happenings since we "broke up" for the summer.

The trip to Egypt was an enjoyable experience. We played two matches there and the best result was a 1-0 win against their national team. The facilities were quite good in a modern stadium, but the heat was something else. When we played in the afternoon, the temperature was 110 degrees and that's the hottest I've known on the football field.

We had the chance of seeing the sights, especially with our hotel only 60 yards or so away from the Pyramids. Some of the lads also went to Sahara City and had a go riding the camels!

From Egypt, we went on to Marbella and for six days, we were able to forget about football for the first time in ten months. But there was no rest for 'Woody' and 'Latch' — they missed the holiday in Spain and returned home for international duty.

Most of the lads then went away with their families — I chose Rhodes in the Greek Islands. Three of us — 'Kingy', 'Woody' and myself — got together again during the summer to take part in a Superteam event in Southampton.

As we were part of a winning side in a BBC series last year, we were invited to meet a team of athletes for a programme which will be shown on TV in the near future.

It's always interesting to compare different standards of fitness required for various sports. When we had finished, Berwyn Price, the Olympic hurdler, was telling us that he had held a pretty low opinion of footballers, possibly because athletes resent us being paid.

However, he said that we had gone up a great deal in his estimation. He was impressed by our professionalism and how much effort we put into the competition. That certainly was the case when things got a bit heated in a basketball match. We're wondering whether the BBC will cut out the scenes where 'Woody' and the massive shot-putter, Geoff Capes, were ready to have a go at each other!

The basketball showed up the different types of fitness. The athletes had natural sprinters like Berwyn Price and Daley Thompson and three of them were county standard at basketball. They were OK when running straight, but they seemed sluggish compared to us in a ball game.

When we came back for pre-season training at Bellefield, we soon had a few changes. We were rather sorry to see Davey Jones leaving for Coventry — he's a great lad — and we also lost Martin Dobson. At his age, he was suited by a move nearer home where he has an interest in the family business.

We also welcomed three newcomers. Liverpool-born John Bailey is quite a character — he does a great send-up of Emlyn Hughes! The other new lads are at home in the North West — Martin Hodge comes from Southport and Eamonn O'Keefe was born not so far away in Manchester.

Although our pre-season games were designed to reach fitness, they had some significance in relation to the UEFA Cup.

Hertha Berlin, who beat us 2-1 although we had eight corners to their one, knocked Dukla Prague out of Europe last season. Then in Belgium, we lost 1-2 but again felt we were the better side against Sparta Prague, who finished only one point behind Dukla in the Czech League. We would not mind meeting them in the UEFA Cup.

In Antwerp, we were delighted to see that about 500 Evertonians had taken their holidays to watch us. Our away support really is fantastic. On that subject, I've had letters from young fans in Leicester who are looking for transport to League matches. If anyone can help, please write to me and we'll put you in touch.

MIKE LYONS

Mike Lyons, 1979/80

Full of opening day optimism ahead of the match against Norwich City, Lyons vowed to go behind-the-scenes for the benefit of Evertonians in his captain's column.

The notes ahead of the Canaries clash included a rundown of summer events, including Lyons' participation in 'Superteam', new signing John Bailey's mean Emlyn Hughes impression and, bizarrely, fans looking for transport to the game from Leicester.

Mike Lyons and his wife, Patricia, pictured with the family pet "Sam".

A Goodison Gallery feature with Mick Lyons (v Nottingham Forest, 1977/78)

GOODISON GALLERY

Competition . . . that's the key word when Mike Lyons looks forward to the new season and discusses his hopes and thoughts for a campaign that promises to be full of excitement for Merseyside soccer fanatics.

● On competition at Everton, he says: "In my specialist department, for instance, we may have sold Ken McNaught, but there are still six central defenders competing for two places."

● On competition in the First Division, he predicts: "Liverpool must still be the team for everyone to better, but there will not be much difference in points between the top six and the rest of the league."

First, let's hear Mike's views on the new season as it affects Everton. "Our supporters," he says, "expect the best and that's what they deserve. For us to achieve that, we must become more consistent, stop giving away stupid goals, and work hard for every point early in the season.

"A good start is so important because you'll generally find that teams will get better and better if they build up confidence early on. The Boss talks about finishing in the top six, but maybe I'm too optimistic . . . I want to finish higher than that, at least qualifying for Europe."

As a defender, Mike is well aware that such ambitions depend on the foundation that is laid at the back. He admits: "One of our faults last season was that we conceded too many sloppy goals. It was largely through lack of concentration and I was as much at fault as anyone."

Significantly, though, Mike points out that "we were a bit more consistent when Gordon Lee brought his influence to the club." And the statistics underline the amount of improvement. In the first 29 games of the season, 48 goals were conceded — an average of 1·65 per game — but under the new management, the figure dropped to 32 in 29 matches — an average of 1·10 per fixture.

"If we can improve on that," says Mike, "we will be some way towards the overall target for the season. Personally, I'm hoping that I will be given the chance of playing in a settled role. I regard myself as an out-and-out centre half and find that I enjoy playing alongside Roger Kenyon.

"Roger has had terrible luck with injuries over the last two seasons but he seems to have come back to fitness and I hope for his sake that nothing goes wrong again. If we play together, and I'm not pre-judging the Boss's thoughts, we seem to work well, partly because I like playing on the right and he prefers the left.

"But there are so many possible permutations in this part of the team that any two from six could be in the side. Apart from Roger and myself, we have Steve Seargeant, Davey Jones (Remember, he captained the England Youth team from this position), Mark Higgins, and Billy Wright.

"Young Billy may not be so well known, but he had a great season in the Reserves and looks a tremendous prospect. The boys, Billy and Mark, could be put in the side any week and none of us would be missed."

With Mike so determined to see Everton pushing forward among the title challengers, it's interesting to hear his observations on the teams to watch.

"Let's face it," he says, "whether Evertonians like it or not, we have to agree that Liverpool, as double Champions of Europe and England, are still the most formidable opposition. I think they have as good a chance as they've ever had of winning the European trophy again, but a lot of us fancied Manchester City for the League last season. They should do well again because they have a fine squad of players and should gain from the signing of Mike Channon.

"Of the other top teams from last season, I think Aston Villa will have another good year because they are basically a young side and should continue to improve. Ipswich Town won't be far away and I regard Manchester United with special interest now that they have Dave Sexton as their new manager.

"United have always been regarded as possibly the most exciting team to watch and with Mr Sexton's coaching, especially his Continental ideas, I fancy they could be even more attractive.

"The promoted teams are worth keeping an eye on this time as well. We will be seeing Nottingham Forest today, so there will be first-hand evidence for my hunch that they could be the surprise team of the season. Maybe Brian Clough could do a Derby County with them.

"Out of the London clubs, Chelsea could also do well. They're a young side, exciting in their approach, and in Butch Wilkins, they have a player who could establish himself for a long time in the England team.

"If Forest and Chelsea are to be fancied, then we must take note of Wolves, who scored more goals than any other team in the Second Division. They have a lot of good players, all with First Division experience, and a man like John Richards can be worth a lot of points with his goals."

Of course, Mike believes that Everton are capable of competing with the best and doing better than most. "We must do better, I'll accept that," he says. "But I think people should remember that last season was our most successful for five years — ninth in the League, finalists in the League Cup and semi-finalists in the FA Cup.

"That's not bad by any standards. How many did better? But the trouble is that we'll always be judged in comparison with Liverpool. If we had done as well in a different part of the country — in London, just to name one major soccer centre — there's no doubt that people would have taken much more notice.

"In the end, I suppose we have to admit that we didn't win anything and the fact that we were so close to winning the League Cup, and the European place that goes with it, is probably a disappointing memory for the fans who gave us such wonderful support in those exciting weeks in March and April.

"I know how they yearn for success because I'm an Evertonian myself. I can't wait for the time when this great club is back at the top."

MIKE BEDDOW

"I WAS SCARED TO DEATH ON MY OWN! I WOULD GO DOWN TO THE LOCAL 'CHIPPY' AND THAT MEANT I WAS PUTTING ON TOO MUCH WEIGHT"

Evertonians learnt much more about their heroes as the decade progressed. The 'Man At Work, Man At Home' series from the start of the decade (see below's Tommy Wright feature) gave way to more traditional family shot-led fare in the Goodison Gallery, as well as receiving questions related to on and off-field matters.

Andy King's was a particular eye-opener (opposite), his move north and living for a spell on his own a factor in his apparent weight gain.

The feature could also vary in format, from Q&A interview to factfile-style questions, the usual favourite food/singers being aimed at Bob Latchford in 1974/75 (overleaf). Answers? T. Bone steak, Jack Jones and Lulu...

At home with the King family . . . Andy and Sue with their family pet, "Carmey."

GOODISON GALLERY

There was something special about the winning goal at Villa Park last Saturday – and not only because it opened up Everton's victory chart for the new season. "A First Division-class goal from start to finish," said Gordon Lee. "The build-up between Andy King and Bruce Rioch was excellent and Duncan McKenzie took the chance very well."

For Andy King, in particular, it was a magical moment. Because, as he admitted just 24 hours before the trip to Villa Park, he needed the confidence that comes from being involved in a slick, goal-making movement.

"My game started to go wrong towards the end of last season," he says. "I thought of all kinds of reasons, but it all comes down to a matter of confidence. That's something I've got to get back for myself.

"When I first came into the side, everything was great. I was scoring goals and it was all fabulous. The main difference was that I was a lot more confident. Because everything was going right, I wanted to try things, like shooting from 40 yards.

"Now I feel I am being too precise and too careful. And what happens? Someone comes along and whips the ball off my toe at the last second. Strikers find that happens to them when they are in a bad patch, but the only answer is to keep working, keep trying.

"Up until Christmas last year, I had my greatest experience in football. I started at the end of the previous season with two goals away at Derby and by Christmas I was up with Bob Latchford in the leading scorers' list. Perhaps I had built such a high standard that I started worrying when the goals stopped flowing.

"Also, because I had scored a few goals, people stopped thinking I was only a midfield player. In this role, I am supposed to score goals but making them is part of the job as well.

"In the end, I was pleased to finish as our top midfield scorer, beating Martin Dobson by 12 to 11. When I started to look back over the season, it dawned on me that this was a good record to have two midfield players scoring more than 20 goals between them.

"Look at Manchester City, for example. Their three most regular midfield men, Asa Hartford, Gary Owen and Paul Power, scored only eight goals between them. Yet, if they had matched our record, they must have won the Championship."

While Andy makes such a self-critical assessment of his progress in his first season in the top division, it would be easy to forget the "plus" marks – an England Under-21 cap in December ("That came at a good time," he says) and an appearance at Wembley.

"It seems as if all ex-Luton players are destined to go to Wembley," says Andy. "I used to go down there on most week-ends, certainly when we played in the Midlands or London, and the talk among the Luton lads was always about me going to Wembley.

"I told them it was just a dream, but it came true and I joined all the other Luton players who got to Wembley with new clubs – Alan Slough and Viv Busby (Fulham), Chris Nicholl (Villa), Bruce Rioch (Villa and Derby), Malcolm Macdonald (Newcastle) and Vic Halom (Sunderland)."

Away from football, Andy found that homesickness was a problem after his engagement last October. "I looked forward to the week-ends when I could see Sue in Luton," he says. "We bought a house in Melling mid-way through the season

and I moved in there on my own until we were married in June.

"Looking back, it wasn't the best idea to be living alone. I wasn't eating properly and, to be honest, I was scared to death on my own. Without thinking about it, I would go down to the local 'Chippy' and that meant I was putting on too much weight.

"Being with Mick so often, I started to join him when he went along to visit kids in hospital. This is something I enjoy doing. If you can get a little smile from a youngster, you feel that you've helped in some way.

"We also go out and make presentations at various functions. I enjoy having a chat and a joke because it takes me back to when I was a kid. The thing I hated more than anything was a personality who ignored you. I try to remember that when the kids want autographs.

Andy has his own special fan club – his mother and father, Bill and Eileen. "Dad hardly ever misses a match, home or away," he says. "He joined the London branch of the Supporters Club and comes up with them on the train. He's never been that much of a football fan, you could call him an Andy King-watcher."

Football, in fact, was the starting point for Andy's romance. "I've known Sue for about nine years," he says. "We went to the same school, but the strange thing is that I didn't really like her at first. I thought she was the teacher's pet. She says the feeling was mutual.

"But we eventually got together when I was playing for a local junior team. The fellow who ran the team lived next door to Sue and his house was my second home."

Incidentally, there was a special celebration for the newly-weds when Andy reached his 21st birthday three weeks ago. Congratulations, Andy!

BOB LATCHFORD

Latchford is a far happier man in mid-September than he was this time
year. The reason, goals. It's all very well for players to play an important
in their club's success but with regard to strikers – it's goals that count.
rtunately for Everton Bob and Joe Royle – the men from whom the bulk
e goals is expected this season – have both got off to great starts and it
rs well for the club when one realises that goals are the staple diet of
ellows like this Evertonian pair.
hen you consider the start Latchford has made this season compared to
then you must realise that he has received a tremendous morale booster
e very right time. Four goals from six matches – at the time of writing –
od news for everyone, particularly Evertonians.
st season when he was a Birmingham player Bob got off to the kind of
t that every striker dreads. He admitted at the time that two goals in the
nine matches didn't do his confidence any good at all.
et's face it," he told us "when you get that kind of start you begin to
der where you're going wrong. Somehow a fear of trying anything creeps
your game. You know that the best thing is to follow the managers advice
ep at it – but somehow that doesn't come off.
was lucky in that I got a good start when I came to Everton. Very quickly
ads and the fans accepted me and I was fortunate enough to get among
goals but that is only O.K. so far.
ou have to look forward to a complete season with another club as a new
lenge. You have to say to yourself that you are aiming at something and
you want to achieve it – both to prove your own ability and to prove right
e friends you have in the side.
Strikers tend to get the headlines but there is an awful lot of work done
thers in the team to create for you the chances that put you in the spot-
t.
What a change this season has been so far to last. Don't get me wrong –
s happy with Birmingham and after all that is my home town – but to get
rom the sprinting blocks like I have done gives you a great feeling.
But the Boss, the team and I myself are all striving for improvement and
is the way it should be. I don't set myself a target of goals for the simple
on that it might be presumptuous of me to do so and secondly because I
'd hate people to think I wasn't trying should I fail to get what I had
icly announced I was aiming at.
What also pleases me is that my own family seems to have got off to a
d start. Dave, who is with Birmingham has recently moved house and is
on the phone but I have been in touch with some of the other lads I used
lay with and they say he's bang in form.
And Peter with Albion seems to be doing well, also. I would think my Dad
ell chuffed with us all at the moment. And I'm sure that we'll all be trying
hardest to keep him that way.
t always takes time for a player to work an understanding with a colleague
I think the pre-season training has given me an additional opportunity
hitting in with the other lads both professionally and socially.
must say, however, that no-one could have wished to have met a friendlier
ch of fellows than I did when I came here. They made you welcome and
appreciated what a move could mean for a one club man like myself.
So at the moment I can also share the feelings of Martin Dobson, our
st signing. I know that he is still feeling his feet. But I'm sure that with
co-operation of the lads here he'll feel at home just as quickly as I did."
Now the date I'm looking forward to is November 30th when we take on
ingham at Goodison Park. I put a couple past my brother Dave when we
here last season. I want to do it again.
Sorry brother".

ll name: Robert Dennis. Birthplace: Birmingham. Date of birth: 18th January,
51. Previous clubs: B'ham C. International record: England Youth and Under 23.
ost memorable game: For Birmingham City when we clinched promotion from
e Second Division by beating Orient, at Orient, by 1-0 and I was fortunate enough
get the goal. Family: Wife's name: Pat. Children: Isobel (5 yrs) Richard (3).
hoolboy Hero: Dennis Law. Best player in my position: Big Chivers when he
on form. Player I most admire: For all round ability and versatility I must go
r Paul Madeley – there aren't many of his type around. Hobbies: Reading –
rillers or any kind of modern novel. Pet Hate: Hanging around hotels and air-
rts and the like. Favourite Artists: Male Singer: Jack Jones. Female Singer:
lu. Actor: Charlton Heston. Actress: Liz Taylor. Group: Beatles. Favourite
V. programme: Morecambe and Wise. Favourite Food: T. Bone steak. Drink:
ger. Car: Austin Maxi 1750.

John Hurst & Howard Kendall

It's always heart-warming to see a dog in human clothing - though whether John Hurst's pooch, Buster, should be allowed to don a sacred England Under-23 cap is another matter! His baby daughter, Samatha, also gets in on the act as we learn of John's love for reading, and looking after the Alsatian.

Howard Kendall was in positive mood for the club ahead of the 1973/74 campaign.

An award-winner with a couple of national newspapers for his performances the previous season, as well as being the holder of Merseyside Sportsman of the Year, Kendall discussed how much of an influence his father was on his career, taking on the captaincy and on the team being able to "make our mark."

On the captaincy, he noted:

"Every time I step out on the field leading the Everton side, I am reminded of the great traditions of the club and the responsibility that lies in my performance."

HOWARD KENDALL

"Injury free - we will give them a chase"

Howard Kendall was voted the most consistent midfield player in England by *The Sunday People* and the *Daily Express* and is also holder of the Merseyside "Sportsman of the Year" award for his exploits in 1972/73. Yet he would be willing to return all these honours for a place in European football.

Howard told us: "Every player in the country takes notice of the various newspaper ratings when they feel they have done well. I, like many others, do not give them a glance when I feel I have had a bad game.

"While players themselves know and realise whether they have had a good, bad or indifferent game, it is always pleasant to have one's own opinion strengthened by a critic's rating – especially if it's a good one.

"Personally it would have been better and more satisfying for me to have won these awards had it meant that Everton would have had a better time. We are beset by injury which makes it difficult, but I am thrilled that so many non-partisan judges thought that I had played well.

"Consistency is one of the main aims of managers and I must say that in this respect, since I was a teenager, my father has been a tremendous help.

"He has always been quick to spot the flaws in my game and to give me advice to remedy them. I have always respected his judgement and have given serious thought and training time to his suggestions.

"At the same time, I have at times received a pat on the head in acknowledgement from him when I have had a good game.

"It should be remembered that last season we were wracked by injuries from start to finish and that, as a stable member of the side, I was bound to attract some limelight. Perhaps the captaincy helped me a lot with regard to my consistency.

"Every time I step out on the field leading the Everton side, I am reminded of the great traditions of the club and the responsibility that lies in my performance. There, again, the glut of injuries that the club suffered last year also presented the more experienced players of the team with a fair challenge.

"We knew that even though the teams were going through a testing time, the experienced professionals had to try to give the newcomers a fair crack, and it must be appreciated that the lads who came into a troubled side did exceptionally well in the circumstances. Not one of them gave less

then 100 per cent for the team and their colleagues in the club.

"Things always go well for the team and the individual player when results are good because success breeds more success.

"The crunch comes when you have to introduce comparative newcomers to the team when results are bad. Everton had to do this last year and came through tremendously.

"But 1972/73 is behind us and we are all confident that, given an injury-free run, we should make our mark in the First Division this season.

"So far we have had only one serious injury – and everybody has got to sympathise with Tommy Wright, our right back, who recently underwent a cartilage operation.

"This type of surgery is bad enough at any time but at this specific stage of the season it is more than heart-breaking because Tommy will have to start all over again with regard to his overall fitness when he is able to resume training."

Howard has already spoken of the minor honours that have come his way.

We are sure that the reputation and the consistent displays he gave last season could well put him in the Munich squad for 1974.

YOUNG BLUES

No 1. KEVIN RATCLIFFE

KEVIN Ratcliffe was just three days past his 18th birthday when he joined Everton's full-time professional staff last month. His promotion fulfilled a schoolboy dream, for Kevin was a supporter at the Gwladys Street End right up to the time he signed as an apprentice in July, 1977.

"One of the last big games I saw as a fan was the League Cup Final at Wembley," he says. "I used to come to Goodison with my Dad. He still watches the first team and also tries to get over from Queensferry when I'm playing at home in the Central League.

Kevin, who was born at Mancot, just outside Queensferry, won schoolboy caps for Wales at Under-15 and Under-18 levels and was wanted by numerous

YOUNG BLUES

NO. 6 STEVE McMAHON

"I COULDN'T imagine working anywhere else," said Steve McMahon as he looked over Bellefield last week. Not even the sub-zero temperature could diminish the enthusiasm of the 17-year-old midfield player who was born almost in the shadow of Goodison in Everton

Kevin Ratcliffe, Steve McMahon, 1978/79 – Young Blues looking to break into the first team

YOUNG BLUES

Several changes have taken place outside the first-team. Apprentice winger Gordon Taylor has been released at his own request so that he can return to his studies at University in Scotland. And we also released two young professionals, Mark Tansey and Nick Banner.

Southport-born midfield player Dave Barton has stepped up to the professional ranks — a move which is also about to be taken by another midfielder, Steve McMahon.

The full list of apprentices for the new season is . . .

Player	Position	Schools team
Paul Garner	Goalkeeper	Liverpool Boys
Philip Ratcliffe	Full back	North Sefton Boys
Michael Imlach	Full back	North Sefton Boys
Dean Kelly	Midfield	England & L'pool Boys
Mark Ward	Outside right	St Helens Boys
Derek Goulding	Centre back	North Sefton Boys
Karl Green	Striker	Bootle Boys
Kevin Richardson	Midfield	Newcastle Boys
Robert Ash	Striker	West Midlands Boys
Gary Stevens	Striker	Cumberland Boys

Youth Stars, 1979/80 – Future first-teamers Mark Ward, Kevin Richardson and Gary Stevens noted on the apprentices list, the latter as a 'striker'

A peak form Joe Royle can devastate any defence. The same can be said of Bob Latchford. Put them in the same attack, as manager Billy Bingham has done, and you're hoping to light the fuse of a spectacular explosion of goal power.

The most successful strikers hunt in pairs, it is often said, and here you have an ideal combination of two strong, mobile players who have abundant power in the air and on the floor. But could the basic similarity in their styles cause any snags?

Joe Royle's answer is, "While I would agree that our clubs have used us as target men with others working off us, and in that respect, our methods have been quite similar. I also think that both of us possess attributes which we employ in our own individual way.

"You can take it from me that in the games we have played since we came back for pre-season training there's never been any instances of us both trying to take up the same position or of us banging into each other in the goalmouth.

"The couple of matches we had in Germany did us a world of good. Bob got three in one and I got a couple in the other and since then we've both managed to break the ice in the League. I know that my goals against Stoke were nothing to write home about, one a penalty and the other not the most spectacular of efforts, but they were goals and that's all that counts to me.

"As a result, I am more optimistic this season and feeling a lot happier with my own form. I know that now Bob has got his break he's feeling exactly the same and confidence will breed confidence and success."

How did Joe re-act when the news broke that the Boss had negotiated a record-breaking deal to bring Bob to Goodison to fill the number nine shirt? "Quite honestly, I had too much to worry about with regard to my own game to start wondering whether there was going to be a place for me.

"And at the back of my mind there was the question of my own personal fitness. I played with Bob towards the end of last season, but did nothing spectacular. That was due to my own personal lack of form, not with the pair of us failing to hit off an understanding.

"It wasn't until the end of last season that I began to feel fully fit. I'm happy to say that this season I've started off feeling much stronger than for some time. That, and the fact that I've got a goal or two, has made a terrific difference.

"It has been mentioned that I was in the

'nervous nineties' waiting for my 100th goal for the club for a considerable time and that I reached my ton with the penalty against Stoke. That it was the 100th was incidental, as far as I'm concerned. Getting it into the back of the net was all that mattered to me.

"Goals are the name of the game as far as Bob and I are concerned. Certainly, we are working at establishing an understanding, but the essence of any partnership we work out will be the number of goals we stick in.

"Even though we can play together and link up with 'one-two' passing and the like, we are both aware that we will be judged on how many times we score. All the pretty stuff in the world means nothing if the ball doesn't end up in the net.

"There's no great rivalry between us as to who gets more goals this season. As far as I am concerned, I shall be delighted every time Bob gets the ball in – as long as I'm getting my share as well. And I know he feels the same about me.

"Let me put it quite frankly. If at the end of the season our partnership has brought 40 goals between us it will be regarded as a success, regardless of how good or bad we may have looked in the process."

Joe was deadly serious when he commented: "O.K. so I've got my 100th for the club. But I prefer to regard it as having made a start towards my 200th."

Full Name: Joseph. Birthplace: Liverpool.
Date of birth: 8th April, 1949.
Previous clubs: None.
International record: Youth, Under 23, Full.
Most memorable game: Last full international against Yugoslavia at Wembley.
Wife's name: Janet.
Children: Lee (3), Darren (6 months).
Schoolboy hero: Charlton (R.) – "all way and every way."
Best player in your position: "It's hard to say. I don't think any two strikers are the same. But men like Bob Latchford, Mike Channon and Malcolm Macdonald will always get goals. And I was very impressed with Geoff Hurst the other night – he's still got a great deal of ability."
Player you most admire: The aforementioned Bobby Charlton.
Favourite ground: Old Trafford.
Hobbies: Records and chess.
Pet Hate: Travelling, particularly on coaches, and full ash trays – I can't stand the sight of them.
Favourite Artistes:
Male Singer: Elton John and Scott Walker.
Female Singer: Barbra Streisand.
Actor: Steve McQueen.
Actress: Barbra Streisand.   Group: Hollies.
T.V. Programme: Most T.V. movies and things like Horizon.
Favourite Food: Chinese.
Drink: Lager.
Car: Volvo.

Joe Royle, 1974/75 – On the hunt for goals, and being a Hollies-lover but not being a fan of full ash trays on the coach...

PICTURE POINT . . . The new Goodison electric scoreboard flashes up the best news of the season, recording our best League win for nearly ten years.

Millions of the "Match of the Day" television viewers shared the pleasure which a large Goodison Park crowd had enjoyed when watching our 3-2 win against Leeds United. The major talking point around the country was Mick Lyons' remarkable diving header for Everton's second goal. Gary Talbot's picture reveals the full extent of Mick's bravery in lunging forward and risking serious injury as Norman Hunter attempted to lash the ball out of the goal-mouth. Another high spot for Evertonians was Steve Seargeant's first senior goal which certainly made him look a happy fellow (Inset).

Mick Lyons' brave diving header in a 3-2 win over Leeds was captured brilliantly in the Newcastle programme of 1974/75

It's enough to make you cry!

Barry Farrell's picture of three young Evertonians is a superb reflection of how we all felt at Anfield last Saturday morning. But, disappointing as the result was, let's give the team full marks for a first-class display at Anfield. Our action pictures show . . . LEFT: Mike Lyons shooting between Steve Heighway and Emlyn Hughes. RIGHT: George Telfer releasing a shot which clipped the post. FAR RIGHT: Martin Dobson trying for goal.

EVERTON ACTION

BOLTON WANDERERS 1, EVERTON 1 (Match Abandoned at Half-time)

TERRY MEALEY'S camera clearly shows the impossible conditions as snow piled up on the Burnden Park pitch on New Year's Day. Andy King (above) goes for a snow-slide over the outstretched legs of Bolton defender Paul Jones . . . then we see a shot from Andy (top right) sticking in the snow as Tony Dunne clears the danger. Trevor Ross (bottom right) might not have been so happy about the abandonment, for this goal is one that doesn't count for the record books!

Bob's
30...
goal
by
goal

1 Leicester 10.9.77

2 Man City 1.10.77

3 W.B.A. 4.10.77

4 Q.P.R. 8.10.77

5 Q.P.R. 8.10.77

6 Q.P.R. 8.10.77

7 Q.P.R. 8.10.77

8 Newcastle 29.10.77

9 Newcastle 29.10.77

10 Birmingham 12.11.77

11 Birmingham 12.11.77

12 Coventry 26.11.77

13 Coventry 26.11.77

14 Coventry 26.11.77

15 Chelsea 3.12.77

16 Middlesbrough 10.12.77

17 Middlesbrough 10.12.77

23 Leeds 25.3.78

27 Coventry 8.4.78

18 Manchester Utd 26.12.77

24 Manchester Utd 27.3.78

28 Ipswich 15.4.78

19 Arsenal 31.12.77

25 Manchester Utd 27.3.78

29 Chelsea 29.4.78

20 Leicester 4.2.78

26 Derby 1.4.78

30 Chelsea 29.4.78

21 Leicester 4.2.78

22 Newcastle 24.3.78

1971-73

With European Cup football on offer in 1970/71, the Toffee Shop appeared to have increased their range – including a Blue Doll and a bemused-looking Blue Teddy Bear. Coach travel to Stoke City was also on offer, while Ford dealer Blakes insisted that they 'ARE ALWAYS TOP OF THE LEAGUE'.

A goalscoring football scene with happy workers either side hovered in the background of Ford's latest match programme recruiting campaign, THAT'S WHAT HAPPINESS IS!

A new, short-lived innovation at Goodison was a travel agents, with the 1972/73 Manchester City programme acting as a marketing tool for said business. Keith Prowse set up shop on Bullens Road, with the Everton Holiday Club set to launch soon after.

The bizarre-looking 'Soccer Sam' could not be ignored in the same programme, the mascots made from 'soft, high quality materials'. Made in two sizes, 'stumpy' or 'streaky', most club colours were catered for.

Away travel to Arsenal was also advertised on the same page, with the most noticeable point being the contrast in travel times between rail and bus – and for 40p difference: £2.10 bus, leaves 11.30pm the night before; £2.50 train departs 10.08am, returning 6.13pm.

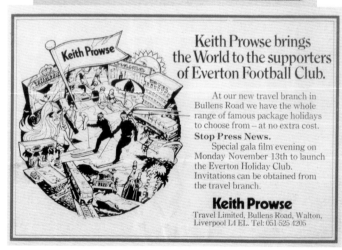

Visit **LIVERPOOL'S PREMIER NITE SPOTS!** *members notice*

| **WOOKY HOLLOW** 051 236 0330 *INTERNATIONAL CABARET* every night, see Local Press for Details | **WISPA** 051 928 8771 *Liverpools Liveliest Nite Spot* Mon to Sat OVER 30s Mon and Thurs | **PEZ ESPADA** 051 236 9580 *INTIMATE CANDLELIT ATMOSPHERE* of Liverpools Friendliest Nite Spot | **BOBBINS** 051 427 7128 stag nights disco nights cabaret nights there's a night to suit YOU! | **MR. PICWICKS** DANCE CABARET/ SPECTACULAR mon to sat over 30s nights: mon and sat 051 207 4605 | **ALLINSONS** 051 928 7442 *3 hours TOP cabaret 1½ hours dancing every night* |

Blue or Red you know your brown when you down a

Double Top

HIGSONS

INDEPENDENT BREWERS ON MERSEYSIDE SINCE 1780

1972/73

A who's who of Liverpool 'premier nite spots!' made an appearance in the Merseyside derby programme, while Higsons focused on both sides of Stanley Park in their advertising.

Cigarette promotion was still a key player in the advertising industry – and Everton and Manchester City fans were left in no doubt who 'the best in smoking' was...

How many people knew that Soccerbus had been running since the early 1970s? The scheme appeared to be confined to Bromborough, where you could leave your car before transferring to the bus.

NEW SOCCERBUS PARK AT OLD HALL ROAD BROMBOROUGH
off Bromborough by-pass
TO AND FROM THE GAME'S NO FUSS... ...WHEN YOU USE A SOCCERBUS
* A new bus service brought to you by MPTE in conjunction with the Club's management...
HOW IT WORKS
DRIVE YOUR CAR TO THE NEW BROMBOROUGH SOCCERBUS PARK - PARK IT AND GET A SOCCERBUS - IT DROPS YOU RIGHT OUTSIDE THE GROUND AND BRINGS YOU BACK. NO TUNNEL FEES!
ONLY 30p CAR & DRIVER
LEAVES - 1.45 RETURNS - 4.50 approx.
Merseyside Passenger Transport Executive, 24 Hatton Garden, Liverpool L3 2AN. Tel: 236 7606.

Embassy
FILTER VIRGINIA

the best in smoking

EVERY PACKET CARRIES A GOVERNMENT HEALTH WARNING.

GOOD LUCK EVERTON -Radio City Sport

Dave Clements in the Radio City Studios

A message from Everton mid-field star and Radio City presenter, Dave Clements:-

"Merseyside is the most exciting and demanding soccer city in the World and if you want to keep right up to date with all the news about Everton and Liverpool, the behind the scene stories, and hear us talk about each other and the next match, tune in to the Independent Radio Station on Merseyside, Radio City, broadcasting 24 hours a day on 194 metres on the medium wave band and 96.7 on the VHF band and that's also in stereo.

"Just before the match, tune in to my own show on Radio City. It's on every Saturday between 9.00 a.m. and 11.00 a.m. If you'd like a mention on the programme, a record dedication, or you've got a question about Everton or the game in general, why not drop me a line to:-

Dave Clements,
Radio City,
P.O. Box 194,
Liverpool L69 1LD."

194 RADIO CITY
INDEPENDENT RADIO ON MERSEYSIDE

194 metres med.wave
96·7 VHF and stereo

24 Hours a day

1974-77

The launch of Radio City was big news in Liverpool – as was the decision to involve players from both of the city's clubs – Dave Clements turning his hand to DJ-ing according to this advert.

Caribbean Evenings were all the rage in the Sportsmans Cabaret Lounge at Goodison – in January 1977 – while you could buy your outfits at Littlewoods, or something for the little one via Kadix.

The opportunity to see Frank Sinatra live at the Royal Albert Hall was a tempter, the chance to experience 'The Night Of A Lifetime.' Prices started at £99...

WHY NOT JOIN US FOR A
Caribbean Evening

IN THE SPORTSMANS CABARET LOUNGE ON THUR. 27 JAN

Speciality dinner plus Cabaret of Los Caribos and dancing to the Wilberforce Steel Band. Tickets available from the Promotions Department or the Restaurant Manager Tel. 051-521-2020 or 051-525-7455

for the best in childrens wear buy
KADIX

Well saved!
Shop at Littlewoods where quality and value mean real savings

KEYNOTE
FOR QUALITY
AT OVER 100 LITTLEWOODS STORES

LITTLEWOODS
YOUR LOCAL STORES · LIVERPOOL · KIRKBY · RUNCORN · WALLASEY
BIRKENHEAD · CHESTER · ELLESMERE PORT

SUPERSPORTS
TRAVEL
INVITE YOU TO AN EVENING WITH
FRANCIS ALBERT SINATRA
March 1st-5th 1977 (Royal Albert Hall, London)

Spend a night at the fabulous 5-star Royal Grand Hotel

Bottle of champagne on ice awaits your arrival

Chauffeur-driven car to take you to the concert (and back again)

Best seat in the house to see SINATRA

A-la-carte dinner in the Royal Roof Restaurant, where you can wine, dine and dance till 2.00am.

Full English breakfast before you depart the following morning

THE NIGHT OF A LIFETIME
£99.00 per person, all-in

**For further details ring
SUPERSPORTS TRAVEL LIMITED
(01) 568-3478 (London)
(061) 236-8606 (Manchester)**

SPONSOR A GAME AT GOODISON

The Sponsorship package consists of:-

- 6 Directors Box seats
- 50 seats in the Main Stand
- Acknowledgement on front cover of programme
- Advertisement space inside programme
- 4 advertising display boards around playing area
- Announcements over public address system
- Announcements on the Electronic Scoreboard
- 2 passes for Car Park
- Exclusive use of Directors private guest room between the hours of 11 a.m. and 2 p.m. (at 2 p.m. the Sponsor's guests will be joined by the other guests of the Directors)
- Buffet luncheon and bar

For full details of fixture availability and prices contact:-

WILLIAM J. HENRY (Advertising) LIMITED
26 NORTH JOHN STREET,
LIVERPOOL, L2 9RZ.   051-236 7741/2/3

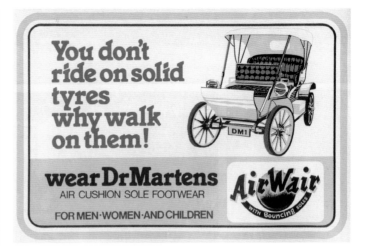

You don't ride on solid tyres why walk on them!

wear Dr Martens
AIR CUSHION SOLE FOOTWEAR

AirWair WITH Bouncing SOLES

FOR MEN·WOMEN·AND CHILDREN

Higsclusive Bitter

only Merseysiders can enjoy Higson's bitter

Real Merseyside pubs - real Merseyside beer

PLAY THE INSTANT LOTTERY GAME

with EVERTON F.C.

£4000 TO BE WON IN EACH LOTTERY

£1000 JACKPOT DRAW

OVER 3000 PRIZES TO BE WON IN EACH LOTTERY

Win £500 instantly

TICKETS 25p

FROM ALL MERSEYSIDE NEWSAGENTS WHERE YOU SEE OUR SIGN ▶

FIRST LOTTERY ENDS 31st. MARCH

EVERTON FOOTBALL CLUB 25p

INSTANT LOTTERY

WIN UP TO £500 INSTANTLY THOUSANDS OF PRIZES

ALL INSTANT GAME WINNERS ENTERED IN £1000 JACKPOT DRAW

OFFICIAL VENDOR

1977/78

The chance to sponsor a game at Goodison, or play the 'Instant Lottery Game with Everton FC' were two club initiatives advertised to fans.

Dr Martens encouraged supporters to stop wearing solid-soled shoes, while Higsons 'Higsclusive Bitter' was presumably brewed specifically with Merseysiders in mind.

BUY BRITISH! Or else it didn't say... while Arnold Palmer was happy for fans to make one exception in the form of his fashion shirts...

Put your money where your job is!

BUY BRITISH!

A sound economic truism from the
London Executive Placement Bureau

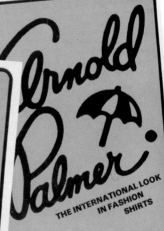

Arnold Palmer

THE INTERNATIONAL LOOK IN FASHION SHIRTS

1978/79

Anybody following the fans away from Goodison after the fixture with Leeds United would not have been surprised to find themselves at St Johns Centre in Liverpool – had they read the small print on the ad. Meanwhile the Holiday Inn copywriters were busy shoe-horning in a link to their 'world championship' credentials and the potential prizes on offer to the city's big two.

Higsons' staples Rock Ferry, Albert Dock and Gwladys Street became the faces of Merseyside bitter, while the Everton Official Annual 1979 was now available for £2.45 in the Toffee Shop.

The latter half of the campaign saw updates from SMC and Holiday Inn. Prices at the former are comparable with certain low-cost fashion outlets today – while we'll have to 'take their word for it', that there really was 'cheap beer and lager' available at The Warehouse.

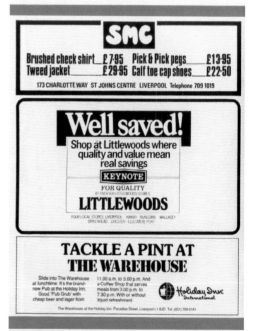

SOUVENIRS FOR CHRISTMAS

ASA
Supporters Jacket
36"-38" only
£10.45

Tee Shirt
£2.25

Hats £1.40
Scarf £1.55

Everton F.C.
Sweaters
£6.75
£7.25

Everton F.C.
Sweat Shirt
£6.25

All items available from the Souvenir Shop in Goodison Road — Monday to Saturday, 9 a.m. to 5 p.m.

1979/80

The relaxed pose, the casual, coy smile – yet it's still John Bailey who catches the eye donning questionable headwear.

There's more from SMC, while club sponsors Hafnia offered fans the chance to have lunch with the players, receive a tour of the ground plus win a signed ball, just by answering six 'true or false' statements on Everton and Hafnia. Revision of the blurb may have been required for statement 2:

HAFNIA account for over 15% of all Danish Cooked Meats eaten in the UK.

EVERTON IN CHILE

A TOTAL OF 150,000 SPECTATORS RECENTLY SAW AN EVERTON TEAM INSTALLED AS FOOTBALL CHAMPIONS OF . . . CHILE!

Club Everton de Deportes were named after THE Liverpool-based Everton in the early 1920's and news of their championship success reached us in a letter from Mr. Eric Davies, O.B.E., an exiled Merseysider, who lives at Casilla 16057, Correo 9, Santiago, Chile.

"My family was a Liverpool family," writes Mr. Davies. "One uncle, P. G. Davies, was Mayor of Wallasey in World War II. Another, Trevor Davies, was a Wesleyan Minister who went to Canada. My father, J. L. Davies, went to Chile and was a Director in a Liverpool firm, Duncan Fox & Co. Every one was an Everton fanatic.

"I have been an Everton supporter since 1906 (I am now 81). I write to you about another Everton, here in Chile, formed a few years after World War I by a group of British and Chileans in Vina del Mar, a beautiful resort near the port of Valpariso.

"Everton of Chile won the Final for the Chilean First Division yesterday (27th November). Everton and Union Espaniola (1975 Champions) had tied for first place in the League and had to play off on Thursday, 25th November. After extra time, they drew 0–0. The replay was yesterday and Everton won 3–1 after tremendous excitement and three spectacular goals.

"There were 80,000 spectators at the first match and 70,000 at the second; 20,000 Everton fans came by car, train and bus.

"There were no problems with the crowd. This is not exceptional for Chile. It is just CHILE! The excitement in Vina del Mar (where I lived for 35 years) was terrific.

"There is no other soccer club in Chile (I don't think there is one in South America) named after a British club and I thought you might be interested. The President is: Senor Antonio Martinez, Presidente Club Everton de Deportes, Viana 161, Vina del Mar, Chile.

"Two years ago Everton of Chile were in the Second Division. They got promotion, re-formed their ranks and achieved success through — 1: Complete co-operation between the Board, the manager and players. 2: Tremendous loyalty from their fans.

"My memories of THE Everton go back to 1901 when I watched them play Bury at Goodison. I think Everton won 2–0. I also saw them lose the Cup Final to Sheffield Wednesday, 2–1, having beaten Newcastle in 1906, 1–0, with a goal scored by Jack Sharp. I remember many of the players around that time — Scott, Balmer, Makepeace, Bert Freeman, 'Sandy' Young and others.

"I listen in to the B.B.C. every Saturday evening for news of the team. I believe there is another club in Liverpool, but I don't bother about them — nor ever have! Best wishes for Everton. I shall never change."

WE WOULD LIKE TO ADD OUR CONGRATULATIONS TO THE EVERTON OF CHILE AND HOPE TO SEND COPIES OF THIS PROGRAMME ARTICLE TO THEIR PRESIDENT IN TRIBUTE OF HIS CLUB'S SUCCESS.

EVERTON IN CHILE

£300,000 RECORD BREAKER

Martin Dobson's transfer to Everton on Tuesday set a new British cash record of £300,000 — and he looked a happy fellow when he took his wife Beatrice onto the Goodison pitch, where he hopes to display the form which took him into the England team.

The former Burnley skipper had completed the transfer forms, much to the delight of Manager Billy Bingham and Secretary Chris Hassell.

Burnley League Record:
220 appearances (3 subs.), 42 goals.
International Under 23 v. Bulgaria 1970.
Full International 1974 — East Germany, Bulgaria and Yugoslavia.
Football League v. Scottish League 1974.
Plays cricket – Ribblesdale League.

Pictures by Liverpool Daily Post & Echo

Top: Reports of success for Everton – Chile edition – 1976/77
Right: Everton swoop for Martin Dobson, 1974/75

CLUB NEWS

TICKET ARRANGEMENTS

BOLTON WANDERERS v EVERTON
LEAGUE CUP SEMI-FINAL (2nd LEG)
TUESDAY, FEBRUARY 15th, 1977

This is an all ticket game and all Season Ticket Holders and Club Members will be able to purchase one ticket for each book held. Tickets will be allocated on the following basis:–

All Ground, Paddock & Enclosure Season Ticket Holders: 1 x 90p Ground Ticket.

	*Ticket Serial Number Ending 5 & 8	*Ticket Serial Number Ending 0, 1, 2, 3, 4, 6, 7, 9
300 & 500 Club Members	1 x £2 Stand Ticket	1 x £1 Enclosure Ticket
Main Stand & Top Balcony Season Ticket Holders	1 x £1·80 Stand Ticket	1 x £1 Enclosure Ticket
Upper Bullens Road Centre A & B Season Ticket Holders	1 x £2·00 Stand Ticket	1 x 90p Ground Ticket
Lower Bullens Road & Gwladys Street Season Ticket Holders	1 x £1·50 Stand Ticket	1 x 90p Ground Ticket

* Note Ticket *Serial Number* not *Seat Number*.

Personal applications with voucher number **31** should be made between Monday, January 17th and Wednesday, January 26th as under:–

	Monday – Friday (Non-Match Days)	First Team Match Days
Goodison Road Ticket Office	9.30 a.m. – 4.30 p.m.	Available from both offices up to 3 hours before kick-off and after the game.
Bullens Road Ticket Office	Closed	

Postal applications must also include a stamped addressed envelope and the correct remittance. Please mark the envelope BOLTON TICKETS. An announcement will be made later regarding the general sale of the balance of ground tickets available.

CLUB NEWS

CHEERS TO BOB

Bob Latchford became the first Evertonian to receive a case of whisky from the makers of "J and B", who are offering a similar prize to every player who scores a hat-trick in League football this season. Bob collected his dozen bottles before the Bristol City match (pictured above), but it was not a signal for a party in the Latchford household.

"It's not the taste for me," he told us. "I've shared the bottles around the lads who played against QPR and helped me score the four goals."

Bob's hat-trick goal at QPR. *Picture by Liverpool Daily Post and Echo Ltd.*

ROUNDABOUT

The arguments raged on for weeks in the pubs and clubs of Merseyside, but someone HAD to make a final decision on the composition of an "All-Time Great" Everton team.

For many positions, the choice was simple. Who has seen a better centre forward than William Ralph "Dixie" Dean? Who has seen a more consistent goalkeeper than Ted Sagar? Who has seen a more complete half-back line than Cliff Britton, T. G. Jones and Joe Mercer? Who has seen better wingers than Albert Geldard and Jackie Coulter?

At least, in the opinion of the Judges, these players were automatic choices for the final team. There was some discussion before Billy Cook, a specialist right back, was preferred to Warney Cresswell, normally a left back, for the No. 2 shirt. Ray Wilson, in turn, had to win the vote over Cresswell at No. 3.

The inside forwards caused most deliberation. Finally, Alan Ball was chosen as the perfect modern player and Alec Stevenson went in at No. 10 because he played alongside the elected left winger, Coulter.

THE VOTING

GOALKEEPERS

Ted Sagar 100%

FULL BACKS

Warney Cresswell	31½%	Ray Wilson	31½%
Alex Parker	30%	Billy Cook	5%
Benny Williams	2½%		

CENTRE HALVES

T. G. Jones	95%	Charlie Gee	5%

WING HALVES

Joe Mercer	42%	Cliff Britton	38%
Tony Kay	8%	Jimmy Gabriel	5%
Jock Thomson	5%	Charlie Gee	2½%

CENTRE FORWARDS

W. R. 'Dixie' Dean	89%	Tommy Lawton	10½%

INSIDE FORWARDS

Roy Vernon	23½%	Alan Ball	21%
Jimmy Dunn	13%	Alec Stevenson	10½%
Alex Young	8%	Bobby Collins	5%
Wally Fielding	6%	Tommy Johnson	5%
Duncan McKenzie	5%	Tommy Lawton	2½%

WINGERS

Albert Geldard	29%	Jackie Coulter	21%
Tommy Ring	15½%	Alex Young	8%
Terrey Gillick	5%	Jimmy Stein	5%
Jimmy Caskie	2½%	Sam Chedgzoy	2½%
Teddy Critchley	2½%	Alec Stevenson	2½%
Dave Thomas	2½%	Alec Troup	2½%

All percentages to the nearest ½%.

THE JUDGES

We decided that the Panel had to be made up by experts who could go back on pre-war knowledge of the old-time Everton stars. Mr. Jack Sharp, a former Chairman of the club and, of course, still a much-respected Director, was joined in the difficult task by George Watson, a former player and later member of the coaching staff, and Alan Storey, the Head Groundsman at Goodison Park, who succeeded his father and has served the club for more than 30 years.

They are pictured above (from left to right): Alan Storey, Jack Sharp and Gordon Watson.

OUR WINNERS

We did not receive a single entry which corresponded exactly to the final verdict of the Panel, but three readers were selected for the prizes on the basis of getting nine players correct. They are:

Tom Billson, 14 Brickwood Road, Croydon CR0 6UL: Sagar; Cresswell, Wilson; Britton, T. G. Jones, Mercer; Geldard, Dunn, Dean, Stevenson, Coulter.

George Bordessa, 11 Eastdale Road, Wavertree, Liverpool L15 4HN: Sagar; Parker, Wilson; Britton, T. G. Jones, Mercer; Geldard, Ball, Dean, Stevenson, Ring.

Chris McCarron, 6 Spinney View, Kirkby, Liverpool L33 7XX: Sagar; Parker, Wilson; Britton, T. G. Jones, Mercer; Geldard, Ball, Dean, Young, Coulter.

They will be contacted individually for details of their prizes.

ALL-TIME TEAM

1 TED SAGAR
2 BILLY COOK
3 RAY WILSON
4 CLIFF BRITTON
5 T. G. JONES
6 JOE MERCER
7 ALBERT GELDARD
8 ALAN BALL
9 W. R. "DIXIE" DEAN
10 ALEC STEVENSON
11 JACKIE COULTER

To keep the discussion boiling, Mr. Sharp immediately pencilled out the following alternative team: Gordon West; Alex Parker, Warney Cresswell; Jimmy Gabriel, Charlie Gee, Jock Thomson; Terrey Gillick, Bobby Collins, Tommy Lawton, Alex Young and Wally Boyes.

Clockwise from top left: Bolton ticket details, 1976/77; drinks are on Bob, 1977/78; Everton's all-time greatest side, 1977/78

DUKLA

THE Juliska Stadium was packed to its 28,000 capacity and the Dukla officials told us this was a record crowd for them.

By English standards, this figure may seem a little low but even though Dukla have been at the top of their league all the season, the normal attendances are nearer 10,000.

The reason for the sell-out on Everton's visit was explained by an official who said: "The Czech people still regard English football as the best in the world. If we had played a top Italian side, like Juventus, the attendance would have been around 15,000."

Apart from the packed crowd in the Stadium — hundreds climbed a steep slope next to the impressive stand — the game was watched live on Czech television. They must take their football, for another live transmission of a European Cup-tie between Brno and Krakow, was on the TV screen by the time we reached the airport at 8 o'clock!

It looked as if Father Christmas had arrived a few weeks early when Jim Greenwood engaged the help of the Press party to carry out the gifts presented by the Dukla club at a function on Tuesday evening.

Each member of the official group and the players received a beautiful cut-glass vase — a sample of the craft for which Czechoslovakia is most famous among tourists.

Before we left the Inter Continental Hotel, a superb, American-developed building on the banks of the river which makes Prague so eye-catching, we pictured Jim Greenwood with the presents from Dukla. He is displaying the glassware which will have a place in the Goodison Boardroom.

Patience is the by-word for travellers moving in and out of Iron Curtain countries.

On the outward trip from Prague Airport, we had to go through three official checks — and no one is in a hurry! The first control examined a currency exchange form and the next dealt with Passports and Visas.

We never did discover the purpose of the third inspection by a man who darted to the head of the queue and asked for Passports as we prepared to go down the steps to the Aer Lingus jet!

Someone asked Mike Lyons if he was suffering from a cold or sore throat when they heard him speaking on the return flight. Back came the reply: "No — this is what happens after two games sitting on the bench. I've shouted myself hoarse!"

Our tight travelling schedule — 34 hours from Speke to Prague and back — gave the players little time to have a look around the sights of the Czech capital. A breath of fresh air on the morning of the match

strolled by one of the many bridges crossing the River Vltava.

Martin Dobson and George Telfer.

It seemed there was a welcoming party for Everton when we spotted large numbers of children on the public viewing gallery at Prague Airport. Later, however, we learned that the reception was for a visiting dignitary from Moscow who was in Prague for the celebrations of the 61st anniversary of the Russian Revolution.

Even so, the team was greeted by many young football followers who all seemed very well versed with the personalities in England. Some of them continued to pop up at the hotel and were there again for the departure from Prague.

Our picture below shows the players in the Terminal Building on arrival.

Two Evertonians from Childwell hitch-hiked from Liverpool and completed their four-day trek to Prague just in time to arrive at our hotel as the team was ready to

Jim Greenwood with glassware...

was all they managed. Pictured above right) were among those who

Players arrive at Prague.

depart for the match.

Steve Bird and his brother, Mark, started out on Sunday and made their way to the English Channel by way of London and Dover. They continued across France, Belgium and West Germany via Calais, Brussels, Liege, Aachen and Nuremburg.

They then caught a train into Czechoslovakia, and on this leg of the journey they teamed up with an exiled Evertonian, Neil Maslin, who works in Munich.

Two other supporters, Frank McGinnty, from Maghull, and his nephew, Paul McGinnty, from Birkenhead, drove from Merseyside to Prague. They set out on Monday and reached the team's hotel on Wednesday lunchtime.

They then earned full marks for nerve by following the team coach from the city centre and driving into the Juliska Stadium car park. Frank and Paul pictured below.

On the subject of supporters

travelling independently to games in Europe, we must underline the problems that can be caused when people arrive without tickets. Whilst we have every admiration for their adventure in undertaking a journey of 1,000 miles, the club is concerned that these fans are taking a big chance, especially in Iron Curtain countries.

The golden rule is to book through our official excursions. Only then can we guarantee a ticket to the match.

Despite the early kick-off — half past three on English time — the match was played under floodlights throughout. The Stadium is situated on the side of a hill and the playing area, surrounded by a running track, is on a plateau etched into the slope. On a clear day, you would see for miles from the main stand, but mist obscured the valley and also made life difficult for our photographer, Terry Mealey.

Martin Dobson still manages to get in his shot while evading tackle from Pelc.

Dave Thomas skips over dual penalty as he runs into the Dukla penalty area..

Micky

Two fans and car...

All I Want For Christmas is...Everton behind the Iron Curtain in the following round, v Nottingham Forest (League Cup), 1978/79

Inset, top right: Park End redevelopment – the final phase

A GREAT SPORTSMAN

The legend of Everton's most famous player is to be perpetuated by a permanent tribute at Goodison Park.

It is the intention of the Directors that the name of William Ralph Dean should be commemorated on the ground where he played for Everton from 1924 to 1938 — and where he died a fortnight ago. But the precise form of the dedication, and its location, will be decided only after careful consideration.

Secretary Jim Greenwood explained: "The Chairman has pointed out that quite a bit of re-development is planned for Goodison Park in the future, and the immediate feeling is that the club's tribute could take the form of naming some part of the stadium in his memory.

"Because of Bill Dean's unique place in the history of Everton, the Directors will consider the matter in detail and would be pleased to receive suggestions from supporters. It would be all too easy to put a plaque somewhere in the ground, but the achievements of Bill Dean should be honoured by a more suitable dedication.

The respect for Bill Dean is probably greater than for any player of his lifetime. He achieved that distinction not only by being an outstanding footballer, but also by his stand for sportsmanship and friendship in the game that he enjoyed so much.

The *Liverpool Echo* is to commemorate these much-admired qualities by instigating *The Dean Award for Sportsmanship in Professional Football*. Already, Joe Mercer and Bill Shankly have agreed to serve on the panel of judges who will be looking each year for a professional player who fulfills the requirements of character, attitude to the game and sportsmanship.

The Award is open to footballers with Merseyside connections, although not necessarily a current member of staff with a local club.

In welcoming the *Echo's* initiative, the Everton Chairman, Mr Philip Carter, said: "Any award that focuses the attention of the game on the need for fair play and sportsmanship must be for the good of football. To present such a trophy in the name of William Ralph Dean is most appropriate."

The *Echo* expect to appoint as many as six judges, including members of their staff. "We would hope the Award will have a certain prestige and that the winner each year treasures his nomination as he would the PFA Footballer of the Year trophy," said Charles Lambert, of the *Echo's* football reporting team.

Mr Lambert added: "The Judges would necessarily see a player week in and week out, and, indeed one isolated incidence of sportsmanship could be highlighted, rather than a whole season. The system is elastic and does not necessarily rule out players booked for offences of a technical nature."

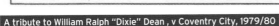

A tribute to William Ralph "Dixie" Dean , v Coventry City, 1979/80

Roundabout

"Playing against Joe Royle keeps any centre half occupied for the full 90 minutes, for Joe has ability in every department of his game. His control, passing and work-rate are every bit as good as his shooting and heading. Joe will be England's centre forward in Munich '74 and will probably win the Cup for them."—Southampton's former Evertonian, Jimmy Gabriel, writing in the Southern Evening Echo.

●

The cost of being a football director is something that cannot be measured only in money but also in a thousand small ways — not the least being the consumption of time which could cost a businessman personal profit. But, when brought to basics, it is the financial investment which is important — and Bob Harris, of Thomson Newspapers, got to grips with the subject in the South Wales Echo.

Millionaire Harold Needler is hoping to celebrate his 25th year as chairman of Hull City, by realising his greatest ambition — seeing his club gain promotion to the First Division for the first time in its history.

If they do make the top grade it will be a triumph not only for the players, but for the whole Needler family as well, for on the Board with Harold are brothers John and Henry and son Christopher.

It will also be just reward, for in his 24 years as "Mr. Hull City", Harold Needler estimates that he has pumped nearly half a million pounds of his own personal fortune into the club, justifying it by saying: "Some people buy yachts – I like football."

Without him it is more than likely that there would be no Hull City today. During the war the old Hull stadium was bombed and although the club had acquired a new site there was nobody prepared to put forward the necessary finance to develop it.

As a 'terrace supporter since 1921, Harold Needler could not bear to see the club sink into oblivion and, with John and Henry and a few friends, they decided to make an offer for the assets of Hull City.

"For £10,500," said Mr. Needler, "We bought ourselves the site for the new ground at Boothferry Park, membership of the Third Division and one player – Billy Bly.

"We formed a complete new company with 200,000 five-shilling shares, many of which were purchased by the directors. With donations of £50,000, we were left with £100,000 with which to build the new ground. By the time it

was fit for League football we had little left to spend on players.

"I did not realise how expensive it would be, but I have never regretted it. It would have left a terrific void in the City if there had been no League club."

Now, with Hull beaten only twice in the first 13 matches, will there be reward for Mr. Needler's patience, ambition . . . and judgment of character? For it is that final quality that could have turned the key for Hull. In the summer he appointed former Arsenal skipper Terry Neill as player-manager with Cliff Britton leaving the team to look after administration. Mr. Needler told Bob Harris: "Terry is a man who impresses me more than anyone in the game. He has ability, a dedicated personality, he is a good speaker, and is very intelligent. If anyone can get us First Division football, it is Terry Neill."

●

"Well over half a million people have watched Newcastle United in a mere dozen games put on under the European banner. And while United guard gate receipt figures like Fort Knox gold, I reckon they have picked up around £250,000 from the increased admission prices."—John Gibson, of Evening Chronicle discussing Newcastle United's financial bonanza in the Fairs Cup.

●

For the second half TV rights of our European Cup match in Monchengladbach, the West German Champions were reported to have received a fee of around £7,000 . . . about ten times the fee paid by the BBC for Match of the Day. The London Evening News reported Crystal Palace manager Bert Head's viewpoint on this subject:

"Football is being sold on the cheap. Clubs get approximately £750 from the BBC Match of the Day and around £250 for ITV's The Big Match. What would Humperdinck or Tom Jones demand for that length of time?

". . . We often get letters from supporters in faraway places like Hong Kong, New Zealand and Australia, saying: 'We saw you on the telly.' So the films of our matches must be despatched around the world . . . I think the day is not far off when TV payments will have to be re-assessed."

TOFFEE TALK

CENTENARY RECEPTION

THE last week of October 1978 will be indelibly engraved on the memories of Evertonians as "The week we did it" – beat Liverpool for the first time in seven years. But for shareholders of the club, that envied band of some 300 people, the week contained another memorable event: the Centenary Reception given for them by the directors.

This was a glittering and nostalgic evening in the staff restaurant at Littlewoods' JM Centre on Monday, October 23. Each shareholder brought a guest and, swelled by the ranks of current and past players, the number present was nearly 700.

Mr. Philip Carter, chairman, welcomed the guests and Gordon Lee made a sincere and forceful speech which earned a great ovation. But the note of approval were reserved for the gallery at past greats — more than 30 ex players introduced from the stage by Brian West and headed, of course, by Dixie Dean. Mr. Peter Perry chairman of the Shareholders' Association, presented Mr. Carter with a shield to mark the centenary.

The former players Brian introduced were: Dixie Dean, Joe Mercer, Gordon Watson, Ted Sagar, Alec Stevenson, Brian Labone, Johnny Morrissey, Gordon West, Tommy Wright, Brian Harris, Dennis Stevens, Jackie Grant, Tommy Clinton, Jimmy Harris, Tommy Jones, Jimmy O'Neill, Jimmy Tansey, Derek Temple, George Burnett, Harry Leyland, Eddie Wainwright, Harry Catterick, John Hurst, Dave Hickson, Ray Wilson, Alex Parker, Peter Farrell, Tommy Eglington, Bobbin Collins, Cyril Lello, Norman Greenhalgh, George Commins and Colin Harvey.

Below Left: Mr. Peter Perry, chairman of the Shareholders' Association, presents Mr. Carter with a shield to mark the centenary. Below Right: Sign here, please! Dixie Dean had a busy evening autographing copies of the Official Centenary History for shareholders. Above: Evertonians all! Dixie Dean poses with, left to right, Mr. John Moores, Gordon Lee, Harry Catterick and chairman Philip Carter.

11

GOODISON OPINION

THE distressing heat of an Arabian desert seems a million miles away from Goodison Park as we wrap up against the icy blasts of an English winter.

But there is a link between Everton and a small cluster of rocks in an isolated corner of Saudi Arabia. As you can see from today's inner picture, an unknown supporter saved the world by painting an "Everton Are Magic" slogan in a prominent position alongside the desert highway.

The discovery was made for us by John Smith, a Sunderland supporter from Workshop who works in a chemical engineer for the Arabian American Oil Company. He thought that at the Sunderland at home would be interested to know that Everton have plenty of followers finding at the far end of the world.

Mr Smith told us: "I took the picture in November of last year in the Middle of the South Desert of Saudi Arabia — the longest in the world. I came across the work, and its message, in the desert region of Eastern Province whilst

driving to a remote location south of a village called Uthaiyfuat.

"There are quite a few in-activities like myself working within the area as engineers, operators and maintenance staff. With some of the staff spending up to four months in the desert region before taking some leave, it helps to keep us morale if you see following a successful football team.

"The Saturday evening football meals are sadly missed as the radio and distributed around the area. The could clearly between supporters of different clubs exist — and an Everton supporter so certainly leads in conversations with his 'first painting'?"

It would seem that Mr Smith enjoys only the spirit of soccer rivalry in Saudi Arabia, for he signed off his letter by saying: "I wish Everton Football Club well in the League this season but can only hope that their Cup campaign ends at Sunderland."

We wonder what the "Unknown Evertonian" would have had to say about that? Also, we wonder whether anyone knows of the mystery supporter's identity. We would like to hear from him — telling us how he manages to follow Everton from so far away from home. A picture would be welcome, too.

TOFFEE TALK

THE DESERT SIGN-WRITER

EXILED Evertonian Bob Tonbridge can only watch The Blues when he is on leave from his job with an oil company in the Middle East.

So it was an amazing coincidence when he turned up for the Bristol City match at Goodison Park — and saw the programme cover photograph of a slogan which he had daubed on a rock in the Saudi Arabian desert last year.

Bob, who lives at Okerminster Close, Great Sankey, Warrington, then called in to see Promotions Manager Ralph Williams and identified himself as the 'mystery man' who had painted the "Everton Are Magic" sign thousands of miles from Goodison Park.

He was back in England on three weeks' leave and later told in the story behind his highly individual advertising for the club in Saudi.

Bob explained: "I had seen similar graffiti by Welshmen and the Saudis. And most of the chaps I work with are from the North East, supporting Middlesbrough, Newcastle or Sunderland. I was getting a little bit fed up with them and one day, I decided to stop and mark this rock alongside the main road. Since then, we've done two or three more. But I think I'll have to go back to the original and smarten it up. Plenty of people can see it because extra traffic goes along the road to a new oilfield further south."

Strangely, for one who is so keen on promoting the Everton cause, Bob is not a Merseysider. He was born in Kent and came to the Liverpool area 13 years ago. His support for the club began nine years ago while he was working for ICI at Runcorn. "Some of the chaps asked me to go to the football one Saturday", he says. "It just happened to be at Goodison Park – and since then I've watched Everton as much as I can."

Bob, who is married with two children, spends six weeks at a time working in Saudi and then has three weeks at home. "We work for 42 days straight through, averaging between 12 and 14 hours a day," he explains. "My contract is up in May, but I've been

or two are a little bit too serious. We also play matches between the 'in-pats' and the Saudis. Football is very popular with the locals and, more recently, we've played against Koreans and Turks from overseas.

"When Bob is back in England, he watches Everton at every opportunity, travelling to the away games on his motor cycle. "I know most of the grounds now," he says. "So I know where someone will watch my bike for me!"

One of his favourite matches was last season's 5-1 victory over Leicester at Filbert Street — and it seems he couldn't see enough of that goal-rush. He explains: "I went to Leicester for the game and than I watched it again on TV the next day. About two weeks later, I was back in Saudi and the match turned up on the Video films which the company fires out to us! It's a good job we won 5-1 and didn't lose by a score. Ha Ha."

TOP: Bob Tonbridge pictured on his recent leave in Liverpool. ABOVE: The slogan he painted in Saudi Arabia.

offered another two years – and I will be signing on again."

His latest spell of leave in the English freeze-up provided a stark contrast in weather conditions. Even in winter, the temperatures in the desert is 85 degree Fahrenheit and, in the summer, it goes up to around 110 degrees. He keeps up to date with the football scene at home by listening to the BBC World Service on Saturdays and Sundays for a run-down on the results. In addition, there is a flight in from England every Monday and he can catch up on Everton's form in the papers from London.

"We have a lot of rivalry between supporters of the various clubs," adds Bob. "It's all done in good fun, but one

ALL RECORDS played on Radio Goodison are supplied by Robert Crease, 14, County Road, Walton, Liverpool (two minutes from the ground).

WILLIAM RALPH DEAN
A MAN FOR THE BIG OCCASION

"A big man for the big occasion." That was Joe Mercer's simple tribute to Billy Dean on "Match of The Day" last Saturday, after the Everton Legend had died in the very ground where he scored so many great goals.

Billy — he disliked the nickname "Dixie" by which he was universally known — was at the derby match almost by accident. Earlier in the day he had attended a luncheon for about 80 soccer enthusiasts at the Holiday Inn, which had been addressed by Bill Shankly.

Having agreed to attend the lunch with other Everton and Liverpool "greats", Billy subsequently accepted an invitation to come on to Goodison for the match, which he watched from his wheelchair at the top of the steps to the Directors' Box.

I spoke briefly with him before the game, when he was his usual kindly self. On his way into the main stand he had readily agreed to be taken first to the sponsors' lounge, to meet Jake Foods and their guests. I found him there, surrounded by admirers, patiently signing autographs.

His handshake was as firm as ever, the eyes bright and missing nothing. "How are you, young man? Me? I'm fine". Under two hours later it was hard to accept Brian Labone's information, delivered to a stunned press box: "Billy Dean's dead".

One could write almost endlessly about William Ralph Dean, and the press have eulogised him deservedly this past week. He has two chapters to himself in John Roberts' "Everton – A Centenary History" and a place in English football's hall of fame which is forever secure. Joe Mercer, who loved the maestro who took such an interest in his own burgeoning Everton career, called him a "goal machine" in his TV tribute and his epitaph, in a game which is all about goals, is best summed up in his record:

Dixie Dean with left to right Mr John Moores, Gordon Lee, Harry Catterick and Mr Philip Carter at the launching of the Everton Centenary History.

Dixie Dean (Centre)

	For Everton		For England	
	Played	Goals	Played	Goals
	431	377	16	18
60	League goals in a First Division season (1927-28).			
100	League goals before the age of 21.			
200	League goals in 199 games (aged 23).			
300	League goals in 310 games.			
37	Hat-tricks.			
18	Goals in 16 Liverpool derbies.			

A grand total of 473 League, Cup, International and Charity match goals in a career spanning 502 games.

God bless you, Billy, as you nod them in, in that great sky.

The Historic Goal, September 2nd, 1936. W. R. Dean heading his 353rd goal in League football! Note the 3 defenders on the goalline yet they were unable to prevent the conversion of Coulters corner kick. This goal beat the previous record held by Steve Bloomer.

"AN EVERTON SUPPORTER CERTAINLY LEADS IN ONE-UPMANSHIP WITH THE 'ROCK PAINTING'"

1 **'Roundabout' (v Nottingham Forest, 1970/71)**
The page was essentially a news round-up of the goings-on in and around football. These snippets include talk from former Blue Jimmy Gabriel (on Joe Royle: 'Joe will be England's centre-forward in Munich '74 and will probably win the Cup for them'), the ambitions of 'Mr Hull City' Harold Needler, Newcastle United's lucrative European nights and the fact that some of the Blues' European Cup tie at Borussia Moenchengladbach was televised – earning the West German champions a fee 10 times that paid by the BBC for *Match of the Day*.

2 **Everton centenary celebrations (v Chelsea, 1978/79)**
October 1978 brought together the finest names in the club's history as they club marked 100 years since its formation. Dixie Dean was the star attraction at Littlewoods' JM Centre, while more than 30 former stars were also officially saluted by nearly 700 guests.

3 **Everton Are Magic (v Bristol City, 1978/79)**
A mystery Evertonian had apparently daubed said phrase on a rock in the middle of the South Ghawar oil-field. Sent to the club by a Sunderland supporter working in Saudi Arabia, the shot was used on the front of the programme. The Goodison Opinion piece also appealed to the mystery fan to come forward and tell all. Would anybody respond?

4 **When graffiti was endorsed?! (v QPR, 1978/79)**
It appears our exiled Evertonian was actually at the match, and had seen his handiwork 'first hand'. Bob Tunbridge duly told the full story, as well as what life was like supporting Everton at home and overseas. The usual lines of communication were covered, including the BBC World Service for finding out results. When at home though he revealed he travelled to watch away games on his motorbike. 'I know most of the grounds now, so I know where someone will watch my bike for me!'

5 **Obituary for Dixie Dean (v Ipswich Town, FA Cup, 1979/80)**
The club's greatest-ever player passed away the week before, attending a Merseyside derby at Goodison. The tribute was poignant, noting his goalscoring exploits, and how loved he was at Goodison. Joe Mercer had summed it up on *Match of the Day* – and his words were repeated here: "A big man for the big occasion."

EVERTON 74-75

FIRST TEAM SQUAD

Back Row (Left to Right): JOHN SMITH, DAVE IRVING, PETER SCOTT, DAI DAVIES, GORDON WEST, DAVID LAWSON, GARY JONES, GEORGE TELFER, BILLY KENNY.

Middle Row (Left to Right): STEWART IMLACH, JOHN HURST, JIM PEARSON, JOE ROYLE, MIKE LYONS, BOB LATCHFORD, JOHN CONNOLLY, RAY HENDERSON.

EVERTON 1977-78

BACK ROW (from left to right): Mike Lyons, Mark Higgins, Steve Berkenshaw (Coach), Bruce Rioch, MIDDLE ROW: Mike Pejic, Andy King, Steve Seargent, ON GROUND: Mark Coffey, Billy Kenealy, Bertt Wallace, Ken McNaught (with son Alex, with Neville Southall, David Smallman, Jim Pearson, Bob Latchford, Roger Kenyon, David Jones, Mick Buckley, Ronnie Goodlass, Dai Davies, Martin Wright, David Lawson, Drew Brand, Terry Darracott, George Telfer, Mike Bernard, Jim McGregor, Gordon Lee (Manager), Nigel Greame, Duncan McKenzie, Teddy Wheeldon, Roy Deakin, Martin Murray, Billy Wright, Neil Robinson.

Back row: John Barton, Mike Lyons, Georg
Centre row: Eric Harrison (trainer), Andy King, B
Garry Stanley,
Front row: Trevor Ross, John Bailey, Go

Everton first-team squad picture, taken at Bellefield, 1979/80

...artin Hodge, Mark Higgins, Brian Kidd.
...d, Geoff Nulty, Peter Eastoe, John Gidman,
...or (physio).
...anager), Asa Hartford, Billy Wright.

CHAMPIONS

ARCHIE GEMMILL, SKIPPER OF DERBY COUNTY'S 1974-75 TITLE-WINNING SIDE, DISPLAYS THE TOP TROPHY IN ENGLISH SOCCER.

EVERTON WELCOMES ASTON VILLA

DENNIS MORTIMER

TOMMY CRAIG

ASTON VILLA FACTS

TOTTENHAM

Terry Yorath

Ricardo Villa, now playing to full extent.

THE INTERNATIONAL LOOK IN FASHION SHIRTS

KADIX

... the best in Children's

OPPOSITION NOTES...

Away supporters were well served by the Everton programme, being offered action spreads and in-depth profiles of their squad and manager rather than just the cursory offerings of many other sides' matchday publications in the First Division.

As the decade progressed, the club dabbled in colour print, while other innovations included player statistics, as well as previous encounters between the two clubs. It is also unlikely today to hail the visit of the reigning league champions with a salute in the opposition notes...or indeed on the front cover, as we did ahead of the 1974/75 encounter with Leeds United (p64).

EVERTON STA

date	fixture	att.	res.	Pts	Pos	1	2	3
Aug.	20 **NOTTINGHAM FOREST**	38,001	1—3	0	—	Wood	Jones	Pejic
	23 Arsenal	32,954	0—1	0	—	Wood	Darracott	Pejic
	27 Aston Villa	37,806	2—1	2	15	Wood	Darracott	Pejic
	30 Sheffield United (LC2)	18,571	3—0	—	—	Wood	Darracott	Jones
Sept.	3 **WOLVERHAMPTON W.**	36,636	0—0	3	15	Wood	Darracott	Pejic
	10 Leicester City	16,425	5—1	5	10	Wood	Darracott†	Pejic
	17 **NORWICH CITY**	34,405	3—0	7	5	Wood	Darracott	Pejic
	24 West Ham United	25,296	1—1	8	6	Wood	Darracott	Pejic
Oct.	1 **MANCHESTER CITY**	43,286	1—1	9	8	Wood	Darracott	Pejic
	4 **WEST BROMWICH A.**	34,582	3—1	11	5	Wood	Jones	Pejic
	8 Queens Park Rangers	20,495	5—1	13	5	Wood	Jones	Pejic
	15 **BRISTOL CITY**	39,230	1—0	15	3	Wood	Jones	Pejic
	22 Liverpool	51,668	0—0	16	4	Wood	Jones	Pejic
	25 **MIDDLESBROUGH (LC3)**	32,766	2—2	—	—	Wood	Jones	Pejic
	29 **NEWCASTLE UNITED**	37,574	4—4	17	3	Wood	Jones	Pejic'
	31 Middlesbrough (LC3 replay)	28,500	2—1	—	—	Wood	Jones	Pejic
Nov.	5 Derby County	29,335	1—0	19	2	Wood	Jones†	Ross
	12 **BIRMINGHAM CITY**	37,783	2—1	21	2	Wood	Jones	Pejic
	19 Ipswich Town	22,795	3—3	22	2	Wood	Jones	Pejic†
	26 **COVENTRY CITY**	42,279	6—0	24	2	Wood	Jones	Pejic
	29 Sheffield Wed. (LC4)	36,079	3—1	—	—	Wood	Jones	Pejic
Dec.	3 Chelsea	33,899	1—0	26	2	Wood	Jones	Pejic
	10 **MIDDLESBROUGH**	38,387	3—0	28	2	Wood	Jones	Pejic
	17 Birmingham City	22,177	0—0	29	2	Wood	Jones	Pejic
	26 **MANCHESTER UNITED**	48,335	2—6	29	2	Wood	Jones	Pejic
	27 Leeds United	45,500	1—3	29	2	Wood	Jones	Pejic
	31 **ARSENAL**	47,039	2—0	31	2	Wood	Darracott	Pejic
Jan.	2 Nottingham Forest	44,030	1—1	32	2	Wood	Darracott	Pejic
	7 **ASTON VILLA (FAC3)**	46,320	4—1	—	—	Wood	Darracott	Pejic
	14 **ASTON VILLA**	40,630	1—0	34	2	Wood	Darracott	Pejic
	18 Leeds United (LC5)	35,020	1—4	—	—	Wood	Darracott	Pejic
	21 Wolverhampton W.	23,777	1—3	34	3	Wood	Darracott†	Pejic
	28 Middlesbrough (FAC4)	33,652	2—3	—	—	Wood	Jones	Pejic
Feb.	4 **LEICESTER CITY**	33,677	2—0	36	2	Wood	Jones	Pejic
	18 **WEST HAM UNITED**	33,826	2—1	38	2	Wood	Jones	Pejic
	25 Manchester City	46,817	0—1	38	3	Wood	Jones	Pejic
Mar.	4 **QUEENS PARK RANGERS**	33,861	3—3	39	3	Wood	Jones†	Pejic
	11 Bristol City	25,986	1—0	41	2	Wood	Jones	Pejic
	15 Norwich City	19,502	0—0	42	2	Wood	Jones	Pejic
	24 Newcastle United	27,103	2—0	44	2	Wood	Darracott	Pejic
	25 **LEEDS UNITED**	45,020	2—0	46	2	Wood	Jones	Pejic
	27 Manchester United	55,317	2—1	48	2	Wood	Jones	Pejic
Apr.	1 **DERBY COUNTY**	38,213	2—1	50	2	Wood	Jones	Pejic
	5 **LIVERPOOL**	52,759	0—1	50	2	Wood	Jones	Pejic
	8 Coventry City	26,025	2—3	50	2	Wood	Jones	Pejic
	15 **IPSWICH TOWN**	33,402	1—0	52	2	Wood	Jones	Pejic
	22 Middlesbrough	15,969	0—0	53	2	Wood	Robinson	Jones
	25 West Bromwich Albion							
	29 **CHELSEA**							
May	6 F.A. Cup Final							

FIRST-TEAM APPEARANCES – 1977-78

	League App.	Gls.	FAC/FLC App.	Gls.	Ev. Career App.	Gls.			
Brand	—	—	—	—	2		Dobson	36	6
Buckley	10	2	3	—	126	10	Higgins	25	1
Darracott	19	—	3	—	131	—	Jones	29	—
							Kenyon	7	—
							King	40	8
							Latchford	37	28

Home fixtures in CAPITALS   Everton's score first   Name in bold—scorer   Superior

STICS 1977~78

5	6	7	8	9	10	11	12
enyon	Higgins	King	Darracott†	**Pearson'**	McKenzie	Thomas	Goodlass
enyon†	Rioch	King	Pearson	Latchford	McKenzie	Thomas	Higgins
iggins	Rioch	King	Pearson	Latchford	**McKenzie²**	Thomas	Jones
iggins	Rioch	**King'**	Pearson	**Latchford'**	**McKenzie'**	Thomas†	Robinson
iggins	Dobson	King	Pearson	Latchford	McKenzie	Thomas	Jones
iggins	Rioch	**King²**	Dobson	**Latchford'**	**McKenzie'**	**Thomas'**	Jones
iggins	**Rioch'†**	King	**Dobson'**	Latchford	**McKenzie'**	Thomas	Jones
iggins	Rioch	King	Dobson	Latchford	**McKenzie'**	Thomas†	Jones
iggins	Rioch	King	Dobson	**Latchford'**	McKenzie	Thomas	Pearson
iggins'	Pearson	**King'**	Dobson	**Latchford'**	McKenzie	Thomas	Buckley
iggins	Pearson	King	Dobson	**Latchford⁴**	**McKenzie'**	Thomas	Darracott
iggins	Buckley†	**King'**	Dobson	Latchford	Pearson	Telfer	Darracott
iggins	Rioch	King	Dobson	Latchford	Pearson	Thomas	Darracott
iggins	Rioch	**King'**	Dobson	Latchford†	Pearson	Thomas	**Telfer'**
iggins	Rioch	King	Dobson	**Latchford²†**	Pearson	Thomas	Telfer
iggins	Buckley	King	Dobson	Latchford	**Pearson'**	Thomas	Telfer
iggins	Buckley	King	Dobson	Latchford	Pearson	Thomas	Seargeant
iiggins	Buckley	King	Dobson	**Latchford²**	Pearson	Thomas	Ross
iggins	**Buckley'**	King	Dobson	Latchford	**Pearson'**	Thomas	Ross
iggins	Buckley	**King'**	**Dobson'**	**Latchford³**	**Pearson'**	Thomas	Ross
iggins	Buckley	King	**Dobson'**	Latchford	**Pearson'**	Thomas	Darracott
iggins	Buckley	King	Dobson	**Latchford'**	Pearson	Thomas	Ross
iggins	**Buckley'**	King	Dobson	**Latchford²**	Pearson	Thomas	Ross
iggins	Buckley	King	Dobson	Latchford	Pearson	Thomas	Darracott
iggins	Buckley	King	**Dobson'**	**Latchford'**	Pearson†	Thomas	Ross
iggins	Ross	King	**Dobson'**	Latchford	McKenzie	Thomas	Darracott
Kenyon	Ross	**King'**	Dobson	**Latchford'**	McKenzie	Thomas	Jones
enyon†	**Ross'**	King	Dobson	Latchford	McKenzie	Thomas	Jones
iggins	**Ross'**	**King'**	Dobson	**Latchford'**	**McKenzie'**	Thomas	Jones
iggins	Ross	**King'**	Dobson	Latchford	McKenzie	Thomas	Buckley
iggins	Buckley†	King	Dobson	Latchford	McKenzie	**Thomas'**	Jones
enyon	**Ross'**	King	Pearson	Latchford	McKenzie	Thomas	Jones
enyon†	Ross	King	Dobson	Latchford	**Telfer'**	Pearson	McKenzie
iggins	Ross	King	Dobson	**Latchford²**	McKenzie	Telfer†	Wright
iggins	Ross	King	Dobson	Latchford†	**McKenzie'**	**Thomas'**	Telfer
iggins	Ross	King	Dobson	Pearson	McKenzie	Telfer	Kenyon
enyon	**Ross'**	**King'**	**Dobson'**	Pearson	McKenzie	Thomas	Telfer
enyon	**Ross'**	King	Dobson	Latchford	McKenzie	Thomas	Telfer
arracott	Ross	King	Dobson	Latchford	McKenzie	Thomas	Telfer
ones	Ross	King	Dobson	**Latchford'**	**McKenzie'†**	Telfer	Pearson
arracott	Ross	King	Dobson	**Latchford'**	**McKenzie'**	Thomas	Pearson
arracott	Ross	King	Dobson	**Latchford²**	McKenzie	Thomas	Pearson
arracott	Ross	King	**Dobson'**	**Latchford'**	McKenzie	Thomas	Pearson
arracott	Ross	King	Dobson	Latchford	McKenzie	Thomas	Pearson
arracott	Ross	King	Dobson	**Latchford'**	McKenzie	Thomas	Telfer
obinson	Buckley	King	Dobson	**Latchford'**	McKenzie	Thomas	Pearson
'right	Pearson	King	Dobson	Latchford	Telfer	Thomas	McKenzie

48	24	Lawson	—	—	—	—	124	—	Ross	18	5	2	1	18	5
27	1	Lyons	40	4	7	3	238	36	Smallman	—	—	—	—	19	6
58	1	McKenzie	28	9	3	2	45	14	Telfer	5	—	2	2	68	17
0	6	Pearson	21	3	5	2	76	16	Thomas	36	2	6	1	36	2
'9	17	Pejic	38	1	6	—	55	2	Wood	40	—	7	—	40	—
3	81	Robinson	2	—	—	—	7	—	Wright	1	—	—	—	1	—

† goals scored   * Denotes substituted player   ● Own goal

22nd April

STATISTICS 1976/77

STATISTICS — ALL DETAILS UP TO AND INCLUDING SATURDAY, 8th JANUARY, 1977

date	fixture	att.	res.	Pts	Pos	1	2	3	4	5	6	7	8	9	10	11	12
Aug. 21	Queens Park Rangers	24,449	*4-0	2	—	Davies	Bernard*	Jones	Lyons	Kenyon	McNaught	King	Dobson	Latchford²	Pearson	Telfer	
24	IPSWICH TOWN	33,070	1-1	3	—	Davies	Bernard	Seargeant	Lyons	McNaught	Kenyon	King	Dobson	Latchford	Pearson	Telfer¹	
28	ASTON VILLA	32,058	0-1	3	10	Davies	Bernard	Jones	Lyons	McNaught	Kenyon	King	Dobson	Latchford	Pearson†	Telfer¹	
30	CAMBRIDGE UTD. (LC2)	10,899	3-0	—	—	Davies	Bernard	Jones	Lyons	McNaught	Kenyon	King	Dobson¹	Latchford²	Pearson†	Telfer	Smallman / Hamilton
Sept. 4	Leicester City	22,277	3-1	4	7	Davies	Bernard	Jones	Lyons	McNaught	Kenyon	King	Dobson¹	Latchford	Goodlass	Telfer	
11	STOKE CITY	21,572	1-0	6	7	Davies	Bernard	Jones	Lyons	McNaught	Kenyon	King	Dobson	Latchford	Goodlass	Telfer²	
18	Arsenal	34,076	3-3	6	9	Davies	Bernard†	Jones	Lyons	McNaught	Kenyon	King	Dobson	Latchford	Goodlass	Telfer³	Darracott
20	Stockport County (LC3)	16,408	1-0	—	—	Davies	Darracott	Jones	Lyons	McNaught	Hamilton	King	Dobson¹	Latchford	Goodlass	Telfer¹	
25	BRISTOL CITY	25,761	1-0	8	6	Davies	Darracott	Jones	Lyons	McNaught	Hamilton	King	Dobson	Latchford	Goodlass¹	Telfer	
Oct. 2	Sunderland	34,670	0-1	8	6	Davies	Jones	Higgins	Lyons	McNaught	Hamilton	King	Dobson	Latchford	Goodlass	Telfer	
5	MANCHESTER CITY	31,370	0-1	9	11	Davies	Darracott	Jones	Lyons	McNaught	Bernard†	King	Dobson	Latchford	Goodlass	Telfer	Pearson
16	Liverpool	55,141	1-3	9	11	Davies	Darracott	Jones	Lyons	McNaught	Bernard	King¹	Dobson†	Latchford	Goodlass	Telfer	Pearson
23	WEST HAM UNITED	23,163	2-2	11	6	Davies	Bernard	Jones	Lyons¹	McNaught	Hamilton	King	Dobson	Latchford	Goodlass	Telfer	
26	COVENTRY CITY (LC4)	21,572	3-0	—	4	Davies	Bernard	Jones	Lyons¹	McNaught	Hamilton	King²	Dobson¹	Latchford¹	Goodlass	Telfer	
30	Tottenham Hotspur	26,027	2-3	11	8	Davies	Bernard	Jones	Lyons	McNaught	Hamilton	King¹	Dobson	Latchford	Goodlass	Telfer†	Darracott
Nov. 6	LEEDS UNITED	32,618	0-2	14	8	Davies	Bernard	Jones	Lyons	McNaught	Hamilton†	King†	Dobson	Latchford¹	Goodlass	Telfer	Buckley
20	DERBY COUNTY	23,020	0-0	14	10	Davies	Bernard	Jones	Lyons†	McNaught	Kenyon	King¹	Dobson	Latchford²	Hamilton	Smallman†	Darracott
27	West Bromwich Albion	31,208	1-4	16	13	Davies	Darracott	Jones	Lyons†	McNaught†	Kenyon	King²	Dobson	Latchford	Goodlass	Telfer	Telfer
Dec. 1	Manchester United (LC5)	21,025	0-3	—	—	Davies	Darracott	Jones	Lyons†	McNaught	Kenyon	King¹	Dobson¹	Latchford	Goodlass	Telfer	
11	Coventry City (2)	57,738	3-0	16	13	Lawson	Darracott	Jones	Rioch	McNaught	Kenyon†	King	Dobson	Latchford	McKenzie¹	Goodlass	Hamilton
18	BIRMINGHAM CITY	18,970	2-2	17	13	Lawson	Darracott	Jones	Lyons	McNaught	Kenyon¹	King	Dobson†	Latchford	McKenzie	Goodlass	
27	Manchester United	56,786	0-4	17	14	Lawson	Darracott	Jones	Lyons	McNaught	Rioch	King	Dobson	Latchford	McKenzie	Goodlass	
29	MIDDLESBROUGH	28,189	2-2	18	18	Lawson	Jones	Seargeant	Seargeant	McNaught¹	Rioch	King	Dobson	Latchford¹	McKenzie	Goodlass	
Jan. 8	STOKE CITY (FA Cup 3)	32,952	2-0	—	—	Lawson	Robinson	Jones	Lyons¹	McNaught¹	Rioch	King	Dobson	Latchford	McKenzie¹	Goodlass	
15	Ipswich Town																
18	BOLTON W. (LCSF)																
22	QUEENS PARK RANGERS																
29	Swindon (FA Cup 4)																
Feb. 5	Aston Villa																
12	LEICESTER CITY																
15	Bolton W. (LCSF)																
19	Stoke City																
26	ARSENAL (5)																
Mar. 5	Bristol City																
12	SUNDERLAND (LCF)																
19	Manchester City (6)																
22	LIVERPOOL																
April 8	MANCHESTER UNITED																
9	Middlesbrough																
11	NEWCASTLE UNITED																
16	Derby County																
23	WEST BROM. A. (SF)																
30	Norwich City																
May 7	COVENTRY CITY																
14	Birmingham City																
21	F.A. Cup Final																
	NORWICH CITY—to be arranged																
	Leeds United—to be arranged																
	TOTTENHAM—to be arranged																

Everton's score first   Name in bold—scorer   Superior figure—No. of goals scored   * Own goal   † Denotes substituted player

Home fixtures in CAPITALS

These fixtures are the copyright of the Football League Limited

EVERTON FIRST-TEAM APPEARANCES — 1976-77 (Up to and including matches played 8th Jan. 1977)

	Everton League Career App.	Gls.	1976-77 League App.	Gls.	1976-77 FLC/FAC App.	Gls.		Everton League Career App.	Gls.	1976-77 League App.	Gls.	1976-77 FLC/FAC App.	Gls.
Bernard	136	9	11	1	2	—	Latchford	100	45	20	9	5	2
Brand	1	—	—	—	—	—	Lawson	112	—	3	—	1	—
Buckley	109	8	—	—	—	—	Lyons	176	30	19	2	5	1
Darracott	100	—	8	—	2	—	McKenzie	4	2	4	2	—	—
Davies	73	—	17	—	4	—	McNaught	42	2	20	—	2	—
Dobson	92	13	20	3	5	2	Pearson	46	9	3	—	—	—
Goodlass	18	1	16	1	4	—	Rioch	—	—	4	—	—	—
Hamilton	29	5	7	—	2	—	Robinson	4	—	1	—	—	—
Higgins	1	—	2	—	—	—	Seargeant	73	1	2	—	—	—
Jones	30	—	19	—	5	—	Smallman	19	6	1	—	1	—
Kenyon	240	6	11	—	2	—	Telfer	60	17	14	4	3	—
King	23	7	20	5	5	5	Own Goal			5			

LEADING DIVISION 1 SCORERS

Gray (Aston Villa)	22
Hales (Derby)	18
Macdonald (Arsenal)	15
Burns, K. (Birmingham)	14
Mariner (Ipswich)	14
Pearson (Manchester Utd.)	13
Latchford (Everton)	**11**
Stapleton (Arsenal)	11
Burns, M. (Newcastle)	10
Ferguson (Coventry)	10
Hill (Manchester Utd.)	10
King (Everton)	**10**
Little (Aston Villa)	10
Tueart (Manchester City)	10
Worthington (Leicester)	10

(Including Lge. & Lge./F.A. Cup games)

CENTRAL LEAGUE 1979-80

	P	W	D	L	F	A	Pts
Liverpool	38	20	12	6	65	40	52
Man. Utd.	40	20	11	9	68	44	51
WB Albion	40	18	14	8	72	47	50
Coventry	39	20	9	10	84	54	49
Nottm Forest	37	19	10	8	63	39	48
Everton	39	19	9	11	70	43	47
Aston Villa	39	16	13	11	58	46	45
Wolves	36	19	6	11	55	40	44
Man. City	41	15	14	12	61	55	44
Burnley	39	17	9	13	44	46	43
Derby	41	13	16	12	58	57	42
Sheff. Wed.	36	15	7	14	60	54	37
Stoke	38	10	15	13	42	45	35
Huddersfield	38	12	9	17	51	61	33
Blackburn	40	13	7	20	57	83	33
Blackpool	37	11	10	16	54	64	32
Newcastle	38	12	8	18	46	51	32
Bury	39	11	9	19	37	46	31
Preston	38	8	11	19	46	76	27
Leeds	38	9	8	21	45	69	26
Bolton	38	8	9	21	43	70	25
Sheff. Utd.	38	6	10	23	46	96	22

(Up to and including Saturday, 19th April)

FIRST-TEAM APPEARANCES 1979-80

	79-80 League A	G	79-80 Cups A	G	Everton League Career A	G
Bailey	38	–	13	–	38	2
Barton (J)	6	–	5	–	15	–
Eastoe	19	6	10	2	26	6
Gidman	25	1	8	1	31	1
Hartford	31	–	8	1	31	1
Heard	1	–	–	–	7	1
Higgins	19	–	5	–	66	2
Hodge	23	–	7	–	23	–
Kidd	31	10	11	8	40	12
King	29	9	10	2	150	38
Latchford	23	6	7	7	214	100
Lyons	31	–	13	–	304	43
McBride	14	1	–	–	14	1
Megson	12	–	5	1	12	1
Nulty	9	–	6	–	22	2
O'Keefe	2	1	–	–	8	1
Ratcliffe	2	–	8	1	2	–
Ross	27	3	–	1	71	13
Stanley	20	–	6	–	20	–
Todd	10	–	–	–	32	–
Varadi	2	1	8	–	2	1
Wood	15	–	–	–	99	–
Wright	36	1	11	–	78	3
Own Goal	–	2	–	3	–	–

(Up to and including Saturday, 19th April)

FIRST DIVISION TABLE 1979/80

	P	Home W	D	L	F	A	Away W	D	L	F	A	Pts
Liverpool	38	14	6	0	42	8	7	3	8	23	21	55
Man. Utd.	40	15	1	3	39	16	7	9	5	27	25	54
Ipswich Town	40	13	4	3	42	13	8	5	7	24	24	51
Arsenal	40	13	3	4	25	11	5	7	8	27	24	46
Aston Villa	37	8	10	2	28	18	8	0	9	22	27	42
Southampton	38	10	5	4	44	24	4	8	7	21	27	41
Wolves	39	12	2	6	41	21	4	9	6	18	27	41
Nott'm Forest	37	7	6	5	37	11	10	1	8	26	21	40
W.B.A.	36	13	2	3	37	17	2	9	7	18	29	39
Middlesbrough	37	8	9	2	25	14	4	5	9	17	23	39
Crystal Palace	37	9	9	1	23	13	2	5	11	17	40	39
Coventry	39	9	3	7	33	21	4	5	11	15	30	38
Leeds United	40	9	7	4	28	17	4	4	12	17	32	38
Tottenham H.	39	11	5	4	34	28	2	6	11	17	32	36
Norwich	39	9	8	3	38	24	2	6	11	14	38	36
Brighton	40	8	7	5	24	24	4	5	11	16	32	35
Man. City	40	7	6	7	26	24	4	4	12	16	32	32
Stoke	39	8	4	7	28	24	2	8	11	16	36	32
Everton	38	6	8	6	26	26	2	5	14	12	36	31
Derby	40	8	6	7	33	28	2	2	16	13	43	28
Bristol City	40	8	8	5	17	19	1	5	14	19	51	28
Bolton	40	5	10	5	19	21	0	5	16	19	51	24

(Up to and including Saturday, 19th April 1980)

"MAY I COMPLIMENT YOU ON THE DECISION TO BAN STANDING 'AIDS' FROM GOODISON"

With the 1970s publication offering increased content for supporters, there were a variety of snippets that caught the eye.

The family theme the club were keen to portray even included players attending christenings, with Brian Labone's daughter in safe hands - namely goalkeeper Gordon West's - a man who was apparently always 'in charge on the big occasion'.

Blue Mail became a staple feature of the programme, with early issues in the 1970/71 campaign including the refusal of entry to Goodison due to young supporters attempting to take small stools into the ground.

On the flip side, a supporter was complimentary towards the club in this decision, noting how farcical the situation had become.

'It started in a minor way but has accelerated this season out of all proportions with the use of milk crates, boxes, ladders and even a table which I regarded as the last straw!'

Blue Mail

Those Stools

I have recently been refused entry into the Goodison Road Enclosure on the grounds that my young sister, my friend's little brother and myself had small stools. This also applied to a lady in her late thirties who told the police on duty that she was not paying 7/– to see the backs of the crowd and immediately returned home with her husband. As a small person myself who usually takes 3 or 4 young persons to the match I agree with this lady. Not once in the past three or four seasons have supporters complained about us standing on our stools up against the wall. I could afford to go in the stands but the children I take could not and their parents would not allow them to go on their own in the boys pen, so why should I and many other small people be the victims of the minority of young hooligans.

Miss I. Roberts,
16, Northcote Street,
Everton, Liverpool L5 4PD

EDITOR:—We sympathise with your point Miss Roberts but here is the opposite view.

May I compliment you on the decision to ban standing "aids" from Goodison Park. In the past I have had reason to complain on a number of occasions about the people who stand on various contrivances around the surrounding area of the pitch. It started in a minor way but has accelerated this season out of all proportions with the use of milk crates, boxes, ladders and even a table which I regarded as the last straw! These articles were frequently used as stepping stones to get on to the pitch and it is noticeable that since they were banned the invasions have become far fewer.

As a season ticket holder and an Everton Supporter for 20 years I feel I have a right to a good view of the match without the risk of breaking my leg on the way out.

R. Barnett,
50, Richmond Road,
Hindley Green, Wigan.

In safe hands

Everton team-mates attended the christening of Brian Labone's daughter, Rachelle Patricia, recently. Gordon West is one of Rachelle's God-parents and Gary Talbot's picture shows Brian and Gordon "in charge" on the big occasion.

Brian's Night

Brian Labone, pictured here with the managers and players before his Testimonial Match between Everton and Liverpool, sends his warmest thanks to all those who made up an attendance of 25,609 at Goodison last month. It was possibly Brian's final public appearance on the ground where he served Everton so brilliantly – and the fans showed their appreciation to the extent of cash receipts in the region of £15,000.

Picture: Gary Talbot

It was a big night for Brian Labone in March 1973, his testimonial between Everton and Liverpool attracting over 25,000 to Goodison – although as the above clipping shows, there were some stern and bemused faces from some of the players.

The Toffee Shop continued to show off its wares in the match programme, a seemingly rotating advertising section highlighting some of the items fans could purchase. The main product to catch the eye (right) is the sinister-looking 'Everton Footballer', a 'blow-up man 33 inches high'.

Another advertising snippet for Keith Prowse travel taken from the Manchester City programme of 1972/73, 'Talkabout' focused on the day-to-day job of travel agent Hilary Watson, daughter of Everton stalwart Gordon, as well as informing fans of what the company could do for them. As Hilary accurately noted: "We are deeply conscious of the fact that there is nothing worse than a ruined holiday."

Toffee Shop

START THE NEW YEAR WITH THESE EVERTON SOUVENIRS

Scarf	...	£1.35
Everton Footballer	...	£1.10
(Blow-up man 33 inches high)		
Diary	...	30p
Picture	...	25p
Jig-saws	...	50p
Mascot	...	90p
Cuff Links	...	£1

talk about with... Hilary Watson

ROYAL NAVY scores top

The Navy teaches you a trade that can last a lifetime. And pays you while you learn. All this plus travel and adventure. Get the facts from your local Navy Careers Office

New at Goodison, 1970/71

With the development of the new Main Stand nearing completion, it wasn't the only new facility offering supporters the opportunity to contribute to their club.

The new club shop was officially opened by vice-chairman Jim Hacking, with young supporter Michael Hughes, who had travelled nearly 200 miles with his father, being one of the first customers.

Situated on the Bullens Road side of Goodison, there were over 100 souvenirs available for fans – including a giant Alan Ball poster (below).

Also noted was the opening of the 300 Club at the end of February, offering the best in hospitality for club officials, guests and members of the Press.

The pictures showcase some of the scenes, including director Norman Coffey pouring himself a pint...

Toffee Shop

Everton Vice-Chairman Mr. Jim Hacking performed the official Opening Ceremony of our "Toffee Shop", the official souvenir premises on the Bullens Road side of the ground. On the left, Mr. Hacking cuts the tape, watched by Promotions Manager David Exall (left) and Sales Manager Bill Townsend (far right).
One of the first customers was a "long-distance" supporter, nine-year-old Michael Hughes, who had travelled over 200 miles with his father to be at the Opening Ceremony. Michael, who lives at Midsomer Norton, near Bath, Somerset, was presented with a scarf in Everton colours and he is seen above, receiving the gift from P.... Secretary I.... Mr. Hackin.... are also in t....

16

....ose Goodison

● Dateline: 27th Feb. Opening of Everton's "300 Club" and new Guest Room facilities.

1 Everton Chairman George Watts pulls the first pint in the "300 Club" lounge.

2 Director Norman Coffey seen at the new Directors' Room Bar.

3 Trainee Chef Graham Ward cuts a sirloin in the kitchen of the new club room.

4 Members of the "300 Club" enjoy a pre-match meal and toast to the success of Everton.

5 At the "300 Club" Bar.

6 In the lounge area.

7 The New Press lounge where newsmen Colin Wood, Don Kendall, Ray Matts and Don Hardisty relax before the game.

26

Toffee Shop

B on the BALL !

with this giant colour Poster of the Everton skipper – just 7/6 or 9/6 by po...

One of over 100 souvenirs of your favourite ... you cannot afford to miss !

Pop in and see us after the game – we are in ... Road, and open 9.30 to 5.30 every day Mo... Saturday, or send stamped addressed envelope... Champion Autograph Sheet and full list available.

27

EFC Scenes, 1974-76

Love was in the air in 1976 when Julie Dodds proposed to her boyfriend via the scoreboard during a friendly against Dundee. He responded in the affirmative - after she pointed out said message - having apparently been too engrossed in the action...

It was 'safety first' at Goodison as the crush-barriers were strengthened on the terracing (1974/75), while ticket prices were released for the AC Milan UEFA Cup tie the following year - maximum price £2.

There was also the revelations from Toffee Girl Lorraine Styles, that she 'could hide under the match ball every time the fans whistle after me'.

LOVE MATCH

Julie Dodds was determined to 'got her man' under the powers of the Leap Year licence granted to young ladies—and she asked Everton for help. Her request was unusual to say the least... she wanted to propose to her boyfriend, Terry, with a St. Valentine's Day message on the electronic scoreboard at Goodison Park!

The idea was put forward to Promotions Manager

Mike Skinner and he happily played a part in the Goodison love match by arranging for seven magic words to be flashed on the board during the friendly match against Dundee. Even then, Julie had a problem—because Terry was concentrating on the game and didn't notice the message. "I had to nudge him to have a look in the right direction," says Julie. "I think he nearly fainted, but then he did say 'Yes'!"

Pictures: Barry Farrell.

TERRY BE MY VALENTINE
AND MARRY ME
JULIE DODDS

Lorraine Styles, the Everton "Toffee Girl" for the past two seasons, loves to go round with the sweets which are donated by Barker & Dobson for every match, but she has just one minor complaint. "I could hide under the match ball every time the fans whistle after me," says the pretty 17-year-old from Huyton! Lorraine comes from a family of Evertonians— one brother, three sisters —and her boyfriend, Terry Smith, watches every Everton match, home and away. "Everton will definitely win something this season," claims the confident Lorraine, who makes a quick change from the "Toffee Girl" dress before dashing to her regular place in the Gwladys Street stand.

SAFETY FIRST

Work is continuing on strengthening and re-siting of the crush-barriers around the ground and by the end of the season it is anticipated that Goodison Park will meet all the provisos set out in a government Green Paper 'Guide to the Safety of Sports Grounds' which was issued in 1973.

Everton, assisting jointly with local authorities, police and the government working party, actually helped to formulate the recommendations of the finished report and whilst they have not been mandatory to formulate the recommendations of the public to implement what had been recommended. Work on the crush-barriers is just the tip of the iceberg for the club's architects and advisers have been consulted on every aspect of crowd safety which embraces exits and entrances, the terraces

UEFA CUP
FIRST ROUND — FIRST LEG
EVERTON
AC MILAN

At Goodison Park, on WEDNESDAY, 17th September, 1975. Kick-off 7.30pm (19.30 hrs).

PRICES

Seats £1.80* and £2* (Goal Stand and North End Stand cash at the turnstiles).

Paddock and Enclosure £1; Ground 80p; Boys Pen 40p.

*bookable in advance

Season Ticket Holders

Applications for tickets are now invited from Season Ticket Holders. Please enclose priority booking card and stamped addressed envelope plus remittance as follows:

Main Stand, Top Balcony, Centre 'A' and 'B' £2.

South End, Lower Stand and Gwladys Street £1.80.

300 500 Club Members

No action is necessary as membership covers all UEFA Cup matches at Goodison Park. Voucher number 22 should be surrendered at the turnstiles on the day of the match.

General Applications

Advance bookings will be accepted as outlined above— prices £1.80 or £2 plus stamped addressed envelope.

CLUB SCENE

FROM EMLYN HUGHES . . .

We were pleased to receive the following letter from Liverpool skipper Emlyn Hughes . . .

"The day I could have bitten off my tongue . . . I sincerely hope that the many thousands of Everton supporters will accept my heartfelt apologies for the stupid remarks I made at the official welcome home celebrations after our European Cup Final in Rome. It was said on the spur of the moment and I now deeply regret the incident.

"I now realise that many people, including our own supporters, took offence, and quite rightly, for it spoilt an otherwise happy occasion, and I can only say again how much I regret it."

QUIZ SPOT . . .

The winner of Quiz Spot No 26 (v Sunderland) was B. Dutton, of 196 Halton Road, Runcorn, Cheshire, who correctly answered that we beat Sheffield Wednesday 1-0 and drew 0-0 with Sunderland in the last two matches of the 1969–70 Championship season. The winner of Quiz Spot No 27 (v Newcastle) was Paula McShane, of 29 Marbury Road, West Vale, Kirkby, Liverpool L32 0UE, who was correct in naming Terry McDermott as the Liverpool-born player who had played for Newcastle and Jimmy Husband as the Newcastle-born forward who had played for Everton. Both winners will receive two tickets for our game against Wolves.

Blue Mail...Emlyn 1976-78

As well as an 'ode' to the Blues, written by Mrs J. I. Rathbone's son and his friend, some fans noted how much improved the atmosphere might be on the Gwladys Street should a roof be erected.

There was the chance to win an autographed ball, as the second Goal Of The Month competition was in operation - although from the goal descriptions and picture angles it appears to have been a tough month for long-range strikes...

The first game of the 1977/78 season made reference to comments made by Liverpool skipper Emlyn Hughes, in the wake of his side's first European Cup triumph. He offered his apologies: "It was said on the spur of the moment and I now deeply regret the incident."

BLUE MAIL

From: Mrs. J. I. Rathbone, 16 Broadway Avenue, Wallasey, Merseyside.

I thought you might like to see this "ode" written by my son, Steven, and his friend, who are strong Evertonians along with their respective fathers. – Could this be a preview of next Tuesday's m

It's 7.30 and all is tense,
For the match that follows hence.
Out they run amid the cheers
Dispelling all the players' fears.
Supermac stands next to Lawson.
Latchford and King make a foursome.
The Referee blows, away we go
And the game begins to flow.
1-2-3 it's in the net
The ball the keeper has to get.
Goodless to Latchford, Latchford to score
And sure enough the crowd does roar.

Written By: Steve Rathbone & Jon Duffey — Aged 15. (Avid supporters)

Irving Nattrass gives a very bad pass,
And in comes roaring Ronnie Goodlass.
The shot he hits strikes the bar
But the ball goes back too far
Mickey Pejic sends a cross
Against the sun the Keepers lost.
Davey Jones gives it a smack
It falls right out to Supermac.
McKenzie flicks, it looks like magic,
But for Newcastle downright tragic.
Two-nil it ends, fair and square,
Leaving the Geordies to curse and swear.

From: Pete Wells, Moreton, Wirral, Merseyside.

During the semi-final replay, I was hit in the eye by a beer can. It made me think how well behaved Evertonians are. I wonder just how well they would have behaved had we beaten them 3-0!

I think we all deserve a pat on the back for the excellent support given to the team, even when all w lost – "The song of Everton came riding on the breeze." Did anyone hear the famous Kop on the Saturde when the score was 2-2? Take away their roof – and what are they?

But the day of reckoning is coming soon, lads, and then we'll take up the chant: "Oh, where's you famous Kop!"

● **EDITOR: Strong words, Pete. But let us hope that your "day of reckoning" – a peaceful one, remember – is not far off. Incidentally, Pete touched on the subject of a roof echoing sound, as did the following readers. For the moment, however, we cannot promise any further ground development while the financial climate of the country is so difficult. We only have to remember the trouble other clubs found after spending more money on the ground than the team.**

From: B. O. Malley, 52 Stone Barn Lane, Palace Fields, Runcorn, Cheshire.

I think a word of praise to the Everton supporters is not out of place here. The way they have continually cheered and encouraged the team has been magnificent. I feel sure that if the Gwladys Street End had a roof like the Kop, we would prove we are the loudest in the country.

From: Stephen Rose, 7 Cowper Way, Huyton, nr. Liverpool.

I think I am correct to say that Everton have given the fans a great season and the fans have repaid them with their tremendous support. But how about a proper roof over the Gwladys Street End? Then we could shout for our team without the sound being muffled by the Lower Stand.

goal of the month

GOAL A — Andy King scores the second in a 2-2 draw against Manchester City. With the entire City team on the goal line for an indirect free kick, two shots were charged down before Andy stabbed the ball home.

GOAL B—Martin Dobson puts away the first goal against Manchester City. Martin ran to the near post where he met a corner from Ronnie Goodlass and placed his header into the far side of the net.

GOAL C—Mike Lyons hammers home the first g 3-2 victory over West Ham. From a throw-in b Dobson, Bob Latchford took the ball into the was tumbled over and the rebound was tucke the Everton skipper.

GOAL D—Andy King on target again with the first goal in the 3-0 win against Coventry. Andy's first shot was pushed away by the goalkeeper, but he followed up to score comfortably.

GOAL E—Andy King gets his second against Coventry. Put clear by Ken McNaught's clearance, which was helped on by a defender. Andy took the ball round the goalkeeper and calmly rolled it into the net.

Busy Bruce, Dave Jones, Higgy 1977-80

Bruce Rioch had a gift for groundsman Syd McGuinness' growing collection of football shirts after returning to Bellefield ahead of the 1977/78 season, a Brazil shirt picked up during Scotland's friendly in South America over the summer. According to the midfielder, who had been on national duty, he had been in his new Blundellsands home for only four days since the end of the season until mid-July.

Tickets for the Merseyside derby were available at prices from £1-£3, while Terrace Talk contained a snippet concerning Evertonian Dave Jones, now turning out at Coventry City:

'When I played with Coventry Reserves at Anfield, the game was over by quarter to four. And I couldn't miss the chance to see the lads at Goodison. So I dashed down there and saw the second half of the first-team match.'

Meanwhile Mark Higgins was reflecting on the untimely end to his season in 1979/80, a freak accident at Aston Villa resulting in his ankle being broken in two places and torn ligaments.

SUMMER RUSH

Bruce Rioch adds a Brazilian jersey to the collection of international shirts belonging to Bellefield groundsman, Syd McGuinness.

TERRACE TALK

BLUE MAIL

Send your letters to: "Blue Mail," Everton FC, Goodison Park, Liverpool L4 4EL.

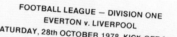

FOOTBALL LEAGUE — DIVISION ONE
EVERTON v. LIVERPOOL
SATURDAY, 28th OCTOBER 1978, KICK-OFF 3 p.m.

THIS WILL be an all ticket match and admission prices will be as for normal league fixtures:—

Ground £1.00
Paddock/Enclosure £1.10.
Main Stand, Top Balcony + Bullens Rd. Centre A + B £2.20.
Gwladys Street Stand + Park Stand, Bullens Rd. Lower + North + South End Stands £2.00.
Joint Adult/Juvenile £3.00

Main Stand, Top Balcony + Gwlayds Street Stand voucher/ticket stub holders: Goodison Road Ticket Office

Bullens Road Stands + Park End Stand voucher/ticket stub holders: Bullens Road Ticket office
Ground, Paddock + Enclosure voucher holders: Bullens Road Turnstiles

MARK MAKES A DATE...
"I'll be back next August"

1980-1990

As glory returned on the pitch, it was a great era to be a Goodison match-goer...but it wasn't just the players who were sweeping all before them in the pursuit of trophies

The matchday programme continued to improve throughout the decade, a period that produced the greatest side in Everton history.

National recognition was achieved for the first time, with *Programme Monthly* voting the publication the prestigious title for the first time in 1984/85, followed by second the following season and third in 1987/88. The publication was also Programme of the Year winner for five seasons in succession from 1984/85, and landed the Northern Programme Club prize in 1985/86.

The continual utilisation of fans' contributions and the freshening up of features remained key elements. The ability to involve the first-team squad was maintained – the fans were even invited into the family home of most players – and humorous elements including the popular Player Profile section, Neville Southall's responses in particular are worth noting later in this section.

Colour print also became more prominent throughout the official matchday programme, with the first all-colour programme introduced for the 1988/89 season.

Some of the most iconic covers were also produced during this period, partly due to the success of the side between 1984-1987, but also to note the Merseyside derby in May 1989 (see overleaf), Liverpool's first competitive game following the Hillsborough Disaster.

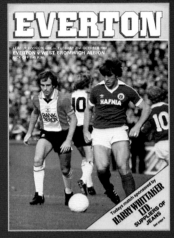

EVERTON

LEAGUE DIVISION ONE – TUESDAY 21st OCTOBER 1980
EVERTON v WEST BROMWICH ALBION
KICK-OFF 7.30 P.M.

Todays match sponsored by
HARRY WHITTAKER LTD
SUPPLIERS OF JEANS

EVERTON

EVERTON v MANCHESTER UNITED
SATURDAY 10th APRIL 1982 – 3.00 p.m.
FOOTBALL LEAGUE DIVISION ONE
OFFICIAL MATCHDAY MAGAZINE 30p

TODAY'S MATCH
SPONSORED BY
Bass
North
West

EVERTON

EVERTON v TOTTENHAM HOTSPUR
FA CUP 5th ROUND
SATURDAY 19th FEBRUARY 1983 – 3pm
OFFICIAL MATCHDAY MAGAZINE 30p

EVERTON

EVERTON FOOTBALL CLUB   OFFICIAL PROGRAMME 40p

EVERTON v

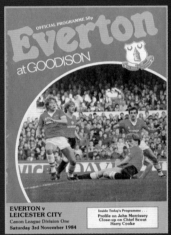

OFFICIAL PROGRAMME 50p

Everton
at GOODISON

EVERTON v
LEICESTER CITY
Canon League Division One
Saturday 3rd November 1984

Inside Today's Programme . . .
Profile on John Morrissey
Close-up on Chief Scout
Harry Cooke

EVERTON

NEC
OFFICIAL
PROGRAMME
50p

EVERTON v
LUTON
FA Cup Sixth Round Replay
Wednesday 12th March 1986

Everton

OFFICIAL PROGRAMME 60p

FOOTBALL LEAGUE DIVISION ONE – TUESDAY 2 SEPTEMBER 1986
EVERTON v OXFORD UNITED

NEC

EVERTON

NEC

PETER REID   JOHN BARNES

TODAY'S MATCH SPONSORS
MANFAST

FA Cup Round Five – Sunday 21st February 1988
EVERTON v LIVERPOOL
Official Programme 60p

EVERTON

NEC

BARCLAYS
LEAGUE

TODAY'S
MATCH
SPONSORS:
sayers
the Bakers

Barclays League Division One EVERTON v NEWCASTLE UNITED Sunday 27th August 1989
OFFICIAL PROGRAMME PRICE 80p

Selected covers, this page, clockwise from right: v
Birmingham City, 1981/82; v Gillingham (FA Cup),
1983/84; v Bayern Munich (European Cup Winners' Cup),
1984/85; v Aston Villa (League Cup), 1983/84;
v Southampton (FA Cup), 1980/81; (centre programmes,
left to right): v Tottenham Hotspur, 1981/82;
v Manchester United, 1982/83

Opposite page covers, clockwise from left:
v Southampton, 1985/86; v Luton Town, 1986/87; v
Nottingham Forest, 1987/88; v Tottenham Hotspur,
1988/89; v Manchester United, 1989/90; v Aston Villa,
1989/90; v Liverpool, 1988/89

EVERTON

FOOTBALL LEAGUE DIVISION ONE
SATURDAY 29th AUGUST 1981 — KICK-OFF 3.00 p.m.
EVERTON v BIRMINGHAM CITY
OFFICIAL MATCHDAY PROGRAMME — PRICE 30p

Inside today's matchday programme
News Desk, Howard Kendall
Action from last Saturday
Spotlight on Birmingham
Travel details, Statistics

FA CUP FIFTH ROUND REPLAY
EVERTON v SOUTHAMPTON
Tuesday 17th February 1981
Kick-off 7.45 p.m.
OFFICIAL MATCH DAY PROGRAMME PRICE 30p

EVERTON v TOTTENHAM HOTSPUR
SATURDAY 30th JANUARY 1982 - 3.00 p.m.
FOOTBALL LEAGUE DIVISION ONE
OFFICIAL MATCHDAY MAGAZINE 30p

EVERTON v MANCHESTER UNITED
LEAGUE DIVISION ONE
TUESDAY 19th APRIL 1983 - 7.30 pm
OFFICIAL MATCHDAY MAGAZINE 30p

EVERTON v GILLINGHAM
Saturday 28th January 1984
FA CUP FOURTH ROUND

EVERTON

MILK CUP
SEMI-FINAL
FIRST LEG
OFFICIAL PROGRAMME 40p

EVERTON v ASTON VILLA
WEDNESDAY 15th FEB 1984
KICK-OFF 7.30 P.M.

The Milk Cup

The two captains, Mark Higgins
and Allan Evans.

TODAYS MATCH SPONSORED BY British TELECOM

Everton at GOODISON

OFFICIAL PROGRAMME 50p

EVERTON v BAYERN MUNICH
European Cup Winners' Cup
Semi-final — 2nd Leg
Wednesday 24th April 1985

Inside Tonight's Programme . . .
PROFILE ON NEVILLE SOUTHALL
IN COLOUR – ACTION AND NEWS
FROM THE FIRST LEG IN MUNICH

EVERTON v SOUTHAMPTON
Canon League
Division One
Saturday
3rd May 1986

FREIGHT TO IRELAND

TODAY'S MATCH SPONSOR:
LIVERPOOL ECHO

EVERTON
OFFICIAL PROGRAMME 60p

THE TODAY LEAGUE

CHAMPIONS AGAIN!
See Howard Kendall on page two

THE TODAY LEAGUE DIVISION ONE – SATURDAY 9 MAY 1987
EVERTON v LUTON TOWN

NEC

EVERTON

BARCLAYS

NEC

Barclays League Division One – Sunday January 3rd 1988
EVERTON v NOTTINGHAM FOREST
Official Programme 60p

EVERTON
TODAY'S MATCH SPONSORS
HAFNIA DANISH COOKED MEATS
NEC

EVERTON
NEC
Barclays League Division One ◆ EVERTON v MANCHESTER UNITED ◆ Saturday 9th September 1989

BARCLAYS

EVERTON
NEC
Barclays League Division One ◆ EVERTON v ASTON VILLA ◆ Saturday 5th May 1990

BARCLAYS LEAGUE

TODAY'S MATCH SPONSORS
TELECOM

OFFICIAL PROGRAMME ◆ PRICE ONE POUND

Barclays League Division One ◆ Wednesday 3rd May 1989 ◆ Official Programme Price 80p

EVERTON v LIVERPOOL
TONIGHT'S MATCH SPONSORS: HAFNIA DANISH COOKED MEATS

Matchfacts

EVERTON
Royal Blue Shirts, White Shorts

1	NEVILLE SOUTHALL
2	GARY STEVENS
3	PAT VAN DEN HAUWE
4	KEVIN RATCLIFFE
5	DEREK MOUNTFIELD
6	PETER REID
7	TREVOR STEVEN
8	ADRIAN HEATH
9	GRAEME SHARP
10	PAUL BRACEWELL
11	ALAN HARPER
12	

JACK SHARP SPORTS LIVERPOOL

MANCHESTER UTD
Red Shirts, White Shorts

1	GARY BAILEY
2	MIKE DUXBURY
3	ARTHUR ALBISTON
4	REMI MOSES
5	KEVIN MORAN
6	GRAEME HOGG
7	BRYAN ROBSON
8	GORDON STRACHAN
9	MARK HUGHES
10	ALAN BRAZIL
11	JESPER OLSEN
12	

MATCH OFFICIALS

REFEREE
GEORGE M. TYSON
Sunderland

LINESMEN:
D. R. FARRALL
Nantwich
(Red Flag)

E. HART
Leyland
(Yellow Flag)

BALL BOYS

Today's Ball Boys are provided by the Norris Green Junior Football League and Everton FC Supporters' Club.

EVERTON MASCOT

The selection of today's Everton mascot was donated to Radio City's Give-a-Child-a-Chance Scheme. They have chosen seven-year-old Barry O'Hare, of The Paddock, Gateacre, Liverpool 25. The matchday mascot's kit is supplied by Le Coq Sportif, who have kindly agreed that it should be retained as a lasting souvenir of the occasion.

TOFFEE GIRL

Sweets distributed by the Everton Toffee Girl are by courtesy of Barker and Dobson.

FOOTBALL AT GOODISON

CANON LEAGUE DIVISION ONE

EVERTON v LEICESTER CITY

Saturday 3rd November
Kick-off 3.00 p.m.

CAR PARKING

Supporters driving to matches at Goodison Park are advised that the National Car Park in Priory Road will be open for every home game.

v Manchester United, 1984/85 – Two-goal No. 11 Kevin Sheedy had been a pre-match doubt...

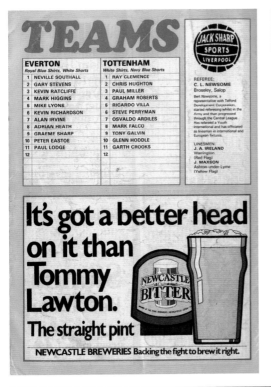

TEAMS

JACK SHARP SPORTS LIVERPOOL

EVERTON		TOTTENHAM	
Royal Blue Shirts, White Shorts		White Shirts, Navy Blue Shorts	
1	NEVILLE SOUTHALL	1	RAY CLEMENCE
2	GARY STEVENS	2	CHRIS HUGHTON
3	KEVIN RATCLIFFE	3	PAUL MILLER
4	MARK HIGGINS	4	GRAHAM ROBERTS
5	MIKE LYONS	5	RICARDO VILLA
6	KEVIN RICHARDSON	6	STEVE PERRYMAN
7	ALAN IRVINE	7	OSVALDO ARDILES
8	ADRIAN HEATH	8	MARK FALCO
9	GRAEME SHARP	9	TONY GALVIN
10	PETER EASTOE	10	GLENN HODDLE
11	PAUL LODGE	11	GARTH CROOKS
12		12	

REFEREE:
C. L. NEWSOME
Broseley, Salop

Bert Newsome, a representative with Telford Development Corporation, started refereeing whilst in the Army and then progressed through the Central League. Has refereed a Youth international and has officiated as linesman in international and European fixtures.

LINESMEN:
J. A. IRELAND
Warrington
(Red Flag)
J. MAXSON
Ashton-under-Lyme
(Yellow Flag)

It's got a better head on it than Tommy Lawton.
The straight pint

NEWCASTLE BITTER

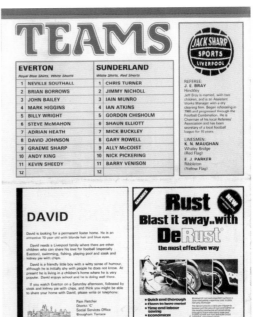

TEAMS

JACK SHARP SPORTS LIVERPOOL

EVERTON		SUNDERLAND	
Royal Blue Shirts, White Shorts		White Shirts, Red Shorts	
1	NEVILLE SOUTHALL	1	CHRIS TURNER
2	BRIAN BORROWS	2	JIMMY NICHOLL
3	JOHN BAILEY	3	IAIN MUNRO
4	MARK HIGGINS	4	IAN ATKINS
5	BILLY WRIGHT	5	GORDON CHISHOLM
6	STEVE McMAHON	6	SHAUN ELLIOTT
7	ADRIAN HEATH	7	MICK BUCKLEY
8	DAVID JOHNSON	8	GARY ROWELL
9	GRAEME SHARP	9	ALLY McCOIST
10	ANDY KING	10	NICK PICKERING
11	KEVIN SHEEDY	11	BARRY VENISON
12		12	

REFEREE:
J. E. BRAY
Hinckley

Jeff Bray is married, with two children, and is an Assistant Works Manager with a dry cleaning firm. Began refereeing in 1965 and progressed through the Football Combination. He is Chairman of his local Referees' Association and has been secretary of a local football league for 16 years.

LINESMEN:
K. N. MAUGHAN
Whaley Bridge
(Red Flag)
F. J. PARKER
Ribbleton
(Yellow Flag)

DAVID

David is looking for a permanent foster home. He is an attractive 10 year old boy with blonde hair and blue eyes.

David needs a Liverpool family where there are other children who can share his love for football (especially Everton), swimming, fishing, playing pool and steak and kidney pie with chips.

David is a friendly little boy with a witty sense of humour, although he is initially shy with people he does not know. At present he is living in a children's home where he is very popular. David enjoys school and he is doing well there.

If you watch Everton on a Saturday afternoon, followed by steak and kidney pie with chips, and think you might be able to share your home with David, please write or telephone:

Pam Fletcher
District 'C'
Social Services Office
Brougham Terrace
West Derby Road
Liverpool 6
Tel: 263 3421

CITY OF Liverpool

Rust
Blast it away..with
DeRust
the most effective way

- Quick and thorough
- Clean to bare metal
- Time and labour saving
- economical
- Drive in or phone

BOOTLE
051-207 0011

Clockwise from above: v Tottenham Hotspur, 1981/82; v Sunderland, 1982/83; v Middlesbrough, FA Cup third-round replay, 1989/90; v Chelsea, 1986/87

MATCHFAX...

EVERTON	v	CHELSEA		SCORECHECK	
Royal Blue Shirts, White Shorts		Jade Shirts and Shorts		A	Arsenal v West Ham
NEVILLE SOUTHALL	1	TONY GODDEN		B	Coventry v Nottm F
ALAN HARPER	2	DOUG ROUGVIE		C	Leicester v Newcastle
PAUL POWER	3	KEITH DUBLIN		D	Manchester C v Aston Villa
KEVIN RATCLIFFE	4	STEVE WICKS		E	Norwich v Tottenham
DEREK MOUNTFIELD	5	JOE McLAUGHLIN		F	Oxford v Manchester Utd
KEVIN LANGLEY	6	JOHN BUMSTEAD		G	QPR v Liverpool
TREVOR STEVEN	7	PAT NEVIN		H	Sheffield W v Southampton
ADRIAN HEATH	8	KEITH JONES		J	Watford v Charlton
GRAEME SHARP	9	KERRY DIXON		K	Wimbledon v Luton
PAUL WILKINSON	10	KEVIN McALLISTER		L	Birmingham v Oldham
KEVIN SHEEDY	11	DARREN WOOD		M	Blackburn v Sheffield Utd
	S			N	C Palace v Grimsby
				O	Derby v Ipswich
				P	Huddersfield v Brighton
				Q	Hull v Stoke
				R	Millwall v Leeds
				S	Portsmouth v Bradford C
				T	Reading v Barnsley
				U	Shrewsbury v Plymouth
				V	Sunderland v WB Albion
				W	Chester v Brentford
				X	Port Vale v Wigan
				Y	Crewe v Wrexham
				Z	Tranmere v Swansea

MATCH OFFICIALS
Referee: GEORGE TYSON, Sunderland
Linesmen: G. BANWELL, Eccleshall (Red Trim)
D. M. CHARNLEY, Failsworth (Yellow Trim)
Stand-By Official: G. M. CARROL, Liverpool

Ring Everton Club Call. Tel: 0898 121199.

EVERTON
Everton & NEC
Technique and Technology
NEC Corporation.
The company in Computers and Communications.
NEC

MATCHFACTS
F.A. Challenge Cup
Third Round Replay
January 10th 1990

Mitre

EVERTON	v	MIDDLESBROUGH
Royal Blue Shirts, White Shorts		Red Shirts and Shorts
NEVILLE SOUTHALL	1	STEPHEN PEARS
IAN SNODIN	2	GARY PARKINSON
NEIL McDONALD	3	COLIN COOPER
KEVIN RATCLIFFE	4	TONY MOWBRAY
DAVE WATSON	5	SIMON COLEMAN
NORMAN WHITESIDE	6	STUART RIPLEY
PAT NEVIN	7	BERNIE SLAVEN
STUART McCALL	8	MARK PROCTOR
GRAEME SHARP	9	ALAN KERNAGHAN
MIKE NEWELL	10	MARK BRENNAN
PETER BEAGRIE	11	PETER DAVENPORT
	12	
	14	

Referee: BRIAN HILL, Kettering
A Wages/Cost Accountant. Began refereeing in 1965 and reached Football League list in 1975. Refereed the FA Cup Final in 1989 and was reserve referee for the Littlewoods Cup Final in 1987.

Linesmen: D.W. MANSFIELD, Macclesfield (Yellow/Red Trim)
R.D.FALEY, Huddersfield

MASCOT
Tonight's Everton mascot is Philip Hall, aged 9, of Mawdsley Close, Formby, Liverpool
The mascot's kit is kindly supplied by Umbro and is retained as a lasting souvenir of the occasion.

BALL BOYS
Today's Ball Boys are provided by the Rainhill Junior League and Everton FC Supporters' Club.

EVERTON CLUB CALL
0898 121 199

EVERTON
Everton & NEC
Technique and Technology
NEC Corporation.
The company in Computers and Communications.
NEC

Howard Kendall

It's a pleasure to welcome a club of Bayern Munich's standing to Goodison Park tonight for the second leg of our semi-final in the European Cup-Winners' Cup.

The first thing to say about Bayern is that they are a very good side, possessing so many international players of real quality.

We knew they would be very difficult to beat in their own stadium in Munich, but full credit to our lads for getting the result that we did achieve.

There were chances for us to sneak a goal, while they had a couple of near-things, including one off the line by Kevin Richardson which, incidentally, was good defending and not good luck.

No doubt they expected to bring a lead to Goodison, which they haven't done, but our job is only half complete, although the draw in Germany does give us a tremendous opportunity to go through to the Final.

We have to put them under as much pressure as possible while making sure we are not caught on the break. The situation, though, is a little bit different from playing the first leg at home. That's when you need to build up a lead and when nothing happens, you tend to become anxious, which Bayern did a fortnight ago.

But, in our position tonight, we will not have to keep forcing if we get one goal. It's not as if we are looking for two or three goals to take a lead into an away leg, as we were in our last home European game against Fortuna Sittard.

Having said that, a 1-0 lead would not leave any room for error. In fact, we are back to the first round situation against the Irish team. We got an early goal but failed to add to that, and if UCD had scored, then we would have been out.

In our last programme, I didn't have time to reflect on the FA Cup semi-final in any detail. Obviously, we are delighted to be going back to Wembley and I can only praise all the players for the way they worked to put things right after not playing well in the first-half against Luton.

I felt their goal was the result of a foul on Gary Stevens and was surprised that people made much more fuss about the free-kick leading to our equaliser. Also, I didn't think enough was made of Neville Southall's brilliant save from Ricky Hill early in the second-half.

However, we have to agree that Luton would have been unfortunate if they had not gone in at half-time with a lead. We accept that we had a very disappointing first-half, but we did play a lot of good football later in the game.

People were asking questions about our physical fitness following the midweek trip to Munich, but there was no way the players suffered from that. The extra night in Munich meant they were not up until the early hours of the morning, and it was a comfortable start to Thursday, not leaving the hotel until 9.30 am.

The lads went home to rest on Thursday and came in for light training on Friday afternoon, before travelling to Birmingham and having another good night's sleep.

From the semi-final, we moved back to League matters with a 4-1 win against West Bromwich Albion. And what a start it was for Ian Atkins to score after only two minutes on his first home appearance!

There was an awkward bounce but he volleyed it home tremendously well. It looked like a goal of a natural striker which, of course, he was for a time when he was at Shrewsbury.

The early boost was followed by a period in which we looked sloppy, and not just at the back. Albion had chances and, fortunately, Neville Southall was up to the job. He was outstanding for a spell of about 15 minutes.

Then, we made it 2-0 from a defensive slip, and, to be honest, that was rather flattering. However, in the second-half, we did much better by playing to our strengths. Although Kevin Sheedy's shot took a deflection, it was originally on target, and then we got a fourth when Pat Van den Hauwe was brought down for a clear penalty.

The result left us seven points clear, with two games in hand, but it's nonsense for people to say the Championship is all over. To be absolutely certain, we still have to win five of the last nine games.

What we did do against Albion was to increase the points difference, increase the goal-difference, increase Graeme Sharp's position as leading scorer and increase Neville Southall's reputation as a goalkeeper.

● We have released Terry Curran from his contract to enable him to make a fresh start and I believe a Swedish club are interested in him. He didn't have the best of times with injuries while he was here and we wish him all the best in the future.

● We have offered a new contract to John Bailey and we are hoping that he will be signing.

Howard Kendall's programme notes from a famous night against Bayern Munich, European Cup Winners' Cup, 1984/85

"NO DOUBT MUNICH EXPECTED TO BRING A LEAD TO GOODISON, BUT OUR JOB IS ONLY HALF COMPLETE"

The decade began with Gordon Lee as the man in charge and an FA Cup semi-final appearance hinted at better times to come - only for the struggles of the 1980/81 campaign to signal the end for Lee and the appointment of a former favourite who had been making waves in East Lancashire with Blackburn Rovers.

Howard Kendall's arrival in May 1981 was a welcome boost for Evertonians, and his early notes signalled a planned return to winning football.

Despite ups and downs, the period from 1984-1987 is seen as the most productive in the Blues' history, with two league titles, an FA Cup and European success - as well as numerous other trips to Wembley. Kendall was never afraid to tackle issues in the football world, as well as hail the success of his players.

His successor, assistant Colin Harvey, battled to maintain the club's place at the top table of English football. Hamstrung by the European ban and having struggled to replace the ageing players from the mid-1980s side, his notes also highlighted the injury woes that took a toll.

HOWARD KENDALL

With interests in three cup competitions, and at least a European qualification in mind in the League, Tottenham Hotspur face a minimum of 29 matches in the last 16 weeks of the season.

They are one of the best footballing teams in the country, and in welcoming them to Goodison Park today, I look forward to this opportunity of measuring our progress since we lost 3-0 at White Hart Lane in September.

We took a certain amount of criticism for our performance that day, but I felt that the final score was unjust in that we were beaten by three late goals, scored from set pieces.

Whilst accepting that we did not pose many problems for them, I think it also fair to say we weren't in any particular trouble. In fact, I was very pleased with our defensive work.

An interesting aspect of today's fixture is that Garth Crooks and Adrian Heath will be on opposing sides. They were good friends at Stoke and I know they will be looking forward to this meeting.

Adrian has played two games for us since his transfer from Stoke and I am very pleased with him. I see great things in him; the amount of ground he covers, the way he breaks things up and starts us moving. He is just what we needed in midfield.

I formed a tremendous respect for him when we were together at Stoke, where I had a close look at what he can do. I rated him as a fine prospect in those days and it was no surprise to see the headway he made in the last couple of seasons.

He was top of my list when Asa Hartford and Mickey Thomas left Goodison Park, but we had to wait a while after Stoke had turned down our original offer. There was an agreement that Stoke would contact us if the position changed and I received that call on the Monday after they had gone out of the FA Cup.

It's amazing how fortunes change in football. I am sure that Stoke's exit from the Cup influenced the deal, for I think that Richie Barker realised that he needed to make changes and that Adrian would have to leave.

I believe we have value for money in Adrian, who is only just 21 and joining us at a similar age to Alan Ball on his arrival here in 1966.

We have bought him as a midfield player, but he can play in an attacking role, and it is always handy to have someone so adaptable. It makes it a lot easier to select the substitute, knowing that we do not have to reshape the side to a great extent in the event of an injury.

If Adrian approaches anywhere near to "Bally's" standards, I will be delighted — and I think he has that potential, for he is an all-action player, with a good brain and a nice change of pace.

The three games since we went out of the FA Cup provided further encouragement in maintaining a good run in the League. We gave an excellent performance against Manchester United, coming so soon after the disappointment of defeat at West Ham.

It was tremendous, the way the lads adapted, and they were very unlucky to drop two points. There is no doubt we were the better side and played some good football, which we now want to maintain.

Having set that standard, this is the level we want to improve on. The pleasing thing is that we are looking like a team, and that was something that was lacking a short while ago when we lost our way after being forced to change our system of play because of injuries and departures.

There were a lot of good things in our first-half display against Southampton, but they came into the game in the second half when I felt we dropped too deep and gave their midfield too much ground.

It was disappointing to concede a goal in the last two minutes, but it was one that could have been prevented. Looking at the video afterwards, we saw that some players jogged back for the corner instead of sprinting to their positions. The lesson is that we must concentrate for 90 minutes.

Having lost four points I thought we deserved in two drawn games, it was good to go to Wolverhampton last week and win so emphatically. This took us into fifth place, and whilst realising that other teams can catch us with games in hand, I am delighted to have the points.

Alan Irvine gained a boost in confidence from scoring his first League goals at Molineux and Kevin Richardson was on target for the second time in the week. He strikes a good ball and his two goals were both shots from set pieces, creeping just inside the post.

It was unfortunate that the game at Molineux was held up by demonstrations by Wolves' supporters. I feel sorry for Wolves, for this was more off-putting for the home side. They could find themselves in a position where the players do not want to play at home.

Finally, just a note to say that I am pleased to see that Martin Hodge did well by keeping a clean sheet in his first few games for Preston. At the time of writing, we have to decide whether to extend his loan, but we have made John Barton available for transfer, and Eamonn O'Keefe has joined Wigan. They both felt they needed regular first team football and I fully understood their position.

Notes from Howard Kendall's early days as boss as he states how impressed he is with Adrian Heath, v Tottenham Hotspur, 1981/82

COLIN HARVEY

OUR great city has been united in grief and compassion since that awful moment when it became clear that so many Liverpool supporters had lost their lives at Hillsborough.

My sympathy goes to the bereaved families, to Liverpool Football Club and to all Merseyside people who stood shoulder-to-shoulder in their response to disaster.

Football people around the country always marvelled at the way Everton and Liverpool supporters could gather together as both friends and rivals at derby matches. This was a special quality in happy times and in the last two-and-a-half weeks it has been a great strength in tragedy.

The mourning will continue for a long time and the events of Saturday April 15th will never leave the memory. Playing football again is a strain on the emotions. We felt that when we resumed at Tottenham a week later and the players of both clubs will probably shed a tear this evening.

There couldn't be such a thing as an ideal fixture for Liverpool to start playing again, but I'm sure a derby match is as good a time as any. It is a Merseyside occasion and we will all stand together in respect for those who died and with thoughts for those who lost loved ones at Hillsborough.

At Villa Park that day, we went from top to bottom on the emotional scale after winning an FA Cup semi-final and then returning to our dressing room to hear the devastating news from Hillsborough.

It really hit me when I watched TV that night. What we had achieved on the football field seemed meaningless. It still does in many ways, but the game goes on and we have to try to get back into our regular routine.

With that in mind, the rest of this article includes reflections on matches in the normal way. The two games prior to the semi-final brought mixed results - a defeat at Arsenal and a win at home against Charlton.

At Highbury, we went a goal down within three minutes, but we ought to have got something out of a good spell in the first half. We had Arsenal on the ropes for half-an-hour, and if we had

scored in that period, I'm sure that we would have beaten them or at least got a draw.

The second goal clinched it for them and we finished looking a bit short in terms of organisation at the back. That was when we missed Kevin Ratcliffe and Dave Watson, but full marks to those who did a good job for the side despite playing out of position.

Stuart McCall came in at right back and we moved Neil McDonald into the middle with Pat Van den Hauwe. I did consider bringing in Eddie Youds, but after weighing everything up, I decided to go for experience.

It was a big game and the last thing we wanted was to put Eddie in a situation which could have affected his confidence. Of course, young players have to be introduced at some stage, but I think it's important to choose the right time to ease them in.

The Charlton game was memorable for Graeme Sharp when he scored his 100th league goal in a little under 250 full appearances. Congratulations to him on reaching his century at a very good striking rate in modern football.

Graeme, of course, is more than an out-and-out goal-scorer. He makes things happen for others, as we saw when he played his part in a marvellous goal for Pat Nevin in the same match.

He beat two opponents and then played a one-two with 'Sharpy' before flicking the ball over the 'keeper as he came out. That was one for the fans to enjoy and I'm sure there's more to come from Pat. He can go past people as if they aren't there and he has a good scoring record for a winger.

The encouraging point recently is that we have started to spread the goals around. Kevin Sheedy is scoring consistently, and if Pat can continue to get his share, we will have a much better balance to the attacking side of our game.

After the semi-final, we didn't do a great deal of training and it was always going to be a difficult game at Tottenham. We tried to do a professional job and the result was less than we deserved. A draw would have been much fairer reflection of our performance.

■ As you'll read elsewhere in tonight's programme, the 'A' team have won the Lancashire League title. I'd like to add my congratulations to everyone concerned in an achievement which has to be a promising sign for the future.

Every manager would love to have five or six local-born players in the first team, but youth development is a long process and so much depends on how whether youngsters go on to make the most of their ability.

The next step for the 'A' team lads is to go into the Central League side and then start to show something something at that level over a period of time.

John Ebbrell is one who has come through that building-up phase and now he's beginning to break through in the first-team squad. As I mentioned earlier, Eddie Youds is also nearing that stage, having travelled with us on a few occasions.

Only exceptional prospects play regular First Division football at 18 or 19. For instance most of the youngsters blooded by Manchester United this season are 20 or 21 and have served a long apprenticeship in the Central League.

Even then, it was really only because of injuries that they got in. They took the chance when it came, but if everyone had been fit, I doubt that so many of them would have had a look-in.

Colin Harvey's tribute to the Liverpool fans who died at Hillsborough, v Liverpool 1988/89

CAPTAIN'S COLUMN

By KEVIN RATCLIFFE

Hello again! It's a very special occasion for Everton tonight — the first-ever European semi-final at Goodison Park — and we're all looking forward to what could be a cracking match with Bayern Munich.

It was a tremendous performance to go over there a fortnight ago and come back with a 0-0 draw. From my experience with Wales, I know how difficult it is to get results away from home at this level. The attitude of the lads was brilliant.

We knew Bayern were a good team and that not many sides had held them in the Olympic Stadium in the past.

As we expected, they put us under a lot of pressure in the first-half, but we defended well and gradually came more into the game, trying not to rush things, but always looking as if we might sneak a goal.

With no disrespect to the other teams we have played in Europe, Bayern are a far better side and we are not under-estimating what we have to do tonight if we are to go through to the Final.

I think it will be our turn to put them under pressure, but we will have to keep a sharp eye on them when they break. They have players with a lot of pace and have a good touch on the ball.

Like ourselves, Bayern are going for their League Championship and are through to their Cup Final as well. But I must admit that we nearly came unstuck in our semi-final against Luton.

The first-half at Villa Park was probably the worst we have played all season — and it would have to be in a semi-final before 30,000 of our own fans.

All credit to Luton, of course. We were playing against the wind in the first-half and they used their advantage very well. We were lucky to concede only one goal, but the lads pulled themselves together and showed great character.

Mind you, it was a close thing when Kevin Sheedy equalised with only a few minutes to go. I had that feeling that we were never going to score, never going to win. I haven't had that for a long time, and I don't want it again!

Yet, once we got into extra-time, there was no way we were going to lose. Because we had been behind for such a long while, the celebrations afterwards seemed a little bit more special than when we beat Southampton in last year's semi-final.

Looking back now, it was something of a turning point when we pushed Derek Mountfield up front. To be honest, I was surprised that Luton pulled Mick Harford back to mark him. Most teams do that for corners and free-kicks but not in general play.

Perhaps they were worried about us and sensed that we were going to get a goal back.

It was nice to book our Wembley place and know that we had five weeks in which to concentrate on the League. We've got that much on our plates that the only reminder of Wembley will be the requests for tickets!

With two Cup competitions on the go, our League football seemed to be only in little spasms of two or three games at a time. Fortunately, when we haven't played, we have still been on top.

In fact, we have held the lead by not playing. Whenever the others were in a position to overtake us, they missed their chance. Having said that, there is still a lot to do as we start to make up on our games in hand.

Tonight's match is our 52nd of the season, not counting the Charity Shield, and we still have nine — hopefully, 10 — to come. There's also an international programme next week, when Neville Southall and myself will be hoping to upset Spain's World Cup hopes. Trevor Steven, too, will be looking for another England cap in Romania.

Kevin Ratcliffe, 1985

Fresh from a goalless draw at Bayern Munich and with the league title all-but sealed, focus was very much fixed on the return leg of the European Cup Winners' Cup semi-final at Goodison.

'With no disrespect to the other teams we have played in Europe, Bayern are a far better side and we are not under-estimating what we

have to do tonight if we are to go through.'

The skipper also noted the victory over Luton Town in the FA Cup semi-final, and the fact the team had seemingly saved their worst performance of the season for the first half. In reference to Kevin Sheedy's late equaliser that took the match to extra time:

'I had that feeling that we were never going to score, never going to win. I haven't had that for a long time, and I don't want it again!'

Kevin Ratcliffe, 1989

In 1989 the Hillsborough Disaster was very much on the minds of everybody on Merseyside.

Ratcliffe's notes recall the day - Everton were playing Norwich City in the other semi-final at Villa Park - and of getting to hear the tragic news.

'There has been a huge show of strength, and dignity, on Merseyside in these recent sad days. May it bring a better future for the game and its supporters, and never again should we ever have to hear someone vowing "Never again."'

CAPTAIN'S COLUMN

IT should have been one of those moments which stay in your mind forever; that magic, precious time when you know you are on your way to Wembley.

And it was - until we reached the dressing room at Villa Park.

Then, and only then, did we have our first news of the Hillsborough disaster. Never has a team reached the F.A. Cup Final in so much silence. And rightly so.

The disaster has come close to overwhelming the city of Liverpool but in the end, as so often before, everyone has closed ranks, shed their tears, blinked, bit their lips - and then faced the future.

I don't think the enormity of the tragedy really hit home until we saw the Sunday papers. You see, nobody wanted to listen to the radio on the coach returning us to Merseyside from Birmingham; we were still too numbed by it all.

But the papers, and their pictures, brought it all home. The tragedy overshadowed everything and yet, even almost a week later when we stopped off at Anfield to pay our respects on the way to our game with Spurs, the enormity of the disaster, and the tidal wave of emotion, hit us more than ever as we left our own floral tribute.

I am proud that Everton F.C. and Evertonians throughout the country have stood shoulder to shoulder with our friends and colleagues at Anfield during the worst moments of their club's history.

There has been a huge show of strength, and dignity, on Merseyside in these recent sad days. May it bring a better future for the game and it's supporters, and never again should we ever have to hear someone vowing "Never again". Enough is enough.

Now we are picking up the threads again, I am left with a feeling that our journey to Wembley was clinched by a very professional performance against a Norwich City team which has a great capacity to surprise.

The 1-0 scoreline at Villa Park was too close for us to relax, but I never felt that we were in danger of losing. We always felt comfortable, and that's always a true test of our composure and confidence.

The F.A. Cup Final would give the club, and it's supporters, the chance to end the season on a high note, though I would not be true to my own conscience if I did not acknowledge how disappointed we all our by our overall showing this season.

We can do better - and will. But just how and where we went wrong is something for us to thrash out among ourselves - not in the club programme.

Right: Trevor Steven takes on Norwich's Andy Linighan at Villa Park

NEVILLE SOUTHALL - Q: YOUR FAVOURITE ITEM OF CLOTHING? A: LEFT SOCK

A popular fans' feature, the Player Interview was one of the few opportunities supporters were given to learn about one of their heroes in media form. The internet and blanket TV coverage were still yet a distant possibility, while matchday coverage remained the domain of print and radio.

As well as the usual career/season overview format, there were other player-related features which provided common currency in the match programme. Player Factfiles and Opinions were among the more eye-opening, with certain players adopting a tongue-in-cheek tone. Alternative interviews and profiles were also utilised, such as that opposite, celebrating Peter Reid's PFA Player of the Year award in 1985.

A regular feature, continued from the mid-late 1970s, saw players pictured at home, often surrounded by family and, in some instances, questionable furnishings...

PLAYERS' NUMBER ONE

Peter Reid was lifted to the peak of his profession a fortnight ago – voted Players' Player of the Year.

The highest individual honour in the game was bestowed upon him at the annual gathering of members of the Professional Footballers' Association at The Hilton Hotel in London.

Yet, Peter, both proud and modest at the same time, reminded his illustrious audience that he was receiving the award, not only for himself but on behalf of his Everton colleagues.

'As I said in my speech, it was an award for what Everton have achieved in the last 18 months,' he was anxious to point out when congratulated on becoming the first Everton player to win the trophy. Andy Gray, of course, was with Aston Villa when he received the accolade.

'Four or five of our lads could have won it,' added Peter. 'I was just fortunate enough to be the one elected above the others.'

Although the destination of the prize is never revealed until the big night itself, Peter was privately asked to make sure that he was in

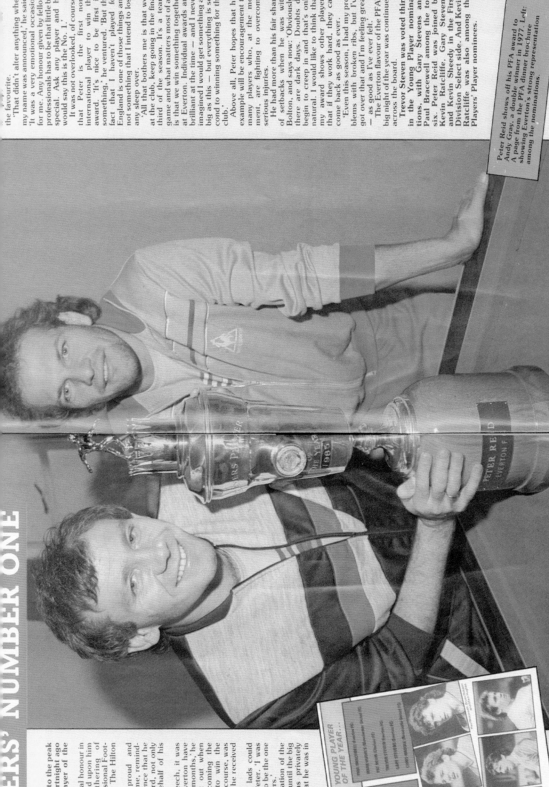

attendance when my name was announced,' he said.

'It was a very emotional occasion for me. Any honour given by fellow professionals has to be that little bit special. Ask any player and he would say this is the No. 1.

It was not overlooked, of course, that Peter is the first non-international player to win the award. 'It's nice to be first in something,' he ventured. 'But the fact that I haven't played for England is one of those things and not something that I intend to lose any sleep over.

'All that bothers me is that we, at the club, keep going in the final third of the season. It's a team game and what matters most of all is that we win something together at Everton. Individual awards are brilliant at the time – and I never imagined I would get something as big as this – but everything is second to winning something for the club.'

Above all, Peter hopes that his example will be encouragement to many players who, at the moment, are fighting to overcome serious injuries.

He had more than his fair share of setbacks when he was with Bolton, and says now: 'Obviously, there are dark days. Doubts do begin to creep in and that's only natural. I would like to think that my award shows other players that if they work hard, they can come back as good as ever.

'Even this season, I had my problems with broken ribs, but I've got over that and I'm feeling great – as good as I've ever felt.'

The Everton flavour of the PFA's big night of the year was continued across the board.

Trevor Steven was voted third in the Young Player nominations, with Gary Stevens and Paul Bracewell among the top six. Peter Reid was joined by Kevin Ratcliffe, Gary Stevens and Kevin Sheedy in the First Division Select side. And Kevin Ratcliffe was also among the Players' Player nominees.

'That didn't alter anything when

PLAYERS' PLAYER OF THE YEAR...

YOUNG PLAYER OF THE YEAR...

PROFILE

A newspaper cutting supplied by two of Neville Southall's old school pals is evidence of the astonishing progress made by the Everton goalkeeper on a complicated route to the First Division.

Today, for example, he could be facing Osvaldo Ardiles and yet, four years ago, when the gifted Argentinian was a World Cup winner, Neville was only just switching from the Vale of Conwy League to the Welsh League as his 20th birthday approached.

Even now it seems that his journey to the top, via five non-League clubs, is not as well recognised as it should be in his home town.

For we received the following plea recently from his ex-school mates, David Vale and David Hughes . . . 'People don't believe us when we tell them that Neville is from Llandudno, but if you publish this newspaper item, they will know it is true.'

These former pupils at Ysgol John Bright School added: 'All the lads Neville played football with in the school team and on The Oval wish him all the best and hope he stays with Everton for a long time.'

Their good wishes brought back memories. Neville is now a well-built 6ft 1in and yet he recalls that he was smaller than anyone else at school. But he was always a goalkeeper and lived for football because 'I wasn't very good at anything else.'

Despite his lack of inches, he started playing for Llandudno Swifts in the Vale of Conwy League at 13 and had hopes of going to a League club on leaving school. He had a trial at Crewe and also went to Bolton for two trials — 'but I didn't hear anymore.'

Instead he combined local football with numerous jobs after starting work in the Government's Youth Opportunities Scheme. 'I did some of the cooking and served meals at an hotel, then I was hod-carrier and a bin-man — what they call Refuse Disposal these days!'

At 18, Neville stepped up into the Northern Premier League with Bangor City but spent only a season there, a pattern that was to be repeated with each of his clubs leading up to Everton. 'Perhaps I get fed up easily,' smiled the amiable Welshman.

His subsequent trail took him to Llandudno Rangers (Vale of Conwy League), Conwy United (Welsh League) and Winsford United (Cheshire County League).

It was with Winsford that Howard Kendall first spotted his potential but Blackburn Rovers had sufficient goalkeepers at the time and Bury moved in to sign him in the summer of 1980.

'I had heard that one or two League clubs were watching me but the only definite knowledge was when Bury came along,' says Neville. 'Dave Connor was their manager at the time and he told me he wanted me to play in the first team straight away.

'But he got the sack almost as soon as I had signed the forms and I wondered what my situation would be with the new boss, Jim Iley. Well, he started the season with the regular 'keeper, John Forrest, but it wasn't long before he gave me my chance in the League.

Southall gets a boost from boss

FORMER Llandudno Swifts and Conwy United goalkeeper Neville Southall, who was promoted to the No. 1 goalkeeping position by Everton for last Saturday's game against Football League champions Aston Villa, must have had a tremendous boost to read his manager's comments in the daily newspapers that morning.

For Goodison Park boss Howard Kendall was quoted as saying 'I think Neville could be as

'He could eventually be as good as Shilton'

day he had made only one previous First Division appearance — in the win over Ipswich when previous regular choice Jim Arnold was out through injury.

Arnold was dropped for the Villa game on Saturday, and Kendall was quoted as saying 'Maybe the break will do

very nervous. It was understandable because he was playing at Goodison Park for the first time.

'But he has that game behind him, and now it is up to him.'

Neville kept a clean sheet as Everton beat Villa and — viewers to the BBC Match of the

started in Welsh League football at the age of 16 with Llandudno Swifts. After a spell in the Northern Premier League with Bangor City, he went on to play for Llandudno Rangers, Conwy United and Cheshire League club Winsford.

After the game, Neville said he 'thoroughly enjoyed it' and hoped to keep his place for the exciting Day league match against Manchester United at Old Trafford.

Commenting on the

Reaching for the top . . . a cutting from a North Wales newspaper.

'From when I first played in September, I stayed in the side the rest of the season. At first, we were down the bottom en[d] the Fourth Division, but we got a good run going from the Fri[day] before Christmas and finished halfway up the table.'

Neville's League experience amounted to 39 games and [the] last thing he expected was to be in the First Division within [?] months. That was the time span between his last appeara[nce] for Bury and his League debut for Everton in October.

'The transfer came as a complete surprise in the summer, [he] says. 'The first I knew about it was back home in Wales. I pick[ed] up a paper on a Sunday morning and read that Everton [were in]terested. I went back to Bury the next day and signed here [at] Goodison Park on Tuesday.'

This completed a year of remarkable advancement. He [left] Winsford for £6,000 and joined Everton for a reported £150,0[00]. He had also moved into the Welsh international picture, hav[ing] been named as stand-by 'keeper for a World Cup match [in] Turkey last March.

'I thought it would take a while to get into the first team he[re] he says. 'I also missed one or two early Reserve matches with [an] ankle injury and had played very few games when I deputised [for] Jim Arnold against Ipswich.

'I was very nervous that day. It was a bit like going to the d[en]tist — and wondering what all the fuss was about afterwa[rds]. The atmosphere was great but I was disappointed in gen[eral] with my performance.'

He went back to the Reserves for a couple of months [and] made further strides with Wales by travelling to Russia as [a] reserve to Dai Davies. With Dai now approaching the la[ter] stage of his career, Neville is clearly a front-runner in the race [to] become the number one 'keeper in the future.

'Naturally, I hope to play for Wales but the club comes [first] and, in any case, thee are two other good Welsh 'keepers [in] Martin Thomas at Bristol Rovers and Eddie Niedzwieck[i at] Wrexham,' he says cautiously.

'For now, I am just happy to be with a club like Everton. [It's] nice to come here and train. The facilities are marvellous and [the] skill of the players is unbelievable. People say there is no [?] these days but take Peter Eastoe as an example. I have ne[ver] seen anyone with such ability.'

● PERSONAL NOTE . . . As a non-driver, Neville w[as] delighted to get a house in West Derby, close to Bellefield. [It's] only a short walk in for training and much better than when I w[as] at Bury. I lived four miles from Gigg Lane and I either had to g[et a] lift with one of the other lads or catch a bus.'

For the family album . . .
Neville Southall pictured
with his wife, Eryl.

UMBRO SPORTSWEAR
THE CHOICE OF CHAMPIONS

Alan at home with his wife Paula and children Natalie (5) and twins Zoe and Mellissa (4).

Alan Ainscow & Billy Wright

One of Howard Kendall's 'Magnificent Seven' upon signing for the Blues in August 1981, Alan Ainscow spent two years at Goodison without really establishing himself as a first-team regular. However, as part of the programme's player feature, he was pictured at home with his wife and children.

Defender and one-time captain Billy Wright was another who got the treatment with his wife Ann and unnamed pet collie...

Billy pictured at home with his wife Anne.

Adrian Heath & Pat Nevin

Adrian Heath was able to forget his injury worries to 'pose' for this photo with nurse Karen Harper during late autumn of 1984.

Pat Nevin's profiles were often illuminating, with this profile from the final game of the 1989/90 season a case in point. The winger refers to his disappointment at not making a more positive impact, and noting the influence of fanzines as part of fan culture.

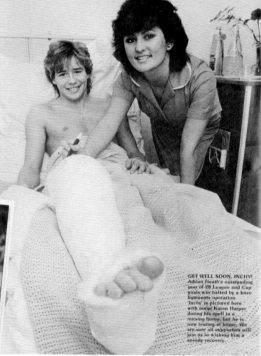

GET WELL SOON, INCHY! Adrian Heath's outstanding year of 28 League and Cup goals was halted by a knee ligaments operation. 'Inchy' is pictured here with nurse Karen Harper during his spell in a nursing home, but he is now resting at home. We are sure all supporters will join us in wishing him a speedy recovery.

Fact File

No. 14 GARY LINEKER
Full name:
Gary Winston Lineker
Birthplace/date:
Leicester on 30th November
1960.
Engaged: To, Michele
Cockayne.
Where live: Southport.
Car: Toyota Celica Supra.

Nickname: 'Links'.
Previous club: Leicester City.
International honours:
10 Full caps, 1 'B'.
Club honours: Second
Division Championship, FA
Charity Shield.
*Best English stadium
played in:* Wembley.

*Best foreign stadium
played in:* Aztec, Mexico
City.
Magic moment in football:
Winning my first Full cap.
Worst moment in football:
Being relegated with
Leicester.
Most memorable match: It
has to be scoring a hat-trick
for England against Turkey.
Player for the future:
Ian Andrews, the Leicester
goalkeeper.
Favourite other team:
Leicester City.
Favourite other player:
Frank Worthington.
Club supported as a boy:
Leicester City.
*Biggest influences on
career:* My parents, Barry and
Margaret.
*What would you like to
change in football:* We all
want to see the end of crowd
trouble.
Favourite other sports:
Snooker and cricket.
*Favourite other sports
personality:* Willie Thorne.
Favourite TV show: Any
sports programme.
TV shows you like least:
Coronation Street.
Favourite reading: Novels,
especially by Jeffrey Archer
and Frederick Forsyth.
Musical taste: Dire Straits
and Slade.
Best film seen recently:
Beverley Hills Cop.
Dislikes/likes:
People who knock football/
Going out for a meal with
Michele.
Hobby: Playing snooker
(Gary has twice registered
a century break).
Holiday Spot this year:
Crete.
Favourite food/drink:
Dover Sole/Wine.
Pre-match meal:
Poached eggs on toast.
*Who would you most
like to meet:*
Barry McGuigan.

Gary Lineker, 1985/86 – Leicester influence apparent,
and a penchant for the musical stylings of Noddy Holder

More action from our Cup-Winners' Cup semi-final against Bayern Munich at Goodison and the *Daily Express* headline that said it all! Graeme Sharp causes problems in this picture, right: Kevin Sheedy forces a diving save from Pfaff. Below: Andy Gray, close marked by Bayern defenders. Below right: Trevor Steven breaks through the German defence.

Magnificent...

1981/82

Geoff Hurst, the 1966 World Cup final hat-trick hero himself, urges fans to follow England in 'sunny Spain' ahead of the tournament that summer. Included in the Tottenham programme in late January, 'Special Rates for Everton Supporters' proclaims the advert – while the opportunity to 'take part in this, the greatest soccer spectacular in history', with 'TICKETS SELLING FAST!' will have been the clincher to watch Ron Greenwood's side shorn of any Everton player involvement.

The other selected advert from the campaign was from the Manchester United programme in April. The back cover team listings included this piece of product placement for...Newcastle Bitter, noting the north-east city's then most famous footballing export.

1982/83

The Milk Marketing Board became the first sponsor of a major cup competition in England when they took on the League Cup. This was the first season of the contract, and the advertising copywriters weren't unduly pressed by linking their 'bottle' product with the cup format.

Le Coq Sportif and Everton — a winning combination

22/24" Shirt	9.99	27/28" Shorts Size 70	5.99
26/28" Shirt	10.99	29/30" Shorts Size 75	6.99
30/32" Shirt	10.99	31/32" Shorts Size 80	6.99
34/36" Shirt	12.99	33/34" Shorts Size 85	6.99
38/40" Shirt	12.99	Small Boys Socks	2.25
42/44" Shirt	12.99	Youths Socks	2.25
23/24" Shorts Size 60	5.99	Mens Socks	2.75
25/26" Shorts Size 65	5.99		

Available from Souvenir Shop or send now with SAE for mail order price list to
Souvenir Shop, Everton FC, Goodison Road, Liverpool L4 4EL

PLANTERS Nuts
The sporting nut for Sporting Nuts

A GREAT SHAPE TO BE IN

Over 50 years ago in France, a company manufacturing sports apparel for famous sporting teams was born. Five years ago the same company was launched in the international market as a fashion/leisure brand.

Since then, success has been synonymous with the name Le Coq Sportif in the UK. So it was only natural when Everton decided to join the ranks at the beginning of last season, past glories would once again return to Goodison.

Now that Le Coq Sportif is established as a brand leader in the fashion/leisure market it would be easy for the company to sit back. But continued promotional and advertising programmes have ensured Le Coq Sportif will always be in the fore in the world of sport . . . whether it's football, running or the creation of stylish sporting fashions, Le Coq will always be there.

Le Coq Sportif, now based in Cheshire, is delighted to be associated with Everton and wishes the club and its supporters an enjoyable — and rewarding remainder of the season —

ESCLA
Everton Supporters Club London Area

Support Everton's
LARGEST SUPPORTERS CLUB
outside Merseyside.
Existing membership 500 + throughout the
UK and overseas

Newsletters ● ESCLA Wallets
Quality enamel badges
(limited edition)
Consideration for big match
tickets
(subject to availability)
Cheap travel from London to
home and overseas matches.

Enquiries welcomed from Evertonians everywhere. For membership details and application form please write to:
ESCLA Membership Secretary
43 Dickerage Road, Kingston
Surrey KT1 3SR.

le coq sportif®
a great shape to be in

Le Coq Sportif and Everton — a winning combination

1984/85

Le Coq Sportif were keen to push the sale of kits ahead of the most successful season in the club's history, with Kevin Richardson in FA Cup final action used to encourage fans to snap up the iconic strip in the Coventry City programme. Later in the campaign, Andy Gray (right) was used to show off the amber away strip.

The memorable Manchester United fixture (top right) included a page not only including text espousing the virtues of the sportswear label but some salted snacks – and Everton's London Supporters' Club.

le coq sportif®
a great shape to be in

Le Coq Sportif
and Everton —
a winning
combination

1984/85 & 1985/86

Other Le Coq Sportif adverts included more away kit action shots from Leicester City, with Peter Reid holding off Alan Smith in this shot used in the Sunderland programme. Kevin Sheedy's late equaliser in the Luton Town FA Cup semi-final was used in the Norwich City edition, although the company appeared keener on promoting the 'shape' of their product than the kit detail.

The 1985/86 season saw many changes, with the adoption of a new kit (below) - the much-derided 'bib'.

With the loss of European football, clubs who missed out played in a replacement competition, the Screen Sport Super Cup (below left). The advert was included in the Tottenham SSSC programme, as an exercise in public awareness. An early satellite TV incarnation, low attendances and viewing figures suggested that fans lacked the appetite for another domestic competition, with the final eventually completed the following season.

le coq sportif®
a great shape to be in

SCREEN
SPORT
SUPER CUP

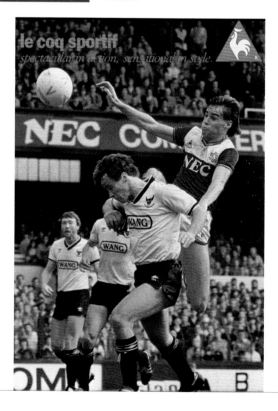

le coq sportif
spectacular in action, sensational in style.

Like 91 Football League clubs we're behind Everton.

NEC Corporation. The Computers and Communications Company congratulate Everton F.C. on a year of great achievement. We hope our partnership will be as successful in the future.

The new sponsors of Everton NEC NEC Corporation

SHOW YOUR SUPPORT

Unique – the team's very own look for sports and leisure. With the distinctive style, quality and prestige of the match kit, training and off the field wear worn by the players themselves. Made by Umbro, the club's official supplier. There are designs and sizes to suit most members of the family. There's no mistaking the real thing – every garment bears the authentic team badge and the distinctive Umbro diamond trade mark.

IT'S ONLY AUTHENTIC IF IT'S UMBRO

umbro

NEC AND EVERTON THE ONES TO WATCH.

The quality and style of our TV and Video are becoming known to an ever widening and appreciative audience. Like Everton we've built up a superb team. Here's one of our star performers: FS 1502 PI Colour Television at £269.00 or lower. High Fashion · High Flying · High Tech · Timer TV · Great value for money. Now available from **COLORVISION** Branches in Liverpool and surrounding areas.

NEC

The one to watch

EVERTON LEAGUE CHAMPIONS 1986-1987 SEASON

Congratulations to Everton from their biggest supporter.

The biggest name in Computers and Communications.

NEC Business Systems (Europe) Ltd., 35 Oval Road, London NW1 7EA.

NEC

CONGRATULATIONS TO EVERTON F.C. ON BECOMING THE 1986 - 1987

TODAY

LEAGUE DIVISION ONE CHAMPIONS

WHEN IT COMES TO SOCCER COVERAGE **TODAY** IS IN A LEAGUE OF ITS OWN

WHEN YOU BUY YOUR NEWSPAPER TOMORROW MAKE SURE IT'S **TODAY**

One of the most dramatic stories in sport...

EVERTON WINTER MEXICAN SUMMER

A Football Diary

PETER REID

with Peter Ball

Everton at the top of the League... Wembley for the third year running... England in Mexico for the World Cup... a unique day-by-day record of an eventful season for Everton and England midfield dynamo Peter Reid.

IN BOOKSHOPS NOW AT £8.95

Macdonald Queen Anne Press

1986/87

The shirt sponsorship pages were mainly basic affairs, with standard tag lines reflecting on-field success. One incidental about the advert top right, was that a letter in the programme asked who the man in the TV was – Paul Power perhaps?

The availability of leisurewear as well as the usual home and away kits for Evertonians became an increasing trend as the decade progressed, with 'The Everton Collection' a popular choice for many fans.

NEC and league sponsors Today newspaper were quick to sing the praises of the new champions in the Luton Town programme, while Peter Reid's 'Everton Winter Mexican Summer' was still a must-have tome in spring 1987.

JOIN THE TEAM

Unique – the team's very own look for sports and leisure. With the distinctive style, quality and prestige of the match kit, training and off-the-field wear worn by the players themselves.
Made by Umbro, the club's official supplier.

There are designs and sizes to suit most members of the family.
There's no mistaking the real thing – every garment bears the authentic team badge and the distinctive Umbro diamond trade mark.
Join the team – with Umbro.

IT'S ONLY AUTHENTIC IF IT'S UMBRO

EVERTON
SPORTS AND LEISUREWEAR

RUGBY-STYLE JERSEY AVAILABLE

umbro

1987/88-1989/90

The rarely used third strip was used in the 1987/88 advertising for the Everton 'sports and leisurewear', the removal of the head shot adding to the curiosity.

Official 'savoury' suppliers Sayers, with their familiar 'So Fresh We're Famous' tagline was a staple matchday advert in the 1988/89 programme, although the heat of the opening-day triumph against Newcastle United may have meant a slow sales day at Goodison for pies and sausage rolls.

The models were ditched – and the England strip added – in Umbro's kit promotion ad in 1988/89 (bottom left), while NEC focused on the league the following season.

sayers
the Bakers

OFFICIAL SUPPLIERS TO EVERTON F.C.

sayers

SO FRESH WE'RE FAMOUS!

LOOK GREAT IN THE LINE-UP.

UMBRO Repli-kit – The Choice of Champions
Step out in style with the authentic product, made by Umbro the sportswear people – the top teams choice.
There's no mistaking the real thing – every garment bears the authentic team badge and distinctive Umbro trade mark.
Make sure you're wearing the winning kit – REPLI-KIT.

umbro

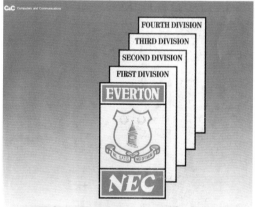

CdC Computers and Communications

FOURTH DIVISION
THIRD DIVISION
SECOND DIVISION
FIRST DIVISION

EVERTON

NEC

WE'RE IN A DIFFERENT LEAGUE.

NEC believes in success. That's what put us at the top of the electronics league.

And that's why we're sponsoring Everton, one of the most successful clubs in football history.

For Everton and NEC only the best has ever been good enough. Together, we aim to go one better.

NEC. The Company in Computers and Communications

NEC (UK) Ltd., NEC House, 1 Victoria Road, London W3 6UL.

PERSONAL COMPUTERS · PRINTERS · DISK DRIVES · FACSIMILE · PBX
KEY TELEPHONES · MOBILE TELEPHONES · RADIO PAGERS · TV AND VIDEO · DBS

TEAM SPIRIT-
REPLI-KIT.

REPLI-KIT
TOP TEAM REPLICA FOOTBALL KIT

umbro
THE CHOICE OF CHAMPIONS

ALL THE GAMES
ALL THE GOALS
FOR & AGAINST
HOME & AWAY

NOW! A feast of football
entertainment from your team! **Reserve
your copy today** and it will be despatched
to your home within 10 days of the end of
Everton's last game of the season.

This Official Football League Video brings you the
best of the action in every single game played by
Everton during the 1989-90 Barclays League
Division One season.

● See every goal scored – for and against, home
and away.

● Coverage of every game your team played
in is featured, with all the facts and
figures as well.

● Relive the excitement, the near misses, the
controversy, the great saves.

All on a single VHS first generation video available to
you now for just **£11.99** + p&p!

PLUS!

**3 GREAT VIDEOS THAT
ALL SOCCER SUPPORTERS WILL
WANT IN THEIR COLLECTION,**
EACH AT £9.99

ALL THE GAMES · HOME & AWAY · ALL THE GOALS FOR & A

EVERTON

THE OFFICIAL REVIEW OF BARCLAYS
LEAGUE DIVISION ONE · GAME BY GAME · 1989/9

CBS
FOX

SO EASY TO ORDER!
Simply send your cheque/postal order for
£11.99 plus £1.95 postage, packing and
insurance today to: **World Sports Action,
FREEPOST,** Wellingborough, Northants
NN8 2YX, together with details of your name
and address.

If you prefer to pay by credit card
(Access or Visa), please send details
of your card number and expiry
date and we will do the rest.

VISA

**OR RING OUR HOTLINE NUMBER
FOR 24 HOUR ORDERING ON**
☎ **0933 442056**

SPECIAL BONUS!
No matter how many videos you order, a
once and for all charge of £1.95 is made for
postage, packing and insurance.

Offer applies only to UK. Please allow 14 days for delivery

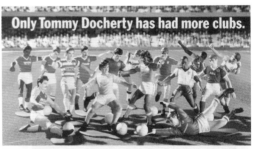

Only Tommy Docherty has had more clubs.

SPORTSTARS

Students of the game will have realised that the Sportstars collection comprises almost as many
clubs as The Doc's. (Obviously quite some collection.)

In it you'll find over sixty lifelike figures, sporting no less than fourteen authentic team strips.
(And we've got plans for more.) All of which begs the inevitable question. Who will end up with the
most clubs? Sportstars or The Doc? **Sportstars. Collect the players who collect the trophies.**

1989/90

Graeme Sharp was all smiles (top) as the new 1989/90
strip was shown off, with Umbro's 'Repli-Kit' range
adding the Scotland strip to their Everton advertising.

The final-day Aston Villa clash included a full-page
season review advert, the Everton 1989/90 video being
made available along with the general 'Goals Galore!',
'Saves Galore!' and 'Race For The Championship'
videos.

The other new advert from the same programme
trumpeted the virtues of 'Sportstars', its range of
figures being compared favourably to the number of
teams Mr Docherty had managed...

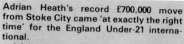

NUMBER ONE AGAIN...

The Programme of the Year title remains at Goodison Park for a record-breaking fifth year in succession.

The 1988-89 award was confirmed last week when MATCH magazine announced that Everton had once again held off the challenge of Aston Villa.

'Unbeatable Everton' was the MATCH verdict after compiling the marks from nine judges in a competition which is run in comnjunction with the Football League Executive Staffs Association.

The MATCH report continued: 'Ever-excellent Aston Villa made a determined bid to unseat their Mersey rivals; Norwich stormed an amazing 17 places up the top twenty chart; and the slick, inventive West Ham programme again caught the eye.

'But it was Everton's crisp, colourful and informative matchday production which emerged triumphant from a comprehensive marking system taking into account factors including design, presentation, photography, features, statistical content and value-for-money.'

The top twenty were:
1. EVERTON
2. Aston Villa
3. Norwich
4. West Ham
5. Watford
   Derby County
7. Leeds
8. Liverpool
9. Chelsea
10. Tottenham
11. Sheff Wed.
12. Wolves
13. Arsenal
14. Sheff Utd.
15. QPR
    Wrexham
17. Soton
18. Brighton
19. S'land
20. Man C.

Adrian Heath's record £700,000 move from Stoke City came 'at exactly the right time' for the England Under-21 international.

Joining Everton four days before his 21st birthday was the perfect 'key of the door' present for a talented midfield player who swept into national prominence by scoring two goals on his England debut last April.

The transfer to Goodison Park (breaking Everton's previous cash record, paid for John Gidman in October 1979) was welcomed by Adrian as 'a great move' at a time when he was a little disappointed with his form.

'I started the season quite well but gradually my form was coming down,' he explained. 'I think this was partly due to problems between myself and the new manager, Richie Barker. We didn't always see eye to eye.'

It was also unsettling to read reports of interest from a number of major clubs, including Manchester City, Arsenal and Aston Villa. 'But there was 'nothing concrete,' says Adrian. 'I kept hoping that something would happen — and then came news that Everton had made an offer for me a few weeks before Christmas.

'It seemed a reasonable bid to me, considering that I hadn't cost Stoke anything, and I was a bit frustrated when it was turned down.'

But everything worked out favourable when Stoke accepted an increased offer after being knocked out of the FA Cup.

Adrian was delighted to sign for Howard Kendall. They had joined Stoke at much the same time in 1977 and Adrian recalls that the current Everton manager assisted his progress to a first team debut when he was still a 17 year old apprentice in October 1978.

The boss started to take training at the time

I was in the Reserves and on the ve breaking through into the first team,' he 'I trained with the senior players for tw a week and made my debut in a Leagu tie at Northampton. We won 3-1 scored.'

Born at Newcastle-under-Lyme, played for Staffs Schools and had tri England before signing schoolboy for Stoke at 14. His early days at the V Ground coincided with a difficult peri the club, as relegation ended a 14-year t the First Division.

He met four managers in less than 12 ths. 'Tony Waddington signed me on a and left on Monday. George Eastham over for a time and then Alan A'Cour caretaker manager before Alan Durba the job.'

Adrian says that Mr Durban was the bi influence on his career so far. He gave A a couple of outings during the prom season in 1978-79 and launched him as team regular in the First Division in the fo ing campaign.

Last season there was an added dime when he switched from midfield to pla front alongside Lee Chapman. 'I was p that position because there was a shorta players, he explains.

'A couple of strikers were out of the and it was really a case of Mr Durban dec I was the one who might do best as a st in. I had the enthusiasm for the job; it v new challenge and I did reasonably well time. But eventually that wore off and I glad to go back into midfield.'

However, it was as a striker, partne Garry Thompson, of Coventry City, Adrian started his England Under-21 c with two goals against Rumania at Swin He has been an ever-present since that m and, in fact, is the only player to have bee the field for every minute of the last five i nationals.

Thompson, Remi Moses and Billy Gi were also selected for all five games but w either substituted or went on in the No shirt.

England were unbeaten in games aga Rumania, Switzerland, Hungary (home away) and Norway. Now Adrian hopes to capped again in this season's Europ Championship quarter-final against Polan

'It was a big boost in my career to selected by England,' he says. 'My ga seemed to improve 100 per cent when I w back to the Stoke team.'

GETTING BETTER

Alan Ainscow, out of action for two m ths with a knee injury sustained in November match at Notts County, wa lot happier with life after beginning comeback with a Reserve outing agai Bolton a fortnight ago.

He had been reasonably free from inj during his ten years as a League player this season's setback was not his long period on the sidelines. 'I only missed games when I had a cartilage operation Blackpool,' he says.

Alan's knee problem turned out to be

New signing — ADRIAN HEATH

Selected news snippets from the decade included (right) Adrian Heath's record signing (v Tottenham Hotspur, 1981/82) and (above) Programme of the Year success (v Liverpool, 1988/89)

A LIFETIME WITH THE BLUES

t's a funny thing," said Bill Kenwright, "but I'd almost made up my mind to go and live in Los Angeles before I was invited to join the Board."

The call that changed his thoughts came from chairman Philip Carter when Everton's newest director returned from a two-week business trip to California.

"It was an extraordinary moment when Mr Carter said: 'Do you want to be a director?' Straightaway I thought back to when I was a kid in the Boys' Pen and asked myself: 'Did I ever believe in those days that this would happen to me?'"

Mr Kenwright, who was educated at Liverpool Institute along with Paul McCartney and George Harrison, went to London at 18 to pursue his ambitions as an actor and stayed to become a major figure in the British theatre.

In those early years, he would hitch-hike to Goodison because he couldn't afford the train fare, but nowadays he's a regular on the 9.20 from Euston. Usually he has lunch with his parents, and after the game, he rushes to catch the 17.32 from Lime Street which gets him back in time to see one of his shows in the evening.

Smash hits such as Blood Brothers and Shirley Valentine are among nine of his productions currently being staged in England, America and Australia.

The business takes him round the world and whether it's London or New York, he's in the theatre every night. But there is always room for Everton in his incredibly hectic schedule.

Three years ago he flew back from Australia to see the FA Cup Final, and on another trip Down Under to direct a musical, he arranged to have a Radio City commentary piped down the telephone line to his room in a Melbourne hotel.

"That was the time when Adrian Heath equalised from the famous Kevin Brock back pass at Oxford," he recalls. "It was 4 o'clock in the morning in Australia and there I was, standing in the middle of the bed screaming and shouting!"

In 1986, when he had to miss a derby at Anfield while he was directing an opera at Sadlers Wells, he arranged with a good friend at London Weekend to have a video of the match sent round to his flat that evening.

"I had it all set up so that I could watch the game without knowing the result," he says. "I got all the company at Sadlers Wells together, told them I was missing my first derby for years, and said that they should ignore me that night if they knew the score.

"They all kept quiet and when the performance was over, I couldn't wait to get home, but just as I left the theatre, a fan went past and shouted: 'Hey, Bill, what a great result that was!' If I had gone out a second later, I would have been safe."

Mr Kenwright corrects anyone who calls him an Everton supporter. "No, I'm an Everton fanatic," he reminds them. Yet it's true that he was actively considering whether he should put his film interests in America before his beloved Blues.

"I have always wanted to make movies and that was the choice facing me when I came back from the States last month," he says. "I was asking myself whether I could cope without seeing Everton and I must admit a house on Malibu Beach was inviting.

"But Mr Carter's call settled everything. Now I'll have to find a few more dates in my diary for the Board meetings. In my business, I always say I've got a team of 11 plus two subs and I have a feeling they won't be seeing so much of the Boss as they used to. I've already told them that they'll have to come up with some production ideas of their own.

"I certainly wouldn't have accepted the invitation to join the Board if I had felt unable to make a full contribution. To be honest, I'm not a committee-man type, never have been, but this is one job I couldn't turn down."

The journey from the Boys' Pen to the Boardroom took 33 years almost to the day. On October 27th 1956 he saw Everton beat Arsenal 4-0 on his first visit to Goodison Park and on October 21st 1989 he celebrated another victory over Arsenal in his first match as a director.

"You can imagine how I felt," he says. "Not only did we win 3-0 but one of my best friends, David Dein, is an Arsenal director, and we went to the top of the League! I didn't quite believe it was all happening to me."

◆ Mr Kenwright was appointed to the Board to fill the vacancy created by the retirement of Bill Scott, who becomes a Vice-President.

NEWS DESK

86, FA Cup semi-final)."

By the way, we had to smile at Stephen's sign-off line: *"With all this talk about Ian Rush, not many people realise that Everton didn't lose a game when Andy Gray scored for us, though the same could be said for Neil Pointon!*

NEVILLE IS NO 1 ...

Neville Southall (pictured below right) broke the longest sequence in the history of the PFA awards when he was named in the First Division Select XI.

The country's professionals had solidly given their goalkeeping vote to Peter Shilton for the previous nine years – a run which began when he was PFA Player of the Year for 1978.

Shilton was the first-choice 'keeper as long ago as 1975, when he was with Stoke City, and Southall now joins Ray Clemence and Pat Jennings, the only other players to have pipped Shilton in the past 12 seasons.

Southall is the sixth Everton player to appear in the First Division Select XI in three years. The others: Gary Stevens (2), Kevin Sheedy (2), Gary Lineker, Peter Reid and Kevin Ratcliffe.

QUIZ NIGHT ...

Everton Supporters' Club are holding a Quiz Night on Wednesday 29th April (8.00 p.m.).

All the questions will be on Everton and supporters are invited to form teams of up to four players (entry fee: £2 per team). For further details, please contact the Supporters' Club.

ESC are also looking for players to join the club's quiz team. We are told that interested parties should ha[ve] a good general knowledge [of] football and be prepared to spend hours studying the Rothmans Football Yearboo[k].

FAN CLUBS ...

Rachel Kelley is organisin[g] fan clubs for Kevin Sheed[y] and Ian Snodin.

Membership is £1 per ye[ar]. For further details please w[rite] to Rachel (enclosing s.a.e.) Warden's Bungalow, Pemb[roke] House, Hampstead Road, Liverpool L6 8NG.

SCHOOLBOY SIGNINGS

Welcome to our latest gro[up] of associate schoolboy signings ...

Terence McGuirk, mid[field] Sefton Under-14s, Bootle H[igh] School; Iain Jenkins, mid[field] St Helens Under-14s, Rain[hill] High School; Ian Horriga[n,] midfield, Liverpool Under[-14s,] De La Salle School; Carl Spelman, right back, Live[rpool] Under-15s, Broadgreen Comprehensive.

SHARP RESEARCH ...

We never cease to be amazed at the statistical output of our supporters.

A typical example of the care and detail that goes into their hobby was sent in recently by Stephen Gilmore, of Mill Lane Parbold.

His subject: Graeme Sharp (pictured above) and his scoring record from his first goal for The Blues in November 1981 up until his recent injury.

Read on for Stephen's findings . . .

"Of his 109 goals, 69 were scored at home and 57% of those at the Gwladys Street End.

"53% of his goals have come from shots, 33% from headers and 14% from the penalty spot.

"Incredibly, in the last four seasons, almost a third of his goals have been scored in the last ten minutes and altogether 70% in the second half.

"His favourite opposition is Manchester United (9 goals), then Watford (7 goals, all away from Goodison) and Aston Villa (7 goals).

"He has scored in 90 games and 69 of them have been won, with only seven defeats.

"It would be interesing to hear of fans' favourite three goals from 'Sharpy'. Mine are: 1 – volley v Liverpool (Oct 84); 2 – volley v Spurs (Jan 82); 3 – volley v Sheffield Wednesday (April

A news desk which includes Graeme Sharp goals research and Neville Southall: PFA Number One (v Newcastle United, 1986/87)

MOVING WITH THE TIMES

I T is understandable that followers of the two major Merseyside football clubs should be anxiously awaiting official reaction to the proposed construction of a 67,000 all-seater stadium on the site of Kirkby Golf Course.

We recognise that supporters will wish to make their feelings known and, to this end, we are throwing the debate open today by publishing in a letter from a Gwladys Street season-ticket holder who has clearly given the matter a great deal of thought

Mr Paul Smith, of Wootton Road, Childwall, lists what he sees as the merits and objections to ground-sharing and objections to the conclusion that such a scheme is "of dubious viability and is, furthermore, not actually desirable".

In summary, he suggests that there are a number of sound reasons why Everton should remain at Goodison Park and aim to re-develop the stadium. And he signs off by saying: "I believe the reasons given cannot and should not be dismissed as merely 'emotional' or 'sentimental'".

Supporters may be influenced one way or the other, but let us know what you think by writing to: Stadium Debate, Everton FC, Goodison Park, Liverpool L4 4EL.

We should stress that ALL the points raised in this feature represent Mr Smith's personal opinion. The club's position will be made known at a later date.

IN FAVOUR

1 - FACILITIES

◆ Such a scheme would allow for the planned provision of modern facilities comparable with the best of European stadia Catering, toilet and entertainment facilities (improved public address system, video screen etc) could be provided to a standard in keeping with current expectations.

As the stadium would be all-seater, it would comply with the Taylor Report's recommendations.

2 - CAPACITY

◆ The planned capacity would mean that public demand to watch even the biggest games would be comfortably met by the number of seats available.

3 - ACCESS

◆ The proposed location would have obvious advantages in terms of:
(a) improved access via the motorway network.
(b) The availability of land for the provision of car parking adequate to meet both present and future demand.

4 - PRESTIGE

◆ For Merseyside, there would be the prestige of having within its boundaries one of the finest sporting facilities in Europe, a stadium that would undoubtedly be used for cup semi-finals and ultimately for international matches (once the FA is free from its contractual obligations to Wembley Stadium).

AGAINST

1 - FINANCE

◆ A massive outlay is required (the estimated cost being £125m). Assuming the necessary loans could be obtained to get the scheme off the ground, the interest payments would be enormous.

The stadium would be privately owned and therefore private investors would presumably seek to re-coup their money via revenue from executive box facilities and stadium advertising - traditional sources of additional income for football clubs.

Furthermore, presumably the owners would set the rent that the clubs would have to pay. What controls would there be on rent levels? AC Milan and Inter Milan share a stadium but it is owned by the local authority, and in setting the rent paid by the clubs, the council is not motivated by commercial interests.

The original press release regarding the "super" stadium stated that it would primarily be a football venue, staging only the occasional pop concert or Rugby League match. Since then, there has been some suggestion that there will also be a large indoor arena. It seems to me that such a massive financial expenditure that, in footballing terms, would be unlikely to be used more than 60 times a year, is hardly practical - is not the growing diversification of the use of Wembley Stadium evidence of this?

2 - ACCESS

◆ The new stadium would be more accessible for those, like myself, who travel to matches by car. However, the implication that nearly everybody travels by this means is certainly not justified. For those that travel by bus, or walk from areas near the present stadia, such a relocation of their football clubs would not improve accessibility!

Could either Everton or Liverpool say with certainty what percentage of their support travels by car and what percentage by other means? Until they can, a move to the outskirts of the city would surely be unwise.

---

3 - CAPACITY

◆ A stadium for 67,000 would, in my opinion, represent gross over-capacity.

In 1987-88, Liverpool averaged 40,000 - their best average attendance for a decade. In 1984-85, and 1986-87, Everton averaged slightly under 33,000, on each occasion when winning the League championship.

The current averages of Liverpool and Everton are 36,000 and 28,000 respectively, a combined total of 64,000, i.e. 3,000 below the proposed capacity of the new stadium.

Visualise 31,000 empty seats, on current average, at each Liverpool game and 39,000 empty seats at each Everton game.

At each Everton game, on current average, there would be 13,000 more empty seats than the current total number of seats at Goodison Park.

This takes no account of a possible further reduction in attendances due to the greater expense of attending matches at an all-seater stadium.

Such a situation, with capacity far exceeding average demand, could only lead to a very poor atmosphere inside the stadium - and again raise serious doubts about its practicality.

4 - PRESENT STADIUM FACILITIES

◆ It seems to me that Everton Football Club are in a fortunate position with regard to Goodison Park.

Setting aside the poor toilet and catering facilities (men want decent toilets as well as women), three sides of the ground provide good facilities, and, in the case of the Gwladys Street End and Bullens Road, should lend themselves fairly readily to an all-seated provision.

The area where work is required is the Park End, originally built in 1906, modernised to some extent in the 1960s but now very inadequate compared with the other stands. Much of the terrace has been blocked up since the early 1980s presumably intended only as a temporary measure?

There is clearly much wasted capacity in the existing stand and, should that be demolished, there is potential to expand.

THE ambitious plan to build Britain's first all-seater super stadium on Kirkby Golf Course at a cost of £125m was given an extremely cautious reception by Merseyside's two soccer giants today.

The plan, drawn up by a company called Stadium Mersey Ltd and backed in principle by Liverpool City Council, would involve development of a 200-acre site.

Managing Director Bill Young says it is hoped the stadium would be completed in time for the 1993-94 season and that it would be able to house both Liverpool and Everton football clubs on a regular basis.

Neither Liverpool nor Everton were consulted about the project in advance, and they heard about it for the first time yesterday when called to a special presentation.

"We cannot say much until we have a great deal more information," said Everton chairman Philip Carter.

"We shall have to look into all the aspects with a great deal of care. Quite apart from the costs involved and the practicality of the scheme, we have to consider our own position and what would happen to our own club and our existing stadium at Goodison."

Liverpool Chief Executive Peter Robinson was equally non-committal, but pointed out that a great many risks were involved.

The club have to make a decision by mid-summer on whether or not to press on with the development of the Kemlyn Road stand at a probable cost of at least £5m, and they would have to be satisfied about the new stadium's credibility before they abandoned their own plans.

By Ian Hargreaves

£125m plan unveiled for Kirkby golf course

Right: A cutting from the Liverpool Echo.

---

for this is the only part of the stadium which has any significant space behind it.

I would suggest that most Evertonians would be far more excited by the prospect of the construction of a new Park End Stand, similar in architectural style to the Gwladys Street End, linking in the same way with Bullens Road, and of similar size to the Street End, than they are by the proposed 'super' stadium.

Such an enlarged, all-seated Park End would maintain the architectural unity of the stadium and would enable the capacity to be expanded to about 45,000. This would adequately meet demand and do so in a far more realistic way.

The atmosphere would also be greatly improved by allowing Evertonians to sit in the upper tier of this new Park End Stand. Segregation would be maintained by allocating the lower tier only to away fans.

5 - TRADITION AND IDENTITY

◆ I have deliberately left this until the end. The media has often criticised football fans for being stubborn and "emotional" in clinging to their existing "Victorian" grounds. Despite this, I will nevertheless state the case for Everton AND Liverpool fans.

I believe that English football grounds have a quality which is lacking even at the most sophisticated foreign stadia.

Each ground has a unique atmosphere and appearance. The different shapes and designs of the various stands give a sense of special location and provide each ground with a characteristic.

Each stadium is physical embodiment of the history and fortunes of its team. It represents to the fans the status and durability of their club and, more importantly, it is a place of memories. It is, simply, the "home" of the fans and the club, not merely a stadium.

Furthermore, the stadia of most of the big English clubs are not Victorian - most have been considerably modernised. I would argue that it is better, and more realistic, to continue that process of modernisation (in the absence of Governmental financial support for more ambitious projects), thereby enabling tradition and identity to be retained.

'EARLY DECISIONS'

◆ Everton's Chief Executive, Jim Greenwood, says: "All these points, particularly as far as financial propositions are concerned, will be exercising the minds of both clubs in the next few weeks.

"In fairness to everyone concerned, it is essential that firm decisions as to the feasibility are taken at a very early stage."

The new stadium debate was alive and well in the 1989/90 season (v Norwich City)

1 NEWS DESK

FIRST MEDAL

Adrian Heath came home from the UEFA Under-21 Championship Final last week with the first medal of his career — and his right ankle strapped up as a two-welcome legacy of a competitive match against West Germany in Bremen.

It was nice to get the first medal and particularly in a competitive which England had never won before, he said.

But the after-glow of England's triumph was quickly replaced by a return to the treatment table under the supervision of physiotherapist John Clinkard.

John wished really hard the previous week to get me fit for the Manchester City game, said Adrian. I had no problem, and the ankle stood up to a couple of early knocks in Germany.

It was tough out there because their defenders were coming through all the while with their tackling. I was eventually caught again and that did the damage when I fell over on my ankle. Even if I had not had a knock before, that would have still have been painful.

Nevertheless, Adrian enjoyed his part in an English triumph. He said: Everybody was agreed, even the coaches, when you remember that the Germans beat us 1 (Holland and Spain, with news substitutes the following night in the full international at Wembley. We were in a battle to the wall situation, but we didn't sit back on our lead and always looked very dangerous on the break.

His involvement with England over the last two seasons — he played in seven of the Championship matches — has whetted his appetite for more international football. There were three Germans made over the two years, but, basically, we had much the same squad and we had a terrific spirit.

So much so that it was also a sad occasion after we had won the trophy. We all realised that it was probably the last time we would be together, although we all hope to meet up again in the senior side one day.

Looking at the team Bobby Robson picked last week, there must be hope for everybody with a manager who is so prepared to experiment. I'm sure that some of the Under-21 lads will go through and play for England!

NEW SCOREBOARD

Today we proudly launch our new Bulova Scoreboard on the Park End Stand.

The new scoreboard, sponsored by Bulova Watches, replaces the one which has three positive service since 1971 but which, in recent seasons, has been increasingly temperamental.

The new system confuses the marvel of the microchip and the latest computer technology to give a really improved information service. Two messages can be run simultaneously, moving in stationary, and there is also a 'countdown' digital clock which will show how much time remains in the half.

Our operator, Jeanette Wollhman, sees an electric handover keyboard to assemble messages on a visual display unit (TV screen). When she has checked out the message, she can either release it instantly to one of the scoreboard's memory disks. Each disk will hold up to 50 messages.

The new board is available to assist teams in addition to the latest greetings. The top is £50 for three of 'commercials' and the facility will be available to private individuals to wish all Evertonians success. So, if you would like to dedicate a birthday to wish, send a message to a singer or a pal, contact Ralph Williams, Promotion Manager, at Goodison Park.

DOWN MEMORY LANE

The new A-Z series on past Everton players and club history is pouring intensive with our readers and prompted a note from Mr Max Bryan, JP, recalling the career of his father, Lettie Frederick Bryan, who signed for Everton in 1908-29.

His son recalls: 'He was a regular in the Reserves until 8th October 1921, when he was chosen to play against Liverpool at Anfield in the Liverpool Senior Cup.

'Unfortunately, my father was in a collision with Hodgson and was carried off on a stretcher. Despite Everton paying for numerous operations, it was in the 1902-03 season, an advice from a specialist, that his professional career was ended at the age of 32.

In 1948, he returned to Everton as a part-time scout for a period of 15 years.

'He is still living in Port Sunlight and, at 73, still takes a good deal of interest in Everton.'

REGULAR VISITOR

Youth coach Graham Smith and his family lost a badger when Joe Mills info signed for Rotherham United in August.

'... but the Scottish winger is still a regular visitor to the South household.

'He comes most to see us most weekends,' says Graham. 'He says he is enjoying his football at Rotherham and he's just about to fix up a flat over there.'

2 VS DESK

INTERNATIONAL GALA

Apart from congratulations, Kevin Ratcliffe on another international call we are sure pleased that Neville Southall and his so-pleased player at the World record, not should be having a professional career... ...

LUCKY SAVE!

... ...

FAIRER SLOT

David Johnson couldn't see properly for several days after an unfortunate incident in two home games at Villa Park... He managed had a scuffle with Mike Ferron, had a season... and both came blows... and both had his nose injured, which came and both had sight all day disturbed of adding a shift... ...

HONORARY MEMBER

Michael Kenworthy, a local on Doers' shop School, Blackhill is our latest signing on probationary forms. He is a fine player in a very exciting career position which the Dean had some concern for... ...

... ...

GORDON'S HALF CENTURY

... ...

SPOT THE FACE

Recognise an Evertonian football figure among this group of future cricketers from the Merseyside schools. ... ...

BARNSLEY NEXT

... ...

GOOD! & SON by Jim.
I AGREE. I'VE YET TO SEE HIM SOIL HIS JERSEY. HE IS A CLEAN PLAYER
GOOD! & SON by Jim
SON I KNOW THERE'S A GOOD SIDE, BUT HE DON'T ALL WANT TO BRING HIS SHIRTS!

SPECIAL DEAL FOR EVERTONIANS

This advertisement could be worth £100 or more off your next family holiday. Special departures have been arranged with P &O. Cruises in substantial faith discounts, call in at any Towns branch for our special P & O. Cruise leaflet giving full details.

Towns Travel Services Ltd.

4 News Desk...

TOP OF THE HOT SHOTS!

Adrian Heath's musical tastes ranges from Bruce Springsteen to Frank Sinatra... and of course, the Everton FC 'choir'!

Once again, the players are aiming to be Top of the Pops with a new Cup Final recording — 'Everybody's Cheering The Blues.'

And 'Inchy' is quite sincere when he bangs the drum on behalf of the Goodison 'group' of lyric singers.

'Personally,' he says, 'I think it's the best football song I've heard. Maybe that's for the people who buy the record to decide, but I'm sure that when they hear it, they'll buy it even if they are not interested in football.'

The song is the work of Tony Hiller, who has written for Andy Williams and other top singers, and was nominated as the musical director for England in the Euro contest.

The song is the work of Trevor Steven, a midfield dynamic, maybe, but surely not a Moscow Dynamic!

MERSEYSIDE OR MOSCOW?

There was a rush for the dictionary when the Sunday Times' correspondent, Brian Glanville, introduced an unfamiliar word into his coverage of the Everton v Arsenal match.

Well, what would YOU have made of his reference (see caption below) to 'the mathchorchus Trevor Steven'?

Our search for his meaning took us to the Oxford Dictionary, which listed a mathchorchus as 'a writer who increases his output to an exceptional extent, and so gains special awards.'

Then, it was on to an encyclopedia to discover that the word emanates from the Russian Stigichevich Stakhanov, a Russian coalminer who in 1935 organised his work gang to increase its daily production unverified.

Now there's a thought for Trevor Steven — a midfield dynamic, maybe, but surely not a Moscow Dynamic!

The field-markers leading up to Wembley. This season, he is fit but wondering whether he will be in the squad on the big day next weekend. That's the strange thing about the year,' he says. 'I've played more games but in some ways, I felt I made a bigger contribution last time because I was a regular and the injury...

'I'm quite pleased with my performances and, obviously, I'm delighted when I get a chance to help towards winning things. That's the best part about coming on and scoring goals it doesn't matter whether you're on from the start or for the last couple of minutes.

Had it not been for the performance of Lukic in Arsenal's goal in the second half, Everton would have gone ahead long before the substitute Heath got the ball of the match after 81 minutes. In Everton's ranks, it might have been more impressive than the stakhanov-ite Trevor Steven.

SKY-HIGH FOR FOOTBALL

◆ Football League clubs were meeting this week to discuss a proposal which would complete a package of television contracts for ALL competitions until 1992.

Sky TV tabled a prospective £4.5m, three-year deal for coverage of the Zenith Cup and the Leyland DAF Cup, beginning with this season's competitions.

Sky's eleven approach is another indication that the satellite companies regard sport as the key to attracting new viewers. Only last week they announced plans to show this winter's Test series in the West Indies.

The market can only expand when their rivals, BSB, go on the air next year in partnership with the BBC, who have access to the FA Cup and England's international matches.

TV contracts are like any other business arrangement. Competition increases the market value, which was the case as soon as BBC and ITV negotiated independently for live League matches.

Another factor is the demand for more events to fill the vast capacity of all-sport satellite channels. In turn, this will attract new sponsors looking to put their name to competitions which may not have had a high profile in the past.

The Full Members' Cup was never particularly popular with supporters under its original title or when it became known as the Simod Cup for two years. Indeed, we expressed reservations about the format, even when we reached the final last season.

Consequently, we are among seven First Division absentees as the competition continues under a new sponsorship with Zenith Data Systems, who are paying £100,000 this season, with an option for a two-year extension.

The structure has been revised, with the 37 participating clubs being divided into north and south divisions. The regional winners will meet in the final at Wembley on Sunday 25th March.

Ten clubs will compete in Round One in order to reduce each section to a neat-and-tidy 16-club format from the second round.

Nottingham Forest, who won the Simod Cup in April after a thrilling match with The Blues, are one of only five First Division clubs in the 19-strong northern section. They are at home to Manchester City in the second round.

Goalmouth action from last season's Simod Cup Final as Tony Cotton and Steve Sutton fight for a loose ball.

3 HARRY CATTERICK — A PERFECTIONIST

Harry Catterick, like Dixie Dean before him, was with Everton to the last.

He collapsed and died on Saturday 9th March at Goodison Park, five years to the month since Dixie passed away in the very ground where he created a legend.

If Dixie was the most famous player to wear the Royal Blue colours of Everton, Harry Catterick was undoubtedly the most respected and most successful manager in our history.

Goodison Park was brought to a stunned silence when players, officials and guests heard of his death immediately he had watched the FA Cup quarter-final against Ipswich Town. He was 65.

Howard Kendall sought and found the words we were all looking for. 'We had just witnessed a great Cup-tie, but the game will never be foremost in the minds of people who were present,' he said.

'I will remember him as a hard man who was very demanding of his players. We all have our different ways and Harry's record proves that his was the best. Above all else, I thought he was a tremendous judge of a player.

Harry Catterick first joined Everton as a promising centre-forward in 1937. His first-team career was confined to the immediate post-War years and he left in 1951 to become player-manager of Crewe Alexandra.

His management reputation grew in subsequent spells with Rochdale and Sheffield Wednesday before he returned to Goodison Park as manager in April 1961. In the next decade, Everton won the League Championship twice and appeared in two FA Cup Finals, winning the trophy in 1966.

It was only the club's concern for his health — his friends at Goodison believed that he worked too hard for his own good — that prompted his switch to a consultancy role in April 1973. He remained with Everton on that basis until 1975 when he took his last management post with Preston North End.

The club's debt to Harry Catterick was expressed this week by chairman, Philip Carter. 'His death was a sad day for Everton and for football in general,' he said.

Men at the top in the 1960s... Chairman Sir John Moores and manager Harry Catterick.

'He was the outstanding manager who took Everton to greatness. I would also link that to the fact that during his period of management, Howard Kendall and Colin Harvey were signed by the club.

'Now they are following in his footsteps, having produced a team with the exciting style of play favoured by Harry.

He often expressed his admiration for the present team and we all hope that the side will maintain the momentum that he managed to achieve.'

Those who knew and worked with Harry Catterick would probably agree on his epitaph...

'A perfectionist, a great man and a great manager.'

PLAYER:
From Stockport 1937: To Crewe 17.12.51 (player-manager).
First match for Everton 9.3.40 (A) Manchester City 2-2
First League match for Everton 31.8.46 (H) Brentford 0-2
Last match for Everton 27.8.51 (A) Brentford 0-1
War-time appearances: 71. Goals: 55.
League appearances: 59. Goals: 19.
FA Cup appearances: 12. Goals: 6.

MANAGER:
From Sheffield Wednesday April 1961. Consultant 1973 to 1975. To Preston September 1975.
Best wins   Home: 8-0 v Southampton (1971-72).
             Away: 6-2 v West Bromwich Albion (1967-68).
Worst defeats Home: Several games 0-4.
              Away: 0-6 v Arsenal (1963-64).

League record:	HOME							AWAY					
	P	W	D	L	F	A		P	W	D	L	F	A Pts
	506	154	63	36	503	224		72	78	105	297	373	591
League Champions: 1962-63, 1969-70.													

FA Cup record:						
P	W	D	L	F	A	
55	34	9	12	41	43	

FA Cup winners: 1966. Runners-up: 1968.

GORDON SMAILES

6 LIGHTING UP GOODISON

◆ Tonight's meeting between Everton and PSV Eindhoven cements a business connection as well as a football link between two clubs who have proudly displayed major European trophies during the 1980s.

For both reasons, it is an ideal fixture to formally celebrate the appearance of the new floodlights at Goodison Park.

PSV are the sports club arm of the giant Philips electronic and electrical company who were the contractors for the previous lighting system and for the £700,000 modernisation project this year.

The update enabled us to take advantage of advancements in technology. The bulbs are smaller but more powerful, running costs are lower and yet the illumination is better than before. Indeed, Philips confirm that the Goodison system now matches up to the highest standards at sports grounds in Europe.

Everton's Chief Executive, Jim Greenwood, says: 'We were pleased to place the contract with Philips because they had always given excellent service over a period of many years. 'In the early days, the television companies were keen to come to Goodison because of the superb lighting provided by Philips. This was important for TV at the time because their cameras were not as flexible as those which nowadays obtain excellent results from inferior lighting.'

'PSV put in a new system last year and we were invited to view their set-up before placing an order. The one difference is that they are still using four towers as opposed to our lamps mounted on the stands.

'It was during the original discussions with Philips that a match with PSV was first discussed and we are delighted that it has come about so soon.'

'The first Goodison Park floodlights were officially opened by a match with Liverpool which celebrated the 75th anniversary of the Liverpool County FC on October 9th 1957.

'The original towers were replaced in 1971 by a sideligthing system and at the same time the Bullens Road Stand was given a new roof.'

"HE WAS THE OUTSTANDING MANAGER WHO TOOK EVERTON TO GREATNESS"

1 **A first for Heath, new scoreboard (v Sunderland, 1982/83)**
The Everton frontman was a happy man after helping England Under-21s to victory over West Germany. Meanwhile, there was also mention of a new-look scoreboard at the Park End, which 'utilises the marvel of the microchip and the latest computer technology'. Incidentally, David Johnson was the first Everton goalscorer to be recognised – he had been the first noted '7' when the Blues beat Southampton 8-0 in 1971.

2 **Wales call-ups, Johnson woe, Bails (v Swansea City, 1982/83)**
Note was made of Neville Southall's international squad selection, despite being on loan at Port Vale. Meanwhile David Johnson was unable to eat properly, which 'ruled out any chance of eating a nice, juicy steak' following a tackle with Aston Villa's Allan Evans. John Bailey was also spotted, pictured at a charity event for a local kids home.

3 **Obituary for Harry Catterick (v Arsenal, 1984/85)**
Everton's greatest manager (at that point) passed away while attending the FA Cup sixth-round tie with Ipswich Town at the previous home game earlier that March. Both Howard Kendall and chairman Philip Carter led the tributes, with his epitaph stating: 'A perfectionist; a great man and a great manager.'

4 **Pop stars, stakhanovite Steven (v Southampton, 1985/86)**
With the all-Merseyside FA Cup final looming, Everton's players were aiming for a repeat of their *Here We Go* success with follow-up *Everybody's Cheering The Blues* ("...the best football song I've ever heard" – Adrian Heath). There was also an observation taken from Brian Glanville's Arsenal v Everton Sunday Times report of Trevor Steven's eye-catching contribution.

5 **TV takeover (v Millwall, 1989/90)**
Notice was made of the emergence of a satellite broadcaster keen to dip their toe into football. Whatever happened to Sky TV and then rival BSB?

6 **The bright lights of Goodison (v PSV Eindhoven, 1989/90)**
The low-key December friendly with the Dutch giants was arranged as a celebration of the club's new Philips floodlights – with PSV being the 'sports club arm' of the company. It was also a then rare opportunity to witness a top continental side at Goodison due to the then ongoing ban for English clubs from European football.

Kevin Ratcliffe, complete with tash, circa 1981

Kevin Richardson peruses his record collection for the benefit of the cameras, circa 1983

UMBRO SPORTSWEAR
THE CHOICE OF CHAMPIONS

It was the year of a thousand and one memories — and seven trophies.

There's never been a season like 1984-85 in Everton's history, and for the first time we are able to present an exclusive photograph of the major club and individual awards.

Kevin Ratcliffe, representing the players, displays the Canon League trophy and the *France Football/Adidas* award to the European Team of the Year.

And from left to right, we have . . .

Mick Heaton, with the FA Charity Shield;
Peter Reid, the PFA Players' Player;
Howard Kendall, the manager of the Year;
Neville Southall, the Footballer of the Year;
Colin Harvey, with the European Cup-Winners' Cup.
And surely we can vote this the Everton Picture of the Year!

Already, this season, two of the most important individual awards are back at Goodison Park thanks to Gary Lineker's marvellous double as the PFA Players' Player and Footballer of the Year.

Since the PFA first honoured fellow-professionals in 1974, there have been five instances of one club sweeping the board by winning the League Championship and the three top individual prizes.

The full chart is as follows:

Year	Champions	Manager of Year	Footballer of Year	Players' Player
1985*	Everton	Howard Kendall	Neville Southall	Peter Reid
1984*	Liverpool	Joe Fagan	Ian Rush	Ian Rush
1983*	Liverpool	Bob Paisley	Kenny Dalglish	Kenny Dalglish
1982	Liverpool	Bob Paisley	Steve Perryman	Kevin Keegan
1981	Aston Villa	Ron Saunders	Frans Thijssen	John Wark
1980*	Liverpool	Bob Paisley	Terry McDermott	Terry McDermott
1979	Liverpool	Bob Paisley	Kenny Dalglish	Liam Brady
1978*	Nott'm Forest	Brian Clough	Kenny Burns	Peter Shilton
1977	Liverpool	Bob Paisley	Emlyn Hughes	Andy Gray
1976	Liverpool	Bob Paisley	Kevin Keegan	Pat Jennings
1975	Derby	Ron Saunders	Alan Mullery	Colin Todd
1974	Leeds	Bill Shankly	Ian Callaghan	Norman Hunter

* All four trophies won by the same club.

EVERTON 84·85

Back row (left to right): Derek Mountfield, Neville Southall, Jim Arnold, Andy Gray.
Middle row: John Clinkard (Physio), Paul Bracewell, John Bailey, Kevin Richardson, Graeme Sharp, Gary Stevens, Alan Harper.
Terry Curran, Peter Reid, Colin Harvey (Coach), Mick Heaton (Coach).
Front row: Kevin Sheedy, Trevor Steven, Mark Higgins (Club Captain), Howard Kendall (Manager), Kevin Ratcliffe (Team Captain), Adrian Heath, Alan Irvine.

MERSEYSIDE UNITES

This joint-photograph was produced by the Prudential Assurance Company in an endeavour to promote the image of the sport here on Merseyside. Full-size colour posters of the photograph will be available on application to any Prudential representative or local Prudential office.

Back row (left to right): Gary Stevens, Graeme Sharp, Ian Rush, Jim Beglin, Bob Mimms, Bruce Grobbelaar, Neville Southall, Gary Gillespie, Mark Lawrenson, Derek Mountfield, Pat Van den Hauwe.

Centre row: Trevor Steven, Adrian Heath, Jan Molby, Craig Johnston, Neil Pointon, Kevin Richardson, Ronnie Whelan, John Wark, Alan Harper, Gary Lineker.

Front row: Kevin McDonald, Paul Bracewell, Peter Reid, Steve Nichol, Alan Hansen (Liverpool Captain), Kenny Dalglish (Liverpool Manager), Howard Kendall (Everton Manager), Kevin Ratcliffe (Everton Captain), Kevin Sheedy, Paul Walsh, Sammy Lee, Paul Wilkinson.

INSIGHT is the platform for Everton's Trevor Steven to talk about international teammate Ian Snodin.

The appearance of the 21-year-old Doncaster Rovers captain means that this afternoon's Cup-tie is expected to feature three members of England's midfield quartet in the last Under-21 game in Turkey.

Trevor played wide on the right, Ian and Paul Bracewell linked up in the middle and the odd man out, only in terms of today's match, was Wayne Fereday, of Queens Park Rangers.

'From what I have heard, Ian has been having a very good, consistent season with Doncaster, impressing everyone in the Third Division,' says Trevor.

'I'm not surprised, having seen him play in Turkey. He's the type of player who spreads the ball around — a typical central-midfield player who likes to defend and attack.

'It was a difficult game for the side against a very aggressive Turkish side and on an awkward pitch, but Ian played very well, especially as it was his first international at this level.'

Trevor and Ian almost played in the same England Youth team three years ago, but the Everton man, who was then with Burnley, was injured when Snodin won a cap against Scotland at Ibrox. Trevor played in the return leg at Coventry, but the Doncaster player was not in the side on that occasion.

'We were in the same Division that season (Burnley won the Division Three Championship) but I seem to remember that I missed both games through injury,' added Trevor.

Having made the step-up to the First Division himself, Trevor believes that Ian is among a number of Third Division players who could reach the top.

'There are a certain amount of lads who should get an opportunity,' he says. 'Some miss the chance because they are ignored for some reason, but the fact that Ian Snodin and Stuart McCall, of Bradford, were in the last Under-21 squad shows that the selectors are taking notice.'

Doncaster manager Billy Bremner has been excited by Snodin since giving him his League debut when he was a 16-year-old apprentice. Now he and his elder brother, Glynn, are key men in Doncaster's Cup bid.

'Ian has exceptional talent,' says Mr Bremner. 'To be honest, I'm flabbergasted that he is still at this club. Maybe I'm a wee bit biased, but at 21, there are not many facets of the game that Ian is lacking in. And his brother is not far behind him.'

Ian was born at Thrybergh, Rotherham, in August 1963, and joined Rovers as an apprentice in August 1979. He made his debut against Bournemouth in March 1980 and scored his first goal at Aldershot a month later.

He was only 17 when first selected for the England Youth team in a tournament in Yugoslavia in 1981.

INSIGHT, the feature in which an Everton player comments on one of today's opponents, turns the spotlight on Leicester City's prolific marksman, Gary Lineker. Expert opinion comes from Kevin Ratcliffe.

Gary Lineker has progressed from being the 'odd man out' in Leicester City's attacking permutations to a place in the England World Cup squad.

It was not much more than three years ago that the Leicester-born striker did not appear to figure in the plans of former manager Jock Wallace, who opened the season with £250,000 Scots Jim Melrose and Alan Young as the main goal-hunters.

But Lineker won that battle to score 19 goals in the 1981-82 campaign. A year later, he won an Adidas Golden Shoe as the Second Division's top scorer with 26 League goals. And last season his 22 goals in the First Division swept him to a first England cap.

Everton skipper Kevin Ratcliffe was captain of Wales when Lineker was confined to the subs' bench at Wrexham last May. But he had already formed a favourable opinion of the Leicester man and was not surprised when he was given an international debut three weeks later against Scotland.

'He played against us only once in the League last season and scored Leicester's equaliser at Goodison,' recalls Kevin. 'He played pretty well that day. He's a quick striker with a good touch and I'd say he is definitely one to look out for at the highest level.'

Spurs were reported to be among the big clubs making transfer enquiries at the start of the season, but Filbert Street boss Gordon Milne was said to have placed a prohibitive price-tag on the club's major asset.

'He was bound to be noticed after scoring 22 goals in his first season in the First Division,' added Kevin. 'He seemed to have a very good understanding with the other striker, Alan Smith.

'Smith went for the high balls and Lineker was always looking to use his speed to beat the defence for the knock-ons.'

Unfortunately for Leicester, the combination misfired recently and after five weeks without a League goal from either striker, Smith was dropped against Villa last Saturday — but Lineker responded with a hat-trick.

Lineker, who will be 24 at the end of this month, confessed he was unhappy with his own form when Bobby Robson called him in as replacement for Trevor Francis in the recent international against Finland.

Yet he had still scored five times in the first six League matches of the season and was well established as Leicester's most successful goal-scorer since the days of Arthur Rowley in the 1950s.

'It's certainly a compliment to be talked about in the same breath as Arthur Rowley, but it's impossible to say whether I would be scoring goals regularly in the fifties or whether Arthur would be today,' he said.

Lineker, incidentally, is something of a hot-shot outside football. He practices regularly on the snooker table with Leicester ace Willie Thorne and has been close to making a century break.

The 1984/85 programme included an opposition feature where one of the current Everton squad noted their experiences of one of their star men. Third Division Doncaster Rovers visited Goodison in the FA Cup that campaign, featuring an England Under-21 international (opposite) - while a speedy Leicester City striker caught the eye of the club captain

NEWPORT

The fact that Newport County are still in existence as a Football League club is a source of pride for manager Colin Addison, in his second term of office at Somerton Park.

Five years ago, they stayed in business only with the help of £8,000 raised from a 'save the club' friendly with Manchester United. And the position was still critical when Mr Addison took over as team manager in the Fourth Division basement in January 1977.

He performed a major rescue act by steering Newport clear of the re-election zone and laid the foundation for recovery before departing to become assistant manager to Ron Atkinson at West Bromwich Albion in May 1978.

Len Ashurst carried on the revival by leading Newport to promotion in 1980, and the following season brought tremendous excitement as County reached the quarter-final of the European Cup-Winners' Cup before losing only by a single goal to Carl Zeiss Jena.

Things continued to look good when the ... started the Third Division pro... three successive wins last season — their best start in 47 years — but from that point, County slid down the table and were out of four Cup competitions by mid-December.

The directors then decided to make major changes. Trainer-coach Jimmy Goodfellow had left in November and was followed in February by Mr Ashurst who was replaced by the return of Mr Addison from a spell as No. 1 at Derby County.

There were still some anxious moments to come, for Newport were in danger of relegation until their escape was clinched by six wins, seven draws and only three defeats in the final 16 games. This form seems to have been carried over into the current campaign and hopes are high in South Wales that Newport may join Cardiff City in a dual promotion challenge.

A number of the players who featured in the European success are still in a squad which was assembled for around £140,000, which was spent during Mr Ashurst's reign as manager.

The top fee was paid in October 1980, when Wales Under-21 goalkeeper Mark Kendall arrived from Tottenham for £45,000. He made 29 League appearances whilst at White Hart Lane and, last season, he was the only Newport player to turn out in every first-team match.

Next on the price scale is £40,000 striker Dave Gwyther, who will complete 16 years in League soccer in January. He won two Welsh Under-23 caps a decade ago and has scored more than 150 goals in over 450 League games. Now 33, he has been at Somerton Park since December 1979.

Tommy Tynan, a 26-year-old Liverpudlian who started his career as a member of an FA Youth Cup Final team at Anfield in 1972, has also been a reliable marksman in the lower Divisions. A £25,000 signing from Lincoln City in February 1979, he notched 45 League goals for Newport by the start of this month.

Tynan was then disputing the top scorers' spot with another Merseysider, John Aldridge, who was the club's top sharpshooter in his first season after leaving South Liverpool for a small fee in April 1979. He has had injury problems in the last two years but announced his return to form this season with five goals in his first four appearances.

Another scoring outlet for Newport comes from club captain Keith Oakes, a Midlander who moved from Peterborough for £15,000 in September 1978. Although he is a specialist defender, he has chipped in with 30 League and Cup goals in his time in South Wales.

Kevin Moore, a Lancastrian from Blackpool, is the only other player to have cost a significant fee. And Newport's £12,000 investment in February 1979, was more than justified ... he helped them to promotion in ... season. That was his third ... in three years, for he ... Swansea City ...

... the first team defence.

Stroud topped 300 League appearances in 11 years as a professional at Swindon, while 23-year-old Vaughan Jones completed a century of League games and won Welsh Under-21 honours in his time with Bristol Rovers.

Newport will be well pleased if they are as successful as Huyton-born left-back John Relish, who has reached over 230 League matches since his free move from Chester in May 1974. The prospect of playing at Goodison Park is a dream come true for a one-time Everton supporter, who, by a happy coincidence, had his 29th birthday on the day we visited Somerton Park this month.

Three other free signings are giving Newport excellent service. Karl Elsey, a former Welsh League player who spent 18 months with QPR, has been at the club since July 1980; defender Grant Davies, an apprentice at Preston, was County's Player of the Year last term; and midfield man Neil Bailey, an apprentice at Burnley, has been a regular for four years apart from missing a period last season with a pelvic injury.

Newport are equally conscious of the need to find their own players and they have appointed their former player, Graham Reynolds, to step up schoolboy scouting.

They will now be hoping to find youngsters as good as winger Steve Lowndes, who scored in a famous Welsh Under-21 victory in Holland in 1980, and midfield player Nigel Vaughan, who graduated to the Under-21 side with two caps last season. Already they have high hopes for Ceri Williams, a teenager who played in their Milk Cup win against Exeter in September.

...TY STATISTICS 1982-83

League/Cup record 1982-83 ... Goals ...

NEWPORT COUNTY 1982-83

Back row (left to right): Vaughan Jones, Mark Kendall, Karl Elsey.

Middle: Colin Addison *(Manager)*, Dave Gwyther, Jeff Johnson *(on loan to Gillingham)*, John Aldridge, Neil Bailey, Nigel Vaughan, Bobby Smith *(Assistant Manager)*, Dave Williams *(Trainer-Coach)*.

Front: Ray Bishop *(now with Torquay United)*, Steve Lowndes, Tommy Tynan, Keith Oakes, Grant Davies, John Relish.

Picture: Colin Dowd

MERSEYSIDE CONNECTION . . .
John Aldridge (left) started with South Liverpool; Tommy Tynan (right) is a former Liverpool apprentice and professional; John Relish (centre) was born in Huyton and previously played with Chester.

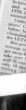

BAYERN MUNICH

BAYERN MUNICH face Everton in the European Cup-Winners Cup with the uncertain knowledge — as if the first leg hadn't proved the point — that British opposition does not always bring out the best in them.

Their record so far in Anglo-German meetings in the 1980s bears that out. In the 1981 Champions' Cup finals they lost on the away goals rule to Liverpool; in the 1982 Champions' Cup Final they went down 1-0 to Aston Villa in Rotterdam; the next season they lost 0-0, 2-3 against Aberdeen in the Cup-Winners' Cup quarter-finals; and last season they were knocked out 1-0, 0-2 by Tottenham in the UEFA Cup third round.

Now Bayern have a long-running score to settle, and they approach that task with a team entering its fourth degree of glory. Team No. 1 was the one who beat Glasgow Rangers 1-0 in extra-time in the 1967 Cup-Winners' Cup Final in Nuremberg. The goal was scored by Franz Roth and the team included great names such as goalkeeper Sepp Maier, sweeper Franz Beckenbauer and goal-grabber Gerd Müller.

Team No. 2 dominated European football through the mid-1970s. Three years in a row they won the Champions' Cup — beating Atletico Madrid of Spain 4-0 in a replay in Brussels in 1974, after a 1-1 draw; beating Leeds 2-0 in a notorious match in Paris in 1975; and then defeating Saint-Etienne of France by 1-0 at Hampden in 1977. Beckenbauer and Maier were then at the height of their powers, as was Müller. And joining them now were full-back/midfielder Paul Breitner, tough centre-back Georg Schwarzenbeck and wandering striker Uli Hoeness (now Bayern's general manager).

They also had a youngster just starting to make his way in the game, named Karl-Heinz Rummenigge. He had an unimpressive outing against Saint-Etienne but coaches Udo Lattek and then Dettmar Cramer had spotted his potential. Two more years and Rummenigge was one of West Germany's outstanding players at the 1978 World Cup.

CLUB DETAILS

Founded: 27th February 1900.
President: Willi O. Hoffmann.
Vice-President: Karl Plab.
Treasurer: Prof Dr Fritz Scherer.
Manager: Uli Hoeness.
Secretary: Karl Hopfner.
Trainer: Udo Lattek.
Co-Trainer: Egon Coordes.

Bayern had in the meantime lost their European grip. But not their ambition. Breitner was bought back after spells in Spain with Real Madrid and in West Germany with Eintracht Frankfurt. He was a midfield general now, not a full-back and he quickly became Bayern's captain and controller.

With Rummenigge approaching his peak, Bayern returned to the Champions' Cup Final in 1982. Eight years earlier Bayern's stars had won the European club trophy and the World Cup for West Germany a few weeks later. But this time the 'double' which fell to Rummenigge, Breitner, full-back Wolfgang Dremmler and company wasn't such a happy one: Bayern lost 1-0 to Aston Villa in the European Cup Final and then, with West Germany, finished runners-up to Italy in Madrid in the World Cup Final.

That team could be called Bayern No. 3. Now they have had to rebuild again. Breitner retired, Rummenigge went to Italy to join Internazionale of Milan last summer and injury forced Schwarzenbeck to retire.

Bayern have, however, led the West German League throughout the season and their quarter-final victory over Roma both home and away in the Cup-Winners' Cup proves they are still very much a force to be reckoned with.

Founded on 27th February 1900, Bayern's success is a comparatively recent phenomenon. Only ... the War did ... Champi... was appalled. He said: 'You can't want to put that elephant in with my thoroughbreds!' But Neudecker insisted and Müller of course came up with the goods, being seven times the League's top scorer.

Bayern entered the Bundesliga in 1965, won the Cup in that first season and the Cup-Winners' Cup a year later. Now, in just under 20 years they have built up a record which looks like this:

- ★ World Club Champions 1976;
- ★ European Champions 1974, 1975, 1976, runners-up 1982.
- ★ Cup-Winners' Cup 1967;
- ★ European Super Cup runners-up 1975, 1976;
- ★ West German Champions (1932), 1969, 1972, 1973, 1974, 1980, 1981;
- ★ West German Cup-winners 1957, 1966, 1967, 1969, 1971, 1982, 1984.

The man who holds the reins now is UDO LATTEK. He is 49 and enjoyed a low-key playing career with Wipperfürth, Osnabrück and Bayer Leverkusen — whom Bayern beat 3-1 recently to reach the German Cup semi-finals — before qualifying as a coach in 1965.

Lattek was immediately taken on by the West German federation (DFB) as an aide to national manager Helmut Schön and ran the Youth, Under-23 and amateur selections. In March 1970, however, he took the plunge and entered club football with Bayern.

Under Lattek Bayern won the Champions' Cup for the first time in 1974, before he moved on to Borussia Mönchengladbach in 1975, taking them to the UEFA Cup in 1979.

But personal tragedy struck. Lattek's teenage son died of Leukaemia and to get away from it all he went to Spain to take over Barcelona after a br... with Borussia Dortmund ... only 18 months wi... falling ... pow...

HANS PFLUGLER

BAYERN IN THE CUP-WINNERS' CUP 198...

4-1	h	v Moss (Norway) — Pflügler 2, Wohlfarth, ...	
2-1	a	v Moss — Wohlfarth, Rummenigge ...	
4-1	h	v Trakia Plovdiv — Wohlfarth ...	
0-2	a	v Trakia	
2-0	h	v Roma — Au...	
2-1	a	v Roma ...	
0-0	h	...	

BAYERN MUNICH PLAYING STA...

	Birthplace	Born	Full	B	U-21	Youth/Schools	Amat...
GOALKEEPERS							
Raimond Aumann	Augsburg	2.10.63	–	–	[illegible]	[illegible]	[illegible]
Jean-Marie Pfaff	Lebbeke (Belg)	4.12.53	44	–	[illegible]	[illegible]	[illegible]
DEFENDERS							
Klaus Augenthaler	Furstenzell	26.9.57	4	8	[illegible]	[illegible]	[illegible]
Bertram Beierlorzer	Erlangen	31.5.57	–	1	[illegible]	[illegible]	[illegible]
Wolfgang Dremmler	Salzgitter	12.7.54	28	–	[illegible]	[illegible]	[illegible]
Bernhard Dürnberger	Kirchanschoring	17.9.53	–	6	[illegible]	[illegible]	[illegible]
Norbert Eder	Wurzburg	7.11.55	–	1	[illegible]	[illegible]	[illegible]
Wolfgang Grobe	Braunschweig	15.6.56	–	–	[illegible]	[illegible]	[illegible]
Bernd Martin	Stuttgart	10.2.55	1	9	[illegible]	[illegible]	[illegible]
Holger Willmer	Lubeck	5.9.58	–	6	[illegible]	[illegible]	[illegible]
MIDFIELD							
Soren Lerby	Copenhagen	1.2.58	43	–	[illegible]	[illegible]	[illegible]
Lothar Matthaus	Erlangen	21.3.61	26	4	[illegible]	[illegible]	[illegible]
Norbert Nachtweih	Bangerhausen (DDR)	4.6.57	–	–	[illegible]	[illegible]	[illegible]
Hans Pflugler	Freising	27.3.60	–	–	[illegible]	[illegible]	[illegible]
FORWARDS							
Calle Del'Haye	Aachen	18.8.55	2	6	[illegible]	[illegible]	[illegible]
Achim Forster	Wurzburg	30.3.62	–	–	[illegible]	[illegible]	[illegible]
Hans-Werner Grunwald	Hausham	2.12.63	–	–	[illegible]	[illegible]	[illegible]
Dieter Hoeness	Ulm	7.1.53	2	2	[illegible]	[illegible]	[illegible]
Ludwig Kogl	Penzberg	7.3.66	–	–	[illegible]	[illegible]	[illegible]
Reinhold Mathy	Bietigheim	12.4.62	–	–	[illegible]	[illegible]	[illegible]
Michael Rummenigge	Lippstadt	3.2.64	1	–	[illegible]	[illegible]	[illegible]
Manfred Schwabl	Holzkirchen	18.4.66	–	–	[illegible]	[illegible]	[illegible]
Ugur Tutuneker	Bursa (Turkey)	2.8.63	–	–	[illegible]	[illegible]	[illegible]
Roland Wohlfahrt	Bocholt	11.1.63	–	–	[illegible]	[illegible]	[illegible]

International honours as at the start of season 1984-85.

NEWCASTLE

Form-check...

Newcastle United opened a survival path by staying unbeaten in March and lifting themselves off the bottom of the table for the first time in three months.

Apart from a four-week spell before Christmas, they had spent all season in the bottom three until they reached make-or-break time with five home games out of six.

After taking only one point out of 27, they were in the classic win-or-bust situation on the first Saturday in March – tailed off by five points at the bottom before meeting the 21st club, Aston Villa, at St James's Park.

But England ace Peter Beardsley gave them a lifeline with a brilliant winning goal and they went on to take a point at Manchester City before winning other vital home matches against fellow-strugglers Southampton and Leicester.

The improvement coincided with some relief from a cruel run of injuries (*see next column*).

The international experience of John Anderson and David McCreery was restored in defence and midfield, and 19-year-old Paul Gascoigne came back to boost the engine room. This also meant that Beardsley, who had often helped out in midfield, was released to form a top-class striking partnership with Paul Goddard.

Goddard, a club record signing at £415,000 from West Ham, scored his 100th League and Cup goal during a profitable spell of nine goals in 13 games.

That made him top scorer above Andy Thomas, who delivered a burst of seven goals in five minutes not long after his £100,000 move from Oxford earlier in the season. United later paid an extra £25,000 when he had completed 25 appearances, but the attacking midfield man lost his place last month.

Internationals...

Peter Beardsley, now an automatic choice alongside Gary Lineker in the England attack, heads a list of eight United players who have been involved in international football this season.

Goalkeeper Martin Thomas deputised for Neville Southall in Wales' first European Championship fixture in Finland, while World Cup men, David McCreery and Ian Stewart, have added to their caps for Northern Ireland.

Defender John Anderson returned to the Republic of Ireland team in Bulgaria last month and three of the younger players have appeared in under-21 games.

Neil McDonald won two caps for England; Darren Jackson was in the Scottish squad before his £40,000 transfer from Meadowbank; and Gary Kelly, son of former Everton coach, Alan, has kept goal for the Republic of Ireland.

Injuries...

Former Everton full back John Bailey was a long-term casualty with Achilles tendon trouble after playing in the first nine games of the season.

Long-serving defender Jeff Clarke and young midfielder Paul Gascoigne were each out for over four months with groin injuries, while former Welsh international Alan Davies (groin) and Scottish newcomer Albert Craig (collarbone) could miss the rest of the season.

Ian Stewart had a cartilage operation in December and fellow-Irishman David McCreery struggled with a persistent groin injury.

John Anderson played only two games in three months because of a foot problem but Paul Goddard missed only one match despite having an Achilles tendon injury put in plaster for nearly a fortnight.

With the squad so stretched, a number of young players were introduced for the first time. In fact, two teenagers made debuts against Everton – Tony Nesbit in the Full Members' Cup in December and Jeff Wrightson in the League meeting on Boxing Day.

The Management...

Willie McFaul is now in his 21st year with Newcastle United and is completing his second season as the club's 11th post-war manager.

The 43-year-old Ulsterman was signed from Linfield for £7,000 in November 1976 and made 290 League appearances for United, winning six full caps, before switching to the coaching staff.

He was the Magpies' goalkeeper when they won the European Fairs Cup against Ujpest Dozsa in 1969 and also played in their last FA Cup Final appearance against Liverpool in 1974.

After finishing his playing career in April 1975, he became reserve coach and then right-hand man to successive managers, Bill McGarry, Arthur Cox and Jack Charlton.

When Mr Charlton suddenly announced his departure in August 1988, Mr McFaul was appointed as caretaker and got the job within a month, leading United to their highest First Division placing in nine years.

Support...

The proud football people of the North East have continued to give Newcastle tremendous support despite their problems this season.

More than 120,000 fans flocked to St James's Park for a recent run of five home games, and at that point, United's average gate of over 24,000 was the seventh best in the country.

The figure is almost 1,000 per game up on last season, and the supporters' loyalty was apparent only a couple of weeks ago when a relegation battle against Leicester pulled in 23,360. It was the second highest gate of the day, topping the turnout for two attractive fixtures in London – Chelsea v Everton and Spurs v Norwich.

With support on that scale, it would be a tragedy if Newcastle were to slip back to the Second Division.

PETER BEARDSLEY

UNITED

Manchester United's challenge for their first League Championship for 15 years faltered in the least expected place.

They lost the habit of winning at Old Trafford in the two months leading up to Easter. Four home games produced just one goal — and that from defender Kevin Moran — as United dropped nine points out of 12 to Arsenal (0-0), Manchester City (1-1), Coventry City (0-1) and Sunderland (0-0).

It was a particularly barren period for their million-pound strikers. Frank Stapleton's last home goal was three months ago, when Everton drew 1-1, and Garry Birtles has to go back to 28th November for his last success at Old Trafford.

Yet United could do little wrong on their travels. With just one setback at Swansea in January, they won four games in five trips. And the goals went in nicely for the front runners — three for Birtles, two for Stapleton and three for England winger Steve Coppell.

Fortunately, United's home defensive record is the best in the First Division — only eight goals conceded in 16 matches — and this enabled them to stay unbeaten for seven months until Coventry inflicted only their second League defeat at Old Trafford this season. But they won only seven times, compared with six drawn games.

It's not like the old days when United were almost invincible with the tidal wave of support from regular 50,000 crowds. And it's a problem that has caused much debate in recent weeks.

Former Everton full-back John Gidman placed his viewpoint in the *Manchester Evening News*. He said: 'Manchester United is the place to be. It's the cream of clubs in Europe and a team everyone wants to play for. And when we've scored an early goal at Old Trafford, it's like playing in paradise, but when we don't, it can be purgatory.'

RON ATKINSON

'Giddy' reckons that life is tougher at the top. 'This time last year with Everton, we were fighting for points to stay in the First Division. The worry and pressure were tremendous. Now, with United, we are almost at the top and yet the pressure is twice as great.

'. . . if we don't score in the first 15 minutes, we get too anxious and perhaps press forward so much that we get caught out and concede a goal. All the players went home feeling guilty after the Coventry game. We knew that we had let people down and that three points had gone down the drain.'

Gidman, of course, is not the only individual connection between United and Everton. Physiotherapist Jim McGregor is now looking after the injury situation at Old Trafford and Eric Harrison, first team coach at Goodison last season, is in charge of United's Youth team.

The rest of the backroom staff has links with West Bromwich Albion. Manager Ron Atkinson's move from the Hawthorns last summer also involved assistant manager Mick Brown, who was previously in charge at Oxford United, and Brian Whitehouse, who spent much of his career with Albion, as a player and coach and even had a spell as temporary manager after the departure of Don Howe seven years ago.

More publicised is the fact that United have two of the players who took Albion to fourth place in the First Division last season. Bryan Robson, one of the more automatic selections for the England team, and Remi Moses, a Mancunian who won England Under-21 honours whilst in the Midlands, cost more than £2 million earlier this season.

With a further massive fee spent on Stapleton, United committed themselves to borrowing at a reported cost of £5,000 per week in interest. 'We cannot allow an overdraft of our size to drift on indefinitely,' said chairman Mr Martin Edwards in the *Manchester Evening News*.

'Our running costs are high at the moment for two reasons. We have taken new, highly-paid players on to the payroll without losing any major wage earners. Then, of course, there is the overdraft itself. But if we sell players, we get a twofold effect. We reduce the wage bill and we reduce the overdraft.'

Mr Atkinson made the first moves in this direction by selling popular Irishman Sammy McIlroy to Stoke City for a reported £400,000. He might have made further savings, but Sunderland could not afford a £250,000 fee after having Jimmy Nicholl on loan and Ashley Grimes, once a target for Brighton, was sidelined for months by illness.

In practice, United have maintained a top position in the table by picking the side from only 13 players during the last couple of months.

Gary Bailey, among the exclusive set of goalkeepers tipped for future England honours, is the undisputed No. 1, and Paddy Roche, the former Eire international, continues, as he has done for some years, as the ever-faithful deputy. He had three games this season in the pre-Christmas period.

Gidman and Scotsman Arthur Albiston are virtually automatic choices at full-back and it seems that the talented Irishman, Kevin Moran, is slowly becoming the first centre-back on Mr Atkinson's team-sheet. Over the last five months, he has always been in the side, apart from the odd break through injury.

STEVE COPPELL

Martin Buchan, who missed only five of the first 30 League games, has usually played alongside Moran, but he lost the captaincy in recent weeks and faced extra competition when fellow Scott, Gordon McQueen, made an impressive return a fortnight ago.

Ray Wilkins, the new captain, is the only ever-present in midfield but Robson has been a fixture since his arrival from West Bromwich. Coppell, as he does for England, plays the linking role between midfield and orthodox winger, while Mike Duxbury, a local youngster who came forward last season, and Moses have shared the other midfield job.

Moses had three months out of the League line-up when troubled by injury but displaced Duxbury, also an England Under-21 cap, for the last three games of March.

Lou Macari, one of United's best signings of the last decade, had a brief return to the first team in January, following the sale of McIlroy, but the player most on the fringe of the side now is Scott McGarvey. A Scottish Youth international last season, the teenage forward made his full debut against Everton in January and has since had a number of substitute appearances.

While a shortage of goals may frustrate United's ambitions, they can never be accused of negative thinking. On their last visit to Merseyside, Mr Atkinson announced, 'we're going for a win,' and they did just that by beating Liverpool with goals from Moran and Albiston.

Martin Buchan lends support to West Ham's Billy Bonds. Garry Birtles helps from behind.

EVERTON v MANCHESTER UNITED PREVIOUS MEETINGS

[illegible]

	P	W	D	L	F	A	Pts
Home	52	29	12	11	117	60	70
Away	53	11	13	29	56	100	35
Total	105	40	25	40	173	160	105

OPPOSITION NOTES...

Retaining a similar format throughout the decade, opposition features usually concentrated on club overviews and records, form and signings, squad notes and statistical comparisons between the Blues and said opponents.

'The Insider' feature was one fresh angle in the mid-1980s, with an Everton player or member of the coaching team talking about an opposition player, usually somebody they had played with at another club or at international level. Notable figures highlighted on the pages previous include future signings Ian Snodin and Gary Lineker – perhaps manager Howard Kendall took heed of his players' advice!

MANCHESTER CITY

Formcheck...

◆ City's return to the First Division was a welcome boost for the North-West in re-establishing the traditional four-club representation for Merseyside and Manchester.

A two-year exile in the Second Division ended with celebrations after a nervy afternoon in May. City needed a point to be sure of taking the runners-up spot behind Chelsea but trailed for an hour at Bradford until Trevor Morley scored a precious equaliser with only four minutes remaining.

The last month of the season was a truly agonising time for Maine Road fans. City were 11 points in front of third-placed Crystal Palace in April but managed only one victory in six games and owed their promotion to a 1-1 draw with the Londoners on May 1st.

If the run-in was rather too dramatic for comfort, there no doubt that City well deserved their triumph after staying in the top two from February onwards.

The general feeling within the club was that they would be better-equipped for First Division football than in the mid-1980s when relegation overtook them after only two seasons back at the top level.

A major reason for the optimism was the success of the youth policy. City won the FA Youth Cup in 1986, took the Central League championship a year later, and reached the FAYC final last season for the fourth time in ten years.

Steve Redmond, David White, Ian Brightwell, Paul Lake and Andy Hinchcliffe graduated through the system to the England Under-21 squad and last season's youth skipper, Gerald Taggart, played for Northern Ireland Under-23s after making his League debut in February.

Even so, City recognised that experience would be an asset in the First Division. Nine of the 13 players who began the season at Anfield were bought at a total cost of more than £3m.

The first four games produced only one point, but there was nothing to worry about when September brought three wins in four games, including a 5-1 walloping of United in the Manchester derby match.

It was in November that things went wrong with a 6-0 trouncing at Derby. Trapped on the rebound from their biggest League defeat for 27 years, City then lost 3-0 at home to Nottingham Forest and went out of the Littlewoods Cup to Coventry.

The sudden slump put them at the bottom of the table even before they went down 4-1 at home to Liverpool on the first Saturday in December.

Transfers. . .

◆ City spent nearly £2m in preparing their promotion-winning team for the First Division.

Clive Allen, the 1987 Footballer of the Year in his 49-goal season for Spurs, moved from Bordeaux, Ian Bishop was signed from Bournemouth and Northern Ireland full back Gary Fleming arrived from Nottingham Forest.

Roughly half of their investment was covered by the departures of Paul Moulden (Bournemouth), Nigel Gleghorn (Birmingham), Carl Bradshaw (Sheffield United), Ian Scott and Wayne Biggins (both Stoke).

A bid to sign Blackburn defender Colin Hendry collapsed in September over personal terms, but the 23-year-old Scot eventually completed a £700,000 move two months later.

City's transfer turnover has topped £7m since their last visit to Goodison Park for a Littlewoods Cup quarter-final nearly two years ago.

Luton goalkeeper Andy Dibble and Wimbledon defender Brian Gayle cost £565,000 in the summer of 1988 and Luton's Australian-born striker, David Oldfield, was added to the squad for £600,000 shortly before last season's transfer deadline.

A £20,000 deal for Ipswich 'keeper Paul Cooper proved just as valuable on the last lap of the promotion campaign. The 36-year-old newcomer played in eight games when Dibble was out with a groin injury and deputised again this season when the first-choice Welshman was absent for two months after breaking three small bones in his back.

Summer signing Clive Allen

12

Management. . .

◆ City added to a long-standing connection with Everton last week when they named Howard Kendall as their 17th post-war manager.

He follows Jock Thomson, Joe Mercer and Ron Saunders on the list of former Everton players who have been in charge at Maine Road in the past 40 years.

City's move to bring Mr Kendall back into English football after two-and-a-half years with Athletic Bilbao was seen as a natural step after they had parted company with promotion-winning manager Mel Machin.

The club's choice was popular with supporters and the chairman, Peter Swales, was delighted to get the man "we wanted right from the off."

Mr Swales added: "The prime objective now is to keep the club in the First Division. In the long term, he has come here to get us up where he took Everton - right to the top and winning trophies."

City last won the League Championship in 1968 with the Joe Mercer-Malcolm Allison partnership, and their last major trophy was the League Cup under the management of Tony Book in 1976.

POST-WAR MANAGERS AT MAINE ROAD

1946-47	SAM COWAN
1947-50	JOCK THOMSON
1950-63	LESLIE McDOWALL
1963-65	GEORGE POYSER
1965-71	JOE MERCER
1972-73	MALCOLM ALLISON
1973	JOHNNY HART
1973-74	RON SAUNDERS
1974-79	TONY BOOK
1979-80	MALCOLM ALLISON
1980-83	JOHN BOND
1983	JOHN BENSON
1983-86	BILLY McNEILL
1986-87	JIMMY FRIZZELL
1987-89	MEL MACHIN
1989-	HOWARD KENDALL

13

FACTS & FIGURES 1983/84

ATTENDANCES AND CANON LEAGUE DIVISION ONE 83-84

Home League Games

Highest	Average			Home						Away					
			P	W	D	L	F	A	W	D	L	F	A	Pts
45,122	31,986	Liverpool	42	14	5	2	50	12	8	9	4	23	20	80
21,141	17,434	Southampton	42	15	4	2	44	17	7	7	7	22	21	77
29,692	17,695	Nottingham Forest	42	14	4	3	47	17	8	4	9	29	28	74
56,121	44,546	Manchester United	42	14	3	4	43	18	6	11	4	28	23	74
27,140	15,518	QPR	42	14	4	3	37	12	8	3	10	30	25	73
48,831	28,139	Arsenal	42	10	5	6	41	29	8	4	9	33	31	63
51,245	19,283	Everton	42	9	9	3	21	12	7	5	9	23	30	62
45,032	28,754	Tottenham	42	11	4	6	31	24	6	6	9	33	41	61
32,555	21,247	West Ham United	42	10	4	7	39	24	7	5	9	21	31	60
39,318	21,243	Aston Villa	42	14	3	4	34	22	3	6	12	25	39	60
22,007	16,515	Watford	42	9	7	5	36	31	7	2	12	32	46	57
26,185	17,422	Ipswich Town	42	11	4	6	34	23	4	4	13	21	34	53
26,826	16,608	Sunderland	42	8	9	4	26	18	5	4	12	16	35	52
25,679	17,078	Norwich City	42	9	8	4	34	20	3	7	11	14	29	51
26,553	14,667	Leicester City	42	11	5	5	40	30	2	7	12	25	38	51
17,275	11,966	Luton Town	42	7	5	9	30	33	7	4	10	23	33	51
27,954	14,781	WBA	42	10	4	7	30	25	4	5	12	18	37	51
24,372	13,870	Stoke City	42	11	4	6	30	23	2	7	12	14	40	50
21,453	12,586	Coventry City	42	8	5	8	33	33	5	6	10	24	44	50
23,993	14,108	Birmingham City	42	7	7	7	19	18	5	5	11	20	32	48
18,745	9,456	Notts County	42	6	7	8	31	36	4	4	13	19	36	41
26,249	12,004	Wolverhampton	42	4	8	9	15	28	2	3	16	12	52	29

FIRST TEAM RECORD

Date	V	Opposition	F A
Aug 27	H	Stoke City	1-0
Aug 29	H	West Ham United	0-1
Sept 3	A	Coventry City	1-1
Sept 6	A	Ipswich Town	0-3
Sept 10	H	West Bromwich Albion	0-0
Sept 17	A	Tottenham Hotspur	2-1
Sept 24	H	Birmingham City	1-1
Oct 1	A	Notts County	1-0
Oct 4	A	Chesterfield (MC 2-1 L)	1-0
Oct 15	H	Luton Town	0-1
Oct 22	H	Watford	1-1
Oct 26	A	Chesterfield (MC 2-2 L)	2-2
Oct 29	A	Leicester City	0-2
Nov 6	A	Liverpool	0-3
Nov 9	H	Coventry City (MC 3)	2-1
Nov 12	H	Nottingham Forest	1-0
Nov 19	A	Arsenal	1-2
Nov 26	H	Norwich City	0-2
Nov 30	A	West Ham United (MC 4)	2-2
Dec 3	A	Manchester United	1-0
Dec 6	H	West Ham Utd (MC 4R)	2-0
Dec 10	H	Aston Villa	1-1
Dec 17	A	Queens Park Rangers	0-2
Dec 26	H	Sunderland	0-0
Dec 27	A	Wolverhampton W.	0-3
Dec 31	H	Coventry City	0-0
Jan 2	A	Birmingham City	2-0
Jan 7	A	Stoke City (FAC 3)	2-0
Jan 14	A	Stoke City	1-1
Jan 18	A	Oxford United (MC 5)	1-1
Jan 21	H	Tottenham Hotspur	2-1
Jan 24	H	Oxford United (MC5R)	4-1
Jan 28	H	Gillingham (FAC 4)	0-0
Jan 31	A	Gillingham (FAC 4-R)	0-0
Feb 4	H	Notts County	4-1
Feb 6	A	Gillingham (FAC 4-2R)	3-0
Feb 11	A	West Bromwich Albion	1-1
Feb 15	H	Aston Villa (MC SF-1L)	2-0
Feb 18	H	Shrewsbury T. (FAC 5)	+3-0
Feb 22	A	Aston Villa (MC SF-2L)	0-1
Feb 25	A	Watford	4-4
Mar 3	H	Liverpool	1-1
Mar 10	A	Notts County (FAC 6)	2-1
Mar 14	A	Nott'm Forest	0-1
Mar 17	H	Ipswich Town	1-0
Mar 20	H	Leicester City	1-1
Mar 25		Liverpool (MC Final)	0-0 1
Mar 28		Liverpool (MC Final R)	0-1
Mar 31	H	Southampton	1-0
April 7	A	Luton Town	3-0
April 9	H	Arsenal	0-0
April 14		Southampton (FAC SF)	1-0
April 17	A	Southampton	1-3
April 21	A	Sunderland	1-2
April 23	H	Wolverhampton W.	2-0
April 28	A	Norwich City	1-1
May 5	H	Manchester United	1-1
May 7	A	Aston Villa	2-0
May 12	H	Queens Park Rangers	3-1
May 14	A	West Ham United	1-0
May 19		Watford (FA Cup Final)	2-0 1

+ Indicates Own Goal   *Indicates substituted pl

CENTRAL LEAGUE RESULTS 1983-84

Aug 31	H	Sheffield Wed	2 - 0
Sept 10	A	Liverpool	2 - 0
Sept 13	H	WBA	1 - 0
Sept 20	A	Stoke City	3 - 0
Sept 28	H	Burnley	3 - 0
Oct 11	H	Sheffield Utd	7 - 0
Oct 18	A	Leeds United	1 - 0
Nov 2	A	Newcastle	2 - 0
Nov 15	H	Bolton	2 - 1
Dec 7	A	Aston Villa	1 - 0
Dec 14	H	Manchester Utd	0 - 1
Dec 17	H	Liverpool	1 - 2
Dec 20	A	Sheffield Wed	2 - 4
Jan 10	H	Newcastle	2 - 1
Jan 18	A	WBA	0 - 1
Feb 8	A	Sheffield Utd	7 - 3
Feb 21	H	Leeds United	0 - 0
Feb 29	A	Sunderland	2 - 0
Mar 6	H	Blackburn	4 - 1
Mar 9	H	Sunderland	1 - 0
Mar 14	A	Blackburn	1 - 2
Mar 22	A	Burnley	0 - 1
April 3	H	Nott'm Forest	1 - 2
April 9	A	Derby County	3 - 0
April 19	A	Nott'm Forest	1 - 5
April 28	H	Aston Villa	0 - 0
May 1	H	Derby County	0 - 2
May 9	A	Bolton	0 - 2
May 14	A	Manchester Utd	2 - 2
May 15	H	Stoke City	2 - 5

RESERVE APPEARANCES 1983-84

	A	G		A	G
Arnold	24		Morris	2	—
Bailey	4	—	Morrissey	21(1)	1
Bateman	30	2	Mountfield	8	—
Bishop	16(7)	2	Mutch	2	2
Coyle	6(1)	—	O'Brien	— (1)	—
Curran	3	—	Oldroyd	8	—
Danskin	1(1)	—	Ratcliffe	1	—
Fielding	7(2)	—	Reid	3	—
Hall	2	—	Richardson	10	—
Harper	5	—	Rimmer N	2(2)	—
Higginbottom	20	6	Rimmer S.	25	15
Higgins	5	—	Sharp	1	1
Hood	5(1)	—	Southall	2	—
Hughes	22	—	Steven	9	5
Irvine	9	2	Stevens	9	—
Johnson	7	4	Stringer	2	—
Kendall	1	—	Wakenshaw	21(1)	4
King	12	4	Walsh	3(1)	—
Macowat	8	—	Own Goal		2
Marshall	12(3)	3			

Substitute appearances in brackets

1st TEAM APPEARANCES 83-84

	League 83-84		Cups 83-84		Everton League Career	
	A	G	A	G	A	G
Arnold	7	—	—	—	48	—
Bailey	33	—	14	—	155	3
Bishop	— (1)	—	—	—	—	—
Curran	8	—	1	—	15	1
Gray	23	5	7(1)	3	23	5
Harper	26(3)	1	7(2)	—	26	1
Heath	36	12	18	6	95	28
Higgins	14	—	5	—	150	6
Hughes	1	—	—	—	1	—
Irvine	19(2)	—	16	2	51	4
Johnson	7(2)	1	1	—	79	15
King	19(1)	2	5(1)	1	193	49
Mountfield	31	3	16	—	32	3
Ratcliffe	38	—	19	—	114	1
Reid	34(1)	2	17(1)	2	41	2
Richardson	25(3)	4	11(1)	3	64	9
Rimmer S.	1	—	—	—	3	—
Sharp	27(1)	7	16(2)	4	96	37
Sheedy	28	4	16	6	68	15
Southall	35	—	19	—	78	—
Steven	23(4)	1	5	1	23	1
Stevens	26(1)	1	16	—	73	2
Wakenshaw	1	1	—	—	1	1
Own Goal	—	—	—	1	—	—

83-84 substitute appearances in brackets
*Career record not including substitute appearances

LANCASHIRE LEAGUE '83-84

Division One

	P	W	D	L	F	A	Pts
Manchester U 'A'	30	24	3	3	90	15	51
Tranmere Res	30	20	7	3	74	32	47
Runcorn Res	30	19	3	8	61	28	41
Manchester C 'A'	30	17	5	8	73	41	39
Liverpool 'A'	30	15	7	8	57	33	37
Barrow Res	30	13	7	10	53	42	33
Southport Res	30	12	5	13	53	51	29
Everton 'A'	30	13	3	14	51	51	29
Burnley 'A'	30	11	7	12	44	45	29
Chorley Res	30	10	9	11	45	56	29
Bolton 'A'	30	11	6	13	46	52	28
Stockport 'A'	30	7	10	13	33	45	24
Crewe Res	30	8	4	18	43	64	20
Rochdale Res	30	9	2	19	45	75	20
UMIST	30	6	2	22	30	118	14
Formby Res	30	2	6	22	23	73	10

FA YOUTH CUP APPEARANCES 83-84

	A	G		A	G
Ashcroft	2	—	Macowat	7	—
Brindle	3	—	Marshall	8	1
Diggle	2	—	McKenzie	— (5)	1
Fielding	9	1	Oldroyd	7	—
Hall	9	—	O'Brien	8	1
Hood	9	1	Richmond	9	—
Hughes	9	1	Rimmer N.	9	2
			Wakenshaw	9	7
			Walsh	4(1)	—

Substitute appearances in brackets

3-84 RESULTS · ATTENDANCES · APPEARANCES AND GOALSCORERS

2	3	4	5	6	7	8	9	10	11	12
Harper	Bailey	Mountfield	Higgins	Richardson	Steven	Heath	**Sharp**[1]	King	Sheedy	Johnson
Harper	Bailey	Mountfield	Higgins	Richardson*	Steven	Heath	Sharp	King	Sheedy	Johnson
Harper	Bailey	Ratcliffe	Higgins	Richardson	Steven	Heath*	Sharp	King	**Sheedy**[1]	Johnson
Harper	Bailey*	Ratcliffe	Higgins	Richardson	Curran	Steven	Sharp	Johnson	Sheedy	Reid
Harper	Bailey	Ratcliffe	Higgins	Steven	Curran*	Heath	Sharp	Johnson	Sheedy	Richardson
Harper	Bailey	Ratcliffe	Higgins	**Reid**[1]*	Steven	Heath	Sharp	Johnson	**Sheedy**[1]	Richardson
Harper	Bailey	Ratcliffe	Higgins	**Reid**[1]	Steven*	Heath	Sharp	Johnson	Sheedy	King
Harper	Bailey	Ratcliffe	Higgins	Reid	Steven	Heath	**Sharp**[1]	Irvine	Sheedy	Richardson
Harper	Bailey	Ratcliffe	Higgins	Reid	Steven	Heath	**Sharp**[1]	Richardson	Sheedy	King
Harper	Bailey	Ratcliffe	Higgins	Reid	Steven	Heath	Sharp	King	Sheedy	Richardson
Harper	Bailey	Ratcliffe	Higgins	Richardson	Steven*	**Johnson**[1]	Sharp	King	Sheedy	Irvine
Harper	Bailey	Ratcliffe	Higgins	Richardson	Irvine	**Heath**[1]	Sharp	**Steven**[1]	Sheedy	Rimmer
Harper	Bailey	Ratcliffe	Higgins	Richardson	Steven	Heath	Sharp	King	Sheedy*	Irvine
Harper	Bailey	Ratcliffe	Higgins	Steven	Irvine	Heath	Sharp	King	Sheedy	Reid
Harper	Bailey	Ratcliffe	Higgins	Steven*	Irvine	**Heath**[1]	**Sharp**[1]	King	Sheedy	Reid
Harper	Bailey	Ratcliffe	Higgins	Reid	Irvine	**Heath**[1]	Gray	King	Sheedy	Stevens
Harper	Bailey	Ratcliffe	Mountfield	Reid	Irvine	Heath	Gray	**King**[1]	Sheedy	Stevens
Harper	Bailey	Ratcliffe	Mountfield	Reid	Irvine	Heath*	Gray	King	Sheedy	Stevens
Stevens	Ratcliffe	Mountfield	Higgins	**Reid**[1]	Irvine	Heath	Sharp	King	**Sheedy**[1]	Harper
Stevens	Ratcliffe	Mountfield	Higgins	Reid	Irvine	King	Sharp	Gray	**Sheedy**[1]	Heath
Stevens	Ratcliffe	Mountfield	Higgins	Reid	Irvine	Heath	Sharp	**King**[1]	**Sheedy**[1]	Harper
Stevens	Bailey	Ratcliffe	Mountfield	Reid	Irvine	Heath	**Gray**[1]	King*	Sheedy	Harper
Stevens	Harper	Ratcliffe	Mountfield	Reid	Irvine	Heath	Johnson	King	Sheedy	Hughes
Stevens	Harper	Ratcliffe	Mountfield	Reid	Irvine	Heath	Gray	Johnson	Sheedy	Richardson
Stevens	Hughes	Ratcliffe	Mountfield	Reid	Irvine	Richardson	Gray	Rimmer	Sheedy*	Steven
Stevens	Bailey	Ratcliffe	Mountfield	Reid	Irvine	Heath*	Gray	King	Sheedy	Richardson
Stevens[1]	Bailey	Ratcliffe	Mountfield	Reid	Irvine	Heath	Gray	**King**[1]	Sheedy	Richardson
Stevens	Bailey	Ratcliffe	Mountfield	Reid	**Irvine**[1]	Heath	Sharp	**Gray**[1]	Sheedy	Richardson
Richardson	Bailey	Ratcliffe	Mountfield	Reid	Irvine	**Heath**[1]	Sharp	Gray	Sheedy	King
Stevens	Harper	Ratcliffe	Mountfield	Reid	Irvine	**Heath**[1]	Sharp	Johnson*	Sheedy	Richardson
Stevens	Harper	Ratcliffe	Mountfield	Reid	Irvine	**Heath**[2]	Sharp	Richardson	Sheedy	King
Stevens	Harper	Ratcliffe	Mountfield	Reid	Irvine	**Heath**[1]	**Sharp**[1]	**Richardson**[1]	**Sheedy**[1]	King
Stevens	Harper	Ratcliffe	Mountfield	Reid	Irvine	Heath	Sharp*	Richardson	Sheedy	Gray
Stevens	Bailey	Ratcliffe	Mountfield	Reid	Irvine	**Heath**[3]	Gray	Richardson	**Sheedy**[1]	Sharp
Stevens	Bailey	Ratcliffe	Mountfield	Reid	Irvine	**Heath**[1]	Gray	Richardson	**Sheedy**[2]	Sharp
Stevens	Bailey	Ratcliffe	**Mountfield**[1]	Reid	Irvine	Heath	Gray	Richardson	Sheedy	Steven
Stevens	Bailey	Ratcliffe	Mountfield	Reid	Irvine	Heath	Sharp	**Richardson**[1]	**Sheedy**[1]	King
Stevens	Bailey	Ratcliffe	Mountfield	**Reid**[1]	**Irvine**[1]	Heath*	Gray	King	Sheedy	Sharp
Stevens	Bailey	Ratcliffe	Mountfield	Reid	Irvine	Heath	Sharp	King	Sheedy	Harper
Stevens	Bailey	Ratcliffe	Mountfield	Reid	Irvine	**Heath**[1]	**Sharp**[2]	**Gray**[1]	Sheedy	Harper
Stevens	Bailey	Ratcliffe	Mountfield	Reid	Steven*	Heath	Sharp	Gray	Sheedy	**Harper**[1]
Stevens	Bailey	Ratcliffe	Mountfield	Reid	Irvine	**Richardson**[1]	Sharp	**Gray**[1]	Sheedy*	Harper
Stevens	Bailey	Ratcliffe	Mountfield	Reid	Irvine	Richardson	Sharp	Gray	Harper	Steven
Stevens	Harper	Ratcliffe	**Mountfield**[1]	Reid	Irvine	Heath	Sharp*	Gray	Richardson	Steven
Stevens	Bailey	Ratcliffe	Mountfield	Reid	Steven	Heath	Gray	King	**Richardson**[1]	Harper
Stevens	Bailey	Ratcliffe	Mountfield	Reid	Irvine	Heath	Sharp	Richardson	Sheedy*	Harper
Stevens	Bailey	Ratcliffe	Mountfield	Reid	Irvine*	Heath	Sharp	Richardson	Harper	King
Stevens	Bailey	Ratcliffe	Mountfield	Reid	Harper*	Heath	Sharp	Richardson	**Gray**[1]	Steven
Stevens	Bailey	Harper	**Mountfield**[1]	Reid	Curran	**Heath**[2]	Sharp	Steven	Richardson	Irvine
Stevens	Bailey	Ratcliffe	Mountfield	Reid	Curran	Heath	Sharp*	Gray	Richardson	Steven
Stevens	Bailey	Ratcliffe	Mountfield	Reid	Curran	**Heath**[1]	Gray	Steven*	Richardson	Sharp
Stevens	Harper	Ratcliffe	Mountfield	Reid	Curran	Heath	Gray	Steven	**Richardson**[1]	Sharp
Stevens	Bailey	Ratcliffe	Mountfield	Reid*	Curran	**Heath**[1]	Sharp	Steven	Richardson	Harper
Stevens	Bailey	Ratcliffe	Mountfield	Reid	Curran	Heath	**Gray**[1]	**Steven**[1]	Richardson	Sharp
Stevens	Bailey	Ratcliffe	Mountfield	Reid	Curran*	Heath	**Gray**[1]	Steven	Richardson	Sharp
Stevens	Bailey	Harper	Mountfield	Reid	**Wakenshaw**[1]	King	Sharp	Steven	Richardson	Bishop
Stevens	Bailey	Ratcliffe	Mountfield	Reid	King	Heath	**Sharp**[1]	Steven	**Richardson**[1]	Harper
Stevens	Harper	Ratcliffe	Mountfield	Reid	Steven	**Heath**[1]	**Sharp**[2]	Gray	Richardson	King
Stevens	Harper	Ratcliffe	Mountfield	Reid	Steven	Heath	Sharp	King	**Richardson**[1]	Wakenshaw
Stevens	Bailey	Ratcliffe	Mountfield	Reid	Steven	Heath	**Sharp**[1]	**Gray**[1]	Richardson	Harper

Statistics

ATTENDANCES & TODAY LEAGUE DIVISION ONE TABLE 1986-87

Home League Games					Home					Away					
Highest	Average		P	W	D	L	F	A	W	D	L	F	A	Pts
48,247	32,639	Everton	40	14	4	1	45	10	10	4	7	27	20	80
44,827	36,281	Liverpool	41	15	3	3	43	16	8	4	8	26	23	76
39,019	25,915	Tottenham H	40	14	3	4	40	14	7	5	7	28	27	71
47,777	29,309	Arsenal	41	12	5	3	30	10	8	5	8	27	23	70
13,447	10,327	Luton Town	40	14	5	1	27	10	4	7	9	17	29	66
23,489	17,913	Norwich City	41	9	10	2	27	20	7	7	6	24	30	65
34,828	19,102	Nottingham Forest	41	11	8	1	34	13	6	3	12	28	37	62
27,000	15,343	Coventry City	40	14	2	3	33	15	3	8	10	15	28	61
23,934	15,755	Watford	41	11	5	4	37	20	6	4	11	29	34	60
15,978	7,704	Wimbledon	40	10	5	5	30	21	7	4	9	23	28	60
54,103	40,895	Manchester United	40	12	3	5	35	17	1	10	9	13	26	52
40,959	23,414	Sheffield Wednesday	41	9	7	4	39	22	4	6	11	19	35	52
20,452	14,948	Southampton	41	11	5	5	44	24	3	4	13	24	43	51
29,301	17,117	Chelsea	40	8	5	7	27	27	5	7	8	22	32	51
24,045	13,983	QPR	41	9	7	5	31	27	4	4	12	16	35	50
29,807	20,652	West Ham	41	9	4	7	31	28	4	6	11	19	39	49
35,078	24,750	Newcastle United	41	10	4	7	33	29	2	7	11	13	34	47
14,211	10,362	Oxford United	40	8	7	5	30	25	2	5	13	11	42	42
19,744	9,074	Charlton Athletic	41	6	7	7	24	21	4	4	13	19	33	41
19,205	11,702	Leicester City	41	9	7	5	39	24	2	1	17	15	52	41
35,336	21,908	Manchester City	41	8	6	7	28	24	0	9	11	8	31	39
32,093	18,172	Aston Villa	41	7	7	7	25	25	1	5	14	19	51	36

EVERTON ROLL CALL 1986-87

Player	Birthdate	1986-87 League Apps	Gls	1986-87 Cups Apps	Gls	Everton League Career Apps	Gls	Previous League Career Apps	Gls
Neil Adams	23.11.65	9(2)	—	7	—	9(2)	—	32	4
Paul Bracewell	19.7.62	(2)	—	—	—	75	5	167	9
Wayne Clarke	28.2.61	10	5	—	—	10	5	240	68
Darrin Coyle	27.3.65	—	—	—	—	—	—	—	—
Jason Danskin	28.12.67	—	—	—	—	1	—	9	—
John Ebbrell	1.10.69	—	—	—(1)	—	—	—	—	—
Alan Harper	1.11.60	27(7)	3	7(1)	—	80(16)	4	—	—
Adrian Heath	11.1.61	39	11	10	4	175(13)	60	95	16
Kevin Langley	24.5.64	16	2	5(1)	1	16	2	168	6
Ian Marshall	20.3.66	—(2)	1	1	—	8(3)	1	—	—
Bobby Mimms	12.10.63	11	—	4	—	21	—	95	—
Derek Mountfield	2.11.62	12	2	6(1)	1	96	18	26	1
Neil Pointon	28.11.64	10(2)	1	4(3)	—	24(3)	1	159	2
Paul Power	30.10.53	40	4	11	—	40	4	365	26
Kevin Ratcliffe	12.11.60	40	—	11	—	233(1)	2	—	—
Peter Reid	20.6.56	13(1)	1	2	—	105(2)	6	225	23
Graeme Sharp	16.10.60	25	4	9	8	192(10)	81	40	17
Kevin Sheedy	21.10.59	28	13	8	3	156	44	54	4
Ian Snodin	15.8.63	13(1)	—	3(1)	1	13(1)	—	239	31
Neville Southall	16.9.58	29	—	8	—	181	—	48	—
Trevor Steven	21.9.63	40	12	12	2	144(4)	34	76	11
Gary Stevens	27.3.63	23	2	4	—	174(1)	8	—	—
Stuart Storer	16.1.67	—	—	—	—	—	—	9	—
Mike Stowell	19.4.65	—	—	—	—	—	—	—	—
Pat Van den Hauwe	16.12.60	9	1	3	—	80	2	123	1
Dave Watson	20.11.61	33	4	7	—	33	4	212	10
Own Goals		—	2	—	1	—	—	—	—

Also played: Kevin Richardson (now Watford) 1 League appearance; Peter Billinge (now Crewe) 2 Cup appearances; Warren Aspinall (now Aston Villa) — (6) League, — (3) Cup appearances; Paul Wilkinson (now Nott'm Forest) 12(10) League, 8(1) Cup appearances, 4 League, 9 Cup goals.

Substitute appearances in brackets for 1986-87 and Everton League career.
Previous League career includes substitute appearances and games while on loan from Everton.

(All statistics up to and including Monday 4th May 1987)

FIRST TEAM FIXTURES 86

Date		V	Opposition	F/
Aug	23	H	Nottingham Forest	2-4
	25	A	Sheffield Wednesday	2-?
	30	A	Coventry City	1-?
Sept	2	H	Oxford United	3-1
	6	H	Queens Park Rangers	0-0
	13	A	Wimbledon	2-1
	16	A	Liverpool (SC Final - 1L)	1-3
	21	H	Manchester United	3-1
	24	H	Newport County (LC2-1L)	4-0
	27	A	Tottenham Hotspur	0-2
	30	H	Liverpool (SC Final — 2L)	1-4
Oct	4	H	Arsenal	0-1
	7	A	Newport County (LC2-2L)	+5-1
	11	A	Charlton Athletic	2-3
	18	A	Southampton	2-0
	25	H	Watford	3-2
	28	H	Sheffield Wednesday (LC3)	4-0
Nov	2	A	West Ham United	0-1
	8	H	Chelsea	2-2
	15	A	Leicester City	2-0
	19	A	Norwich City (LC4)	4-1
	23	H	Liverpool	0-0
	29	A	Manchester City	3-1
Dec	3	H	Newcastle United (FMC3)	5-2
	6	H	Norwich City	4-0
	13	A	Luton Town	0-1
	20	H	Wimbledon	3-0
	26	A	Newcastle United	4-0
	28	H	Leicester City	5-1
Jan	1	H	Aston Villa	3-0
	3	A	Queens Park Rangers	1-0
	10	H	Southampton (FAC3)	2-1
	17	H	Sheffield Wednesday	2-0
	21	H	Liverpool (LC5)	0-1
	25	A	Nottingham Forest	0-1
	31	A	Bradford City (FAC4)	1-0
Feb	7	H	Coventry City	+3-1
	14	A	Oxford United	1-1
	22	A	Wimbledon (FAC5)	1-3
	28	A	Manchester United	0-0
Mar	3	H	Charlton Athletic (FMC4)	°2-2
	8	A	Watford	1-2
	14	H	Southampton	+3-0
	21	H	Charlton Athletic	2-1
	28	A	Arsenal	1-0
Apr	4	A	Chelsea	2-1
	11	H	West Ham United	4-0
	18	A	Aston Villa	1-0
	20	H	Newcastle United	3-0
	25	A	Liverpool	1-3
May	2	H	Manchester City	0-0
	4	A	Norwich City	1-0
	9	H	Luton Town	
	11	H	Tottenham Hotspur	

°Lost 6-5 on penalties

© The Football League Ltd.

KEY TO COMPETITIONS

LC = Littlewoods Cup FAC = FA Cup
FMC = Full Members' Cup SC = Screen Sport Sup

| Aug | 16 | | Liverpool (FA Charity) | 1-1° | 8 |

+ Indicates own goal   °Indicates substitut

STATISTICS SUPPLIED BY NEC COMPUTERS AND COMMUNICATIONS

RESULTS · ATTENDANCES · APPEARANCES AND GOALSCORERS

	2	3	4	5	6	7	8	9	10	11	12
is	Harper	Power	Ratcliffe	Watson	Langley	Steven	Heath	Sharp	Richardson*	Sheedy[2]	Wilkinson ●
is	Harper	Power	Ratcliffe	Watson	Langley[1]	Steven	Heath	Sharp[1]	Wilkinson	Sheedy	Marshall
is	Harper	Power	Ratcliffe	Watson	Langley*	Steven	Heath	Sharp	Adams	Sheedy	Marshall[1] ●
is	Harper[1]	Power	Ratcliffe	Watson	Langley[1]	Steven[1]	Heath	Sharp	Adams*	Sheedy	Marshall ●
is	Harper	Power	Ratcliffe	Watson	Langley	Steven	Heath*	Sharp[1]	Mountfield	Sheedy[1]	Wilkinson ●
is	Billinge	Power	Ratcliffe	Marshall	Langley	Adams	Wilkinson	Sharp	Steven	Sheedy[1]*	Aspinall ● Coyle
is	Mountfield	Power	Ratcliffe	Watson	Langley	Steven	Heath[1]	Sharp[1]	Wilkinson	Sheedy[1]*	Adams ●
is	Mountfield	Power	Ratcliffe	Watson	Langley*	Steven	Heath[1]	Sharp	Wilkinson[2]	Adams	Marshall Aspinall
is	Mountfield	Power	Ratcliffe	Watson	Langley	Steven	Heath	Sharp	Wilkinson	Sheedy*	Adams ● Aspinall ● ● Pointon ●
is	Billinge	Power	Ratcliffe	Mountfield	Steven	Adams	Heath*	Sharp[1]	Wilkinson	Sheedy	Aspinall ● Pointon ●
is	Mountfield*	Power	Ratcliffe	Watson	Langley	Steven	Adams	Sharp	Wilkinson	Sheedy	Aspinall ●
is	Harper	Power*	Ratcliffe	Watson	Langley	Adams*	Steven	Sharp[1]	Wilkinson[3]	Sheedy	Wilkinson ●
is	Harper	Power	Ratcliffe	Watson	Langley*	Adams	Steven	Sharp	Heath	Sheedy[2]	Wilkinson ●
is	Harper	Power	Ratcliffe	Watson*	Mountfield	Steven[1]	Heath	Sharp	Wilkinson[1]	Langley	Aspinall ●
all	Harper	Power	Ratcliffe	Mountfield[2]	Langley	Adams	Heath	Sharp	Steven[1]	Wilkinson	Aspinall
all	Harper	Power	Ratcliffe	Mountfield[1]	Langley	Steven	Heath[1]	Sharp	Wilkinson[2]	Sheedy	Pointon/Adams
all	Harper	Power	Ratcliffe	Mountfield	Langley*	Steven	Heath	Sharp	Wilkinson	Sheedy	Aspinall ●
all	Harper	Power	Ratcliffe	Mountfield	Langley	Steven[1]	Heath	Sharp	Wilkinson	Sheedy[1]	Adams
all	Harper	Power	Ratcliffe	Mountfield	Langley	Steven*	Heath[1]	Sharp	Adams	Sheedy[1]	Aspinall ●
all	Harper	Power	Ratcliffe	Mountfield	Langley	Steven[1]	Heath[1]	Sharp[1]	Adams	Sheedy[1]	Watson Wilkinson
all	Harper	Power	Ratcliffe	Mountfield	Langley*	Steven	Heath	Sharp	Adams	Sheedy	Wilkinson ●
all	Harper	Pointon	Ratcliffe	Mountfield	Power[1]*	Steven	Heath[2]	Sharp	Adams	Sheedy	Wilkinson ●
all	Harper	Pointon	Ratcliffe	Watson	Power	Steven	Heath[1]	Sharp[3]	Adams	Sheedy[1]	Mountfield ● Wilkinson
all	Stevens	Pointon[1]	Ratcliffe	Watson	Power[1]	Steven[1]	Heath[1]	Sharp*	Harper	Sheedy	Wilkinson ●
all	Stevens	Pointon*	Ratcliffe	Watson	Power	Steven	Heath	Sharp	Harper	Sheedy	Wilkinson ●
all	Stevens	Pointon*	Ratcliffe	Watson	Power	Steven[1]	Heath[1]	Sharp	Harper	Sheedy[1]	Reid ●
all	Stevens	Pointon	Ratcliffe	Watson	Power[1]	Steven[2]	Heath[1]	Sharp*	Harper	Sheedy	Wilkinson ●
all	Stevens	Pointon	Ratcliffe	Watson	Power*	Steven	Heath[2]	Wilkinson[2]	Harper	Sheedy[1]	Aspinall ●
all	Stevens	Pointon	Ratcliffe	Watson	Power*	Steven[1]	Heath	Wilkinson	Harper[1]	Sheedy[1]	Aspinall ●
all	Stevens	Pointon	Ratcliffe	Watson	Power	Steven	Heath	Sharp[1]	Harper	Sheedy	Wilkinson
all	Stevens	Pointon	Ratcliffe	Watson	Power	Steven	Heath	Sharp[2]	Harper	Sheedy	Wilkinson Mountfield
all	Stevens	Pointon	Ratcliffe	Watson[1]*	Power	Steven[1]	Heath	Sharp	Harper	Sheedy	Wilkinson ●
all	Stevens	Pointon*	Ratcliffe	Mountfield	Power*	Steven	Heath	Sharp	Harper	Sheedy	Snodin ● Snodin ●
all	Stevens	Power*	Ratcliffe	Mountfield	Snodin	Steven	Heath	Wilkinson	Harper	Sheedy	Pointon ●
all	Stevens	Van d Hauwe	Ratcliffe	Watson	Reid	Steven	Heath	Wilkinson	Snodin[1]	Power	Harper/Aspinall
all	Stevens	Van d Hauwe	Ratcliffe	Watson	Reid	Steven[1]	Heath[1]	Sharp*	Snodin	Power	Harper ●
all	Stevens	Van d Hauwe*	Ratcliffe	Watson	Reid	Steven	Heath	Wilkinson[1]	Snodin	Power	Harper ●
all	Stevens	Van d Hauwe*	Ratcliffe	Watson	Reid*	Steven	Heath	Wilkinson[1]	Snodin	Power	Harper ● Pointon ●
all	Stevens	Van d Hauwe	Ratcliffe	Watson	Reid*	Steven	Harper	Heath	Snodin	Power	Wilkinson ●
all	Van d Hauwe	Pointon	Mountfield	Watson	Harper*	Steven[1]*	Heath	Wilkinson[1]	Snodin	Adams	Langley ● Ebbrel ●
all	Stevens	Van d Hauwe*	Ratcliffe	Watson	Reid	Steven	Heath[1]	Clarke	Snodin	Power	Wilkinson ●
all	Stevens	Van d Hauwe	Ratcliffe	Watson[1]	Reid*	Steven	Heath	Clarke	Snodin	Power[1]	Harper ●
all	Stevens[1]	Van d Hauwe*	Ratcliffe	Watson	Reid	Steven[1]	Heath	Clarke	Snodin	Power	Harper ●
all	Stevens	Power	Ratcliffe	Watson[1]	Reid	Steven	Heath	Clarke[1]*	Harper[1]	Sheedy*	Pointon ●
all	Stevens[1]	Power	Ratcliffe	Watson[1]	Reid[1]	Steven	Heath	Clarke	Harper	Sheedy	Pointon
all	Stevens	Power	Ratcliffe	Watson	Reid	Steven	Heath	Clarke	Snodin	Sheedy[1]*	Harper ●
all	Stevens	Pointon	Ratcliffe	Watson	Harper	Steven	Heath	Clarke[3]	Snodin	Power	Marshall
all	Stevens	Power	Ratcliffe	Watson	Reid	Steven	Heath	Clarke	Snodin	Sheedy[1]	Harper
all	Stevens	Van d Hauwe	Ratcliffe	Watson	Reid*	Steven	Heath	Clarke	Snodin	Power	Harper ●
all	Stevens	Van d Hauwe[1]	Ratcliffe	Watson	Reid	Steven	Heath	Sharp	Snodin	Power	Harper

---

| ms | Harper | Power | Ratcliffe | Marshall | Langley | Steven | Heath[1] | Sharp | Richardson | Sheedy | Adams* ● / Wilkinson |

● Indicates substituted appeared

"MARK WAS A SMASHING LITTLE PLAYER BUT HE JUST DIDN'T GROW AND WE HAD TO LET HIM GO"

All aspects of Everton life appeared to be covered at some point during the 1980s.

Features on Goodison, the coaching staff, new signings and club news were common, while the Blues' youth system also gained column inches during the 1982/83 season (right).

Keen to promote the work done by youth coach Graham Smith, there was also notable mention of a player who didn't quite make it – and another who did:

"We had one lad here called Mark Ward. He was a smashing little player who was always willing to take people on and go past them. But he just didn't grow and we had to let him go. He's playing with Northwich Victoria.

"But on the other hand there are people like Steve McMahon. He wasn't very big or strong when he arrived but he worked hard at all aspects of the game.

"He would come back for extra work and he worked at building his muscles as well as polishing his game with the ball. The result is that he is now a first-team player."

Wintry conditions were the subject of a 1984/85 article in the Everton v Watford programme (right) featuring the Goodison

PROFILE

ON YOUTH DEVELOPMENT AT EVERTON

UMBRO SPORTSWEAR
THE CHOICE OF CHAMPIONS

GO AHEAD GOODISON

No, not the land of the midnight sun... but a wintry scene at Bellefield while Head Groundsman Alan Storey, left, inspects the green, green grass of Goodison.

The mushkin trip to The Gulf was undoubtedly a triumphant flag-waving exercise on behalf of British football. This and other pictures show ... ABOVE: A pre-match Press Conference with Kevin Ratcliffe, Colin Harvey, Mr. Philip Carter, Graham Roberts among those on the top table. BELOW RIGHT: Dave Watson relaxing by the hotel pool. ACTION: Graeme Sharp battles with Rangers' Graham Roberts.

● See News Desk for a report by Mike Ellis.

and Bellefield ground staff. The £70,000 undersoil heating system at Goodison came in for praise, while it was noted how northern clubs were one step ahead of their southern rivals in looking after their home surface.

Bellefield head groundsman Douggie Rose also revealed some of the ups and downs of the role:

"People are in and out during the day, schoolboys come in for training at night, and if the alarm goes off, then I'm the one who is called out."

The League Championship success saw Everton invited to Dubai the following season to play in an unofficial British Championship match against Scottish champions Rangers. Despite eventually losing the match on penalties after a 2-2 draw, fans who purchased the Nottingham Forest programme for the first home fixture of 1988 were at least treated to one or two shots, no doubt warmed by the players' experience in sunnier climes...

From: Barry Spencer, Welling, Kent . . .

Would you please stop publishing letters which advertise fan clubs for ex-Evertonians such as David Johnson and Jim Pearson. They were not the most popular players at Goodison and therefore the letters would seem to be a form of 'mickey-taking'.

EDITOR: We are assured that these clubs are genuine. And there is news of another one in the following letter.

From: The Jim Pearson Appreciation Society, 99 Whetstone Hey, Great Sutton, S. Wirral . . .

I write this letter, still seething from the letter published in Blue Mail from Barry Spencer, Welling, Kent, who wrote denouncing the formation of our Society.

His knowledge of Everton is highlighted when he insinuates that Jim was unpopular at Goodison. On the contrary, as all loyal supporters will remember, Jim Pearson was a well-liked character in the mid-70s.

From: John Collins, 9 Underwood Crescent, Fazackerly, Liverpool . . .

I am writing in response to a letter criticising the Jim Pearson Appreciation Society. I wrote off to the Society, initially expecting little or no reply, but since then, I have received several letters which are very enthusiastically written by fans who have supported Everton over the last 10 years. it seems a pity that such enthusiasm should be subject to such cynicism.

Jim Pearson, 1984/85

Fan club letters were a common sighting, with the top players usually the subject of supporters' enthusiasm. However, when a note in the programme appeared for somebody beginning a fan club for 1970s striker Jim Pearson, the follow-up responses questioned the validity of said appreciation society.

This dismissive reaction ignited a furious response from said society, with supporters assured Jim warranted his own fan club. How long it lasted though is unknown...

FAMILY PHOTO
A must for Christmas! your photog taken with t Everton trop here at Goo Sunday 1st December (p eighth if num demand).

The price for 10" × 8" colo photo in a presentation £3.95. Please or send remit to the Souver Shop in Good Road when yo be given or se time-card to a the 500 Club a have your pict taken.

Trophy picture, 1985/86

A popular photo opportunity for Evertonians, supporters were given the chance to be pictured with the Canon league championship trophy, the European Cup Winners' Cup and the FA Charity Shield, 'a must for Christmas!' The price was a seemingly bargain £3.95 for a 10" x 8" complete with presentation folder.

Meanwhile the club shop was offering merchandise celebrating the success of the 1984/85 campaign. A commemorative medallion, and audio tapes and records for fans keen to 'recapture the exciting atmosphere of last season's highlights' were available for less than a fiver.

SHOP CHRISTMAS WITH EVERTON ...

The Everton shop is packed with exciting gifts, ideal for Christmas presents, to suit all friends and family.
On display here we have an attractive Commemorative Medallion produced for the League Championship and European Cup-Winners Cup double achievement. This is priced at just £4.99.
For fans seeking to recapture the exciting atmosphere of last season's highlights, we have audio tapes and records. Tapes are priced at £4.49 and the LP Record is just 3.99.
There's lots more goodies in stock — pop along to the Club Shop and see for yourself.

Hillsborough, 1988/89

The Goodison derby of May 1989 was an emotional occasion, taking place just weeks after the Hillsborough Disaster. Televised live by ITV, it was also Liverpool's first competitive action since that day, and the tone of the match programme, highlighted by chairman Philip Carter's words, more than matched the emotion of the night.

Littlewoods, 1986-87

Everton's links with the Littlewoods organisation have gone back decades, via the involvement of John Moores. The company also sponsored the League Cup for four seasons during the late 1980s.

First noted in the Southampton programme at the end of the 1985/86 season, Miss Littlewood for the following campaign would be Carolyn Barnes who, coincidentally, was an Everton season-ticket holder.

The following season, Everton's first League Cup programme, against Newport County, showed Neil Pointon and Neville Southall on a visit to Littlewoods' flagship Liverpool store in Church Street, along with the new silverware...

COMMENT

WE extend our usual warm welcome to our friends from Anfield this evening, and with it our deepest sympathy and understanding following the Hillsborough tragedy.

We share their sense of loss and grief because this is a common tragedy which has affected not only Liverpool F.C., but also Liverpool as a city.

There are many families within our city with divided loyalties when it comes to matters of football, but in circumstances which appertain at the moment we are united as only, perhaps, Liverpudlians can be in such adversity.

Like a relative of a bereaved family, we at Everton have understood the immense difficulties that Liverpool F.C. have gone through in the past two weeks, and it has been right and proper that we have stayed in the background, helping where we could and always ready to support whatever was required of us.

We are both part of the family of the City of Liverpool. It is our strength, not only in the past, or in the present but in the future that lies ahead.

Philip Carter,
Chairman, Everton Football Club

QUEEN OF THE BLUES!
Lovely Carolyn Barnes is a beauty with an eye for the boys in blue, of course! Blue is a season ticket holder at Goodison Park, and like her favourite team, she knows all about winning trophies. Carolyn is the reigning Miss Edge Lane and the new Miss Littlewood for 1986-87.

Miss Littlewoods, Carolyn Barnes, holds the Littlewoods Challenge Cup with the assistance of Neil Pointon and Neville Southall outside of Liverpool's Littlewoods store.

Blue Mail, 1984/85

Some choice cuts from the letters page, including praise for sugar-free tea at Goodison (v Arsenal), and a Sheffield Wednesday supporter who enjoyed his visit to Liverpool (v Luton Town).

The Blue Mail page (below) is taken from the Coventry City programme. It includes a complaint about a lack of a full fixture list in the opening-day programme, badge collector requests, Paul Bracewell, Andy Gray and Nevile Southall Fan Club information, a Welsh fan hoping for a lift, an Icelandic fan keen to join a Fan Club, a serviceman confirming his support from Northern Ireland and a baby 'Blue'.

From: Daniel Miller, Dorset Street, Blackpool . . .
May I offer my congratulations to the catering department for providing tea without sugar at selected points? It has long been the policy of most clubs to serve only sweetened tea, thus leaving a significant percentage of the public without a choice. As usual, Everton lead where others follow.

From: Mr P. G. Biram, 24 Hawthorne Close, Barlborough, Nr Chesterfield, Derbys S43 4HR . . .
I would like to let people know that there are still some genuine supporters.
Being a Wednesdayite, I travelled to Goodison Park to watch them play. On my arrival at the ground, I met two (lovely) young ladies who support Everton. We had a good conversation and they directed me to the part of the ground for which my ticket was valid. I would like to thank them.
After taking my seat, my thoughts were on the lady I had approached and not on the match. Now I'm kicking myself for not asking if I could write to her! If she reads this, please would she write to me. I mentioned that I'm a postman, so don't forget the postcode!

BLUE MAIL IS THE FEATURE THAT BELONGS TO THE FANS. Send your views, requests etc to: Blue Mail, Everton FC, Goodison Park, Liverpool L4 4EL.

From: Peter O'Neill, Larch Close, Colney Hatch Lane, London N11 3NN . . .
Not so much a complaint but an observation. As one of the best 'best informed' fans in the entire League (as per the Comment column), I was a bit annoyed not to find a fixture list anywhere in the programme (v Spurs). No doubt one will appear in the next issue, but I personally do not consider this good enough.
I have always found fixture lists difficult to come by, even when I lived on Merseyside, and I do not consider it right that supporters should have to look to other sources (e.g. The Echo) for this information.
It has bothered me ever since I bought my first season ticket that the club do not supply a fixture list on renewal (at least this is the case when you renew in May, as we are encouraged). I appreciate the difficulties regarding the availability of dates (particularly in May), but would suggest that the least that could be done would be to publish in the first available slot, possibly as a separate enclosure. How about next year?
EDITOR: Point taken, Peter. We will endeavour to publish the fixtures from the *first* programme next season. The reason for not including a list on August 25th, and in previous years, is the pressure on space. There is usually so much to cram into the first issue, especially when the club has had a season as successful as 1983-84.

From: Miss Helen Ingram, 61 Greenwood Lane, Wallasey, Merseyside . . .
With Paul Bracewell's permission, I am organising his Fan Club. Membership is £1; please enclose sae for return of Membership card.

From: John McAllister, 55 Cleveley Park, Belfast BT8 4NB . . .
I am a collector of enamel lapel badges, and with all the branches of Everton Supporters' Clubs, I was wondering if any of these has its own badge. If so, I'd be happy to give other badges or cash in exchange.
I would like to obtain all the badges which have been issued in connection with my favourite club.

From: Claire and Julie, 14 Tancred Road, Wallasey, Merseyside . . .
Many thanks for advertising our Andy Gray Fan Club in the programme. We now have 25 members with lots more enquiries. Write for details enclosing sae.

From: Michael Preece, 24 Brookside Row, Cwmtillery, Abertillery, Gwent NP3 1LW . . .
I am 20 years old and have supported Everton since I was nine. For the last few seasons, I've been travelling to Goodison Park by train, but as I am unemployed, it is hard to get to all the matches.
Please could you feature this letter, as I desperately want to contact any persons travelling to Goodison from the South Wales area.

From: Jacqueline McKenzie, 5 Westleigh Place, Sutton Leach, St Helens, Merseyside WA9 4NJ . . .
I am starting a Fan Club for Neville Southall. If anyone is interested in joining, please write to me enclosing sae.

From: Leifur Gardarsson, Midvangur 106, 220 Hafnarfjordur, Iceland . . .
Hello! My name is Leifur and I am one of the greatest Evertonians on earth! Every Saturday I listen to BBC World Service for news.
Do any of the Everton players have a Fan Club? If so, give me the address, please. Although my favourite player is Adrian Heath, I would like all the addresses of the Fan Clubs.
One more: Does Everton have a Fan Club? Then, give me the address, please.
EDITOR: Perhaps all the Fan Club organisers would like to contact Leifur, who is a subscriber to the matchday programme. The Supporters' Club address is: 38 City Road, Walton, Liverpool 4.

From: 24583029 KGN Lawrence, S, A Coy BL PLT, 1 Kings Regt, NHSM, BFPO 801 . . .
As a member of Her Majesty's Forces serving in Northern Ireland, I still follow Everton as much as I can. But there was a slight problem. I had tickets for both the Wembley appearances last season, but I had to sell them and serve over here instead.
But, rest assured, my support is still with Everton.

From: Mr and Mrs D. McDonald, Birch Road, Haydock, St Helens . . .
Here is our son, Derek, aged 13 months, and as you can see, he already likes the best things in life, by following in his Dad's footsteps and becoming a True Blue. He is pictured with over 400 programmes from 1960 to the present day and an autographed football from Everton FC.

Derek suffers from 'Ondine's Curse', which means he stops breathing when he goes to sleep, and has to be connected to a ventilator at night, but this will not stop him going to watch The Blues when he is old enough.
We would be honoured if his photograph could appear in one of the programmes.

TV Times, Mail Appeals, 1985/86

Note of a piece of TV history was made in the Aston Villa programme, with the February 1986 Manchester City Goodison fixture having become the first midweek league game to be televised. The news was good for the club, as it meant increased exposure – midweek highlights were longer than would have been the case on a Saturday – while extra revenue from advertising was also beneficial.

The final home fixture Blue Mail included a letter calling for the team to play in all blue – with an all white change strip, a letter of gratitude to Howard Kendall and a request that Adrian Heath be allowed to stay.

A little piece of history was made at Goodison Park when the match against Manchester City became the first mid-week League fixture to be televised.

Previously, highlights from League games were shown only from Saturdays, but the new agreement permits mid-week coverage – and Granada moved in smartly when the weather wiped out ITV's scheduled showing of the Milk Cup semi-final between Aston Villa and Oxford.

The Villa match was not postponed until late on the Monday afternoon, but the Granada cameras were rushed into position at Goodison the next morning.

'We had the first call from Granada at about 6 pm on Monday,' says secretary Jim Greenwood. 'We were happy to go on TV and they came back to me at 11 pm to say they had been able to put everything together.

'It was a very hectic time for our advertising people, organising the boards for TV sites, but it was all done at less than 24 hours' notice. 'Commercially, this was a bonus for the club. There was extra revenue from advertising, and it

was very valuable for our shirt sponsors, NEC. Having been off the screen for such a long time earlier in the season, we are obviously anxious that they should have maximum exposure.

'To that extent, the game with Manchester City was very successful. We were on for rather longer than in the normal Saturday-night programmes of highlights. It was timed at approximately 38 minutes, which is almost three times more than the usual coverage.'

The fact that we were able to accommodate the TV request was another reminder of the value we got from the undersoil heating.

Although there has been a lot of talk recently that artificial pitches are the answer to bad weather, there is no doubt that heating offers the best of both worlds. We have a natural playing surface – and the system is far cheaper to install.

It's no exaggeration to suggest that if the heating were to allow us to go ahead with a 'live' TV match in bad weather, it would almost pay for itself through the commercial profits of such an occasion.

THE MERSEYSIDE MANAGERS

Supporters of both Everton and Liverpool have wonderful memories of the Swinging Sixties. It was the era of The Beatles – and the best in soccer entertainment. Merseyside owes a great debt to Harry Catterick and Bill Shankly for creating two teams which brought pride to the area as they won League Championships and FA Cup Finals. A copy of the photograph [re-produced below] is now available [10 × 8in] at a cost of £1.50, inclusive of postage and packing. Apply to: W. F. Free, 22 Hampton Court Road, Liverpool L12 8EL. Please make out PO/Cheques to W. F. Free.

WZAT!

working for the benefit of people in all walks of life.
Duncan, the overall supervisor in a Government-backed scheme based on Everton and Liverpool, explained: 'The important thing is to try and get accepted for everyone in the community on behalf of the two football clubs and also to draw all sports together.

'We had previously taken St Finbar's School on a tour around Goodison Park, and when it came to the girls' cricket team we thought it was appropriate to give them a day out at Old Trafford.

'There wasn't a lot of play because of the weather, but they had a look round the museum, enjoyed a sit-down lunch and were presented with a bat, autographed by Lancashire and Worcestershire.'

There was another pleasing event involving the Community Programme last week when Duncan met Trevor Steven [pictured left] to receive a video recorder presented by NEC in connection with the Everton Player of the Month scheme.

Trevor issued the Community Programme on the charity of his choice and the video will be used to advertise the benefits of the project into other towns and cities around the country.

Duncan says: 'We will be taking it around to show what we are doing here on Merseyside and elsewhere in the North West. Local authorities will be able to see what we are achieving and hopefully be able to copy us in to that the Community Programme eventually becomes nationwide.'

TOP TWELVE

Wayne Clarke carried the banner for Everton when representatives of the 12 founder members of the Football League – including Accrington Stanley – attended a service in Birmingham to mark the Centenary celebrations.

The Everton striker [pictured second left, behind Stoke City's George Berry] lined up in a group with maestro Tom Finney, who took pride of place on behalf of the first champions, Preston North End.

There was a vast amount of experience among the players in the procession from St Philip's Cathedral. Among those in view are Allan Evans [Aston Villa], Paul Dyson [West Bromwich Albion], Alistair Robertson [Wolverhampton Wanderers], Geoff Pike [Notts County] and Mark Wallington [Derby County].

Everton chairman Philip Carter, in his role as President of the Football League, took part in a ceremony to unveil a commemorative plaque in the home city of the League's pioneer, William McGregor, of Aston Villa.
Photograph by courtesy of the Birmingham Post & Mail.

EitC, Howzat, 1987/88

The fledgling Everton in the Community – known as the 'Community Programme in Football' in its early days – took a group of local pupils to Lancashire CCC to see one day of their opening County Championship match of the season – while Wayne Clarke was Everton's representative to commemorate the 12 founder member clubs of the Football League in 1888 (v Charlton Athletic, 1987/88).

1990-2000

A rollercoaster decade of on-field highs and lows at Goodison as changes in programme style were almost as frequent as changes in the managerial hotseat

Football became more 'modern', more 'professional' with the influx of TV wealth and the foundation of the Premier League, with the 1992/93 top-flight campaign the first season of the competition.

The programme scooped the Programme of the Year for the second time in 1990/91, while design began to become more experimental, as content took a back seat in favour of pictures and graphics. The influence of the internet was first apparent, while the growing utilisation of football within the media meant there were now many other competing areas where fans could receive their club news fix.

Re-branding exercises were among the many changes implemented by the Peter Johnson regime in the mid-1990s. The 1995/96 season saw the iconic 'Everton' logo introduced in print for the first time – while the programme was also given a new name as the decade ended, 'Blues Review' being adopted in 1998/99.

The introduction of the special-edition 'Millennium Blues Review' closed out the 20th century (recognised with third place at the Programme of the Year awards), with the first home match of the 21st century, a home encounter with Leicester City, used to tie in with the Millennium Giant celebration. One player from each decade from the 1900s, plus a manager, were awarded 'Millennium Giant' status.

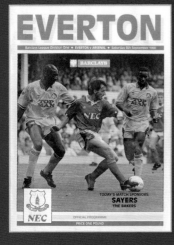

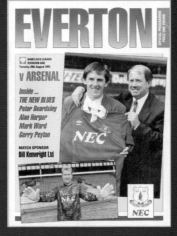

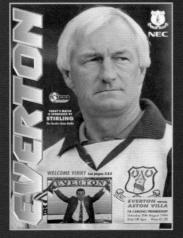

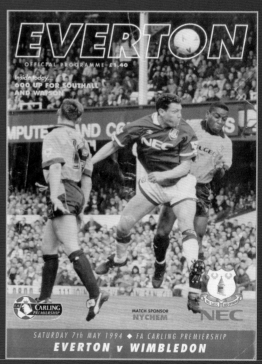

Selected covers, which span the decade. Clockwise from above left: v Woking (FA Cup – away programme, Everton produced the matchday publication with the tie having been switched to Goodison), 1990/91; v Liverpool (FA Cup – second replay), 1990/91; v Wimbledon, 1993/94; v Sheffield Wednesday (Premier League first day), 1992/93

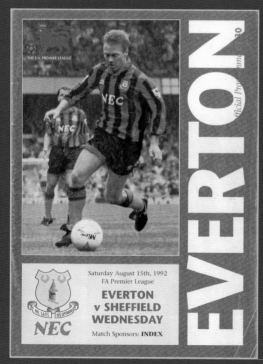

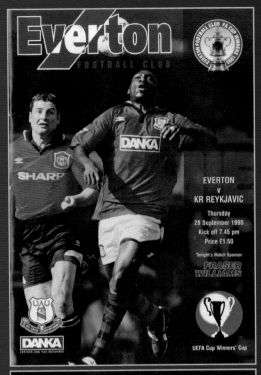

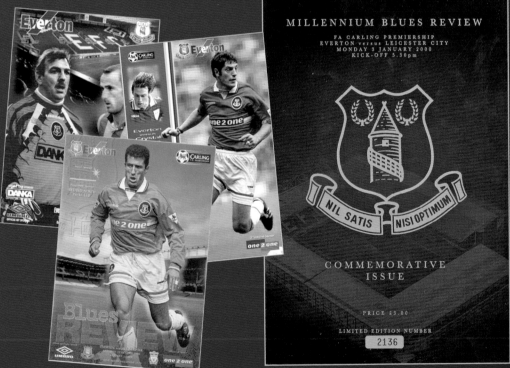

Selected covers, which span the decade. Clockwise from above left: v Liverpool, 1994/95; v KR Reykjavic (European Cup Winners' Cup), 1995/96; v Leicester City, 1999/2000; v Crystal Palace, 1997/98; v Liverpool, 1998/99; v Bradford City (FA Cup), 1996/97

PLAYERS & OFFICIALS
SQUAD CHECK

EVERTON			SPURS	
Royal Blue Shirts, White Shorts			*White Shirts, Navy Blue Shorts*	
NEVILLE SOUTHALL	1	1	ERIK THORSTVEDT	
MATTHEW JACKSON	2	2	DEAN AUSTIN	
ANDY HINCHCLIFFE	3	3	JUSTIN EDINBURGH	
IAN SNODIN	4	4	GHEORGHE POPESCU	
DAVE WATSON	5	5	COLIN CALDERWOOD	
GARY ABLETT	6	6	GARY MABBUTT	
VINNY SAMWAYS	7	7	NICK BARMBY	
GRAHAM STUART	8	8	ILIE DUMITRESCU	
DUNCAN FERGUSON	9	9	DARREN ANDERTON	
BARRY HORNE	10	10	TEDDY SHERINGHAM	
DANIEL AMOKACHI	11	11	RONNY ROSENTHAL	
PAUL HOLMES	12	12	JASON DOZZELL	
JASON KEARTON	13	13	IAN WALKER	
JOHN EBBRELL	14	14	STUART NETHERCOTT	
PAUL RIDEOUT	15	15	DAVID HOWELLS	
DAVID BURROWS	16	16	MICKY HAZARD	
ANDERS LIMPAR	17	18	JURGEN KLINSMANN	
JOE PARKINSON	18	19	KEVIN SCOTT	
STUART BARLOW	19	20	DARREN CASKEY	
GARY ROWETT	21	21	DANNY HILL	
BRETT ANGELL	22	22	DAVID KERSLAKE	
NEIL MOORE	25	23	SOL CAMPBELL	
DAVID UNSWORTH	26	27	STEVE CARR	
		30	CHRIS DAY	

v Tottenham Hotspur, 1994/95

MATCHFACTS

EVERTON v MANCHESTER UNITED

Royal Blue Shirts, White Shorts / *Red Shirt, Black Shorts*

NEVILLE SOUTHALL	1	LES SEALEY
NEIL McDONALD	2	DENIS IRWIN
JOHN EBBRELL	3	CLAYTON BLACKMORE
KEVIN RATCLIFFE	4	STEVE BRUCE
MARTIN KEOWN	5	MICHAEL PHELAN
NORMAN WHITESIDE	6	GARY PALLISTER
RAY ATTEVELD	7	NEIL WEBB
STUART McCALL	8	PAUL INCE
GRAEME SHARP	9	BRIAN McCLAIR
MIKE NEWELL	10	MARK HUGHES
KEVIN SHEEDY	11	DANNY WALLACE
	12	
	14	

Referee: GEORGE COURTNEY, Spennymoor
A Primary School Head Teacher ... Began refereeing in the Auckland Junior League (1960) and reached Football League list in 1972 ... Officiated in World Cup finals in Mexico and Italy, European Championships in 1984 and Asian finals (1989 and 1980) ... Refereed three European club finals plus FA Cup & Milk Cup finals.
Linesmen: R.D. FALEY, Huddersfield (Red Trim), T.A. MOORE, Bradford (Yellow Trim).
Reserve Official: S. WEDGWOOD, Burscough.

TODAY'S MITRE MATCHBALL SPONSORS

MAINSTAY INDUSTRIAL SERVICES LTD.
The No. 1 Industrial Builders of the North East.
Telephone: 051 548 8363.

MASCOT
Today's Everton mascot is Ryan Cookson, aged eight, of Blackthorn Close, Lea, Preston. The matchday mascot's kit is kindly supplied by Umbro and is retained as a souvenir of the occasion.

BALL BOYS
Today's Ball Boys are provided by the South Merseyside Junior Football League and Everton FC Supporters Club.

EVERTON CLUBCALL
0898 121 199
Calls cost 36p/minute cheap, 48p/minute other times

EVERTON v SHEFFIELD WED.

Royal Blue Shirts, White Shorts / *Yellow & Black Striped Shirts, Black Shorts*

NEVILLE SOUTHALL	1	CHRIS WOODS
MATTHEW JACKSON	2	ROLAND NILSSON
ANDY HINCHCLIFFE	3	PHIL KING
JOHN EBBRELL	4	GRAHAM HYDE
DAVE WATSON	5	NIGEL PEARSON
GARY ABLETT	6	PAUL WARHURST
ROBERT WARZYCHA	7	CHRIS WADDLE
PETER BEARDSLEY	8	DANNY WILSON
MAURICE JOHNSTON	9	DAVID HIRST
MARK WARD	10	PAUL WILLIAMS
PETER BEAGRIE	11	NIGEL WORTHINGTON
	Sub	
	Sub	
	Sub	

Referee:
KELVIN MORTON,
Bury St Edmunds
Occupation: Group Accountant ... Began refereeing at 16 and reached the Football League list in 1986 ... Reserve official for last season's FA Cup Final ... Linesman for international and UEFA Cup games.

Linesmen:
P.M. ROBERTS, Bobington (Yellow Trim)
J.R. ROBINSON, Whalley, Wigan (Red Trim)

Reserve Official:
F. HUSSIN, Liverpool

MATCHBALL SPONSOR
NORTHWEST KITCHENS
*THE CATERING EQUIPMENT CENTRE
Showrooms: 276/278 Smithdown Road, Liverpool. Tel. 051 734 5500.
Liverpool's leading catering equipment suppliers.*

MASCOTS
♦ Today's Everton mascot is Michael Griffith, aged 9, of North Drive, Heswall. The Sheffield Wednesday mascot is Kevin Reaney, aged 10, of Hatfield House Lane, Sheffield. The Everton matchday mascot's kit is kindly supplied by Umbro and is retained as a souvenir of the occasion.

BALL BOYS
♦ Today's Ball Boys are provided by the Craven Minor League and Everton FC Supporters Club.

Caption: Clockwise from above: v Manchester United, 1990/91; v Sheffield Wednesday, 1992/93; v Sheffield Wednesday, 1998/99; v Chelsea, 1995/96

SQUAD CHECK

MATCH OFFICIALS

REFEREE
Mr ROBERT HART
Darlington
Began refereeing in the Auckland League in 1971 and appointed to the Football League list in 1986 after officiating as linesman at the Merseyside FA Cup Final. Refereed the Autoglass Trophy Final (Stoke v Stockport) in 1992 and the FA Vase Final (Bridlington v Tiverton) a year later.

Linesmen
Mr A J Hill
Blackpool
Mr E J Walsh
Rubery, Worcs

Reserve Official: Mr D Enright
Belfast

TODAY'S MASCOT
Today's mascot is ALEXANDER KELLY aged 9 of Stockport, Cheshire. All mascots are chosen from members of our Worldwide Fan Club. Today's Ball Boys are supplied by Bootle Netherton Junior Football League and members of The Worldwide Fan Club. Today's Toffee Girl is CHERYL DEMPSEY aged 12 of Liverpool.

MATCHBALL SPONSOR
HENDRE MYNACH
*TOURING CARAVAN & CAMPING PARK
Llanfair, Barmouth, Gwynedd, Wales.
Telephone: 01341 280262.
Camping & Caravaning near the mountains... near the beach.*

SAFETY MESSAGES
All announcements made on the Public Address system which affect the safety of spectators on the premises will be preceded by a two tone signal.

EVERTON		CHELSEA
Neville Southall	1	Dmitri Kharine
Earl Barrett	2	Steve Clarke
Andy Hinchcliffe	3	Scott Minto
David Unsworth	4	Ruud Gullit
Dave Watson (Capt.)	5	Erland Johnsen
Gary Ablett	6	Frank Sinclair
Graham Stuart	7	John Spencer
Paul Rideout	8	Mark Hughes
Duncan Ferguson	9	Mark Stein
Barry Horne	10	Gavin Peacock
Anders Limpar	11	Dennis Wise
Daniel Amokachi	12	Craig Burley
Jason Kearton	13	Kevin Hitchcock
John Ebbrell	14	Paul Furlong
Matthew Jackson	15	Andy Myers
Vinny Samways	16	David Rocastle
Andrei Kanchelskis	17	Nigel Spackman
Joe Parkinson	18	Eddie Newton
	19	Jakob Kjeldbjerg
Tony Grant	20	David Lee
Craig Short	21	Anthony Barness
Peter Holcroft	22	Mustafa Izzett
Alex Smith	23	Gareth Hall
Jonathan O'Connor	24	Dan Petrescu
Neil Moore	25	Terry Phelan
Graham Allen	26	Michael Duberry
Mark Grugel	27	Andy Dow
Chris Price	28	
Andy Weathers	29	
Ged Hennigan	30	
	31	
Mathew Woods	32	
James Speare	33	
Paul Holmes	34	

NEXT AT GOODISON PARK

Tuesday 23 January 1996	Tuesday 6 February 1996
EVERTON v NOTTINGHAM FOREST	EVERTON v STOKE CITY
PONTIN'S LEAGUE	PONTIN'S LEAGUE
Kick off 7.00pm	Kick off 7.00pm

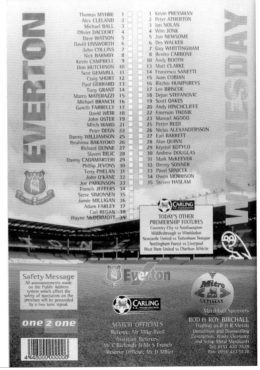

				Kevin PRESSMAN
Thomas MYHRE	1		1	Kevin PRESSMAN
Alex CLELAND	2		2	Peter ATHERTON
Michael BALL	3		3	Ian NOLAN
Olivier DACOURT	4		4	Wim JONK
Dave WATSON	5		5	Jon NEWSOME
David UNSWORTH	6		6	Des WALKER
John COLLINS	7		7	Guy WHITTINGHAM
Nick BARMBY	8		8	Benito CARBONE
Kevin CAMPBELL	9		10	Andy BOOTH
Don HUTCHISON	10		13	Matt CLARKE
Scot GEMMILL	11		14	Francesco SANETTI
Craig SHORT	12		15	Juan COBIAN
Paul GERRARD	13		16	Ritchie HUMPHREYS
Tony GRANT	14		17	Lee BRISCOE
Marco MATERAZZI	15		18	Dejan STEFANOVIC
Michael BRANCH	16		19	Scott OAKES
Gareth FARRELLY	17		20	Andy HINCHCLIFFE
David WEIR	18		22	Emerson THOME
John OSTER	19		23	Manuel AGOGO
Mitch WARD	21		25	Petter RUDI
Peter DEGN	22		26	Niclas ALEXANDERSSON
Danny WILLIAMSON	25		27	Earl BARRETT
Ibrahima BAKAYOKO	26		28	Alan QUINN
Richard DUNNE	27		29	Krystof KOTYLO
Slaven BILIC	28		30	Andrew DOUGLAS
Danny CADAMARTERI	29		31	Mark McKEEVER
Phillip JEVONS	30		32	Danny SONNER
Terry PHELAN	31		33	Pavel SRNICEK
John O'KANE	32		34	Owen MORRISON
Joe PARKINSON	33		35	Steven HASLAM
Franck JEFFERS	34			
Steve SIMONSEN	35			
Jamie MILLIGAN	36			
Adam FARLEY	37			
Carl REGAN	38			
Wayne McDERMOTT	39			

Safety Message
All announcements made on the Public Address system which affect the safety of spectators on the premises will be preceded by a two tone signal.

one 2 one

TODAY'S OTHER PREMIERSHIP FIXTURES
Coventry City vs Southampton
Middlesbrough vs Wimbledon
Newcastle United vs Tottenham Hotspur
Nottingham Forest vs Liverpool
West Ham United vs Charlton Athletic

MATCH OFFICIALS
Referee: Mr Mike Reed
Assistant Referees:
Mr C Richards & Mr S French
Reserve Official: Mr D Miller

Matchball Sponsors
ROD & ROY BIRCHALL
*Trading as R & R Metals
Demolition and Dismantling Contractors, Waste Carriers and Scrap Metal Merchants.
Tel: 0151 420 7529.
Fax: 0151 423 5139.*

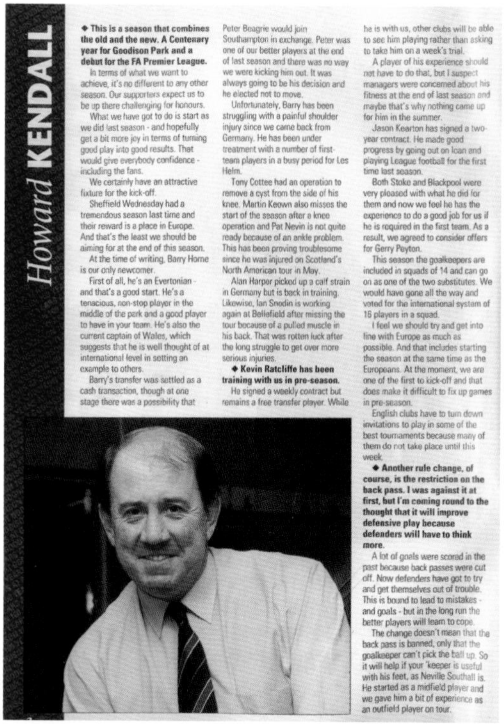

Howard KENDALL

◆ This is a season that combines the old and the new. A Centenary year for Goodison Park and a debut for the club in the FA Premier League.

In terms of what we want to achieve, it's no different to any other season. Our supporters expect us to be up there challenging for honours.

What we have got to do is start as we did last season - and hopefully get a bit more joy in terms of turning good play into good results. That would give everybody confidence - including the fans.

We certainly have an attractive fixture for the kick-off.

Sheffield Wednesday had a tremendous season last time and their reward is a place in Europe. And that's the least we should be aiming for at the end of this season.

At the time of writing, Barry Horne is our only newcomer.

First of all, he's an Evertonian - and that's a good start. He's a tenacious, non-stop player in the middle of the park and a good player to have in your team. He's also the current captain of Wales, which suggests that he is well thought of at international level in setting an example to others.

Barry's transfer was settled as a cash transaction, though at one stage there was a possibility that Peter Beagrie would join Southampton in exchange. Peter was one of our better players at the end of last season and there was no way we were kicking him out. It was always going to be his decision and he elected not to move.

Unfortunately, Barry has been struggling with a painful shoulder injury since we came back from Germany. He has been under treatment with a number of first-team players in a busy period for Les Helm.

Tony Cottee had an operation to remove a cyst from the side of his knee. Martin Keown also misses the start of the season after a knee operation and Pat Nevin is not quite ready because of an ankle problem. This has been proving troublesome since he was injured on Scotland's North American tour in May.

Alan Harper picked up a calf strain in Germany but is back in training. Likewise, Ian Snodin is working again at Bellefield after missing the tour because of a pulled muscle in his back. That was rotten luck after the long struggle to get over more serious injuries.

◆ Kevin Ratcliffe has been training with us in pre-season. He signed a weekly contract but remains a free transfer player. While he is with us, other clubs will be able to see him playing rather than asking to take him on a week's trial.

A player of his experience would not have to do that, but I suspect managers were concerned about his fitness at the end of last season and maybe that's why nothing came up for him in the summer.

Jason Kearton has signed a two-year contract. He made good progress by going out on loan and playing League football for the first time last season.

Both Stoke and Blackpool were very pleased with what he did for them and now we feel he has the experience to do a good job for us if he is required in the first team. As a result, we agreed to consider offers for Gerry Peyton.

This season the goalkeepers are included in squads of 14 and can go on as one of the two substitutes. We would have gone all the way and voted for the international system of 18 players in a squad.

I feel we should try and get into line with Europe as much as possible. And that includes starting the season at the same time as the Europeans. At the moment, we are one of the first to kick-off and that does make it difficult to fix up games in pre-season.

English clubs have to turn down invitations to play in some of the best tournaments because many of them do not take place until this week.

◆ Another rule change, of course, is the restriction on the back pass. I was against it at first, but I'm coming round to the thought that it will improve defensive play because defenders will have to think more.

A lot of goals were scored in the past because back passes were cut off. Now defenders have got to try and get themselves out of trouble. This is bound to lead to mistakes - and goals - but in the long run the better players will learn to cope.

The change doesn't mean that the back pass is banned, only that the goalkeeper can't pick the ball up. So it will help if your 'keeper is useful with his feet, as Neville Southall is. He started as a midfield player and we gave him a bit of experience as an outfield player on tour.

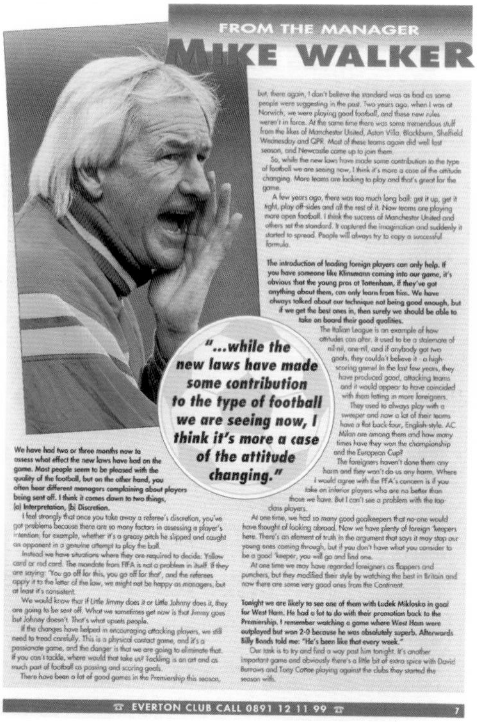

> *"...while the new laws have made some contribution to the type of football we are seeing now, I think it's more a case of the attitude changing."*

but, there again, I don't believe the standard was as bad as some people were suggesting in the past. Two years ago, when I was at Norwich, we were playing good football, and these new rules weren't in force. At the same time there was some tremendous stuff from the likes of Manchester United, Aston Villa, Blackburn, Sheffield Wednesday and QPR. Most of these teams again did well last season, and Newcastle came up to join them.

So, while the new laws have made some contribution to the type of football we are seeing now, I think it's more a case of the attitude changing. More teams are looking to play and that's great for the game.

A few years ago, there was too much long ball: get it up, get it tight, play off-sides and all the rest of it. Now teams are playing more open football. I think the success of Manchester United and others set the standard. It captured the imagination and suddenly it started to spread. People will always try to copy a successful formula.

The Italian League is an example of how attitudes can alter. It used to be a stalemate of nil-nil, one-nil, and if anybody got two goals, they couldn't believe it - a high-scoring game! In the last few years, they have produced good, attacking teams and it would appear to have coincided with them letting in more foreigners.

They used to always play with a sweeper and now a lot of their teams have a flat back-four, English-style. AC Milan are among them and how many times have they won the championship and the European Cup?

The foreigners haven't done them any harm and they won't do us any harm. Where I would agree with the FFA's concern is if you take an inferior players who are no better than those we have, but I can't see a problem with the top class players.

At one time, we had so many good goalkeepers that no-one would have thought of looking abroad. Now we have plenty of foreign 'keepers here. There's an element of truth in the argument that says it may stop our young ones coming through, but if you don't have what you consider to be a good 'keeper, you will go and find one.

At one time we may have regarded foreigners as floppers and poachers, but they earned their style by watching the best in Britain and now there are some very good ones from the Continent.

Tonight we are likely to see one of them with Ludek Miklosko in goal for West Ham. He had a lot to do with their promotion back to the Premiership. I remember watching a game where West Ham were outplayed but won 2-0 because he was absolutely superb. Afterwards Billy Bonds told me: "He's been like that every week."

Our task is to try and find a way past him tonight. It's another important game and obviously there's a little bit of extra spice with David Burrows and Tony Cottee playing against the clubs they started the season with.

We have had two or three months now to assess what effect the new laws have had on the game. Most people seem to be pleased with the quality of the football, but on the other hand, you often hear different managers complaining about players being sent off. I think it comes down to two things.

(a) Interpretation, (b) Discretion.

I feel strongly that once you take away a referee's discretion, you've got problems because there are so many factors in assessing a player's intention, for example, whether it's a greasy pitch he slipped and caught an opponent in a genuine attempt to play the ball.

Instead we have situations where they are required to decide. Yellow card or red card. The mandate from FIFA is not a problem in itself. If they are saying: 'You go off for this', you go off for that', and the referees apply it to the letter of the law, we might not be happy as managers, but at least it's consistent.

We would know that if Little Jimmy does it or Little Johnny does it, they are going to be sent off. What we sometimes get now is that Jimmy goes but Johnny doesn't. That's what upsets people.

If the changes have helped in encouraging attacking players, we still need to tread carefully. This is a physical contact game, and it's a passionate game, and the danger is that we are going to eliminate that. If you can tackle, where would that take us? Tackling is an art and as much part of football as passing and scoring goals.

There have been a lot of good games in the Premiership this season.

Some examples of how the manager's programme notes looked in the 1990s including (clockwise, from above): v Sheffield Wednesday, 1992/93 - the opening day of Premier League action; v West Ham United, 1994/95 - Mike Walker's final notes; v Aston Villa, 1995/96 - the final match of the campaign

JOE ROYLE TALKING

From the Top

■ One of the most important factors has been our away form and it was enjoyable to close that part of our programme in style with five goals for the thousands of Evertonians who made the journey to Hillsborough.

Our away support has been tremendous throughout the season and the players couldn't fail to respond to a wonderful turn-out in Sheffield. We got off to a flyer with the early goal from Daniel Amokachi and then we were treated to a hat-trick by Andrei Kanchelskis. His 16 goals have come from 31 League appearances - a remarkable return for a winger and more in keeping with the ratio expected of a top striker.

No-one would have guessed that we were without so many senior players at Hillsborough because the whole side played well and dominated the game from start to finish.

We gave Michael Branch a full debut and again he did very well, but we could see that he was tired at half-time and that was the only reason for taking him off. It's been a long season for such a young player and earlier that week he had played for the England Youth team against Scotland.

In that respect it was a good time for our young players. Ian O'Connor won his first Under-21 cap and by all accounts he made a good contribution in the heart that he was on the field. O'Connor and Branch have already shown that they can handle Premiership football, and we have Graham Allen and young John Hills coming along behind them. The club is in good shape at all levels and while I would like to make one or possibly two additions in the summer, I feel the squad we have is ready to challenge for honours. Basically we have had one bad spell, and if we had got anything out of that, we wouldn't be that far away now.

Maybe our home form let us down a little bit earlier in the season, but we were struggling with injuries when Arsenal, Manchester United and Newcastle won here. Otherwise the results at Goodison have been quite reasonable and now want to sign off with a good performance today.

I think we would all settle for a repeat of the first-half in the derby match. I can't praise the team enough for the way they overcame our problems that night. We had three players out there after pain-killing injections, and yet we swarmed all over one of the strongest teams in the country.

We scored one goal and the only disappointment was that we hadn't put Liverpool out of sight by the interval. Perhaps the injuries began to tell on us in the second half and we did come under pressure. In the end a draw was probably the fairest result.

That game reflected our season - a case of what might been. But it also reflected how well we can play. When it comes to derby games, I believe the whole attitude of this club has changed in the last couple of years. There is no fear whatsoever about taking on our neighbours.

As you know, the Liverpool match turned out to be Duncan's last appearance of the season. We wanted him to play in the last two games, and obviously Scotland wanted him for the European Championship, but ultimately the priority had to be the lad's own health.

After speaking with Duncan, the specialist and the Scotland coach, Craig Brown, we all agreed that he needed complete rest to get himself right for Everton next season.

■ We appreciate the support you have given us and let's hope that you have something to cheer this afternoon. Our opponents, Aston Villa, have had an excellent season and, in one way, I am a little envious of them because they started from a similar position to ourselves - and they have won something. It's only a year ago that Brian Little and myself were among the managers sweating on results at the other end of the table. I am sure that Brian would join me when I say that my heart goes out to those who are playing for survival today.

It's a measure of our improvement this season that a win today would secure our best points total for eight years and probably put us in our highest position since the club finished sixth in 1990.

■ The new administration at Goodison Park had been in place for two seasons, each of which has been memorable in its own way. Last year, after the long struggle to preserve our place in the Premier League, there was the joy of winning at Wembley. This season I believe the greatest accolade should go to our supporters.

The average attendance is the fifth highest in the country - a considerable benchmark in a season when we have not been in contention for major honours - but perhaps the greater significance is in comparing the present figure with past performances at Everton (as outlined in the graph below).

Our support is at its highest level for 17 years and, therefore, in excess of the club's following during the hugely successful seasons of the mid-1980s. It's extremely gratifying to have made such progress and now we are in a position to build from strong foundations. I thank you all for your support so far and look forward to its continuation in the years to come. Together we can fulfil all our ambitions.

Peter Johnson
Chairman, Everton FC

CHAIRMAN'S STATEMENT

GOODISON PARK   ATTENDANCES 1976-96

It can be a cruel world down there. Imagine how Ron Atkinson, Alan Ball and Dave Merrington must have felt last week-end when their teams got brilliant results away from home - and then came off the field to find out what the others had done.

If there was one crumb of comfort for them, it was that our result dragged Sheffield Wednesday into the equation. They still need a point to be definitely safe and I know they are very worried to be caught up in that situation.

As for ourselves, we want to finish as high as possible and send all Evertonians into the summer in good spirits for next season.

JOE ROYLE

"ARCHIE KNOX AND MYSELF ARE JUST AS THRILLED AS EVERY EVERTONIAN ABOUT THE NEW SEASON"

The 1990s proved to be the most disruptive period in the club's history, with the manager's office occupied by no fewer than five 'permanent' bosses.

Colin Harvey began the decade in charge, before paying for a miserable start to 1990/91. Howard Kendall was prised from Manchester City for a second spell, with his tenure marred by inconsistency and financial woes.

Mike Walker was next in, a success at Norwich City but who quickly found the step up a bridge too far. The memorable 3-2 comeback victory over Wimbledon on the final day of the 1993/94 season secured survival but he didn't last much longer.

A first win of 1994/95 was finally achieved in November – and weeks later Walker was gone, replaced by Joe Royle. The turnaround proved swift – with survival secured and an unlikely FA Cup triumph. A decade-best sixth place was earned in 1995/96, but the following term he was gone, caretaker player/boss Dave Watson helping secure top-flight status. After a third spell for Kendall, Walter Smith came in for the 1998/99 season.

AN OFFICIAL STATEMENT

"Everton Football Club announce that Colin Harvey, their manager, has left the club.

Mr Philip Carter, the club chairman, thanked Colin Harvey for his contribution over 14 years but stated that the team's recent performance was quite unacceptable.

The position of manager will be advertised and an appointment made as soon as possible.

In the meantime, Jimmy Gabriel, Everton's first-team coach, will assume responsibility for all playing activities throughout the club."

2

EVERTON

A club statement from the QPR programme, 1990/91, as Jimmy Gabriel was handed the caretaker role

The Management

Walter Smith and Archie Knox telling it straight....

❶ For two teams occupying the security of the mid-table comfort zone, this afternoon's end of season clash has an added edge...

Middlesbrough are just one point behind us in the Premiership table and crave that top half of the table finish as much as we do. Both of us know that a victory this afternoon can confirm a top ten placing - and after all our hard work and effort this season it would be a grave disappointment if we let that slip in the final match.

Overall you can say we have made progress this season.

When you look back to this time last year, and take into consideration what we had to try and achieve in a financial sense just to keep the club going, we have enjoyed a satisfactory campaign.

What we must ensure now is that our current position becomes a base from which we can build again next season. That will be a difficult task because the margin for error is so slight.

We had amassed 50 points before this afternoon's match and have been comfortably placed for most of the season.

Last season we finished with 43 - or two wins and a draw less - so you can see that the margin between what is perceived as a relatively good season and one threatened by relegation is very narrow.

Having said that, we must give praise to the players here for what they have done for us this season.

We have not had a big squad of players to play with, but we have shown a commitment and a resolve.

While we may not have the most talented pool of players in the division, I don't think anyone can say we are short of the values I have just mentioned.

One of the players who typifies that kind of attitude is Mark Pembridge, which is why I was disappointed in the reaction to his substitution against Arsenal in our last home match.

Whatever shortcomings people perceive Mark as having, his attitude and approach has been exemplary ever since he came here.

We now have a squad of players in place who want to play for Everton Football Club and that is a quality which should be applauded, not denigrated.

That application and work-rate has to be the basis of further progress, but we have to show an improvement in quality in all areas of the club.

Clearly an improvement in quality in certain areas of the pitch is important - but that has to be matched by improvements off it.

There has to be dramatic improvements to Goodison Park if we intend to stay here and the club's training facilities have to be upgraded.

If the club is going to go forward we can't just apply ourselves to one of those areas, we must try and look at the lot. That is the only way to attract the better quality players to Everton Football Club.

The Worthington Cup was a big disappointment, but I have explained our strategy in that competition several times already.

I felt we didn't have a big enough squad to to sustain a long run in that competition and I was very aware that the most important thing at that time was to secure our place in the Premiership.

Everything had to be geared to that end and I felt it was necessary to change the team we fielded in the Worthington Cup matches.

I would hope that if we can add to our squad in the summer that will not be the case next season and we can launch sustainable assaults on all three domestic competitions.

In the Premiership we lifted ourselves from a team which was flirting uncomfortably around the relegation zone to a mid-table team - which is obviously an improvement.

Mark Pembridge

❷ We have to be reasonably satisfied with the progress we have made throughout the course of this season. If we can maintain the kind of form and application we have shown at Goodison Park for the most part of the campaign, we can celebrate a solid top ten place by six o'clock tonight.

There's no doubt that things may have looked even rosier if we hadn't suffered the loss of impetus the injuries to Kevin Campbell and Francis Jeffers gave us at a crucial stage of the season.

The reaction of the other players in the squad to those blows, however, was excellent.

I think there have only been a couple of occasions this season where our performance level here at Goodison Park has been under-par.

Overall the players have responded superbly, and that was underlined once again at Leeds United on Monday night.

Clearly it is going to be difficult to make that sort of progress immediately.

I may take a little longer than everyone would want, but because of the problems we have had here financially in recent years that's the way it has to be.

Whatever the time scale, though, we must make Everton Football Club an attractive place to come to.

Finally, I would like to thank our supporters once again for their continued and commendable support. During difficult periods of the campaign the one constant which has shone through has been the quality and the consistency of our support and that is hugely appreciated by everyone here at the club.

Hopefully we can reward you with a fitting result and performance this afternoon and the top ten finish which we feel would mark reasonable progress this season.

Have an enjoyable summer - and see you all back here next season.

Walter Smith OBE

❸ Our home record has been one of the foundations of our progress this season and it would be nice to carry that through until the final whistle tonight...

We can now add Leeds to the names Chelsea and Liverpool, as teams who have been in the hunt for Champions League football all season, and who we have remained unbeaten by at home and away.

The result at Leeds was achieved in the most testing of circumstances, but I will have to refrain from commenting on the performance of referee Andy D'Urso for fear of receiving a letter from the FA.

We overcame those problems, however, and the players showed that they have the appetite and the resolve to see the season right through to the finish.

That is the least that excellent supporters deserve and we desperately want to bow out on a high this afternoon.

Middlesbrough have enjoyed a good run of form recently and it should make for an entertaining tussle.

Our home record has been one of our progress this season, however, and it would be nice to carry that through until the final whistle tonight.

Archie Knox

v Middlesbrough, 1999/2000, Walter Smith considers a campaign of improvement

CAPTAIN'S COMMENT

Skipper Dave Watson spoke for all the players when he welcomed Joe Royle back to Goodison Park. "It was a good thing that the club were able to announce a replacement for Mike Walker as quickly as they did," said Dave.

"When Howard Kendall left we were a few weeks without a manager and it inevitably led to a lot of speculation. I think that got to the players in the end.

"It is also a good thing that not only have we appointed a good manager but one who knows the ins and outs of the club.

"As an ex-Everton player Joe Royle has a feeling for the club, he has been through it all and understands the passion of the fans.

"He will be aware of the tremendous gates we have had this season and will know our supporters are just waiting for success. He appreciates the attendances at Goodison and I feel he will get things going here."

Dave is an experienced professional who knows all about the reactions a new manager expects from players. He told us, "We all start off with a clean slate. Every player has to show the manager what he can do and convince him he wants to be part of what the new boss has in mind for the club."

Dave and our new manager are not strangers as they were team mates together for a short time at Norwich. Says Dave, "I remember coming to Goodison with Norwich near the end of the 1980-81 season and winning 2-0 with goals by Joe Royle and Justin Fashanu.

"Joe was a great character with a good influence in the dressing room and he has since had 12 years experience as a manager so I am sure he is the right man for the job. With some decent results behind us there should be some confidence in the side and while a derby game is not the easiest of starts there is nothing like starting at the top."

Dave Watson, 1994 & 1996

Dave took over captaincy duties from Kevin Ratcliffe early in the decade, although like his predecessor, programme contributions were few and far between.

However, Joe Royle's appointment encouraged the skipper to speak, with the speed of the decision welcomed and a challenge to the new man, that the supporters 'are just waiting for success' – something he duly delivered.

The opening game of the 1996/97 season found English football in positive mood after the success of Euro '96 – and the club aiming to build on their Premier League improvement the previous season.

'Everyone is quietly confident about our chances of winning a trophy this term.'

It was also Dave's testimonial campaign, and what better way to begin it than by facing Everton 'scourge' Les Ferdinand, partnering Newcastle United's new £15m striker, Alan Shearer.

Dave Watson, August 1998

With the arrival of Walter Smith, Dave was in positive mood ahead of the opening game against Aston Villa.

Money had been spent on a host of exotic names including Marco Materazzi, one of around 25 or so new centre-halves Dave had apparently seen arrive at Goodison since joining the club in 1986.

The skipper, newly-appointed as first-team coach, was also targeting 500 appearances for the club, insisting he was as fit as ever, though he admitted:

'The hardest thing is the wear and tear on the knee joints as you get older.'

It was also to be Dave's final regular column, his coaching responsibilities meaning he was set to pass the baton to Craig Short for no other apparent reason than it would fit in with the editor's choice of column title for the occasional stand-in skipper: 'Short Cuts'.

This will be the 13th season I've started at Everton – and obviously I'm not superstitious, because I'm looking forward to it every bit as much as every other campaign I've been involved in. The arrival of the new boss and Archie Knox, and the quality of players they have brought in, has given everyone around the place a buzz.

Everyone is lifted when new players arrive – and it also gives players already here an extra incentive that if they don't do the business, they may not be involved in the first team. I'm no different to anyone else in that respect.

The boss has gone out and bought a new centre-half for £2.5m – and Marco Materazzi has done really well in our pre-season games. But I just see it as a challenge for me to try and stay in the side.

During my time at Norwich and Everton, probably 25 centre-halves have been bought and I've managed to hold my own against most of them. This is no different, and I'll be doing everything to convince the boss I'm still worth a starting place.

It's been pointed out to me by one of the lads in the press that I'm getting pretty close to 500 appearances for Everton. To be honest players rarely keep count of things like that and I had no idea how close I was – or how significant the 500 mark is.

Apparently only Neville Southall and Brian Labone have topped that figure, and I would feel immensely proud to be bracketed with players of that ilk.

I certainly feel fit enough to keep going for a few more years yet, although I suppose Neville's 750 is just a bit beyond me now! It's not that hard to stay physically fit. The hardest thing is the wear and tear on the knee joints as you get older.

The running and the general fitness is no problem, I've done everything all the other lads have done in training and I've been up there in the front group. I've never been sharp! But I feel as fit now as I did 10 years ago.

It's been great to get the extra responsibility of being made first team coach. Last year I was helping Viv Busby out with the reserves. But now I've been given the title of first team coach, which means that when I'm not training myself I supervise other groups in training sessions.

The arrival of the new boss and Archie has certainly made a difference around the training ground. For a start the accents are different!

But it's not fair to compare the ways different managers work. The lads here have certainly responded positively to Walter and Archie's methods.

There's nothing in football you can dramatically change anyway. But the arrival of a new manager puts everyone on their toes. He is here to have a look at people and see what their strengths and weaknesses are. It isn't just the lads whose spirits have picked up.

My mates who are Evertonians are looking forward to the new season with a bit more optimism now, after the signings we've made. We're not going to say that we will change straight up the table now, but I'd like to think we'll be able to consolidate, create a solid base and keep building on that for the following season.

I hope to still be pulling on a Royal Blue jersey by then, but you'll be delighted to know I won't be writing this column any more.

I've enjoyed doing it, but with my extra responsibilities as coach now, I've decided to let one of the other lads have a go this season.

From the Tottenham game, Craig Short will become the regular matchday columnist.

I've given him a few tips – like making sure I always get a good mention every now and then.

I hope you enjoy this afternoon's match and we can give you the result today – and the performances throughout the season – your magnificent support deserves.

Dave Watson

EVERTON WORLDWIDE WEBSITE... HIT THE NET: HTTP://WWW.EVERTONFC.COM

We are almost at the end of what we could describe as a season of steady progress. I say almost, because this afternoon's game still has a huge bearing on how our campaign could be perceived. Victory, and a guaranteed top 10 finish, would constitute a meaningful improvement on last season.

Anything less, however, could see us slip down to 14th and take the gloss off what we have worked hard to achieve in the last nine months.

Middlesbrough will come here with exactly the same intentions - so this afternoon's match should contain a little more edge than your average end of season affair. I just hope that whoever is in charge this afternoon referees the match with a little more sensitivity than Andy D'Urso managed at Leeds on Monday.

I rarely, if ever, comment on referees - but even the most diplomatic observer would have to describe his performance as very poor.

It could have proved extremely costly to us, but fortunately we managed to hold out with nine men for a point we deserved. That has set us up with the possibility of finishing the season on a high. Ever since we came from behind on the opening day of the campaign to hold the treble winners Manchester United to a draw, we have been optimistic about our season.

That gave us a lot of confidence to go on and maintain the improvement we have shown. The low point of the season was undoubtedly the FA Cup exit to Aston Villa, but we have to take heart from the consistency of our performances in the Premiership and hope we can improve on that again next season.

With a bit of luck the manager will be given some money to spend in the summer to improve the squad and we can enjoy an even better campaign again.

Having said that, there have still been some outstanding displays this term - and I don't think you can look further than the central defensive partnership of Richard Gough and David Weir for Player of the Season candidates.

Gough came in last summer at the age of 37 and probably raised a few eyebrows. People who had seen him play weren't surprised by his acquisition, however, and our fans were soon won over by his performances.

Alongside him David Weir showed that even though he was signed for a very small fee, he looks every inch a big money player with a string of consistently classy displays.

It would be desperately hard to choose between either of them on last season's performances, but if pushed, I'd probably have to go for Goughie... just.

I'm delighted he has agreed to play on here next season - and with

Middlesbrough certainly won't make things easy for us - but we know we are capable of clinching a top ten place we feel we have earned.

a few more quality acquisitions this summer we will be hoping to build on what has already been achieved.

First, however, we have to ensure we end this current campaign on a high. Middlesbrough certainly won't make things easy for us - but we know we are capable of clinching a top ten place we feel we have earned.

one2one *with* John Collins

John Collins, 2000

Reflecting on the progress of 1999/2000 in his 'one2one' column, the midfielder was hopeful of a top-10 finish with victory over Middlesbrough on the final day.

Citing the highs and lows of the season - added consistency in the league, FA Cup disappointment against Aston Villa - Collins was also fuming over referee Andy D'Urso's performance in the draw at Leeds, although 'I rarely, if ever, comment on referees'.

Collins was delighted with the news that veteran Richard Gough - the skipper's Player of the Season - was set to sign on for another season, and 'with a few more quality acquisitions this summer we will be hoping to build on what has already been achieved.'

"I HAVE BEEN OVERWHELMED BY THE FANTASTIC SUPPORT FROM EVERTON FANS"

The 1990s signalled a shift in player interview style, with the previous family feel making way for more standard 'thought' pieces on the team's current plight, and any topical issues involving said player.

There were fewer 'at home' pieces, while the influx of overseas talent to the game became a rich seam of material in the early 90s, with early 'pioneers' Jason Kearton, Ray Atteveld and Robert Warzycha utilised to highlight the cultural shift in the sport, and the difficulties faced by players unfamiliar with the English game.

Duncan Ferguson remains one of the most popular players to turn out for the club, and his spell behind bars in 1995 due to an on-field incident while playing for Rangers was noted in the programme – with Duncan himself including a personal message to the fans to thank them for their support.

As the decade progressed there were 'In Profile' features, youth players given space to reflect on their progression, while new signings were ever-present material for the programme editor – with Ibrahima Bakayoko's signing in 1998 good news for the headline writers...

"...being so supportive. To be honest, I really didn't realise just how much I would miss Everton and the fans."

Duncan's Message

■ **Duncan Ferguson is due to be released from Barlinnie Prison very shortly, following his three month jail sentence.**

The club's feelings about the decision to jail two of the most popular players have been well documented in the press.

Our own supporters have also made their own feelings very well known.

Duncan, himself, has not wanted any sort of media profile - but felt that he had to express his thanks to the Evertonians who have stood by him during his awful experience.

In the following letter to all Everton supporters, he tells how their support has helped - and how he hopes to see them all soon.

❝ I have been overwhelmed by the fantastic support I have received from Everton fans everywhere.

I can tell you that it has helped to keep my spirits up through this most difficult period in my life. The amount of mail I have received and continue to receive is enormous. I spend a tremendous amount of time reading your letters.

Obviously I am limited on the number of replies I can send out at the moment. But my family have been collecting the letters and taking them away for safe-keeping.

I'm going to reply personally to every supporter who has taken the time and trouble to write to me. Those messages have been coming in by the sackful and it is going to be a major job dealing with them. But the office girls at Goodison will help me and it is something I want to do.

I feel it is very important to tell people just how much those messages have helped to lift my spirits.

I would also like to thank the club for being so supportive. To be honest, I really didn't realise just how much I would miss Everton and the fans. I have been made to feel very much at home on Merseyside since I moved down from Scotland.

Many friends have been wanting to show their support in a personal way by coming to Barlinnie.

But in truth, it's really not the kind of place that I want to see people. For the time being, I'm just happy to receive those letters which keep me in touch

with Merseyside. I was pleased to see my manager Joe Royle, club Chairman Peter Johnson and Director Clifford Finch recently.

They were able to pass on some messages from my team-mates as well as bring me up to date with everything that is happening at the club. In my own way, I have been trying to keep in touch. I've got a radio and I wait anxiously to hear our results.

I was actually able to tune into the Feyenoord game in Holland. The lads played well and I was disappointed for them and our travelling supporters that we didn't get the result we deserved. I would have been given anything to have been out there helping the lads.

I didn't realise just how much I would miss football. Obviously, I have no special privileges up here, but I am trying to keep as fit as I possibly can under the circumstances. I am able to exercise for up to an hour a day and I put as much into it as is possible.

I have been keen to express my thoughts to the thousands of people on Merseyside and elsewhere in the country who have been urging me to keep my head up. I can assure you I am doing just that. I owe it to the Evertonians who are right behind me.

Can I once again thank you all for your continued support. I can't wait to pull on that blue shirt again and repay everybody the only way I know how... on the football field. ❞

Duncan Ferguson arriving at Glasgow Sheriff Court.

◆ **PETER BEARDSLEY** had to take a slightly blinkered view of the publicity surrounding his second big-money transfer in four years. Others jazzed up the blue-and-red rivalry, but for him, it was a career decision.

He says: "I wasn't going to be part of the future at Liverpool and I didn't even think that the move was across the park. That didn't enter into it.

"I've joined a great club; there's no doubt about that. I was very surprised when Everton came in for me but obviously delighted."

One of the most gifted forwards of his generation, the 30-year-old Geordie is an entertaining and highly-productive player in the mould of past Everton greats such as Alex Young.

He scored 129 League goals in 382 appearances for his first three English clubs, Carlisle, Newcastle and Liverpool, and he would love to start his Everton career as he opened his last season at Anfield.

Eleven goals in 12 appearances - including two at Goodison Park in the derby match in September - put him in the top three in the First Division scoring list.

"It was absolutely perfect and hopefully it will be the same this time," he says. "Unfortunately, I got an injury which kept me out for 10 or 12 games and then, because of the way the team was going, it

was hard to get back in. And when I did get in, we started to struggle."

His last two goals for the Reds were scored at Goodison in that 4-4 thriller in February. Like everyone in the 37,000 crowd that night, he will never forget "the greatest-ever FA Cup-tie."

"It was a great occasion to be part of," he recalled. "I hadn't been in the starting team since December and it was a great game, for both sets of fans. But I'm sure there will be other great games to come."

After starting his career with Carlisle and then Vancouver Whitecaps, Peter had a whiff of Manchester United in a season on trial at Old Trafford. Then he fulfilled a boyhood dream by playing for his local club, Newcastle United, in front of the passionate Geordie fans.

Now he joins only a handful of players who have worn theblue and red shirts on Merseyside. "I've been lucky," he says. "I've played for a lot of big clubs. You can never forget these days. This is a new chapter in my life and hopefully it's going to be as good as those in the past.

"The fact that I haven't had to move my home is ideal, but if Everton had been down south - and I know that's hypothetical - I would still have gone. It's not as if I have taken the easy way out because it's across the park. I stayed on Merseyside because I got the chance to join a great club."

◆ **Exactly 11 years after being a front-cover personality in the Everton programme, MARK WARD is at last achieving his ambition to play First Division football for the club he supported as a schoolboy.**

"I'll be so proud to run out there in an Everton shirt at Goodison Park," he says. "My dad was an Evertonian and I was a ball boy. It hurt to be released as a lad but you've got to put these things behind you. It probably made me a better player."

It was in August 1980 that Mark - together with Steve McMahon - was pictured on the matchday magazine cover with other members of the young Everton side which won the Groningen International Youth Tournament.

But at the end of the next season, he was brokenhearted when he was told he would not be retained. That was one of Gordon Lee's last decisions because he left the club later the same day.

EVERTON

4

Peter Beardsley talks about his move from Liverpool to Everton, v Arsenal, 1991/92

■ David Unsworth capped his first full season as an Everton first team player in style - a full England cap, an FA Cup winner's medal, and then a new three year contract at Goodison Park.

But this year David's targets are more down to earth. "I just want to stay in the first team and help us win more trophies," he said.

The advances last season of a player nicknamed "Rhino" added up to a spectacular rise for a youngster who was introduced to the side during the tension-riddled battle against relegation in 1993-94, and who became a permanent fixture until being left out at Nottingham Forest this season with a suspension looming.

It was a meteoric rise, but one which didn't exactly amaze manager Joe Royle.

"David is a very talented footballer," he said "but he had crammed a huge amount into one year and just possibly needed a little rest earlier in the season.

"A couple of injuries kept him out then, but since he has come back he has been as good as ever in two different positions."

After making his name in Mike Walker's side as a speedy and powerful central defender, a position in which he won his England cap, David has played left back in recent months.

It's a position he has looked more and more comfortable in, and at Wimbledon on New Year's Day David was overlapping regularly with Graham Stuart - and provided the cross from which Duncan Ferguson made it 3-0.

With competition for first team places intense, adding to the England cap he won against Japan in May is not the first priority in David's mind, but given the opportunity he'd jump at it.

"It was a great experience and to be honest I didn't expect to get a chance so soon," he said.

"All I wanted to do was play for the Under-21s last year; you set yourself little targets in the back of your mind and that was one.

"I didn't really think about the England situation because it seemed so far off on the horizon. I had a couple of weeks training with them and then came the Umbro Cup match against Japan which capped a fantastic last two or three months of the season for me on a personal basis.

"It was a bit weird walking out down the tunnel. I think I was more nervous for my England debut than against Manchester United in the Cup, even though there were more people at the Cup Final.

"I had varied feelings really. I was very proud to play for my country, but you couldn't really take it all in like the Cup Final because there were only 20,000 people there.

"Mind you I'd play in front of nobody if it meant another cap!

"If the chance comes along again I want to take it. I'm no different to any other player and I'd love to win more caps, especially with the European Championships looming.

"But my main concern is helping Everton and I would do anything for this club.

"When I signed my new contract in the summer the negotiations lasted about 30 seconds. It was something I wanted to get over and done with so I could look to the future.

"I am Everton through and through and have no ambitions to go anywhere else. And I wouldn't have signed if I didn't think we could win more trophies!"

As well as chasing silverware, David is also chasing a few more goals - following four successful penalty kicks since he took over the penalty-takers mantle against Leeds last season.

"I enjoy taking them and, touch wood, would like to carry on for a while," he said.

"My main concern is helping Everton and I would do anything for this club!"

DAVID UNSWORTH
In Profile

TUNE INTO RADIO EVERTON 1602 AM 19 page

Above: David Unsworth, 1995/96, First season reflections, his England debut and commitment to the cause
Right: Michael Branch, 1993/94 – alongside future Premier League players Michael Ball and 'Joe' Barton...

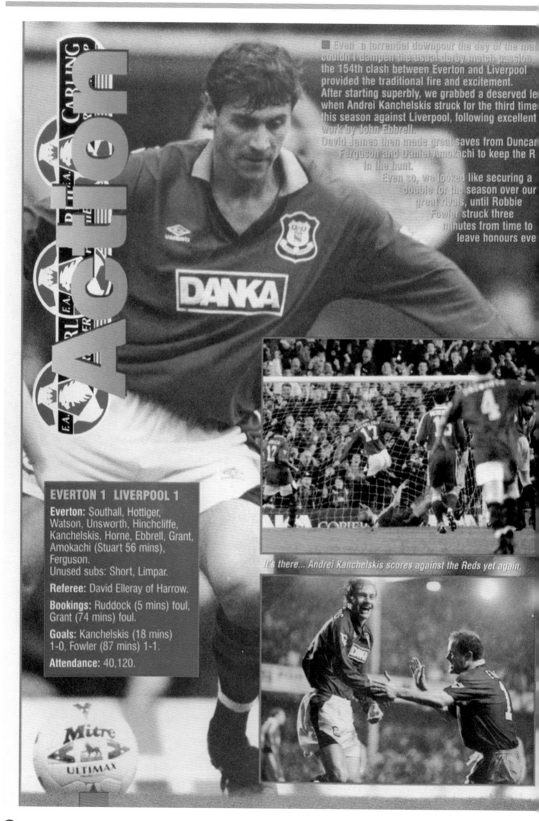

CARLING ACTION

Even a torrential downpour the day of the match couldn't dampen the usual derby match passion, the 154th clash between Everton and Liverpool provided the traditional fire and excitement.
After starting superbly, we grabbed a deserved lead when Andrei Kanchelskis struck for the third time this season against Liverpool, following excellent work by John Ebbrell.
David James then made great saves from Duncan Ferguson and Daniel Amokachi to keep the Reds in the hunt.
Even so, we looked like securing a double for the season over our great rivals, until Robbie Fowler struck three minutes from time to leave honours even.

EVERTON 1 LIVERPOOL 1

Everton: Southall, Hottiger, Watson, Unsworth, Hinchcliffe, Kanchelskis, Horne, Ebbrell, Grant, Amokachi (Stuart 56 mins), Ferguson.
Unused subs: Short, Limpar.

Referee: David Elleray of Harrow.

Bookings: Ruddock (5 mins) foul, Grant (74 mins) foul.

Goals: Kanchelskis (18 mins) 1-0, Fowler (87 mins) 1-1.

Attendance: 40,120.

It's there... Andrei Kanchelskis scores against the Reds yet again.

■ At Hillsborough last Saturday Andrei Kanchelskis celebrated a sweet 16 Premiership strikes - with his first Everton hat-trick.
Our Russian winger was unstoppable, having another 'goal' disallowed and striking the base of the post.
With first half strikes from Daniel Amokachi and John Ebbrell, we romped to our best away win since the last day of the 1992-93 season.

New boy Michael Branch takes on Des Walker.

SHEFFIELD W 2 EVERTON 5

Everton: Southall, Hottiger, Watson, Short, Unsworth, Ebbrell, Grant, Stuart, Kanchelskis, Amokachi, Branch (Rideout 45).
Unused subs: O'Connor, Speare.

Referee: Mike Reed of Birmingham.

Bookings: Sheridan (29 mins) foul, Stuart (31) foul, Watson (36) foul, Short (78) foul, Blinker (81) handball.

Goals: Amokachi (4 mins) 0-1, Hirst (8) 1-1, Ebbrell (9) 1-2, Kanchelskis (22) 1-3, Kanchelskis (55) 1-4, Degryse (64) 2-4, Kanchelskis (66) 2-5.

Attendance: 32,724.

1990-95

A varied selection from the first part of the decade included the standard 'Umbro and Everton' full page – models unknown; the Liverpool Echo's Everton coverage 'six nights a week' was proclaimed as 'the best'; Dave Watson was given the opportunity to awkwardly pose with a Northway Private Hire cab at Bellefield

UMBRO and EVERTON ...the perfect match.

umbro

Sheer Magic

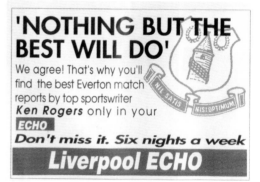

'NOTHING BUT THE BEST WILL DO'
We agree! That's why you'll find the best Everton match reports by top sportswriter **Ken Rogers** only in your ECHO
Don't miss it. Six nights a week
Liverpool ECHO

NORTHWAY PRIVATE HIRE 520 0000

NORTHWAY PRIVATE HIRE ONLY 520 0000

Probably the cheapest taxis in your area

SEE EVERTON FOR FREE

By becoming an Everton FC Agent and selling our Lottery tickets to relatives, friends, neighbours and workmates you could see Everton at Goodison Park for FREE.

◆ For full details phone GOODISON PARK PROMOTIONS on 051 525 4891.

REGISTRATION NUMBER FOR SALE

TOFIIY

The Patrick Collection

SENSIBLE OFFERS ONLY TO 0926-421872

NORMEAT
Danish Cooked Meats

Fresh from the farms of Denmark

◆◆◆◆
TULIP INTERNATIONAL

Proud Sponsors of today's game

NEC. At home in the home of soccer science.

As world leaders in computers and communications NEC are proud to sponsor Everton in their Centenary season at Goodison.

PERSONAL COMPUTERS · PRINTERS · MONITORS · CELLULAR PHONES · FACSIMILE · PAGERS

EVERTON

C&C

NEC

NEC WOULD LIKE TO CONGRATULATE EVERTON F.C. ON THE OPENING OF THE NEW PARK END STAND

Our computers and communications can help everyone reach their goals.

Personal Computers • Printers • Monitors • Cellular Phones • Facsimiles • Pagers

C&C
for Human Potential

EVERTON

NEC

The NEC logo and C&C logo are registered trademarks of NEC Corporation.

EVERTON PROMOTIONS

OFFICIAL
Everton Chocolate & Lemonade

AVAILABLE AT OUTLETS THROUGHOUT THE STADIUM AND THE EVERTON MEGASTORE

GOODISON PARK
ENTERTAINMENT COMPLEX

● LUNCHES ● CONFERENCES ● PARTIES
● SPECIAL OCCASIONS ● TRAINING COURSES
● SPORTSMAN'S DINNERS ● WEDDINGS

FOR DETAILS RING
0151 330 2499

VIDEO SUBSCRIPTIONS

DANKA

EVERTONIAN

this is
Everton
OFFICIAL VIDEO MAGAZINE

BLUE & WHITE STRIKES!

PRICED £7.99

OUT NOW!

ISSUE 2 OF THE ONLY OFFICIAL EVERTON VIDEO MAGAZINE

DANKA

Volume 2 • Issue 6
In your shops
NOW!

Clockwise from top left: 1990/91 – 'See Everton For Free, fancy a number plate? Normeat, proud match sponsors; 1992/93, standard NEC P3; 1995/96, Everton promotions – fans with a sweet tooth need apply; 1994/95, Park End congratulations

1995/96

New shirt sponsor Danka replaced NEC in 1995, a basic 'Perfect Match' message being the supporters' first introduction to the American copier, printer and fax supplier.

It was also noticeable on the below advert how the creative geniuses had been at work to remove the previous sponsor, the shots taken from 1994/95...

Duncan Ferguson's influence continued to dominate Everton merchandise, with 'The Duncan Ferguson Collection' offering t-shirts, pictures and even car stickers...

Everton 'Poster Power' was a popular seller in the club shop, while the issue of unofficial sellers remained a contentious one in and around the club, and the programme carried messages to deter fans from boosting the pockets of people who 'have no connection with your club'.

Clockwise from top left: 1995/96, first edition of the 'Everton Video Magazine; 1998/99, messrs Collins, Phelan, Cleland and Jeffers do a spot of modelling; 1999/00, the shirt sponsors extend terms; fancy a 'one2one' with Kev Campbell?

GWLADYS STREET A SELL-OUT

◆ **Get here early! That's the message from Chief Executive Jim Greenwood to the club's pay-on-the-day supporters.**

The newly-seated Gwladys Street End was closed to cash customers an hour before the kick-off of the game against Manchester United, and this could well be the pattern for the future.

The compulsory seating of the popular former terracing has automatically reduced the capacity at that end and, with the team playing some attarctive early-season football, the new seats are likely to fully occupied on a regular basis.

"The Gwladys Street is the most attractively priced area at £7.00 per head," said Mr Greenwood. "So we expect the capacity to be reached for most games. The message has got to be - 'Get here early and avoid disappointment.'"

Meanwhile, season ticket sales are expected to bring in a record sum, with interest and anticipation running high in the wake of the new signings.

Final figures are not yet available and Mr Greenwood said: "Even if the level of sales stays the same, the revenue would be a new record because of increased prices.

"We are optimistic, however, that numbers will be up, too."

A NEW TURNING FOR DRIVER JIM . . .

◆ **The newcomer in the Everton dug-out at recent matches was a vital part of the "team" on each of the club's visits to Wembley during the 1980s.**

Jim Martin (pictured right) , from Ash-ton-in-Makerfield, travelled thousands of miles each year as our coach driver until he was invited to take a permanent post at Goodison Park at the beginning of December.

In his new role as kit manager - looking after a thousand and one items of training gear in the week and in charge of the play-ing kit on match days - Jim now takes a back seat on the coach to the away games.

It's a big change after nearly ten years at the wheel and 11 trips to Wembley with Everton. "I drove the team to the cup finals, the Charity Shield matches; in fact every time they went to Wembley from 1984," he says.

Jim's new appointment is a spin-off from the days when he helped out with the kit on the coach when the first team or the reserves travelled away.

"I started driving for the club round when Howard Kendall first became man-ager, and soon after he came back this season, I was offered a job here," he added. "We had a little talk about what it involved and I accepted. It's a big step and I'm hoping it's going to be a good step."

When you are dealing with thousands of pounds worth of kit, stock control is as important as keeping up-to-date with the requirements of more than 50 players and staff at the training ground and four teams each playing at least one game a week.

Clubs are gradually recognising the value of having a specialist in this job. Manchester United, Aston Villa, Notting-ham Forest and Ipswich Town are among those who have appointed kit managers.

"I think a big club has got to have one," said Jim as he he began his stocktaking in

his first week. "From what I've seen of all the kit that's been stowed away, it would be impossible for the apprentices to know what's there.

"I had been at it for four days and there was still more to come. I started with all the training gear at Bellefield but there was a lot more kit at Goodison which I hadn't even opened.

"Each team got three kits, so there's quite a lot of money involved. Not just in the playing strip but the training kit and all the big outdoor coats. The match kits go to the laundry but the youngsters take the training kit to the launderette every morning."

Jim played amateur football and has always enjoyed an involevment in the game.

"I watched Everton and Liverpool but I was never one who was really biased," he says. "The coach driving brought in closer contact with Goodison Park and now it's Everton for me all the way. Everything they do is right as far as I'm concerned."

Until he started the driving, he played on Saturdays, but now he runs an under-15 Sunday side called Park Lane Junior FC in Ashton-in-Makerfield.

They were league runners-up and cup winners last season in the Wigan & Dis-trict Junior League.

EVERTON

NORTHERN LIGHTS FOCUS ON GOODISON . . .

◆ **The winter closedown in the Scan-dinavian national leagues increases the interest in English football in that part of northern Europe.**

On each week-end through the winter months, the TV companies in Denmark, Sweden and Norway take a full game from the First Division.

The series began last week from Good-ison Park and, of course, this explained the presence of many foreign advertisements on the perimeter fencing. To complete a Merseyside double, the Arsenal v Liver-pool match on Sunday was also transmi-itted to Scandinavia.

Clockwise from top left: Seating sell-outs in the Lower Gwladys, 1991/92; New role for driver Jimmy Martin, 1990/91; Scandinavian advertising spotted, 1990/91

BEHIND THE SCENES
NEWS DESK

The official opening today of the splendid new Park End Stand is another milestone in the history of Everton Football Club.

The completion of an all-seated stadium - and very few other grounds can, or will, match the 40,000 capacity - is a tribute to the club's forward-thinking in the re-development programme of the past decade.

I'm sure that anyone visiting the ground for the first time would look at the huge stands and come to only one conclusion: this is the home of one of the top clubs in the country.

Evertonians rightly expect the best in everything - and Goodison Park has always lived up to the club's motto. From being one of the largest grounds in the country, it is now among the finest of its kind in another era.

We have a wonderful stage for our team and the next step is to develop a team to match the setting. The brief of our manager, Mike Walker, is to secure the players necessary to ensure - and sustain - success on the field.

Following the re-structuring of the Company this year, funds were made available for the immediate strengthening of the squad. In particular, the signing of Daniel Amokachi was a statement of our intent: we are prepared to go anywhere in the world to identify and then recruit the best available players. It is essential to show everyone that we mean business NOW.

If that means we need to sign half-a-dozen players, then we are prepared to go down that road. But in the longer-term, we would want to to integrate expensive signings with players brought up from the junior teams.

To that end, those who work in youth development are every bit as important as the manager and his coaches at senior level. From my point of view, having come into the club only recently, I find it very encouraging to see David Unsworth in the first team and selected in the England Under-21 side last week.

It must be our aim to produce more young players of this quality, and I am pleased to

say that coaches genuinely believe we have a few more "gems" in the pipeline.

Building a club up to a high level - and that's what we are having to do following the decline in results since the 1980s - is an on-going process. Everything has to be right in all departments.

As far as I'm concerned, you cannot separate one part from another. Commercial development is as important as the success of the team: one thing leads to another.

I realise that supporters are only concerned with the end product on the field. Maybe they are suspicious of "commercialism", but in this day and age, income through the turnstiles is by no means enough to meet running costs at a major club.

Like it or not, times have changed. Some 20 years ago, this club's total income was probably below £1m; by the early 1990s it was above £5m. And we are no exception to the upward spiral.

AN ALTERNATIVE EVERTON XI, JOHN C. SLENSON-TAYLOR, SIR PHILIP CARTER...

Look at the balance sheets from Premiership clubs now and you will see that many clubs have a turnover of more than £10m, even £20m in one or two cases - and at least half of that is generated from commercial activities.

It's a field that covers a multitude of things: sponsorship, television fees, advertising, royalties, executive boxes, corporate entertainment packages, lotteries and replica kit sales.

To improve our income, we have to cater for all fans. The new stand includes a superb new Everton Supporters' Club and we are about to upgrade the Souvenir Shop. For those who want hospitality facilities, we are planning new lounges to serve the Top Balcony.

In the boardroom, it's our job to find ways of meeting

every demand and pull all the parts together for the good of every Evertonian. We want a winning team, a financially buoyant club and tens of thousands of satisfied customers.

Give us time, continue to give us your support, and together we can get it right.

PETER JOHNSON
Chairman, Everton Football Club.

Youth and Reserve

Our Youth Academy footballers reported back to action on Wednesday following a brief winter break. For some, however, it was business as usual.

Young England centre-half Peter Clarke started the season in the FA Youth Academy Under-19 line-up,

progressed to the FA Reserve League side soon after - and kicked off the Millennium on the substitutes' bench for the first team in the Premiership match against Leicester City.

His under 19 team-mates, however, enjoyed a well earned break - after ending the 20th Century with the best possible result, a derby match victory at Liverpool's Kirkby Youth Academy.

Just a fortnight after losing their unbeaten record for the season to The Reds, Colin Harvey's side gained revenge with a lone Leon Osman goal.

Osman struck during the first half, then after the break the Blues battled spiritedly to overcome the loss of central defender David Knowles with a dislocated shoulder.

"We dug in well after that," said Harvey.

"Leon took his goal well and then we defended solidly."

The Blues are next in action in the FA Premier Youth Academy on 22

January 2000 when we travel to Crewe Alexandra.

The Reserves are next in action at the Autoquest Stadium in Widnes on Tuesday 25 January 2000 when Manchester United are the visitors.

UNDER-19 YOUTH ACADEMY 1999-2000 MATCH FACTS

Friday 17 December 1999
Liverpool 0 Everton 1
Scorer: Osman
Everton: Delaney, O'Hanlon, Pilkington, Clarke, Knowles (Price), McKay, Kearney, Osman, Howarth, Dempsey, McLeod.
Liverpool: Crookes, Cavanagh, Porter (McIlroy), Boardman, Jones, Navarro, Partridge, Park, Thompson, Torpey (Foley), O'Mara.

THE FA PREMIER ACADEMY LEAGUE UNDER 19 FIXTURES

AUGUST 1999		
Sat 28 Sheffield Wed	2-0	
SEPTEMBER		
Sat 4 Barnsley	1-1	
Sat 11 Leeds Utd	3-1	
Sat 18 Newcastle Utd	4-1	
Sat 25 Aston Villa	1-0	
OCTOBER		
Sat 2 Liverpool	PP	
Sat 16 Manchester Utd	1-1	
Sat 23 Manchester City	0-0	
Sat 30 Sunderland	2-1	
NOVEMBER		
Sat 6 Crewe Alexandra	3-1	
Sat 13 Bolton Wanderers	3-1	
Sat 20 Blackburn Rovers	7-1	
Sat 27 Liverpool	2-4	
DECEMBER		
Sat 4 Manchester Utd	0-2	
Sat 11 Manchester City	0-1	
JANUARY 2000		
Sat 22 Crewe Alexandra	A	
Sat 29 Middlesbrough	H	
FEBRUARY		
Sat 5 Bolton Wanderers	H	
Sat 12 Blackburn Rovers	H	
Sat 19 Coventry City	A	
Sat 26 Huddersfield Town	A	
MARCH		
Sat 4 Stoke City	H	

UNDER-19 YOUTH ACADEMY APPS & GOALS 1999-2000

	Apps	Gls
CHADWICK	3(7)	3
CLARKE	6(1)	-
CURRAN	4	1
DELANEY	15	-
DEMPSEY	11(1)	3
EATON	2(2)	1
HIBBERT	6	-
HOGG	5(1)	-
HOWARTH	13	5
KEARNEY	5(2)	-
KNOWLES	11	1
McALPINE	3(2)	-
McKAY	5(6)	1
McLEOD	10(1)	3
MANNUS	-(1)	-
O'HANLON	14	1
OSMAN	12	4
PILKINGTON	15	-
PRICE	2(3)	-
SOUTHERN	13	2
WRIGHT	9	-

Up to and including 17.12.99

Above: The 'important' faces at Goodison pose in front of the new Park End stand, 1994/95
Left: Leon Osman the match-winner at youth level, 1999/2000

2 BEHIND THE SCENES
NEWS DESK

Ian Durrant was instantly at home on the big stage. His first Scottish League goal for Rangers was in an Old Firm meeting with Celtic at Ibrox in November 1985. And so it went on...

■ In October 1986, three days before his 20th birthday, he scored in a Skol Cup Final victory over Celtic in front of a 74,319 crowd at Hampden Park.

■ In October 1987, four days before his 21st birthday, he was on the scoresheet as Rangers drew 3-3 with Aberdeen and retained the Skol Cup in a penalty shoot-out. By then he had won his first two caps for Scotland - in Hampden wins against Hungary and Belgium - and the season ended with two more international appearances, notably a 0-0 draw against Spain in Madrid which preserved his unbeaten record at that level.

A substitute outing against Norway in Oslo in September 1988 maintained that run, and in club football, the Glasgow Blues went on to complete a Skol Cup hat-trick - but without Durrant.

The sequence of early birthday celebrations was broken on 8 October when a cruciate ligament was ripped apart in a league match against Aberdeen. A brilliant career was only saved by pioneering surgery in America, and even then, it was to be 32 months before the midfielder re-appeared in first-team football in April 1991.

The road to complete rehabilitation was littered with pitfalls. Season 1991-92 was almost a write-off until he returned in the New Year and won another cup medal, this time in the Scottish Cup Final against Airdrie.

Rangers were champions for a fourth season in succession and went into a revamped European Cup in 1992-93 with a goal for Durrant in a first-round win against Lyngby - his fourth in European competition. The big-match man was back in business in a big way.

More than that, he was back in the Scotland squad after an absence of four years. Sadly, however, it was start of an unsuccessful World Cup campaign: chapter two of his international career included a 5-0 defeat by Portugal in Lisbon. Rangers, though, overcame Leeds in the European Cup - Durrant playing a

full part in home-and-away victories - and only missed out on a place in the final by one point. Marseille went forward to beat AC Milan and two current Evertonians were disappointed after both had scored in the Champions' League.

Daniel Amokachi netted FC Bruges' winner in the opening game against CSKA Moscow and when Amokachi's Belgian club met Rangers, Durrant scored in a 2-1 home victory at Ibrox. The midfielder was also on target against in the away draw with Marseille.

But the Glasgow giants were far from empty-handed. At home they landed a treble and Durrant played in two more cup final wins, both against Aberdeen.

Last season they were desperately close to repeating that achievement, winning the Premier Division for the sixth year in a row and taking the Skol Cup with the help of another goal from Durrant - five days before his 27th birthday. All that was missing was the Scottish Cup which eluded them with a surprise 1-0 defeat by Dundee United.

The season also brought two more caps, making 11 in all.

> "I was a little disappointed to be leaving Rangers, but I welcomed the chance of first team football in the English Premiership."
>
> DUNCAN FERGUSON

Our decision to take Scottish internationals Ian Durrant and Duncan Ferguson on loan from Glasgow Rangers proved to be one of the major stories of the new season.

They are two of the biggest names in British football and their move from Scotland to England intrigued soccer people on both sides of the border.

It is only 15 months ago that Duncan became Britain's highest-priced player when he left Dundee United for four million pounds although that figure has since been topped by Chris Sutton's move from Norwich to Blackburn last summer.

Looking back to his historic move Duncan told us, "It was very exciting at the time. Any player moving to Rangers comes under the spotlight in Scotland but to go for such a big fee put even more pressure on me.

"Suddenly people started looking at me differently. Before the transfer I was just a promising young lad with Dundee United. After it the same people expected a lot more from me and were keen to see just why Rangers thought I was worth so much money."

Other clubs were linked with being

interested in Duncan, including ourselves and Leeds United.

But Duncan says, "Regarding Everton it was only newspaper talk as far as I was concerned. I didn't speak to anybody from the club. Yet I did speak to Leeds but opted for Rangers."

Duncan admits that when Sutton took over as Britain's most expensive player he felt like saying, "All the pressure is now on you Chris."

Yet the luck any player would have needed in Duncan's situation did not move with him. A horrendous series of injuries dogged him during his first season at Ibrox when he was restricted to only 10 appearances, three as a sub.

"I couldn't really have been worse," says Duncan. "I suffered with a hamstring then I chipped a bone in my foot. I had trouble with my groin not to mention a few knocks in general.

"I was just looking forward to the summer and getting fit. But when it was over Mark Hateley was playing so well I couldn't get a regular place in the Rangers side.

"Yet it wasn't all bad as I scored four goals in the five games I played."

So it was with mixed feelings that Duncan heard of our interest. "I was a little disappointed to be leaving Rangers," he said, "but I welcomed the chance of first team football in the English Premiership.

"It offered me good experience and the opportunity to find some form and fitness."

So the 22-year-old striker, just under 6ft 4ins tall, made his debut for us in last week's Coca Cola Cup-tie at Portsmouth and, sad to relate, his luck hasn't changed.

"I thought Everton played well," he said, "and I was pleased with my own performance. But for a good save by the 'keeper I would have had a goal.

"But as it was my first senior game in about six weeks, when I had played for Rangers against AEK Athens, I tired near the end. Then with about 20 minutes to go I took a knock on my foot and it kept me out of the visit to Southampton.

"I stayed on the pitch because I didn't think the injury was too bad. That was because the adrenalin was flowing, but it is when you relax some ten minutes after the final whistle that you really feel it."

Our reputation for classy centre-forwards is well known throughout the game and Duncan admits he is aware of it.

He told us, "The two I am most aware of are Graeme Sharp and Andy Gray, two exceptional players who are also fellow Scots.

"Like me, Andy started his career at Dundee United and if I can half as successful an an Everton Jersey as he was I shall be more than pleased."

At the moment Duncan is scheduled to be with us for three months and he says, "In that time I hope to get myself fully fit and find my best form so I can score some goals for Everton that will ensure a few points."

COTTEE SETS HIS NEXT TARGET...

Tony Cottee deservedly collared the headlines last week when he notched the 200th goal of his career to join an elite band of marksmen.

Tony began the season with 198 goals to his credit for West Ham and Everton so the second of his hat-trick against Sheffield United broke that elusive barrier.

What seemed to go unnoticed was that it was also the 150th League goal of his career and while some players claim to ignore such statistics Tony is not one of them.

"I take great pleasure in scoring goals," he says. "They are what my career is about and I can always aware of what I am doing in that line of business."

Tony has now scored 83 for Everton and he says, "My next target is to complete the ton for the club, hopefully this season. Then I would like to join the 300 club, again along with Everton. I have just signed a new three year contract so it is possible."

Tony knows that if he keeps scoring goals they will ensure his place in the team although he is quick to add, "The manager wants me to contribute as well as score goals and he is quite right.

"I am working very hard on that side of my game and so far it is paying dividends."

On completing the double century, Cottee had made 410 official appearances, plus 41 as substitute, for his two clubs.

From his West Ham debut, against Spurs on New Year's Day 1983, the timetable for goal-scoring landmarks was as follows. . .

ALL COMPETITIONS

Goals	Fixture	Date
50	West Ham v Leicester City	14.9.85
100	West Ham v Luton Town	29.2.87
150	Everton v Queens Park Rangers	7.4.90
200	Everton v Sheffield United	31.8.93

LEAGUE ONLY

Goals	Fixture	Date
50	West Ham v Chelsea	29.3.86
100	Everton v Tottenham	3.12.88
150	Everton v Sheffield United	21.9.93

The 200 barrier was broken with the tenth hat-trick of his first team career - equally divided between the Hammers and Blues. The big scoring days were as follows. . .

Goals	Fixture	Date
4	West Ham v Bury (Milk Cup)	25.10.83
3	West Ham v Wimbledon (FA Cup)	6.3.85

A Carling No 1 Awards panel, including the chief executives of the League Managers' Association (Frank Clark), chose 22 players, one from each club, to celebrate excellence in the top flight of English football.

The Carling No-1 candidate for Everton is Tony Cottee (pictured above), who received a framed full-colour print of himself in action and a magnum of champagne.

The judges said: On his day one of the sharpest strikers around the Everton fans will be hoping he can produce his best this season and help the club return to the trophy-winning days of the mid-80s.

EBBRELL ANSWERS THE CALL...

With two goals in his first three games John Ebbrell has provided a quick response to the manager's call for more

---

inside Goodison

Everton honours two of its most loyal and successful servants this afternoon

YOUTH'S SUCCESS

New Recruits

Putting their Shirts ON THE BLUES

Blues Top Tipsters

"IT'S GREAT TO HEAR THAT FANS ARE BUYING NUMBER NINE SHIRTS WITH MY NAME ON THE BACK"

1 **Cottee's goal (v Aston Villa, 1993/94)**
The Everton striker took his tally to 200 career goals following a hat-trick against Sheffield United early in the campaign. His new target after reaching the landmark? One hundred goals for Everton, and to hit 300 in his career. Although failing on both counts, he did claim a Premier League award for 'excellence in the top flight' – and was also handed the 'honour' of a charity £100 bet on the Blues to land the title.

2 **Loan Rangers (v Coventry City, 1994/95)**
Scottish duo Ian Durrant and Duncan Ferguson were unlikely signings on temporary deals in the autumn of 1994. With both out of favour at their club, and Everton yet to win, Mike Walker moved to strengthen his squad, with both players insisting they were only at Goodison in the short term. Duncan noted: "I hope to get myself fully fit and find my best form so I can score some goals for Everton that will ensure a few points."

3 **Getting shirty (v Coventry City, 1995/96)**
It was all smiles at Goodison as the club confirmed a new shirt sponsorship deal with Umbro, with some of the players forced to line up sporting awkward smiles as the numbers on their backs 'spell' out 2000 – the year the new contract was set to run until.

4 **True legends (v Coventry City, 1997/98)**
There was cause for a salute to two Everton greats. Neville Southall had completed 750 appearances for the club earlier in the campaign, while it was 70 years since Dixie's Dean's famous 60th goal – although the article was keen not to overdo the significance of the game... still, the young Blues had landed the FA Youth Cup earlier that week to provide a timely boost ahead of the relegation showdown.

5 **New Blues (v Manchester United, 1999/00)**
Kevin Campbell's goalscoring impact while on loan at the end of the 1998/99 season ensured the club would do all they could to snap up the centre-forward during the summer – although the signing of a 37-year-old defender hardly set Evertonians' pulses racing. However, Richard Gough was pleased to find somebody older than himself in the first-team ranks at Goodison: "Dave Watson has four months on me, so for the first time in years I've been able to call someone 'dad' at a club!"

EVERTON

Back row (left to right): Kevin Sheedy, Norman Whiteside, Jason Kearton, Martin Keown, Neville Southall, Dave Watson, John Ebbrell, Graham Smith (Youth Manager).

Middle row: Paul Power (Coach), Mike Lyons (Coach), Mike Newell, Graeme Sharp, Neil McDonald, Ray Atteveld, Andy Hinchcliffe, Peter Beagrie, Les Helm (Physiotherapist), Jimmy Gabriel (Chief Coach).

Front row: Ian Snodin, Mike Milligan, Kevin Ratcliffe

EVERTON

FOOTBALL CLUB 1994-95

BACK ROW, Left to right: Vinny Samways, Paul Holmes, John Ebbrell, Gary Rowett, Joe Parkinson, Matt Jackson, Paul Rideout, Andy Hinchcliffe, Graham Stuart. MIDDLE ROW: Jim Martin (Kit Manager), Dave Williams (First Team Coach), Tony Grant, Chris Priest, Stephen Reeves, Neville Southall, Jason Kearton, Gary Ablett, Neil Moore, Jimmy Gabriel (Reserve Team Coach), Les Helm (Physiotherapist). FRONT ROW: David Unsworth, Stuart Barlow, Anders Limpar, Barry Horne, Mike Walker (Manager), Dave Watson (Captain), Ian Snodin, Tony Cottee (now at West Ham), Brett Angell. Also: Daniel Amokachi (top left), David Burrows (top right).

UNICATIONS
EVERTON F
NEC
NEC
NEC
NEC
NEC
NEC
NEC
NEC
NEC
Mitre
PRO MAX

Back row (left to right): Andy Hinchcliffe, Eddie Youds, Neville Southall, Martin Keown, Gerry Peyton, Dave Watson, Alan Harper. *Middle row:* Les Helm (Physiotherapist), Jimmy Gabriel (Reserve Team Coach), Raymond Atteveld, Robert Warzycha, Neil McDonald, Mike Newell, John Ebbrell, Peter Beagrie, Pat Nevin, Colin Harvey (First Coach Coach). *Front row:* Kevin Sheedy, Ian Snodin, Mark Ward, Howard Kendall (Manager), Kevin Ratcliffe, Tony Cottee, Peter Beardsley.

DUNCAN FERGUSON

NEC

HAPPY NEW YEAR

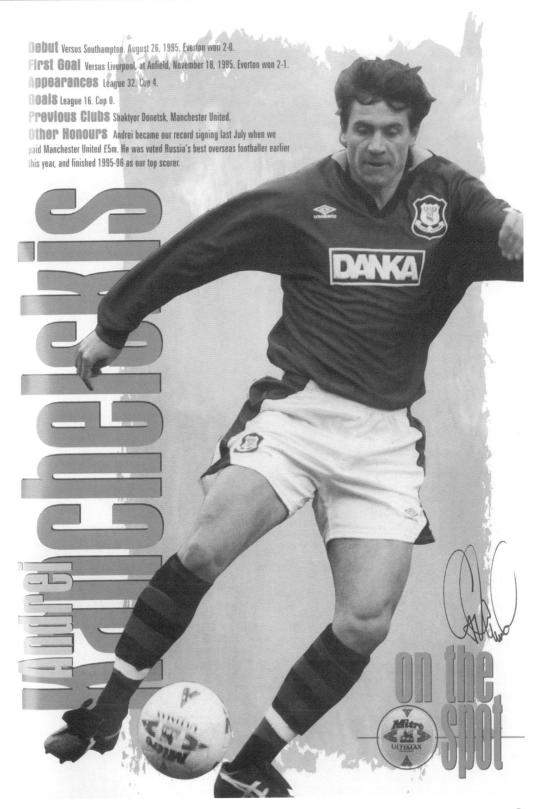

Debut Versus Southampton. August 26, 1995. Everton won 2-0.

First Goal Versus Liverpool, at Anfield, November 18, 1995. Everton won 2-1.

Appearances League 32. Cup 4.

Goals League 16. Cup 0.

Previous Clubs Shaktyor Donetsk, Manchester United.

Other Honours Andrei became our record signing last July when we paid Manchester United £5m. He was voted Russia's best overseas footballer earlier this year, and finished 1995-96 as our top scorer.

Andrei Kanchelskis

on the spot

1990 DIARY

JANUARY

1 Palace are 14th in the First Division after conceding four first-half goals at Arsenal.
6 A tense start on the FA Cup trail until Portsmouth go down to a last-minute penalty by Andy Gray.
20 England 'B' forward Ian Wright (cracked shin) and Eddie McGoldrick (cartilage) go on the long-term casualty list after a 2-0 home defeat by Liverpool.
27 Stand-in striker John Salako scores in a 4-0 win against Third Division Huddersfield in the FA Cup.

FEBRUARY

10 A 3-1 win against Southampton halts a run of four successive League defeats.
17 Phil Barber clinches a place in the last eight in the FA Cup with a second-half goal against Rochdale.

MARCH

3 Wright, absent for six weeks, returns as substitute in a valuable 1-0 win at Tottenham.
10 Geoff Thomas scores the only goal at Cambridge to put Palace through to the FA Cup semi-final for only the second time in their history.
12 The alternative Wembley trail closes with a 4-0 aggregate defeat by Chelsea in Zenith Cup Southern Area Final.
20 More misfortune for Wright, who breaks his shin for the second ti... ...ear in a 1-1 dra...

APRIL

8 An extraordinary semi-final at Villa Park brings an 87th minute equaliser from Gray and then an extra-time winner by Alan Pardew in a 4-3 thriller with Liverpool.
21 A 2-0 win against Selhurst Park tenants Charlton clears up lingering relegation worries.

MAY

8 Wright files his claim for a Wembley place in a reserve try-out at Tooting.
12 Wright starts the Cup Final on the bench but appears after 69 minutes and scores twice in a 3-3 draw with Manchester United.
17 The Cup goes to Old Trafford thanks to a single goal from United full back Lee Martin.

AUGUST

25 Palace begin the new season without Mark Bright (hamstring) and Garry Thompson (suspended) but take a point from Luton with a debut goal by Eric Young.

SEPTEMBER

3 Goalkeeper Nigel Martyn is named in the full England squad to meet Hungary.
8 An unbeaten start gathers momentum with a 3-0 win at Norwich.
22 A cracked bone in an arm keeps Salako out of a 1-1 draw at Tottenham.
29 Palace hold fourth place after another away win at Derby.

OCTOBER

... Wright joins Martyn in the ... to meet Poland. ... Hodges are

Continued from page 15.

Palace's steady rise from the lower reaches of the Second Division is a tribute to the aptitude and dedication of their 35-year-old Liverpool-born manager. Average League attendances have doubled in tandem with promotion and a Cup Final appearance in the last two seasons.

Mr Coppell, an Economics graduate from Liverpool University, began his playing career with Tranmere Rovers in 1973. He moved to Manchester United in February 1975 and was capped on 42 occasions by England prior to his premature retirement through injury.

Transfers. . .

◆ **Palace have spent the better part of £3m on building a new defence in the last year.**

Cornishman Nigel Martyn became the first £1m goalkeeper on moving from Bristol Rovers last November and former Wimbledon FA Cup Finalist Andy Thorn arrived from Newcastle for £550,000 soon afterwards.

In the summer, Thorn revived an old Wimbledon partnership on being joined by £850,000 central defender Eric Young, and Charlton right back John Humphrey cost £450,000 when he made the shortest of moves from one Selhurst Park club to another.

With 22-year-old youth scheme discovery Richard Shaw taking a hold on the No 3 shirt, Palace were able to sell their promotion-year full backs. John Pemberton went to Sheffield United for £300,000 and David Burke re-joined his first club, Bolton Wanderers, for £60,000.

Since their last visit to Goodison, the South Londoners also paid £200,000 for Watford striker Garry Thompson and £410,000 for his former Vicarage Road team-mate, Glyn Hodges.

Shaw and the versatile John Salako were the only home-produced players in last season's Wembley squad. Phil Barber, Alan Pardew and Ian Wright came out of non-League football; Mark Bright, Gary O'Reilly and Geoff Thomas cost a total of £165,000; and Andy Gray returned to his first League club in a £500,000 deal with QPR.

David Madden, a substitute in the Cup Final, joined Maidstone and defender Chris Powell went to Southend. Winger Alex Dyer recently moved to Charlton on loan.

POST-WAR MANAGERS AT SELHURST PARK

1939-47	George Irwin
1947-49	Jack Butler
1949-50	Ronnie Rooke
1950-51	Charlie Slade & Fred Dowes
1951-54	Laurie Scott
1954-58	Cyril Spiers
1958-60	George Smith
1960-63	Arthur Rowe
1963-66	Dick Graham
1966-72	Bert Head
1973-76	Malcolm Allison
1976-80	Terry Venables
1980	Ernie Walley
1980-81	Malcolm Allison
...	...Dario Gradi

Leeds UNITED

A place in Europe is the next target in a 19-month turnround since George Graham returned to management at Elland Road...

Form Guide...

Last season was all about Premiership stability – a mission which was accomplished with six points to spare. This season was earmarked as one for progress – an objective which was secured with a top-eight ranking from September onwards.

A new-look side evolved over the two campaigns, and both results and performances were lifted to a higher level.

Seventeen goals in home-and-away meetings with Blackburn and Derby measured the extent of the improvement.

There may have been an element of necessity in the way George Graham approached the task last season. Leeds conceded 38 goals - six fewer than Manchester United - but scored only 28, the lowest total by any side avoiding relegation from the top division.

The emphasis gradually shifted with an influx of signings last summer. Goalless draws, which were prevalent a year ago, were replaced by a number of high-scoring games. Both Blackburn and Derby were beaten 4-3, and the 5-0 victory in the return fixture at Derby last month would be listed among the best away displays in the Premiership this season.

A UEFA Cup place is a possibility, especially if the threshold moves to seventh position, but a shorter route to success was frustratingly closed after four consecutive home ties ...

next match programme column, Mr Graham conceded that this was "a massive disappointment" but directed the supporters' attention to the broader picture...

"When I look back at this time last year, we have made tremendous progress and we have to continue with that. We've had a very good season in the league and if we can push on and win a place in Europe, that will be a fantastic achievement."

It's only eight years since Leeds won promotion and six since they became the last champions of the old First Division. This led to a couple of European campaigns, the first in the Champions' Cup in 1992 and the other in the UEFA Cup in 1995, but both ended in the second round.

Transfers...

A 0-0 draw at Goodison Park in December 1996 marked the debut of George Graham's first signing for Leeds - the Norwegian international, Gunnar Halle.

The second game with the Blues in March was settled by a goal from £900,000 Dutch defender Robert Molenaar, and before the season was over, the squad was strengthened by striker Derek Lilley, a £500,000 recruit from Morton.

Two Scottish internationals were among five arrivals in the summer. Aberdeen full back David Robertson was capped three times and David Hopkin broke into the World Cup squad shortly before his £3.25m transfer from Crystal Palace.

The versatile Norwegian, Alf-Inge Haaland, cost £1.6m after three years with Nottingham Forest, and the other newcomers came from Portugal. Striker Jimmy Floyd Hasselbaink was priced at £2m after scoring 27 League and cup goals for Boavista last season, ...

market in February when paying a seven-figure sum for Rapid Vienna defender Martin Hiden, who was capped by Austria soon after moving to Yorkshire.

A considerable departure list included Carlton Palmer (Southampton), Richard Jobson (Manchester City), Ian Rush (Newcastle), Brian Deane (Sheffield United), Tony Dorigo (Torino), Tony Yeboah (Hamburg) and Tomas Brolin, who was released before joining Crystal Palace.

Management...

Chelsea's recent success in the League Cup was their first in that competition since a 20-year-old George Graham helped them to victory in the 1965 final.

The Scotsman's distinguished playing career was to bring 12 international caps, a European Fairs Cup triumph with Arsenal and then a League and FA Cup double with the Gunners.

In a total of 455 League matches (106 goals), he also played for Aston Villa (his first club), Manchester United, Portsmouth and Crystal Palace.

As a manager, he won promotion from Division Three with Millwall before landing half-a-dozen trophies on his return to Arsenal. During that time he forged links with David O'Leary, now his assistant at Elland Road.

In Brief...

- Alan Maybury recently won his first full cap for the Republic of Ireland, joining clubmates Gary Kelly and Ian Harte in the squad for a friendly in the Czech Republic.
- Maybury and the exciting Australian international, Harry Kewell, were members of last season's FA Cup Youth Cup-winning team. Other graduates from that squad are Paul Robinson, Lee Matthews, Stephen McPhail and Wales Under-21 cap Matthew Jones.
- Lucas Radebe captained South Africa when the holders were defeated by Egypt in the final of the African Nations' Cup in February.
- David Wetherall, Rod Wallace and Gary Kelly each completed 200 first-team starts for Leeds this season.
- Lee Bowyer captained the England Under-21 side while winning nine caps at that level.
- Former England and Manchester United player Lee Sharpe is on the comeback trail after missing all of this season ...

Andy Gray

...yer

...Premier League ... platform and it will go down as an important marker for all that they expect to achieve...

FORM GUIDE...

Ambitious chairman Steve Gibson wants to win a first major trophy and secure a first European qualification - and he was not to be deterred by the initial disappointments of two relegation years.

Keith O'Neill

Middlesbrough ... First Division ... 1974, continued their development under John Neal, then retreated after a spell of eight years.

The impact of relegation worsened with a slide into Division Three and an accompanying cash crisis which threatened the club's existence. But they survived with two promotions under Bruce Rioch, re-grouped under Lennie Lawrence after another demotion, and moved into a new era of prosperity in a new ground.

The Riverside Stadium opened as a Premier League venue in 1995 and Mr Gibson's vision of an exciting multi-national team was carried out when Bryan Robson pushed through major investments in the likes of Juninho, Ravenelli and Emerson.

It's now history that this squad brought the good times with first-ever Wembley finals in both cups in 1997, only for Boro to go back to the drawing board because of relegation after the deduction of points. Another promoted side called in at the Twin Towers for a League Cup Final on the way back to the Premiership, and this time the acclimatisation process went well with ninth place.

In an ideal world, the Teessiders would have gone forward from there, but this season had a hole in the middle, and a costly one in terms of results and an element of disenchantment among supporters. Cup defeats at Wrexham and Tranmere Rovers were followed by a fall of eight places, from eighth to 16th. This brush with the danger area was the result of one point from six games and hefty home defeats at the hands of Derby County and Aston Villa.

Fortunately, the pressure spot disappeared as quickly as it had appeared. A safe position was guaranteed in a seven-match unbeaten run, culminating in a win at Tottenham, and a more recent away victory at West Ham fitted in among three drawn games.

Three first-teamers, Steve Vickers, Robbie Mustoe and Curtis Fleming, ... signed ... Stockport st... Armstrong and Burnley ... Marlon Beresford were added on the run-in to promotion that year, and Andy Townsend was in and out, arriving from Aston Villa in 1997 and moving to West Brom this season.

For last year's return to the Premiership, two England defenders, Gary Pallister and Colin Cooper, re-joined their first club, and other reinforcements were Crystal Palace wing-back Dean Gordon and Benfica striker Brian Deane, an England player in his Sheffield United days.

A thriving youth policy has also contributed to the club's development. Striker Andy Campbell graduated to a goal-scoring England Under-21 debut this season and local discovery Mark Summerbell enjoyed his longest run in the team after his re-introduction in January.

Robbie Stockdale and Irish defender Jason Gavin are others pressing for places, and more could be on the way, judging by progress to the semi-final of the FA Youth Cup in which Boro were narrowly beaten by Arsenal.

TRANSFERS...

The return of Juninho re-established a link with the high expectations of Boro's previous crack at the Premiership. The Brazilian crowd favourite ...

... season on ... though the "homecom..." muted with a recent stint on the subs' bench.

The South American supply line

Mark Schwarzer

Juninho

MIDDLESBROUGH 1986

Boro

OPPOSITION NOTES...

The usual opposition overviews, player and manager profiles, plus form guide, retained a general standard template during the decade, with only tweaks in format apparent.

Early '90s notes include a diary format for Everton's visitors, while lists of post-War managers remained a feature for several seasons. Presumably the increase in managerial changes during the period necessitated a re-think as the decade progressed...

Former players or links between the two sides continued to be plundered, with Peter Reid's management of Sunderland a particular source of material in the late 90s.

FIXTURES & STATISTICS

FACTS AT A GLANCE...

MILESTONES...
(Premiership games only)

Highest attendance: 43,868 Man. Utd v Sheff. W. 7.5.95
Lowest attendance: 5,268 Wimbledon v Man. C. 21.3.95
Highest home score: 9-0 Man. Utd v Ipswich 4.3.95
Highest away score: 1-7 Sheff. W. v Nottm F. 1.4.95
Five Goals in a match: Andy Cole (Man. Utd) v Ipswich 4.3.95

LEADING SCORERS...
(Including Cup & European Games)

37	Alan Shearer (Blackburn Rovers)
31	Robbie Fowler (Liverpool)
30	Matthew Le Tissier (Southampton)
30	Ian Wright (Arsenal)
29	Jurgen Klinsmann (Totenham Hotspur)
27	*Andy Cole (Manchester United)
26	Les Ferdinand (Queens Park Rangers)
25	Stan Collymore (Nottingham Forest)
25	*Ashley Ward (Norwich City)
23	Teddy Sheringham (Totenham Hotspur)
22	Uwe Rosler (manchester City)
21	Chris Sutton (Blackburn Rovers)
19	Ian Rush (Liverpool)
18	Chris Armstrong (Crystal Palace)
18	*Paul Kitson (Newcastle United)
17	Dean Saunders (Aston Villa)
16	Dion Dublin (Coventry City)
16	Paul Rideout (Everton)

* Includes goals for other clubs

FA CARLING PREMIERSHIP TABLE 1994-95

	HIGH. ATT	AV. ATT	P	W	D	L	F	A	W	D	L	F	A	PTS
BLACKBURN	30545	25271	42	17	2	2	54	21	10	6	5	26	18	89
MAN. UTD	43868	43681	42	16	4	1	42	4	10	6	5	35	24	88
NOTTS FOREST	28882	23537	42	12	6	3	36	18	10	5	6	36	25	77
LIVERPOOL	40014	34175	42	13	5	3	38	13	8	6	7	27	24	74
LEEDS	39426	32964	42	13	5	3	35	15	7	8	6	24	23	73
NEWCASTLE	35626	34691	42	14	6	1	46	20	6	6	9	21	27	72
TOTTENHAM	33040	27258	42	10	5	6	32	25	6	9	6	34	33	62
QPR	18948	14595	42	11	3	7	36	26	6	6	9	25	33	60
WIMBLEDON	18224	10206	42	9	5	7	26	26	6	6	9	22	39	56
SOUTHAMPTON	15210	14689	42	8	9	4	33	27	4	9	8	28	36	54
CHELSEA	31161	21057	42	7	7	7	25	22	6	8	7	25	33	54
ARSENAL	39377	35377	42	6	9	6	27	21	7	3	11	25	28	51
SHEFF. WED.	34051	26595	42	7	7	7	26	26	6	5	10	23	31	51
WEST HAM	24783	20175	42	9	6	6	28	19	4	5	12	16	29	50
EVERTON	**40011**	**31367**	**42**	8	9	4	31	23	3	8	10	13	28	50
COVENTRY	21885	15977	42	7	7	7	23	25	5	7	9	21	37	50
MAN CITY	27850	22747	42	8	7	6	37	28	4	6	11	16	36	49
ASTON VILLA	40154	29756	42	6	9	6	27	24	5	6	10	24	32	48
CRYSTAL P.	18224	14801	42	6	6	9	16	23	5	6	10	18	26	45
NORWICH	21843	18620	42	8	8	5	27	21	2	5	14	10	33	43
LEICESTER	21393	19531	42	5	6	10	28	37	1	5	15	17	43	29
IPSWICH	22559	16907	42	5	3	13	24	34	2	3	16	12	59	27

FIRST TEAM FIXTURES & RESULTS 1994/95

KEY TO SYMBOLS & ABBREVIATIONS
❶ *Goals Scored*   **●₂₂** *Substitute & player replaced*   *FAC = FA Cup*

Date	v	93-94	Opposition (Competition)	Res	Att
Aug 20	H	0-1	Aston Villa	2-2	35,5
Aug 24	A	2-3	Tottenham Hotspur	1-2	24,5
Aug 27	A	0-1	Manchester City	0-4	19,8
Aug 30	H	-	Nottingham Forest	1-2	26,6
Sept 10	A	0-2	Blackburn Rovers	0-3	26,5
Sept 17	H	0-3	QPR	2-2	27,2
Sept 20	H	-	Portsmouth CCC 2 (1)	2-3	14,0
Sept 24	H	-	Leicester City	1-1	28,0
Oct 1	A	0-1	Manchester United	0-2	43,8
Oct 5	A	-	Portsmouth CCC 2 (2)	1-1	13,6
Oct 8	A	2-0	Southampton	0-2	15,1
Oct 15	H	0-0	Coventry City	0-2	28,2
Oct 22	A	-	Crystal Palace	0-1	14,5
Oct 29	H	1-1	Arsenal	1-1	32,0
Nov 1	H	0-1	West Ham United	1-0	28,3
Nov 5	A	0-3	Norwich City	0-0	18,3
Nov 21	H	2-0	Liverpool	2-0	39,86
Nov 26	A	2-4	Chelsea	1-0	28,1
Dec 5	H	1-1	Leeds United	3-0	25,8
Dec 10	A	0-0	Aston Villa	0-0	29,67
Dec 17	H	0-1	Tottenham Hotspur	0-0	32,80
Dec 26	H	0-2	Sheffied Wednesday	1-4	37,08
Dec 31	H	0-0	Ipswich Town	4-1	25,65
Jan 2	A	1-1	Wimbledon	1-2	9,50
Jan 7	H	-	Derby County FA Cup 3	1-0	29,40
Jan 26	A	0-2	Arsenal	1-1	34,74
Jan 21	H	-	Crystal Palace	3-1	23,73
Jan 24	A	1-2	Liverpool	0-0	39,50
Jan 29	A	-	Bristol City FA Cup 4	1-0	19,81
Feb 1	A	0-1	Newcastle United	0-2	34,46
Feb 4	H	1-5	Norwich City	2-1	23,29
Feb 13	A	1-0	West Ham United	2-2	21,08
Feb 18	H	-	Norwich City FA Cup 5	5-0	31,61
Feb 22	A	0-3	Leeds United	0-1	30,79
Feb 25	H	0-1	Manchester United	1-0	40,01
Mar 4	A	-	Leicester City	2-2	20,44
Mar 8	A	-	Nottingham Forest	1-2	24,52
Mar 12	H	-	Newcastle United FA Cup 6	1-0	35,20
Mar 15	H	1-0	Manchester City	1-1	28,48
Mar 18	A	1-2	QPR	-3-2	14,48
Apr 1	H	0-3	Blackburn Rovers	1-2	37,905
Apr 9	N	-	Tottenham FA Cup Semi Final	4-1	38,220
Apr 14	H	0-2	Newcastle United	2-0	34,81
Apr 17	A	1-5	Sheffield Wednesday	0-0	27,880
Apr 29	H	3-2	Wimbledon	0-0	33,063
May 3	H	4-2	Chelsea	3-3	33,180
May 6	H	1-0	Southampton	0-0	36,840
May 9	A	2-0	Ipswich Town	1-0	14,951
May 14	A	1-2	Coventry City	0-0	21,814
May 20	N	-	Manchester Utd FA Cup Final	1-0	79,592

EVERTON SPONSORKIT

3	Andy HINCHCLIFFE
4	Ian SNODIN
4	Earl BARRETT
5	Dave WATSON
6	Gary ABLETT
7	Vinny SAMWAYS
8	Graham STUART
9	Tony COTTEE
9	Duncan FERGUSON
10	Barry HORNE
11	Daniel AMOKACHI
12	Paul HOLMES
13	Jason KEARTON
14	John EBBRELL
15	Paul RIDEOUT
16	David BURROWS
17	Anders LIMPAR
18	Joe PARKINSON
19	Stuart BARLOW
20	Ian DURRANT
21	Gary ROWETT
22	Brett ANGELL
25	Neil MOORE
26	David UNSWORTH
29	Tony GRANT
31	Stephen REEVES
33	James SPEARE

Everton Roll Call

	1997–98 Apps	Gls	Everton Career Apps	Gls	Other Career Apps	Gls
GRAHAM ALLEN	2(3)	-	2(4)	-	-	-
Farnworth, 8.4.77	-	-	-	-	-	-
MICHAEL BALL	21(4)	1	23(7)	1	-	-
Liverpool, 2.10.79	2(1)	-	2(1)	-	-	-
NICK BARMBY	26(4)	2	48(7)	6	129	28
Hull, 11.2.74	2(1)	3	4(1)	4	28	9
SLAVEN BILIC	22(2)	-	22(2)	-	48	2
Croatia, 11.9.68	3	-	3	-	6	1
MICHAEL BRANCH	1(5)	-	15(19)	3	-	-
Liverpool, 18.10.78	-	-	1(1)	-	-	-
DANNY CADAMARTERI	15(11)	4	15(12)	4	-	-
Bradford, 12.10.79	2(2)	1	2(2)	1	-	-
ALEX CLELAND	-	-	-	-	246	12
Glasgow, 10.12.70	-	-	-	-	68	5
JOHN COLLINS	-	-	-	-	380	63
Galashiels, 31.1.68	-	-	-	-	87	12
OLIVIER DACOURT	-	-	-	-	-	-
Montreuil, 25.9.74	-	-	-	-	-	-
RICHARD DUNNE	2(1)	-	8(2)	-	-	-
Dublin, 21.9.79	1	-	2	-	-	-
GARETH FARRELLY	18(8)	1	18(8)	1	18	2
Dublin, 28.8.75	2	1	2	1	1	-
DUNCAN FERGUSON	28(1)	11	97(6)	33	91	30
Stirling, 27.12.71	3	-	12(1)	4	22	11
PAUL GERRARD	4	-	8(1)	-	119	-
Heywood, 22.1.73	2	-	2	-	17	-
TONY GRANT	7	1	30(13)	2	3	1
Liverpool, 14.11.74	2	-	7(5)	1	-	-
DON HUTCHISON	11	1	11	1	182	25
Gateshead, 9.5.71	-	-	-	-	37	6
FRANCIS JEFFERS	-(1)	-	-(1)	-	-	-
Liverpool, 25.1.81	-	-	-	-	-	-
PHILLIP JEVONS	-	-	-	-	-	-
Liverpool, 1.8.79	-	-	-	-	-	-
GAVIN McCANN	5(6)	-	5(6)	-	-	-
Blackpool, 10.1.78	-	-	-	-	-	-
MATT McKAY	-	-	-	-	5	-
Warrington, 21.1.81	-	-	-	-	-	-
MICKAEL MADAR	15(2)	6	15(2)	6	-	-
Paris, 8.5.68	-	-	-	-	-	-
MARCO MATERAZZI	-	-	-	-	-	-
Perugia, 19.8.73	-	-	-	-	-	-
THOMAS MYHRE	22	-	22	-	-	-
Sarpsborg, 16.10.73	1	-	1	-	-	-
JOHN O'KANE	12	-	12	-	22	3
Nottingham, 15.11.74	-	-	-	-	6	-
JOHN OSTER	16(15)	1	16(15)	1	24	3
Boston, 8.12.78	3(1)	1	3(1)	1	1	1
JOE PARKINSON	-	-	88(2)	3	149	7
Eccles, 11.6.71	-	-	17	1	37	2
TERRY PHELAN	8(1)	-	23(1)	-	336	2
Manchester, 16.3.67	-(1)	-	1(1)	-	84	3
CRAIG SHORT	27(4)	-	68(9)	4	310	22
Bridlington, 25.6.68	2	-	12	-	70	8
JOHN SPENCER	3(3)	-	3(3)	-	168	61
Glasgow, 11.9.70	-	-	-	-	46	10
TONY THOMAS	6(1)	-	6(1)	-	257	12
Liverpool, 12.7.71	2	-	2	-	50	2
CARL TILER	19	1	19	1	177	7
Sheffield, 11.1.70	1	-	1	-	42	-
MITCH WARD	8	-	8	-	159	12
Sheffield, 19.6.71	-	-	-	-	27	5
DAVE WATSON	25(1)	1	392(3)	23	212	11
Liverpool, 20.11.61	3	-	98(1)	14	44	4
DANNY WILLIAMSON	15	-	15	-	64	6
West Ham, 5.12.73	2	-	2	-	10	2
OWN GOALS	-	2	-	2	-	-

ALSO PLAYED: Earl **Barrett** (to Sheffield Wednesday) 12(1) apps (Lge); Peter **Beagrie** (loan from Bradford) 4(2) apps (Lge); Andy **Hinchcliffe** (to Sheffield Wednesday) 15(2) apps (Lge), 3 apps (Cup); Jon O'Connor (to Sheffield United) 1 sub (Lge); Gary **Speed** (to Newcastle United) 21 apps, 6 goals (Lge), 3 apps (Cup); Neville **Southall** (to Stoke City) 12 apps (Lge), 1 app (Cup); Graham **Stuart** (to Sheffield United) 14 apps, 2 goals (Lge), 3 apps, 1 goal (Cup); Claus **Thomsen** (to AB Copenhagen) 2(6) apps, 1 goal (Lge), 1 app (Cup).

97-98 Factfile

DATE	OPPOSITION	V	RES	ATT
AUG 9	CRYSTAL PALACE	H	1-2	35,716
AUG 23	WEST HAM UNITED	H	2-1	34,356
AUG 27	MANCHESTER UNITED	H	0-2	40,079
SEP 1	BOLTON WANDERERS	A	0-0	23,131
SEP 13	DERBY COUNTY	A	1-3	27,828
SEP 16	SCUNTHORPE UTD (CCC)	A	1-0	7,145
SEP 20	BARNSLEY	H	4-2	32,659
SEP 24	NEWCASTLE UNITED	A	0-1	36,705
SEP 27	ARSENAL	H	2-2	35,457
OCT 1	SCUNTHORPE UTD (CCC)	H	5-0	11,562
OCT 4	SHEFFIELD WEDNESDAY	A	1-3	24,486
OCT 15	COVENTRY CITY (CCC)	A	1-4	10,087
OCT 18	LIVERPOOL	H	†2-0	40,112
OCT 25	COVENTRY CITY	A	0-0	18,760
NOV 2	SOUTHAMPTON	H	0-2	29,565
NOV 8	BLACKBURN ROVERS	A	2-3	25,397
NOV 22	ASTON VILLA	A	1-2	36,389
NOV 26	CHELSEA	A	0-2	34,148
NOV 29	TOTTENHAM HOTSPUR	H	0-2	36,670
DEC 6	LEEDS UNITED	A	0-0	34,869
DEC 13	WIMBLEDON	H	0-0	28,533
DEC 20	LEICESTER CITY	A	1-0	20,628
DEC 26	MANCHESTER UNITED	A	0-2	55,167
DEC 28	BOLTON WANDERERS	H	3-2	37,149
JAN 4	NEWCASTLE UTD FAC 3	H	0-1	20,885
JAN 10	CRYSTAL PALACE	A	3-1	23,311
JAN 18	CHELSEA	H	†3-1	32,355
JAN 31	WEST HAM UNITED	A	2-2	25,909
FEB 7	BARNSLEY	A	2-2	18,672
FEB 14	DERBY COUNTY	H	1-2	34,876
FEB 23	LIVERPOOL	A	1-1	44,501
FEB 28	NEWCASTLE UNITED	H	0-0	37,972
MAR 7	SOUTHAMPTON	A	1-2	15,102
MAR 14	BLACKBURN ROVERS	H	1-0	33,423
MAR 28	ASTON VILLA	H	1-4	36,471
APR 4	TOTTENHAM HOTSPUR	A	1-1	35,624
APR 11	LEEDS UNITED	H	2-0	37,099
APR 13	WIMBLEDON	A	0-0	15,131
APR 18	LEICESTER CITY	H	1-1	33,642
APR 25	SHEFFIELD WEDNESDAY	H	1-3	35,497
MAY 3	ARSENAL	A	0-4	38,269
MAY 10	COVENTRY CITY	H	1-1	40,109

Everton Roll Call Info: 1st Line: Premiership and Football League games Line: Cup games. Other Career figures include the above competitions as Scottish League and Cup appearances and games while on loan from Eve

KEY TO SYMBOLS & ABBREVIATIONS ● Goals Scored ●s Substitute & Player Replace FAC = F A Cu CCC = Coca-

Player columns with shirt numbers:

3	Andy HINCHCLIFFE
4	Danny WILLIAMSON
5	Dave WATSON
6	Terry PHELAN
7	Graham STUART
8	Nick BARMBY
9	Duncan FERGUSON
10	Gary SPEED
11	John SPENCER
12	Craig SHORT
13	Paul GERRARD
14	Tony GRANT
15	Claus THOMSEN
16	Michael BRANCH
17	Gareth FARRELLY
18	Joe PARKINSON
19	John OSTER
20	Tony THOMAS
21	Mitch WARD
22	Gavin McCANN
23	Carl TILER
24	Jonathan O'CONNOR
25	Michael BALL
26	Graham ALLEN
27	Richard DUNNE
28	Slaven BILIC
29	Danny CADAMARTERI
30	Phillip JEVONS
31	Thomas MYHRE
32	John O'KANE
33	John O'TOOLE
34	Francis JEFFERS
35	John HILLS

Inset labels within grid: Mickael MADAR — 7; Don HUTCHISON — 10; Peter BEAGRIE — 15

...RTON FOOTBALL CLUB WOULD LIKE TO THANK THE FOLLOWING COMPANIES FOR THEIR SUPPORT
...nier Asphalt Ltd, Lever Bros, Jaguar House, Radio City, Manfast Transport , Deans Farm, Fazakerley Rewinds,
...ard Symmons & Partners , Lawtons Ltd, GTB Demolition, KPMG , Sayers the Bakers, Centre Print, IFS Group,
...em, O'Hare Ltd, The Littlewoods Organisation, Express Daries Direct Service, Mitie Group plc, The Royal Bank
...cotland, The Lobster Hotel, Silverbeck Rymer Solicitors, Baker-Petrolite, The Whitbread Beer Co, MJ Quinn
...trical, Kennedy Advertising, Powerflow Hydraulics Ltd, Tradeline Shipping (UK) Ltd, Armstrong Laing Plc,
...n Contract Services, Moore Scott & Co Ltd, David McLean Contractors Ltd, North West Precision Ltd.

EVERTON WORLDWIDE WEBSITE... **HIT THE NET: HTTP://WWW.EVERTONFC.COM**

"GOOD LUCK TO THE BLUES ON SATURDAY. PLEASE, PLEASE GIVE US A WIN"

As noted in the news section, the increasing influence of overseas talent in English and Scottish football continued to attract media interest.

Never a publication to shirk footballing issues, the 'Keeping up with market trends' article in the 1990/91 QPR programme highlighted the issue of escalating prices for English talent, and the option to buy cheaper alternatives from abroad.

The relaxing of regulations regarding overseas players and the political changes in eastern Europe meant a new pool of players was available – with the article concluding on the following note:

'...partly the product of an ever-changing world and undoubtedly an indication that football is becoming more cosmopolitan. What course will be taken in the future is purely a matter of speculation.'

Scandinavian supporters are more commonly associated with other English clubs – but even Everton can boast some of the most loyal followings further afield – or in Finland, as Osmo Tapio Raihala can testify from late 1992/93.

Osmo was bemused by falling attendances, and the disparity between the highest and lowest crowds at Goodison. He noted:

Keeping up with market trends

THIS time last year no British goalkeeper had ever been transferred for £1m. Today there are four in the First Division with seven-figure price-tags.

The barrier was first broken on 15th November 1989 when Nigel Martyn's move from Bristol Rovers to Crystal Palace extended the British record from £600,000 for Chris Woods (Norwich to Rangers, 1986), £750,000 for Jim Leighton (Aberdeen to Manchester United, 1988) and £800,000 for Dave Beasant (Newcastle to Wimbledon, 1988).

All this was not so much representative of inflation as of the law of supply-and-demand.

In another way, it possibly explains why today's Goodison Park visitors, Queens Park Rangers, looked abroad when they found themselves in a chain-reaction situation in the goalkeeping market.

In May they sold David Seaman to Arsenal for £1.3m and within a week the Gunners transferred John Lukic to Leeds United for £1m. Another £1m deal was struck in July when Watford's Tony Coton joined Manchester City.

Faced with this soaraway movement in the home market, QPR's coach, Don Howe, agreed to pay in excess of £500,000 to Sparta Prague for Jan Stejskal, who was Czechoslovakia's No 1 during the World Cup finals in the summer.

By coincidence, Stejskal's national team deputy, Ludek Mikolosko, was already in London, having joined West Ham United from Banik Ostrava for £300,000 last February.

The arrival of two Czech 'keepers was almost a shock to the system because even in the darkest times for British international football there was a sense of pride in our depth of talent in this department, from Banks through to Clemence, Shilton, Southall etc.

Stejskal now makes up a trio of overseas 'keepers in the First Division with Erik Thorstvedt, of Tottenham, and Hans Segers, of Wimbledon.

Taking into account the Welsh and Scottish representatives, as well as the ineligible Bruce Grobbelaar, this means that the England manager can choose from barely a dozen 'keepers in the premier national league.

This problem has always been with us because the Football League feeds four other international teams from the British Isles in addition to England.

Now there are other factors. The European Community is to encourage greater freedom of movement in the labour market and the political changes in Eastern Europe freed previously unavailable players to move to the West.

UEFA, the ruling body of European football, perceived a danger in that the best talent could be monopolised by a handful of countries. This was the thinking behind the new ruling that only four "non-nationals" should be allowed in each squad in European competitions.

Only time will tell how this will influence the transfer policies of individual clubs, but for the moment, all the signs point to a second wave of overseas buying.

The first influx came in the period between 1978 and 1982. British fans admired the skills of Ossic Ardiles and the Dutchmen at Ipswich, Frans Thijssen and Arnold Muhren, but the rush to go international resulted in burned fingers for many clubs.

The tables in this feature reveal that very few overseas players made long-standing or significant contributions. The sample is not meant to be all-encompassing but it covers most of the signings made by clubs at First Division level.

After the initial rush, there was a stock-taking period in the mid-1980s. Only a handful of foreign players were signed from 1982 to 1989 and in the main the shopping was aimed at the better-quality players of current international standing. Jan Molby, Jesper Olsen, Johnny Metgod and Nico Claesen were among the additions who gave good service, and in the main, at a price which was consider-

ably below the British level for players of similar quality.

While our top internationals were commanding fees beyond £1m and eventually topping £2m at home, we began to see prices escalating past two, three and four million pounds for British players who moved to France, Spain or Italy.

Given this situation, it was probably no surprise when First Division managers returned to the alternative market in Europe, notably in Holland and the Scandinavian countries.

This trend gathered in pace in the last two years. As a result, there are now a couple of dozen overseas players with First Division clubs, and for the first time, we have £1m players from abroad, i.e. Anders Limpar at Arsenal and Ronny Rosenthal at Liverpool.

Two Danes, Kent Nielsen at Aston Villa and Lars Elstrup at Luton Town, cost more than £500,000 and now QPR's Stejskal is the most expensive goalkeeper to be brought into English football.

This is partly the product of an ever-changing world and undoubtedly an indication that football is becoming more cosmopolitan. What course will be taken in the future is purely a matter of speculation.

Jan Stejskal organises the Czech defence.

4

THE DAY OF RECKONING

DECISION DAY has arrived. Rarely have we played such an important game on the last Saturday in the season. Quite simply, the club's membership of the Premier League is at stake.

For 40 years the name of Everton has featured in the top division of English football. We are proud of that record, and as one big family of True Blues - management, players and supporters - we want it to continue.

So much has happened since that April day at Oldham in 1954 when John Willie Parker, Dave Hickson and T.E. Jones scored the goals which restored the Blues to the First Division stage.

We have celebrated four Championships, two FA Cup wins at Wembley and a first European success in the Cup-winners' Cup. Of course, there were disappointments but the good times comfortably outnumbered the bad days.

New generations of supporters grew up along the way, and now the children of the 1950s are the parents of the 1990s. The future of the club will be with their children, and on this vital day for all Evertonians, let's hear the optimism of youth.

◆ Jonathan Scally is aged 16. He wants to talk about the new Park End Stand, and his vision of Evertonians at BOTH ends of the ground, cheering on the Blues to victory in the Premiership next season.

He writes: "I would like to know whether Evertonians can have the Park End to sit in during home games, and will the away supporters be staying in the corner of the Upper Bullens Stand?

"If not, I think that Everton supporters should be there because why should away supporters have the best facilities, when they don't see Everton every week?

"Another point is that a lot of away teams don't bring many supporters with them, so a new 6,000-seater stand would look empty with only one or two thousand away supporters. It would look better full of Evertonians."

Rest assured, Jonathan. The Park End will be allocated to Everton fans - and on an exclusive basis for the majority of matches. If it is necessary to accommodate some away supporters, segregation is catered for in the design of the stand.

◆ Philip Rimmer is aged 11. He can't

'If I lived a thousand miles closer to Liverpool, nothing could keep me away from Goodison.'

There was also correspondence noting a dream Evertonian scoreboard scene, the picture taken at the national stadium in Riyadh, Saudi Arabia - note Peter Beardsley's own goal in the Blues' 6-1 victory!

The comment piece from the 1993/94 'Day Of Reckoning' against Wimbledon turned to the new generation of Evertonians to boost spirits.

The first home programme of 2000, against Leicester City, gave special prominence to Everton's Millennium Giants.

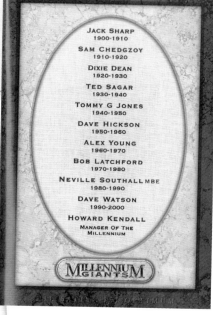

JACK SHARP
1900-1910
SAM CHEDGZOY
1910-1920
DIXIE DEAN
1920-1930
TED SAGAR
1930-1940
TOMMY G JONES
1940-1950
DAVE HICKSON
1950-1960
ALEX YOUNG
1960-1970
BOB LATCHFORD
1970-1980
NEVILLE SOUTHALL MBE
1980-1990
DAVE WATSON
1990-2000
HOWARD KENDALL
MANAGER OF THE MILLENNIUM

MILLENNIUM GIANTS

In SUPPORT

BLUE MAIL

◆ Thanks to everyone for their contributions over the season - but keep writing so that we have plenty of letters for the start of next season. The address: Blue Mail, Everton FC, Goodison Park, Liverpool L4 4EL.

From: Osmo Tapio Raihala, Everton Supporters' Club, Finland. . .
I wonder why Everton fans seem to be the most disloyal to their favourites. The supporters tend to turn away immediately when any silverware is no longer available to the club in the near future.

Last season, in example, the biggest crowd was 37,681 vs Liverpool and the lowest 15,201 vs Southampton. This season it's been the same. The difference between the best and the worst crowd is bigger than the average attendance!

It seems that only the derby match attracts a crowd of 30,000 plus nowadays. The mighty Spurs' visit was watched by only 16,164 spectators. Perhaps it's a question of admission prices?

In my opinion, the fans let down Everton. Somebody might say that the results haven't been much to brag about, but at least the players are trying their best, whatever the conditions. The same can't be said about the fans.

I can't understand why Liverpool attract 35,000 spectators week week out, no matter how poorly they play.

I think that every Scouser with a blue heart, or anybody in the nearhood of Liverpool, should give

everything to get a chance to give his/her support to the Toffees. If I lived a thousand miles closer to Liverpool, nothing could keep me away from Goodison whenever Everton play, and you could hardly call me a woolly-back!

EDITOR: Replies, please, for next season from Merseyside-based fans!

From: Oliver Dalton, Oswestry, Shropshire. . .
I thought you might like to print the enclosed photograph (above) in a forthcoming programme.

My father, uncle and I are all season ticket holders but my uncle has been working over in Saudi Arabia. He had the message printed on the scoreboard at the King Fahd International Stadium in Riyadh.

EDITOR: Like the stadium, like the score, but who's this man Dalton? Sign him on!

From: Mark Belcher, Willenhall, West Midlands. . .
Although I applaud Aston Villa for dropping their admission prices, I feel that it's the away supporters who are still getting a raw deal.

I live about 20 miles from Villa Park and decided to take one of my three daughters with me to the game between Everton and Villa.

It was a good job I only took the one with me. After paying £5.50 in train fares, I was left with £24.50, and when I got to the away supporters' turnstile, to my horror the admission price was £12 - no concessions for children.

Luckily, I just had enough to get in but I didn't have enough left for a cup of tea let alone a programme.

But I must say I was fortunate compared with the man standing behind me in the queue. He had travelled from Liverpool with his wife and three children. So it cost him £60

From: G.Hoople, Lydiate...
Yesterday (18.11.90 v Spurs), I and my two young teenage daughters attended Goodison Park and watched a thoroughly entertaining game of football.

However, it is more than 25 years since I attended a professional match and both my children and I were shocked at the tirade of foul language issuing from the mouths of so-called "dedicated" fans. Yes, I have read the notice in your programme, but I'm not sure if 'they' had, for it made no difference. I wish you luck in your efforts to reduce this element of your fanatics. Perhaps it will be better when I bring my grandchildren.

PS: We did enjoy the game.

Mind Your Language, Cup Vouchers, 1990/91

Frustrations can sometimes get the better of the most placid football supporter – although for one fan, the use of industrial language at Goodison was enough to disappoint as he attended with his family. Still, at least they enjoyed the game...

One other letter caught the eye in a programme from the campaign.

A hand-written letter was received in the wake of the club's decision to distribute vouchers for cup ties – particularly useful for loyal fans in the clamour for Merseyside derby FA Cup tickets...

35 Ryegate Rd
Garston
L'pool 19
27-2-91

I would like to thank the club for the option to buy Cup vouchers with their season tickets. What a boon this has been for the two cup-replays with Liverpool while other people have been queuing for hours all I had to do was turn up on the night and tear out my voucher.

S. Williams.

ADVANCE TICKET ADVANTAGES...
◆ This letter is one of many received from supporters who bought cup-tie vouchers with their season tickets last summer.

The Liverpool replays outlined the advantages. Tickets had to be distributed at short notice, and obviously, it wasn't possible to deal with postal applications.

Season ticket holders who had not taken up the option faced inevitable delays in the queue for tickets. But those in possession of vouchers were able to come along and take up their normal seats, and at a discount on the price of tickets sold in the week of the match.

Chief executive Jim Greenwood says: "We hope more season ticket holders will consider this option for next season. A lot of people may not have been aware of the scheme or felt that it wasn't necessary because they knew they would be able to claim their own seat with a cash purchase at the time of a big game."

Everton are one of the few clubs who provide the latter service for season ticket holders, but it is a laborious task and there are inevitable delays in allocating individual seats to each season ticket holder. This was a particular problem when as many as 30,000 tickets were sold in two days to personal callers for the first Liverpool game.

Mr Greenwood says: "We don't want to discontinue this policy but we may have to reserve the right to withdraw it in certain circumstances. In other words, if we have a situation like the first Liverpool match, playing away on Sunday and replaying on Wednesday, it may not be possible to provide this facility.

It would be to the benefit of all supporters if more season ticket holders took up the voucher option.

The scheme is designed so that there is no obligation to attend what some might regard as lesser occasions. We don't include the Zenith Cup or the first round of the League Cup, so, in the main, you are paying for the bigger games which most likely you would wish to attend in any case.

If there aren't enough cup-ties to use up all the vouchers, supporters receive a credit to be set against their payment for the following year.

YOU BET - FOR THE BLUES!

◆ Peter Beardsley was invited by Ladbroke's to place a bet for charity last week-end. The free wager was £100 on Everton winning the Championship at 50 to 1, the market price at the time the deal struck. Peter is pictured with Ladbroke's staff, Doreen Tench and Graham Purcell.

Blues Bet, 1992/93

A year before Tony Cottee's charity bet, Peter Beardsley was given the honour of backing the Blues for the title – at odds of 50-1...

Numbers Game, 1993/94

A new innovation for the season, the novelty of squad numbers was an oddity the comment article was keen to exploit. The signing of 41-year-old John Burridge by Newcastle as a goalkeeping back-up was recognised thus:

'...he is coming up towards Birthday No 42 – and that's 13 more than his shirt number.'

Meanwhile the Guardian's David Lacey questioned the squad numbering decision:

'Where is the sense in Ian Butterworth, the Norwich captain, being allotted No 17? There would be more logic in Wimbledon making Vinnie Jones 007.' Not far from the truth, as it happened...

A FAVOURITE RETURNS...
COMMENT

Joe Royle is Everton's 11th post-war manager and the third from the 1970 Championship team - following in the footsteps of Howard Kendall and Colin Harvey, who were also among his team-mates in the 1968 FA Cup Final.

The appointment at Goodison Park was an emotional homecoming for an Evertonian who made his mark among the outstanding centre forwards in the club's history with 119 goals 275 appearances in all major competitions.

After nearly 20 years away from Merseyside, the last 12 as manager at Oldham Athletic, he took up residence in the Bellefield office which was built - and first occupied by the legendary Harry

Catterick - during Joe's time as an Everton player.

Old friendships were rekindled with his return, but for his assistant, Willie Donachie, it's a first time at Everton after playing alongside Joe and Norwich and Norwich, and working with him for ten years as player and coach at Oldham.

The hand of coincidence was also at work in reuniting Messrs Royle and Donachie with Dave Watson - a team-mate at Norwich City in the early 1980s.

With words of welcome from Dave, we introduce the new management team on pages four and five in the form of a full statistical breakdown of their careers to date...

CHAIRMAN PETER JOHNSON WELCOMES JOE ON HIS RETURN TO THE CLUB

COMMENT

PLAYING BY NUMBERS TAKE YOUR PICK!

A MAJORITY of clubs, Everton among them, retained some identity with the past in declaring the players' shirt numbers for the new squad system.

Though there always will be changes in personnel, according to form and injuries, Howard Kendall's selection was in a recognisable 1 to 11 format. Full backs at numbers 2 and 3; central defenders at 5 and 6; wide players at 7 and 11; a central striker at 9.

Others, however, have given the impression that numbers were distributed on a "first through the door" process. This, apparently, is much to the annoyance of David Lacey, football correspondent of The Guardian.

He wrote: "Putting players' names on shirts and giving each man a squad number might have been a good idea in theory. In practice it is causing untold confusion.

"The names are illegible from any sort of distance and there is neither rhyme nor reason about the numbering. On the opening day, Sheffield United's back four reportedly lined up wearing 11, 14, 20 and 16. Where is the sense, moreover, in Ian Butterworth, the Norwich captain, being allotted No 17? There would be more logic in Wimbledon making Vinnie Jones 007."

Mr Lacey went off in search of an explanation as to why it was necessary to make a radical change. "It was to help identification, pure and simple," said Mike Foster, the Premiership secretary. "And you can't have names without squad numbering. The two are interlinked."

Mr Foster confirmed that one or two clubs had reservations but, quite rightly, he urged everyone to take their time in passing judgment.

Perhaps some negative reaction was almost inevitable in a country where people feel comfortable with established practices. Essentially we are a nation of traditionalists. After all, it wasn't until 1939 that shirt numbering became compulsory in the Football League.

Finally, a lighter note from Mr Lacey's Talking Point column. Some clubs, he ventured, may have missed an opportunity in their numbering. Why not an Austin 7 at Tottenham? That's Dean Austin, of course, but, as a right back, he has been allocated a rather ordinary No 2!

B RITAIN'S gold, silver and bronze athletes returned from the European Championships with a common plea. In a nutshell they said: Give us the money, give us the facilities and we'll give you even better results.

Appropriate, then, that their homecoming coincided with Michael Parkinson's campaigning on their behalf in The Daily Telegraph - and with no less a subject than the Prime Minister.

Mr Parkinson's opening lines summed the frustrations of many. "The sure way to render most of our politicians speechless is to ask them about sport. In other countries politicians take sport seriously, giving it a place on the political agenda and sufficient funds to ensure a system which affords every facility for those who want to play and watch.

"By comparison, take a look around Britain. What you will find is that our stadiums, though improving in some areas, are third rate and anyone who succeeds in sport in Britain does so, generally speaking, in spite of the system and not because of it."

This was part of the scene-setter leading up to an interview with John Major.

The Prime Minister is known to be a keen follower of sport and straightaway he said: "I think we have undervalued sport and the place it has in our national life."

Conceding that many of his colleagues at Westminster would say sport was "a fetish of mine", he went on to express his hopes for the National Lottery.

"I believe it will produce a good deal of money over the next few years - a quarter of it will go to sport. "That will dwarf any resources sport has had from any government at any stage in the past. I think it will make a great difference to the sporting facilities we have in this country over the next decade or so."

Any influx of new money has to be welcomed, though as we have said before, it remains to be seen how football will fare, especially if existing sources of income should suffer in competition with the lottery.

John Burridge has already staked a claim to being the oldest player in a Premiership squad this season.

Re-signed by Newcastle United as a cover goalkeeper, he is coming up towards Birthday No 42 - and that's 13 more than his shirt number!

Royle Blue, 1994/95

Joe Royle's appointment in November 1994 was greeted with delight by the majority of supporters, the third player from the club's victorious 1969/70 champions to take on the mantle.

Peter Johnson's statement, upon the dismissal of previous manager Mike Walker, was also succinct and to the point - that on the field, performances had not been good enough.

'It would be irresponsible for the directors to let the present situation continue and they believe a change will be beneficial for the club.'

DANIEL AMOKACHI

CAREER
What's Hot: Playing in the World Cup Finals for Nigeria in the USA.
What's Not: Having a difficult time getting into the Everton team last season.

FOOD
What's Hot: Chinese.
What's Not: Having to cook for myself.

MUSIC
What's Hot: Soul/Rap.
What's Not: Heavy Metal.

TELEVISION
What's Hot: Hanging with Mr. Cooper.
What's Not: Coronation Street.

TRAINING
What's Hot: Having to train alongside Andrei Kanchelskis, Anders Limpar and Vinny Samways.
What's Not: Being in the middle with Willie Donachie and having to work extra, extra hard!

HOLIDAY SPOTS
What's Hot: Miami and Malaga.
What's Not: I haven't visited a bad place yet.

FOOTBALL GROUNDS
What's Hot: The Noucamp Stadium, Barcelona.
What's Not: Any Pontins League ground on a wet, cold night!

FOOTBALL CLUBS
What's Hot: Newcastle United.
What's Not: West Ham United.

CLOTHES
What's Hot: The gangster look.
What's Not: Definitely Neville Southall's gear.

TEAM-MATES' DRESS SENSE
What's Hot: I am definitely cool.
What's Not: Neville Southall's and John Ebbrell's underwear.

DRINK
What's Hot: Fruit cocktail.
What's Not: Any alcohol, I have never tasted an alcoholic drink in my life.

GOALS
What's Hot: My goal against Greece in the World Cup.
What's Not: The penalty by Italy's Roberto Baggio which put us out of the tournament.

What's Hot
WHAT'S NOT...

What's Hot, What's Not, 1995/96

A popular series, where a member of the first-team or coaching staff were asked to give an answer to a range of sometimes incidental subjects.

Revelations from Daniel Amokachi included:

TELEVISION: What's Hot – Hanging with Mr Cooper; What's Not – Coronation Street; CLOTHES: What's Hot – The gangster look; What's Not: Definitely Neville Southall's gear; TEAM-MATES' DRESS SENSE: What's Hot – I am definitely cool; What's Not – Neville Southall's and John Ebbrell's underwear...

Dixie, 1995/96

A regular page for younger Evertonians, the content concentrated on taking a more 'sideways' look at what the players got up to off the field – or, usually, on their lack of sartorial elegance.

Supporters could keep up to date with the players' haircut choices, how Duncan Ferguson enjoyed watching Braveheart – and "knew the dates of the battles before they'd even come up" according to Craig Short – and how Daniel Amokachi and Earl Barrett went to a concert at Wembley Arena by stretch limousine.

There was also a piece in the Leeds United programme, the final game of 1995, regarding Everton New Year Resolutions. These included ones for Les Ferdinand ('stop picking on Everton'), Andrei Kanchelskis ('to actually break the sound barrier') and Roy Evans ('accept defeat gracefully after a Merseyside derby').

The name of a relatively obscure Belgian footballer will be forever associated with one of the most far-reaching decisions to affect the game in modern times. I am, of course, referring to the Bosman case.

Millions of words have been written on the subject, but the first point to make is that there is still a long way to go before we become aware of the exact ramifications, as far as they relate to the transfer system, either in an individual country or movement of players across frontiers.

What we can say is that the ruling is likely to have more effect on the lower clubs because they do need transfer money to cascade down the divisions, particularly for the funding of expensive youth development schemes. A prime example is that of Crewe Alexandra, a model to all clubs introducing their own players. But they can only do that with the profit from selling the likes of David Platt, Rob Jones and Craig Hignett.

Because most of the major transfers take place between Premiership clubs, it does not mean that the money is confined to the highest level. For instance, Southend United received a number of sizeable payments from the sale of Stan Collymore, initially from clauses relating to goals scored and international recognition with Nottingham Forest and finally from his move to Liverpool.

I don't believe that the larger clubs will be greatly affected by the changes. Any ambitious player will still want to go to the biggest and best, and will always take his pick from the Evertons, Liverpools and Manchester Uniteds, etc.

Another point to remember regarding Bosman is that we are only talking about players who are at the end of their contracts. Buying and selling will continue as before for players in contract. The question is whether the size of fees will be affected, if they are it may be a step forward in bringing sanity and reality to the transfer market.

Of more immediate concern to the leading clubs - those who may be taking part in Europe next season - is that UEFA are attempting to hold on to the ridiculous restriction on the number of foreign players in teams competing in their three competitions.

I am sure this will fall quite quickly; indeed I wonder how it has lasted so long. I find it quite absurd that someone from Llandudno is classed as a foreigner if he plays football for Everton.

PETER JOHNSON
Chairman, Everton FC

Megastore, Screen, Bosman, 1995/96

Opened in autumn 1995, the iconic club store attracted a trio of centre-forward legends including the then current boss.

The season was also notable for the Bosman Rule change, allowing players greater freedom of movement - an issue the chairman was keen to address.

Meanwhile over 8,500 fans enjoyed the Anfield derby win - watching on a big screen at Goodison...

Everton fans across the world can now benefit from one of the most state-of-the-art football websites around.
The Blues have teamed up with Planetfootball.com the market leaders in official football websites. Amongst the features of the site is full audio commentary of all home and away league matches. Daily interviews with the manager and players, along with statistics and information on everything that is Everton Football Club.
"The launch of our new site has allowed us to give our tremendous fan base across the globe the chance to feel part of the club wherever they are 24 hours a day," says Communications manager Alan Myers.
The websites full time on site reporter Mark Rowan will be in daily contact with Walter Smith. If news breaks Mark will be on hand to deliver it straight away as it happens from the training ground at Bellefield or Goodison Park. With competitions, games and a Community website which is second to none the facility gives fans around the world the chance to interact with each other.
The other exciting aspect of the website is the e-commerce side, which will give Blues fans the opportunity to purchase from the wide range of merchandise on offer in the Everton range, wherever and whenever they want to.
So join Walter on the web at:
www.evertonfc.com

Toffee Joe, Internet Pioneers, 1999/2000

Fans liaison officer Joe Parkinson fronted the campaign to give fans free Toffees ahead of the final game of the season - the club signing a new kit sponsorship deal the reason for the generosity.

The growing influence of online sources had been noted towards the back end of the century - and manager Walter Smith was shown 'getting to grips' with the club website in late 1999, benefiting 'from one of the most state-of-the-art football websites around'.

2000-2013

The modern era – The People's Club – embracing the old, as well as the new in the 21st century

Having celebrated the turn of the Millennium, the first new programme of the first full 21st century season featured a more sober design.

The following four seasons saw the title changed to 'Blue' – the first season being voted third place in the Programme of the Year awards – with publishing partners Tobin helping to launch special edition '100th season in the top flight' publications in 2002/03.

'efc' was adopted for the club's first foray into European competition for a decade, with the 2005/06 corporate-looking designs evolving into a more fan-friendly product the following season. Trinity Mirror Sport Media's initial three-year tenure included special edition European and retro specials, as well as tributes to club legends Brian Labone and Alan Ball in the wake of their passing.

Cre8 Publishing fulfilled programme publishing duties for over two seasons before Trinity Mirror Sport Media were brought back midway through the 2011/12 season. The company continued to introduce retro imagery to covers and were able to offer the programme as a digital download for the first time in 2012/13. The final home match of David Moyes' tenure, in May 2013 against West Ham United, also saw two different programme covers made available: the first a farewell to the retiring club skipper Phil Neville; the second, Moyes himself, saluting the crowd following that final game, made available the following week.

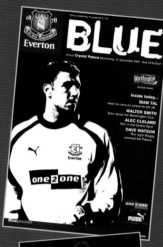

Selected covers, which represent the decade, showcasing the transformation from basic to experimental in terms of design, colour and style. Clockwise from above: v Newcastle United, 2000/01; v Crystal Palace (League Cup), 2001/02; v Crystal Palace, 2004/05; v Stoke City, 2010/11; v Manchester United, 2006/07; v West Bromwich Albion, 2005/06; v Tamworth (FA Cup) 2011/12

Clockwise from top left:
v Chelsea (League Cup),
2007/08; v Fiorentina
(UEFA Cup), 2007/08;
v West Bromwich
Albion, 2013/14; v
Blackpool, 2010/11; v
West Ham United (both
covers), 2012/13; v
Norwich City, 2011/12;
v Stoke City, 2008/09;
(centre programme)
v Manchester United,
2009/10

Everton

Manager: David Moyes

- 1 Carlo Nash
- 2 Tony Hibbert
- 3 Leighton Baines
- 4 Joseph Yobo
- 5 Joleon Lescott
- 6 Phil Jagielka
- 7 Andy van der Meyde
- 8 Segundo Castillo
- 9 Louis Saha
- 10 Mikel Arteta
- 12 Iain Turner
- 14 James Vaughan
- 15 Lars Jacobsen
- 17 Tim Cahill
- 18 Phil Neville
- 19 Nuno Valente
- 20 Steven Pienaar
- 21 Leon Osman
- 22 Ayegbeni Yakubu
- 24 Tim Howard
- 25 Marouane Fellaini
- 26 Jack Rodwell
- 27 Lukas Jutkiewicz
- 28 Victor Anichebe
- 30 John Ruddy
- 32 Dan Gosling
- 34 John Irving
- 35 Kieran Agard
- 36 John Paul Kissock
- 37 Jose Baxter
- 38 James Wallace

Manager: Sir Alex Ferguson

- 1 Edwin Van der Sar
- 2 Gary Neville
- 3 Patrice Evra
- 4 Owen Hargreaves
- 5 Rio Ferdinand
- 6 Wes Brown
- 7 Cristiano Ronaldo
- 8 Anderson
- 9 Dimitar Berbatov
- 10 Wayne Rooney
- 11 Ryan Giggs
- 12 Ben Foster
- 13 Ji-Sung Park
- 15 Nemanja Vidic
- 16 Michael Carrick
- 17 Nani
- 18 Paul Scholes
- 19 Danny Welbeck
- 20 Fabio Da Silva
- 21 Rafael Da Silva
- 22 John O'Shea
- 23 Jonny Evans
- 24 Darren Fletcher
- 26 Manucho
- 28 Darron Gibson
- 29 Tomasz Kuszczak
- 32 Carlos Tevez
- 33 Sam Hewson
- 34 Rodrigo Possebon
- 36 David Gray
- 40 Ben Amos

Safety message

All announcements made on the Public Address system which affect the safety of spectators on the premises will be preceded by a two-tone signal.

evertonfc.com

Everton Prog Oct 25 08 £3

4 3

9 771751 747063

v Manchester United, 2008/09

TODAY'S LINE-UPS

Everton v Tottenham Hotspur

Everton			Tottenham Hotspur	
Richard Wright	1	1	Neil Sullivan	
Steve Watson	2	2	Stephen Carr	
Alessandro Pistone	3	3	Mauricio Taricco	
Alan Stubbs	4	4	Steffen Freund	
David Weir	5	5	Goran Bunjevcevic	
David Unsworth	6	6	Chris Perry	
Niclas Alexandersson	7	7	Darren Anderton	
Tomasz Radzinski	8	8	Tim Sherwood	
Kevin Campbell	9	9	Les Ferdinand	
Duncan Ferguson	10	10	Teddy Sheringham	
Mark Pembridge	11	11	Sergei Rebrov	
Li Tie	12	12	Gary Doherty	
Steve Simonsen	13	13	Kasey Keller	
Idan Tal	14	14	Gustavo Poyet	
Gary Naysmith	15	15	Jamie Redknapp	
Thomas Gravesen	16	16	Antonio Gaspar	
Scot Gemmill	17	17	Oyvind Leonhardsen	
Wayne Rooney	18	18	Ben Thatcher	
Joe-Max Moore	19	20	Jonathan Blondel	
Joseph Yobo	20	21	Mlikenko Acimovic	
Li Wei Feng	21	23	Christian Ziege	
Tobias Linderoth	22	25	Stephen Clemence	
Rodrigo	23	26	Ledley King	
Lee Carsley	26	28	Matthew Etherington	
Peter Clarke	27	29	Simon Davies	
Tony Hibbert	28	30	Anthony Gardner	
Kevin McLeod	29	31	Alton Thelwell	
Nick Chadwick	30	36	Dean Richards	
Leon Osman	31			
Keith Southern	32			
George Pilkington	33			
Sean O'Hanlon	34			
Paul Gerrard	35			

Manager: David Moyes   Manager: Glenn Hoddle

KEJIAN 科健
Main Partner

PUMA
Official Sportswear Partner

Today's Matchball Sponsor
HARVAL CHEMISTS

SAFETY MESSAGE
All announcements made on the Public Address system which affect the safety of spectators on the premises will be preceded by a two-tone signal.

BARCLAYCARD PREMIERSHIP

TODAY'S FIXTURES
Blackburn Rovers v Sunderland
Charlton Athletic v Chelsea
Fulham v Bolton Wanderers
Leeds United v Manchester City
Manchester United v West Brom
Southampton v Middlesbrough

MATCH OFFICIALS
Referee
Mr N Barry

Assistant Referees
Mr A N Butler
Mr N Miller

Fourth Official
Mr P Dowd

FOR THE RECORD

	H/T	F/T
Result		
Everton		
Tottenham		

Everton Scorers:
Tottenham Scorers:
Attendance

---

efc line-ups

09.08.05 v Villarreal

MATCH OFFICIALS
To be confirmed

FOR THE RECORD

	H-T	F-T
Result		
Everton		
Villarreal		

Everton Scorers:
Villarreal Scorers:
Attendance

Everton v Villarreal

Everton				Villarreal	
RICHARD WRIGHT	01		01	JAVIER LOPEZ VALLEJO	
PER KROLDRUP	02		02	GONZALO RODRIGUEZ	
GARY NAYSMITH	03		03	RODOLFO ARRUABARRENA	
JOSEPH YOBO	04		04	CESAR ARZO	
DAVID WEIR	05		05	DIEGO FORLAN	
MIKEL ARTETA	06		06	JOSICO	
MARCUS BENT	07		07	ANTONIO GUAYRE	
JAMES BEATTIE	08		08	JUAN ROMAN RIQUELME	
DUNCAN FERGUSON	09		09	LUCIANO FIGUEROA	
SIMON DAVIES	10		10	ROGER	
JAMES MCFADDEN	11		11	JAVIER CALLEJA	
LI TIE	12		12	JUAN PABLO SORIN	
IAIN TURNER	13		14	HECTOR FONT	
KEVIN KILBANE	14		15	JAN KROMKAMP	
LEE CARSLEY	16		16	ENRIQUE ALVAREZ	
TIM CAHILL	17		17	JAVI VENTA	
PHIL NEVILLE	18		18	ALESSIO TACCHINARDI	
LEON OSMAN	21		19	MARCOS SENNA	
TONY HIBBERT	22		20	ANTONIO VALENCIA	
ALESSANDRO PISTONE	23		22	SANTIAGO CAZORLA	
NIGEL MARTYN	25		23	JUAN MANUEL PENA	
JAMES VAUGHAN	29		24	JOSE MARI	
JOHN RUDDY	30		27	ARMANDO SA	
MARK HUGHES	31		35	MARIANO BARBOSA	
STEPHEN WYNNE	32		36	CESAR ARZO	
CHRISTIAN SEARGEANT	33		37	JOSE MARIA CASES	
SEAN WRIGHT	34		39	PEREIRA JONATHAN	
PAUL HOPKINS	35		31	JUAN CARLOS	
PATRICK BOYLE	36		33	CARLOS ALCANTARA	
JAMES HARRIS	37		44	MARCOS	
VICTOR ANICHEBE	38		46	DAVID FUSTER	

Manager: DAVID MOYES   Manager: MANUEL PELLEGRINI

Clockwise from above: v Tottenham Hotspur, 2002/03; v Villarreal, Champions League third qualifying round, first leg, 2005/06; v Sunderland, 2011/12; v Sheffield United, 2006/07

Everton v Sheffield United

Everton			Sheffield United	
Richard Wright	1	1	Paddy Kenny	
Tony Hibbert	2	2	Leigh Bromby	
Gary Naysmith	3	3	David Unsworth	
Joseph Yobo	4	4	Claude Davis	
David Weir	5	5	Chris Morgan	
Mikel Arteta	6	6	Phil Jagielka	
Andy van der Meyde	7	7	Paul Ifill	
Andy Johnson	8	8	Ade Akinbiyi	
James Beattie	9	9	Rob Hulse	
Simon Davies	10	10	Danny Webber	
James McFadden	11	11	Steven Kabba	
Iain Turner	13	12	Alan Quinn	
Alan Stubbs	15	13	Ian Bennett	
Joleon Lescott	16	14	David Sommeil	
Tim Cahill	17	15	Robert Kozluk	
Phil Neville	18	17	Nick Montgomery	
Nuno Valente	19	18	Michael Tonge	
Leon Osman	21	19	Keith Gillespie	
James Vaughan	22	20	Chris Armstrong	
Alessandro Pistone	23	21	Mikele Leigertwood	
Tim Howard	24	22	Chris Lucketti	
Lee Carsley	26	23	Neil Shipperley	
Victor Anichebe	28	24	Craig Short	
John Ruddy	30	25	Alan Wright	
Mark Hughes	31	26	Derek Geary	
Patrick Boyle	36	27	Christian Nade	
Bjarni Vidarsson	41	29	Stephen Quinn	
		30	Li Tie	
		31	Nicholas Law	
		32	Colin Kazim-Richards	
		33	Jamie Annerson	
		34	James Ashmore	
		37	Colin Marrison	

● Manager: David Moyes   ● Manager: Neil Warnock

Safety message
All announcements made on the Public Address system which will affect the safety of spectators on the premises will be preceded by a two-tone signal.

Everton Prog Oct 21 06 E9

MAN OF THE MATCH
TXT efcmom [name of the player] to 81444 to vote for this afternoon's Evertonmobile man of the match.

9 771751 747063

EVERTON v SUNDERLAND

manager: David Moyes   manager: Martin O'Neill

Everton			Sunderland	
Jan Mucha	1	1	Craig Gordon	
Tony Hibbert	2	2	Phillip Bardsley	
Leighton Baines	3	3	Wayne Bridge	
Darron Gibson	4	4	Michael Turner	
John Heitinga	5	5	Wes Brown	
Phil Jagielka	6	6	Lee Cattermole	
Nikica Jelavic	7	7	Sebastian Larsson	
Royston Drenthe	10	8	Craig Gardner	
Denis Stracqualursi	11	9	Fraizer Campbell	
Marcus Hahnemann	12	10	Connor Wickham	
James McFadden	14	11	Kieran Richardson	
Sylvain Distin	15	12	Matthew Kilgallon	
Tim Cahill	17	14	Jack Colback	
Phil Neville	18	15	David Vaughan	
Magaye Gueye	19	16	John O'Shea	
Ross Barkley	20	17	Dong-Won Ji	
Leon Osman	21	18	David Meyler	
Steven Pienaar	22	19	Titus Bramble	
Seamus Coleman	23	20	Keiren Westwood	
Tim Howard	24	22	Simon Mignolet	
Marouane Fellaini	25	23	James McClean	
Jack Rodwell	26	25	Sotirios Kyrgiakos	
Apostolos Vellios	27	27	Ahmed Elmohamady	
Victor Anichebe	28	28	Stephane Sessegnon	
Joao Silva	29	38	Craig Lynch	
Francisco Junior	30	52	Nicklas Bendtner	
Shane Duffy	34			
Jose Baxter	37			

NIL SATIS NISI OPTIMUM — NOTHING BUT THE BEST

referee: Mr K Friend
assistant referee: Mr D Bond
assistant referee: Ms S Massey
fourth official: Mr A Marriner

"Nights like this are what we are in the game for. I see it as a reward for what the players worked hard to get last season..."

DAVID MOYES

Good evening and welcome to Goodison Park for tonight's match...

We have all been looking forward to this fixture and it is a reminder of just how well the players did last season in qualifying for this tournament. It was an achievement that should not be underestimated because the players worked so hard to give the club this opportunity.

All last season our goal was to attain Champions League qualification, despite many people suggesting that it wasn't going to be possible. The players proved that it could be done and tonight is another night when I'm sure they will show just what they are capable of.

The scenes of celebration after the last home match of last season were terrific, although if you recall we weren't totally guaranteed Champions League football at that stage – we were waiting on an outcome the following day. So maybe tonight is the first time that we've all been back together at Goodison since we officially achieved that 4th placing.

If ever we needed the backing of the famous 'Goodison Roar' then it's tonight. Although it's only early August, this could pan out to be one of our biggest matches of the whole season and the supporters need to play their part as usual. We need you to get behind the boys and really help to push them on. We know that Villarreal will come here and try to slow the game down and that's why we need your help in keeping the tempo high. I hope the atmosphere will be similar to the one we all enjoyed against Manchester United back in April. The tie won't be won and lost this evening but we can try to make a difference at Goodison.

Evertonians have missed out with regard to European football and I know all about the great nights here, such as Bayern Munich 20 years ago, and my aim is to give those experiences back to the supporters. The Champions League offers a new challenge for most people at this club but it's obviously something that we want more of. We want to be accustomed to playing European football.

Our start to this season is just about as tough as it could be! We've got Villarreal tonight and then Manchester United at Goodison. This will be a tough 90 minutes for us, we know that, but I have to say that it's a 90 minutes that the players have earned and that they thoroughly deserve.

Deportivo La Coruña have already been over here to dispose of Newcastle United from the Inter-Toto Cup, so we all know about the strength of La Liga. That Deportivo finished below Villarreal in their table puts the scale of our challenge into context and I think I can justifiably say that this draw is just about the hardest we could have got.

But nights like this are what we are in the game for. I see it as a reward for what the players worked hard to get last season and the priority now has got to be to get some more nights like a.

Get behind the lads tonight, provide that unique Goodison atmosphere and enjoy the game.

David Moyes

David Moyes

v Villarreal, Champions League qualifier, 2005/06 and (below), the first spread from the final notes, v West Ham, 2012/13

The Manager
DAVID MOYES

Everton

Good afternoon and welcome to Goodison Park...

For reasons that everybody is well aware of now these programme notes have changed in the last couple of days.

Today sees me manage Everton at Goodison Park for the last time. It won't be the last time I come to Goodison, and more than anything I want to sign off today with a victory and three points.

My time at Everton started 11 years ago when I was introduced to the crowd before the Fulham game. I still remember that day clearly, the reception I got and the backing the Evertonians gave me from the minute I walked through the door.

I called it The People's Club and if ever there was a statement that's true then I feel this is the one.

You supporters carried that for a long time. I have been incredibly fortunate to work with a club who have people such as Bill Kenwright, Jon Woods, Robert Earl, Sir Philip Carter and Keith Tamlin at board level, who have all supported me and given me great guidance and wisdom throughout my time at Everton.

I must say that my relationship with Bill Kenwright has been something which has made the job at Everton easier. He has been incredibly supportive, desperate for his team and his club to continue improving and I believe he should be congratulated for the way Everton as a football club has moved forward. I will always be friends with Bill and I hope that I will be welcome back through the doors at Goodison.

When you become a football manager you're never sure if someday you'll be sacked and criticised for the work you've done. I hope that most Evertonians would see that we have moved the club into the higher reaches of the Premier League more often than they had been previously.

Over the years we've had brilliant players come through the door but more importantly, I think I have had great men and I would never have been given any opportunity to succeed at Everton if it wasn't for the help that I have received from all the players who have worked under me.

I have brought nearly all the current players to Everton in my time and I do feel disappointed to be leaving them. They are all very much a part of what I have been trying

A message from Bill Kenwright

I am pretty convinced that very few of you need to hear what I think about our manager....!! You have heard little else for over a decade now, but as this is the last Everton programme that will have David's name on it as manager forgive me if I say it again....

Not long after David joined us I said that I believed that he could become one of Everton's greatest managers, not long after that I said that he could become one of football's all-time great managers, he has worked tirelessly throughout his life to achieve his goals, and his 11 years at Everton has proved pivotal to both him, and us, in a mutual journey of respect.

David's immediate task was to guide us away from the lower ends of the table. Having achieved that goal impressively, he set about transforming the squad, introducing and nurturing youth, investing in exceptional talent and building a backroom team around him capable of delivering consistency. As much as anything he has always given us a team, and a squad, that has worn the blue jersey with pride and distinction. Where the jersey matters more than any individual.

Along the way he has given us many great memories in the Premier League, the FA Cup and Europe. As a great personal friend, we have shared the highest of highs and the lowest of lows - and I promise you below that steel-like countenance there is a man of real emotion, who takes defeat as badly as any of us. But who, sometimes miraculously, has managed to pull both himself and his squad together to ensure that our despair has often turned to joy within a short space of time.

As we prepare to bid farewell to David I am sure he will depart with not just the best wishes of everybody at the Club, but also anybody who regards themselves as a member of the Everton family. We will miss him - and indeed his own family, dad David, Pamela, Lauren and young David.

And now, as we begin the search for the next man with the right credentials to manage a Club as special as this one, I know we do so with Everton in great shape - a fact that is in no small part down to David Moyes.

to achieve at Everton and they have all bought into it. I have spoken to them and explained my situation, which they fully understand.

Today's game is also the last at Goodison for Phil Neville. I've no doubt Phil will be back here many more times whether with another club in the future or back at Everton. He has been nothing short of remarkable in the way he has conducted himself and I would have to say that he would certainly be in the group of the best players I have worked with in my time at Everton.

He's a great family man and I am sure in the years to come he'll look forward to spending more time with them...unless he goes into coaching and management, when he'll find he has even less time!

It goes without saying that my only interest is that we try and win the last two games of the season. The players have had a remarkable season and we are very close to ⟩⟩

"I CALLED IT THE PEOPLE'S CLUB AND IF EVER THERE WAS A STATEMENT THAT'S TRUE THEN I FEEL THIS IS THE ONE"

D avid Moyes' 11-year spell as Goodison boss meant fans became accustomed to his notes – a familiarity that had been lacking in the previous decade.

Walter Smith's list of disappointments – injuries, signings, ill-luck – was quickly swept away as Moyes' famous 'People's Club' quote upon appointment in March 2002 set the tone for a more positive approach.

On-field improvement helped matters, with European football back on the agenda at Goodison for the first time in a decade and a succession of top-eight finishes – again, a vast improvement and greater level of consistency than had been the case.

"In total, David Moyes and I sat down together and compiled 258 manager's notes!" said current editor Darren Griffiths, the clubs Media and Publications Manager. "David took his notes very seriously, always insisted on signing them off and often used them to have a thinly veiled dig at the authorities or the opposition!

"His 258th and final set of notes, done as usual in his Finch Farm office, was a bit surreal for me - it really was the end of an era and we both recalled the first set we'd done at Bellefield eleven years earlier."

DAVID MOYES

We've had some memorable nights at Goodison and I still believe the best is yet to come. That may be tonight

G OOD evening and welcome to Goodison Park. The cup is always special for football supporters throughout the country and this game takes on even more significance after the recent draws at Anfield. The one thing you can always be assured of in most cup ties is a strong and feisty level of competition, due to the fact that it's winner takes all and the loser goes out...and, of course, this tie has to be decided one way or the other tonight.

Obviously the fact that we're playing our local rivals adds more intensity and we realise the fact that getting through in the cup will mean so much.

We found ourselves having to come through a big atmosphere at both games at Anfield, which the players handled magnificently. Tonight it is our chance to turn up the heat on Liverpool and see if they can come through the atmosphere in the same way. On that point, I have to praise the two referees for their performances in the two derby matches where they both handled the games in the right manner.

I've been very pleased with the performances of the players and there's a great determination amongst the group and a good feeling that if we continue to play as well as we have then they will get their reward. Every game has to be treated individually and on its own merit and we know that tonight will be one where we'll have to be at our best. The confidence we have at this present time, as we showed against Arsenal in our last game here at Goodison, is high and if we can reproduce that form I will be more than happy.

We have been working closely with a small group of players who have shown great versatility and adaptability to whatever situation they have been put in and they deserve great credit for going about their job like the good professionals they are.

We do not have the numbers in our squad to be able to be so interchangeable – that's something which we cannot match when it comes to some of the top sides. But from that comes a strength and an understanding of what jobs and responsibilities are. That makes you feel part of the club and have a real worth to all the supporters.

We've had some memorable nights at Goodison and I still believe the best is yet to come. That may well be tonight. The way you urged us on against Fiorentina last year made a big difference to the side and the performance, which came very close to getting us into the quarter-finals of the UEFA Cup. It goes without saying that your part tonight will be equally as important as any decision I can make. The players understand the importance of the game and we'll do everything we can to succeed in getting through to the next round of the cup.

We are working together to take Everton Football Club back to the top again and although our process may be slower than some more fortunate clubs, in the end I am sure we will succeed.

'THE ONE THING YOU CAN ALWAYS BE ASSURED OF IN MOST CUP TIES IS A STRONG AND FEISTY LEVEL OF COMPETITION, DUE TO THE FACT THAT IT'S WINNER TAKES ALL AND THE LOSER GOES OUT...AND, OF COURSE, THIS TIE HAS TO BE DECIDED ONE WAY OR THE OTHER TONIGHT'

We played with great confidence against Arsenal

In association with

evertonfc.com/bt

David Moyes' 2008/09 notes v Liverpool for the FA Cup fourth-round replay. Reflections of two draws at Anfield dominated the manager's thoughts – and an appeal for fans to back the side on what would be another big Goodison occasion...

Roberto Martinez

View from the boss

Roberto Martinez

It was a very good starting point towards working to evolve the team

Welcome to Goodison Park for our first home league fixture in the 2013/14 Barclays Premier League.

We have already been working extremely hard for over eight weeks in three different environments preparing for the start of the campaign.

In Austria, at Finch Farm and in the USA we've been able to feel your support, and it is something that straight away I thank you for. It has allowed every single new face in the playing and coaching staff to feel such a part of our football club.

This pre-season we had football exercises in which we've been able to try different things by competing

with the likes of Juventus, Real Madrid, Valencia and Real Betis, and they provided a perfect games programme for our preparations.

Those preparations were highlighted in our opening game last week at Norwich City. In a game where the performance wasn't rewarded with the three points that I thought we deserved, we took many positives from the match. It was a very good starting point towards working to evolve the team.

I don't think many football teams will take the full away allocation at that ground in East Anglia, but your support and colour in the crowd was the perfect way to settle into the game for the players. Four goals in any

game would bring excitement, but the manner that we controlled the ball and created numerous chances was a very impressive aspect of our play.

Goals are always exciting moments in any game but the quality and accuracy of Ross Barkley's strike and the combination and patient play for the second goal, when every player except one touched the ball, were two significant moments in the game.

We are trying to do certain different things in our performances and we need your understanding and patience to make sure that we can master them over the course of the season. We know exactly what we want to do and we know that it may take a little bit of time, and in that time we need your unique support to make sure that we can make the difference on the pitch.

Internally at our football club, you need to know that we are very fortunate with the amount of top professionals that we have in every department. We have huge talent and experience with terrific dedication to help to provide the small margins that can help the players be successful on the pitch. The staff that filled the vacancies we had in the summer have come here full of energy and with a real desire to help. Everyone has been overwhelmed with the welcome that they have all had and they now know what it is to be a Blue!

This afternoon we will all pay a tribute to Dave Hickson before the match. Unfortunately I never got the chance to meet Dave, but I could see from the amount of people who attended his funeral service that he was an Everton legend. He will be sadly missed here at Everton for a long time.

I would like to welcome Steve Clarke and his team to Goodison Park. West Brom enjoyed a very impressive season last campaign in Steve's first full season in charge. They are a side that can play with huge energy and organisation, and their flexibility will make them really competitive throughout the season in every game that they are involved in. The result in the opening fixture for them was one that could have gone either way so we know about the threat that West Brom will cause us this afternoon, and we all have to be ready for a tough encounter.

The speculation and the talk going around up and down the country while the transfer window is open is increasing season after season. I do feel strongly

about how negative it can be to have the window open when the official games have started. It is something that the football authorities must act on to help the situation of everyone involved in the game, and to be able to maintain the values and integrity of the competition.

I always like to be very open and honest about what's happening on that front and we were really pleased in the amount of business that we did early on in the window but once the Premier League starts, it is not healthy to concentrate on and feed all sorts of rumours. All that matters is the preparation for each game and when there is something to inform you of, you will be the first ones to know.

I cannot wait to see the chemistry that we can develop between you and the whole team at Goodison and making sure that we use that key ingredient for our success in the future. We rely on your patience and understanding but we want you to be proud of the team in the process.

Solo lo mejor

Roberto Martinez

---

v West Bromwich Albion, 2013/14, Roberto Martinez's first Premier League manager notes as Everton boss

It would be an understatement to suggest it has been an eventful few days for Everton Football Club. But everyone here, the players especially, must focus on the immediate task in hand which is securing three Premiership points against Fulham this afternoon.

Like all of the lads here, I was very disappointed to see Walter Smith leave. While we haven't enjoyed the best of fortunes in recent years, I still have a huge amount of admiration and respect for him. He was responsible for bringing me to Everton from Turkey – and he also handed me the club captaincy, something of which I am immensely proud. But that's in the past. We have to look forward now.

Our Premiership future is still in our own hands. If we can win enough of our remaining home games – all against teams around us in the table – and pick up the odd point or two away from Goodison Park we will stay up.

We've been in this position before and we know what's needed. When I first came to the club we faced a much bleaker position. We lost at home to Sheffield Wednesday on Easter Monday, a result which dropped us into the bottom three with only six games left. We showed the character and bottle required then to win three successive games and finished our home fixtures with a 6-0 victory over West Ham.

We need the same kind of resolution and resolve now that we showed back then. That spell was a good one for me personally, and I'd love to be involved this afternoon and throughout the remainder of the run-in.

But at the time of writing I still could not be sure about my ankle injury. It's improving, but up until Wednesday I still hadn't even attempted to jog on it. It's been an incredibly frustrating season from that respect, but I'm not alone in that.

Today represents a brand new start for the club. Effectively our season kicks off today, and if we can reproduce the run of results we had at the start of the season proper, when everybody was fit and available, I think you would all be delighted. We've endured a poor run of results ever since we beat Crewe in the FA Cup replay, and we have to end that sequence immediately. With your backing we know we are capable of going on a run which could banish the spectre of relegation quickly. Today's game is vital, but then so is every one of the nine Premiership games we have left. It's up to us all to pull together and make sure there are no mistakes from here on in.

Kevin Campbell

Kevin Campbell, 2002 & David Weir, 2005

Speaking ahead of the Leeds United game, the striker noted previous entertaining encounters between the sides, though 'we'd settle for a 1-0 win with a scrappy goal off somebody's backside!' In Walter Smith's final home game in charge, the result was a scoreless draw...

Grateful for Walter Smith making him captain, Campbell insisted that it was time to move on ahead of David Moyes' first game in charge a fortnight later (left): 'That's in the past. We have to look forward now...Today represents a brand new start for the club.'

Officially made club skipper ahead of the 2005/06 campaign, David Weir was relishing the chance to lead the side in the Champions League, ahead of the qualifier against Villarreal.

'It won't change how I approach the games because obviously my own performance is the most important thing.'

Weir also reflected on a busy pre-season including a tour to Thailand and a trip to Turkey...

CAPTAIN SPEAKING

DAVID WEIR

There is only one way for me to start my first programme notes of the new season and that is to stress what an honour I think it is to be the captain of Everton Football Club.

I have skippered the team before in the past but to be officially asked to be the club captain is something I'm very proud of. It won't change how I approach the games because obviously my own performance is the most important thing.

But as a captain you've also got to help people out, both on and off the pitch... which is something that always goes on here anyway. The kind of lads we've got here means that that we always help each other A Champions League match at Goodison is a great start for me. It's going to be a great occasion, a great challenge and it's a tie that we're all looking forward to... even though we are under no illusions as to the size of the task of the quality of Villarreal.

We watched the draw 'live' on the television in the canteen at the training ground and we all wanted a big name and a big game and that's exactly what we've got.

Villarreal may not be the most well-known side in Europe but anybody who has watched any Spanish football knows full well just what quality they've got.

For ourselves, the summer has gone okay and we've been back for about five weeks now. I personally only had about three weeks off after last season so I just kept myself ticking over.

The trip to Thailand was very good, with the visit to Phuket a particularly humbling experience. Meeting people who had survived the Tsunami really brought home just how devastating the whole experience must have been for them. They have suffered a traumatic time but we were all so impressed at the way they are battling back.

The football in Thailand itself wasn't the best but we emerged unbeaten over 90 minutes in our two matches. We lost only on penalty shoot-outs against Thailand and Manchester City but the games at that stage of the

campaign are all about increasing your sharpness and increasing your fitness levels. We were just getting back into the swing of things and each game, in the warm conditions, was a good workout. The eventual results may not have gone our way but physically we got what we wanted from it. They were both competitive games.

By contrast we were all very disappointed after the Fenerbahce game. Obviously we shouldn't read too much into the game because it was a friendly match but nobody likes getting beaten by five goals. But Fenerbahce played very well on the night and sometimes you just have to hold your hands up and say that you were beaten by a better side. It's better to get that type of match out of the way in July rather than when the season kicks off.

As for tonight, you supporters have a massive part to play. We've all waited so long for a competitive European game at Goodison and everybody has spoken about how good an atmosphere it will be and how much they will enjoy it. Well, it's here now, it's been a long wait and we're all looking forward to it. Get right behind the lads and create the sort of atmosphere that is unique to Goodison Park.

David Weir

"It's going to be a great occasion, a great challenge and it's a tie that we're all looking forward to..."

David Weir, 2006 &
Phil Neville, Phil Jagielka, 2013

Confidence around the club was high in the early stages of the 2006/07 in the wake of derby success:

'There has been a real buzz around the training ground this week and you would expect nothing less after a terrific win here seven days ago.

'The scenes at the final whistle were great and I am sure that all the Evertonians have really relished having the bragging rights in the city this week.'

The end of the 2012/13 campaign brought down the curtain not only on the manager's lengthy tenure at the club, but also on that of skipper Phil Neville. He used his notes against West Ham to thank Evertonians for their support, as well as express gratitude to players, coaching staff and David Moyes.

His successor, Phil Jagielka, began the campaign on a positive note, relishing the beginning of a new era under Roberto Martinez, while also looking to feed on the feeling of positivity around the club.

'The mood is very good and we have to capitalise on that. Everyone's enjoying training, and there is a confidence about the place that is very positive.'

CAPTAIN TALK
David Weir

Delighted with the start but it's still early days

There has been a real buzz around the training ground this week and you would expect nothing less after a terrific win here seven days ago.

Any success against Liverpool is great but to beat them by such an emphatic scoreline was terrific for everyone involved with the club.

I don't think that even the most staunch Liverpool supporter would deny that we thoroughly deserved to take all three points from the game and although they had chances of their own, we really felt that we were full value.

The scenes at the final whistle were great and I am sure that all the Evertonians have really relished having the bragging rights in the city this week.

However, although we all enjoyed last weekend, we quickly put it behind us to start to focus on the challenge that we face from Wigan Athletic this afternoon. They beat us here last season and we are determined to put one over on them this time around.

They were something of an unknown quantity last term but they firmly established themselves as a Premiership force and backed it up with an appearance in the Carling Cup final against Manchester United.

Paul Jewell has recruited well again during the summer and each one of their three games so far in the Premiership this season have been decided by a single goal, either way.

They lost 1-0 at Portsmouth at the weekend and that result put Pompey top of the table so it's safe to assume that Wigan will be difficult to beat again this season.

It will be a bit strange to be playing against Kevin Kilbane this afternoon after his recent switch from Everton.

He will be a real asset to them and he will be determined to put in a good display this afternoon in front of both sets of fans. I am sure he will be given the great reception from our supporters that he deserves. It won't be the first time that I've been in opposition to Kevin because he was at Sunderland, of course, when I first arrived at Everton.

The Premiership table makes pleasant reading for our fans at the moment and although it's nice to see ourselves in the top four, we know that it's still very early days and that it will be a few weeks before the table starts to take what I would define as a 'settled' shape.

But we've got to be delighted with the start we've made, especially when you consider the quality of the opposition that we've already faced. And it doesn't get any easier either with Wigan today and then Newcastle United and Manchester City to come in the next fortnight.

But that's the Premiership for you. You know you will get a stern test every week and there is no question of anyone at this club resting on laurels and basking in the glory of last weekend.

Your support was first-class against Liverpool and all the players were so pleased to give you something to brag about. But that's gone now and we need your full backing, as always, this afternoon. Enjoy the game.

Last season at Goodise: Wigan look the points

The Captain
PHIL NEVILLE

A massive thank you to every Evertonian who has supported me and the team over the last eight years. There are no better supporters in the land than you lot and you should be extremely proud of the way you back your team"

Hello and welcome to Goodison Park.

These are obviously no ordinary set of programme notes because this is obviously no ordinary game.

It was always going to be my last time at Goodison as an Everton player but when that was decided I don't think anyone would have considered that it would also be the gaffer's last one as well.

It's been a somewhat dramatic week for fans of both Everton and Manchester United but that's football for you. We always say that nothing should surprise you in this game but the events of the last few days have taken my breath away.

I am going to attempt to sum up in these notes just what David Moyes has done for me over the eight years I have been at the club, and just how impressed I have been with everything he has done for Everton - but I'm sure I won't do it justice.

In all my years in professional football I have never met a harder-working man than the gaffer. I was told before I arrived at Everton that he had an astonishing work ethic and that his attention to detail would work with him that you realise just how much he puts in to try and win football matches.

He is driven by an insatiable drive to win and his commitment levels are incredible. He just never switches off and I know that he can leave Everton after next week's game secure in the knowledge that every single day of his time here he has given nothing less than 100%.

For me, he has always shown complete faith and confidence in me. He made me the captain of Everton Football Club and that's one of the highlights of my career - I thank him for that.

Even this week he has somehow kept his focus on today's game. Make no mistake about it, David Moyes wants to beat West Ham today and Chelsea next week every bit as much as he wanted to beat Fulham on his first day in 2002.

Phil Jagielka
A word with the captain

There will be quite a few teams in the mix... there's no reason why we can't be as well

Good afternoon and welcome to Goodison Park.

There's always a special atmosphere at the first home game of the season. It's a fixture that the supporters have been looking forward to since May, and there's always a different feeling to it.

We started our Premier League campaign last week with a decent performance at Norwich City. That's never been the easiest of places to go to, and I felt that over the 90 minutes we probably did enough to win the game. There was certainly a touch of good fortune for them when Steven Whittaker's sliced shot found the head of Van Wolfswinkel.

But I can tell you that we returned from Carrow Road dwelling on far more positives than negatives. I always think it's important not to lose your opening fixture and there'll be a few teams who come away from Norwich with nothing.

We've since had a good week's training and we're looking forward to this afternoon. Our form at Goodison Park has traditionally been very good, and that's something we have to maintain if we have any ambition of finishing in a European qualification slot this season.

The mood is very good at the moment and we have to capitalise on that. Everyone's enjoying training, and there is a confidence about the place that is very

positive. But we know we've got another tough game this afternoon.

West Brom did very well last season and after a few yo-yo years they certainly look like a good, strong Premier League team now. That's been proved with some of their summer signings. Nicolas Anelka has played for some of the biggest teams in Europe and I am sure the West Brom fans are delighted to have him. I am equally as sure that our fans will be dreading the sight of him this afternoon. It doesn't matter who he plays for, he seems to score against Everton!

It's been an interesting start to the season in the Premier League and I think this could be the most keenly contested campaign for many years. There will be quite a few teams in the mix as the season progresses, and there is absolutely no reason why we can't be as well.

It's a cliché that there are no easy games at this level, and that's really going to be the case this season. It's so important to have that little bit of luck with injuries so that you can keep your squad as strong as possible. Obviously Gibbo and Hibbo missed last weekend but they won't be too far away, and the gaffer will have serious competition for places all over the pitch, which is exactly what he wants.

Finally, a big thanks on behalf of all the lads to the supporters who travelled to Carrow Road last Saturday. There's no quick and easy way to get there, and to see a packed away end on the first day of the season gave us all a buzz. Your support will be just as important at Goodison Park. You can make a difference by getting right behind the lads from the first whistle.

All the best, enjoy the game and let's have a good season together.

Phil Jagielka

"KNOWING ME, KNOWING YOU ...SAHA!"

The lure of a catchy headline was a growing feature of the player interviews during the period, as well as variety in design and layout.

A mix of action and photo-shoot player pictures remained as standard, while the prominence of an interview was extended, with more pages given over to the first-teamer in question.

Topics generally remained football-related, with content, particularly in the latter phase of David Moyes' tenure, related to the push for Europe - a real sign of progress.

Tim Cahill

The Australian midfielder explains why the Blues have finished the season strongly as he targets a final day victory...

Tim Cahill interview lead-in spread,
v Newcastle United, 2011/12

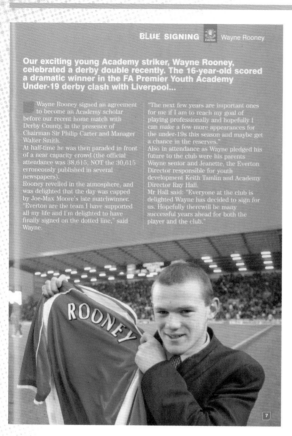

Our exciting young Academy striker, Wayne Rooney, celebrated a derby double recently. The 16-year-old scored a dramatic winner in the FA Premier Youth Academy Under-19 derby clash with Liverpool...

Wayne Rooney signed an agreement to become an Academy scholar before our recent home match with Derby County, in the presence of Chairman Sir Philip Carter and Manager Walter Smith.

At half-time he was then paraded in front of a near capacity crowd (the official attendance was 38,615, NOT the 30,615 erroneously published in several newspapers).

Rooney revelled in the atmosphere, and was delighted that the day was capped by Joe-Max Moore's late matchwinner.

"Everton are the team I have supported all my life and I'm delighted to have finally signed on the dotted line," said Wayne.

"The next few years are important ones for me if I am to reach my goal of playing professionally and hopefully I can make a few more appearances for the under-19s this season and maybe get a chance in the reserves."

Also in attendance as Wayne pledged his future to the club were his parents Wayne senior and Jeanette, the Everton Director responsible for youth development Keith Tamlin and Academy Director Ray Hall.

Mr Hall said: "Everyone at the club is delighted Wayne has decided to sign for us. Hopefully there will be many successful years ahead for both the player and the club."

Wayne Rooney & Mikel Arteta

The emergence of a promising youth-team player was enough to earn column inches in the Manchester United programme of 2001/02.

A 16-year-old by the name of Wayne Rooney agreed an Academy scholarship deal, and he was delighted to see his heroes defeat Derby County at Goodison.

"Everton are the team I have supported all my life and I'm delighted to have finally signed on the dotted line.

"The next few years are important ones for me if I am to reach my goal of playing professionally."

Mikel Arteta was impressing during an initial six-month loan period for the club in the first half of 2005, recently scoring his first goal for Everton against Crystal Palace. He also appeared to be settling in, and enjoyed the backing of the fans:

"The Everton fans have been unbelievable since I arrived here. They have supported me right through every game I've played in. They are always singing and it's very nice because I haven't been here at Everton that long.

"When we play at home they sing all the players' names and I was surprised but it was very, very nice."

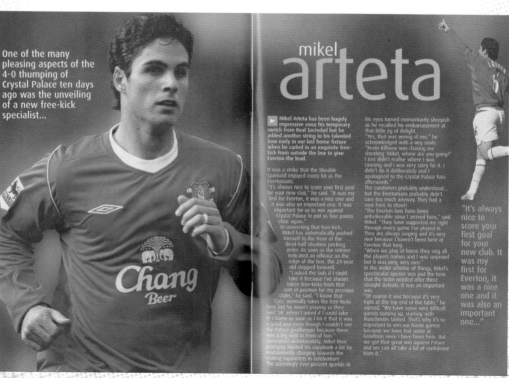

One of the many pleasing aspects of the 4-0 thumping of Crystal Palace ten days ago was the unveiling of a new free-kick specialist...

mikel arteta

Mikel Arteta has been hugely impressive since his temporary switch from Real Sociedad but he added another string to his talented bow early in our last home fixture when he curled in an exquisite free-kick from outside the box to give Everton the lead.

It was a strike that the likeable Spaniard enjoyed every bit as the Evertonians.

"It's always nice to score your first goal for your new club," he said. "It was my first for Everton, it was a nice one and it was also an important one. It was important for us to win against Crystal Palace to put us four points clear again."

In converting that free-kick, Mikel has automatically pushed himself to the front of the dead-ball shutkon pecking order. As soon as the referee indicated an offence on the edge of the box, the 24-year-old stepped forward.

"I asked the lads if I could take it because I've always taken free-kicks from that sort of position for my previous clubs," he said. "I know that 'Cars' normally takes the free-kicks here but he wasn't playing so they said 'ok' when I asked if I could take it! I knew as soon as I hit it that it was a good one even though I couldn't see the Palace goalkeeper because there was a big wall in front of him."

Somewhat unfortunately, Mikel then promptly blotted his copybook a bit by inadvertently charging towards the visiting supporters in celebration! The seemingly ever-present sparkle in his eyes turned momentarily sheepish as he recalled his embarrassment at that little jig of delight.

"Yes, that was wrong of me," he acknowledged with a wry smile. "Kevin Kilbane was chasing me shouting 'Mikel, where are you going?' I just didn't realise where I was running and I was very sorry for it. I didn't do it deliberately and I apologised to the Crystal Palace fans afterwards."

The Londoners probably understood... but the Evertonians probably didn't care too much anyway. They had a new hero to cheer!

"The Everton fans have been unbelievable since I arrived here," said Mikel. "They have supported me right through every game I've played in. They are always singing and it's very nice because I haven't been here at Everton that long.

"When we play at home they sing all the players' names and I was surprised but it was very, very nice."

In the wider scheme of things, Mikel's spectacular opener was just the tonic that the team needed after three straight defeats. It was an important win.

"Of course it was because it's very tight at the top end of the table," he agreed. "We have some very difficult games coming up, starting with Manchester United. That's why it's so important to win our home games because we have lost some at Goodison since I have been here. But we got that great win against Palace and we can all take a lot of confidence from it."

"It's always nice to score your first goal for your new club. It was my first for Everton, it was a nice one and it was also an important one..."

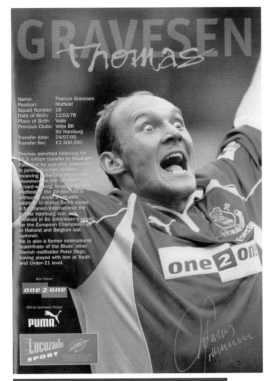

GRAVESEN
Thomas

Name:	Thomas Gravesen
Position:	Midfield
Squad Number:	16
Date of Birth:	11/03/76
Place of Birth:	Vejle
Previous Clubs:	Vejle BK
	SV Hamburg
Transfer date:	24/07/00
Transfer fee:	£2,500,000

Thomas admitted following his £2.5 million transfer to Goodison Park that he was only interested in joining Everton, despite receiving numerous offers from elsewhere on the continent.

A hard-working, tough-tackling midfielder, the 24-year-old is without a doubt a valuable addition to Walter Smith's squad.

A full Danish International the former Hamburg star, was involved in Bo Johansen's squad for the European Championships in Holland and Belgium last summer.

He is also a former international team-mate of the Blues' other Danish midfielder Peter Degn, having played with him at Youth and Under-21 level.

Thomas Gravesen, 2000/01 – A tough tackler only interested in signing for Everton

---

Richard Gough

● The visit of Arsenal to Goodison Park today is one of those fixtures which fills every player with a buzz of excitement and anticipation. The Gunners, along with Manchester United, are still one of the two top sides in the Premiership and the kind of club any self-respecting footballer wants to test himself against.

They turned us over twice last season, but we are going into today's match in a decent spell of form.

We won well at Newcastle, produced half a good performance at Anfield, certainly deserved to beat Aston Villa here a fortnight ago, then won again at Bradford last Saturday. Strangely it has been our away form which has been most impressive this season.

Last time out we collected five away wins all season. This time we already have three in the bank, and with better defending from set pieces at Tottenham and Leeds, might have already equalled that target.

What is a little more reassuring, however, is that we are not drawing quite as many games.

We picked up a single point from matches 14 times last season, which is far too many. If you can convert just three or four of those drawn games into victories it can improve your league position dramatically. For example, a point from each of our two home games against Arsenal and Chelsea would be seen as respectable results.

But if we can pinch a victory from either game that gives you an instantly better return. Arsenal are a quality side, but they are not quite firing on all cylinders like Manchester United at present.

Derby County frustrated them last weekend, and they should hopefully have a number of players away on international duty this week which will not aid their preparations.

As well as the three points at stake, this afternoon's game represents a hugely significant occasion for our fans for another reason.

Like Arsenal, our Board of Directors is considering a move to a new stadium. If a club as traditional and historic as Arsenal can consider a move away from Highbury, I see no reason why we shouldn't do likewise. Personally I think a stadium at the King's Dock site in Liverpool would be a good thing for the club.

I'd love to return to Merseyside in, say 10 years' time, and see Everton based at a magnificent new stadium on the banks of the River Mersey, with a magnificent team playing on it.

Obviously I won't be involved then! I'd just settle for involvement again in a game this season.

This is the longest spell in football I've ever been forced to spend on the sidelines through injury - and it's ironic that it's come in what will be my last season.

Before this knee injury the longest I've been forced to miss was six weeks with a fractured cheekbone.

Right now I'm already at the eight or nine weeks' mark, and there's still a few weeks to go yet.

I can take heart, though, from the example of players like Stuart Pearce who has come back and played at a very good level for West Ham after breaking his leg twice at 36 and 37!

That gives old timers like me great heart!

Richard Gough, 2000/01 – Positive, keen on the King's Dock and the irony of injury in his final season

---

PHIL SIGNS IN

Phil Neville ended an 18-year association with today's visitors Manchester United when he agreed to put pen to paper on a move down the M62 to Everton.

We are delighted to have him and he is just as pleased to be here. "I was frustrated last season," he said. "The manager knew that and we came to an agreement that it would be best if he gave me permission to talk to other clubs.

"David Moyes was the first manager that contacted my father and from day one it was the move that interested me most.

"Leaving United has been the most difficult decision I have ever had to make. But I have come to the decision to sign for Everton and that was an easy decision as they so desperately wanted me to sign."

He added: "I am excited about joining Everton and am relishing my next challenge in football - it is one of the biggest in my career.

"The lure of playing in Champions League and European football is a big factor. I watched Everton last season and having spoken to the manager I admire the work ethic of the team and it fits in with my own.

"I've spent 18 years of my life at United and I would like to thank Sir Alex Ferguson, all the players and the fans for their support.

"I am now going to give my commitment to Everton, David Moyes and the Everton fans. I can't wait for the new season to get started."

Phil Neville, 2005/06 – Delighted to sign, looking forward to European football and promising to work...

Blues follow Jelavic road

Nikica Jelavic has vowed to bring 'goals, goals and more goals' to Everton following his transfer deadline day move to the Blues.

The hitman arrived at Goodison Park for an undisclosed fee, having scored 36 times in 55 appearances for Glasgow Rangers.

It's a run of form he's looking to continue on Merseyside, stating: "This is a big thing for me. It's a new step in my career, a step forward and I can promise the fans and the people at the Club that I will give my very best and score as many goals as possible.

"I'm very excited to be here. It's a new challenge and hopefully I can play some good football, score some goals and win some trophies. In the four-and-a-half years of my contract, I have time to learn."

Asked what he'll bring to the Everton team, the Croatian replied: "Goals, goals and more goals! I know Everton have not scored much this season but I don't feel the pressure, I like a challenge.

"I can bring some good football. In the last couple of seasons I have shown that I have scored goals, hopefully that can continue at Everton.

"I will do my best to score many goals. I am always looking to be better every day and my ambitions are to play well and to be useful for the team and score as many goals as possible. I know David Moyes expects a lot from me and I can promise to do my best and score lots of goals."

Nikica Jelavic, 2011/12 – Targeting goals, and trophies, after signing from Rangers on January transfer deadline day

Barclays Premiership   Everton 3–0 Liverpool 09.09.06

PicturePower

A big Goodison derby win was celebrated to the full with some great action photos, v Wigan, 2005/06

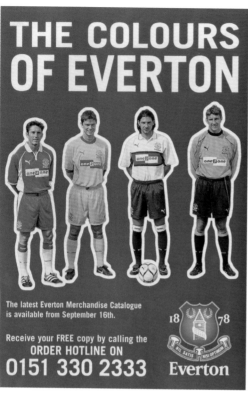

THE COLOURS OF EVERTON

The latest Everton Merchandise Catalogue is available from September 16th.

Receive your FREE copy by calling the
ORDER HOTLINE ON
0151 330 2333

18 78

Everton

2000-03

'The Colours Of Everton' campaign, featuring four first-teamers, lined up to show off the club's new strips ahead of the 2000/01 campaign.

Kevin Campbell remained enough of a favourite to warrant his own official video during the same campaign – while new shirt sponsors Kejian marked a shift towards a more global appeal for the club ahead of the 2002/03 season...

THE PERFECT GIFT FOR ALL EVERTONIANS...

KEVIN CAMPBELL "SUPER KEV"
Official Everton FC Video

"Super Kev" charts Kevin Campbell's Everton career, from his arrival in April 1999, through his turbulent injury, and his eagerly awaited return this season.

This 90 minute special contains footage of all his goals since his arrival at Everton FC and also features Kevin talking about Everton's chances in the 2000/2001 season and of his love for the club. No Everton fan should miss the opportunity to see this sensational striker in action.

ONLY £12.99

Available from The Everton Megastore or call 0151 330 2333 or online at: evertonfc.com

KEJIAN 科健

Are proud of their association
as Main Partner of
Everton Football Club

18 78

Everton

Everton Football Club is suddenly big news in China. And we mean BIG NEWS! Ma Dexing is a journalist with Sports Weekly, the biggest selling sports newspaper in China, and he is over in England specifically to cover Everton.

Kejian is proud to become the main partner of Everton Football Club and be the first company from China to sponsor a football club in the best league in the world.

As one of the few clubs with such remarkable history and traditions, Everton Football Club has long been a name known to millions of football fans in China. However, it has remained to be a club to be far away from Chinese fans.

But now, together with millions of fans halfway around the world from you, we will be cheering and supporting the team with you. Everton Football Club is not simply just a club in the Premier League; it is now our club in the Premier League.

Kejian is probably unknown to you, but we share many views with Everton Football Club in being the best and just as our slogan in Chinese says, "Focus in doing everything right".

I am certain that we will have a great season this year and I wish all of you the very best.

Thank you.

Hao Jianxue
President
China Kejian Company Limited

"We publish an edition three times a week," said Ma Dexing. "And there is massive interest in Everton because, obviously, of the Kejian sponsorship deal and the arrival of two Chinese players.

"Consequently, every Chinese football fan seems to want to know everything about Everton and, in particular, about the two players. So I am over here to want to follow the club." Soccer is an ever-growing sport in China and the number of potential new Evertonians is probably immeasurable.

"Football is very, very popular right now in China," said Ma. "During the World Cup when China played Brazil, more than 40% of the entire population watched the game on television... and that is a lot of people!

"Crystal Palace had two Chinese players a few years ago and when their first match was screened, there was nearly 1 billion people watching. If Li Tie and Li Wei Feng get a chance to play, then I believe more than a billion people would watch it.

"It's very important for Chinese football to have a couple of players in the Premiership. English football is very popular in China but the fans have tended to follow the likes of Manchester United, Arsenal and Liverpool.

"Now though, because of Li Tie and Li Wei Feng, there are now very many Everton supporters."
Li Tie made his Goodison bow last week against Athletic Bilbao and the watching spectators in David Unsworth's Testimonial were very impressed with his brief contribution.

"I have spoken to both players and the only problem they have is the language," revealed Ma. "Everything else is good and they are very satisfied.

"I, too, have been very impressed with Everton. I had been to Britain on six occasions but each time I only visited London. I like Merseyside and I enjoyed looking around Goodison Park.

"There is only one stadium in China that is specifically for football. That is in Shanghai, but other clubs have stadiums that host athletic events and so have a running track around the pitch."

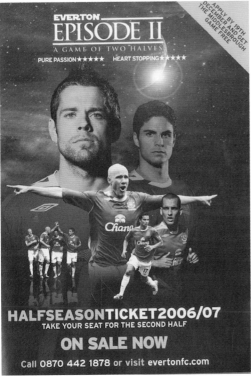

Clockwise, from top left: 2001/02, watch the youngsters home, and away, in the FA Youth Cup final; 2005/06, Evertonia recruitment; 2006/07, half season ticket sales take on a Star Wars theme; 2010/11, new away kit unveiled...

Greatest Ever Everton Team

The fans have voted! We asked YOU to select the GREATEST EVER EVERTON TEAM and we can reveal that this afternoon, the players you have chosen will be here at Goodison Park to take a personal tribute.

Without further ado, in a traditional 4-4-2 formation, the Greatest Ever Everton Team is:

NEVILLE SOUTHALL

GARY STEVENS   **RAY WILSON**

BRIAN LABONE   **KEVIN RATCLIFFE**

TREVOR STEVEN   **KEVIN SHEEDY**

PETER REID   **ALAN BALL**

WILLIAM RALPH DEAN   **GRAEME SHARP**

In this, our 125th anniversary season we thought it would be entirely appropriate to have the Greatest Ever Everton team and the supporters have voted in their thousands. It's a discussion that's taken place a million times whenever Evertonians get together and even though the above line-up has been chosen by the fans, the debate will still rage.

Some will never accept a Greatest Ever Everton without Alex Young, others will insist on Harvey and Kendall joining Ball in midfield, Bob Latchford is still the king in some eyes and the older supporters will wonder why TG Jones or Tommy Lawton are not in there.

Supporters cast their votes via the club's official website, evertonfc.com and used voting slips from the Evertonian, our official magazine. We also received hundreds of postcards and letters from supporters from all over the world.

THE GREATEST EVER EVERTON TEAM WILL BE PARADED IN FRONT OF THE FANS TODAY AT HALF-TIME

(Dixie will be represented by his great-grandson, Daniel)

Some players, like Neville Southall, Kevin Ratcliffe and William Ralph 'Dixie' Dean were landslide selections but some of the others had some fierce competition to contend with.

Big Nev, Footballer of the Year in 1985 and still the only player ever to win two FA Cup winners medals for Everton, was a clear winner of the goalkeeping position, with the only real competition coming from Gordon West and Ted Sagar. At his peak, Neville was undoubtedly the best goalkeeper in the world and this was reflected in the voting.

The battle for the right-back position was a close one.

Tommy Wright played for England in the World Cup and so did Gary Stevens. Both men won League Championship medals and both were members of a winning FA Cup Final side - Tommy in 1966, Gary in 1984. Eventually though, Gary edged out Tommy to take the right-back berth.

The voting for the opposite defensive flank wasn't quite as close.

Ray Wilson is still the only Everton player to win the World Cup and he was, by reputation, the finest left-back in the world when he was at the peak of his powers. His stylish displays were a joy to behold in the 1960s and he is justifiably tagged an Everton legend. His closest rival in the Greatest Ever Team poll was 1984-85 Championship winner, Pat van den Hauwe.

The two central defensive positions attracted a lot of variations. Nobody would argue about the credentials of title-winning/FA Cup winning captains,

Kevin Ratcliffe and Brian Labone, but although the former was on most voting slips, Labby had a fight on his hands. TG Jones pushed him all the way and so did the last Everton player to lift a major trophy, Dave Watson. However, the two greats, Ratcliffe and Labone, who chalked up more than one thousand Everton appearances between them, form the central defensive partnership...and no striker would fancy facing those two in their prime!

On the left of midfield, Kevin Sheedy was a clear winner. The man who we 'rescued' from Liverpool won the hearts of the Evertonians with some memorable performances and vitally important, goals. Like his right-wing team-mate in the glorious mid-80s, Trevor Steven, Kevin polled significantly more votes than any of his closest rivals.

One player who did well, and polled more votes than any other foreigner, was Andrei Kanchelskis. The Russian illuminated the 1995-96 season and although his star only shone briefly, it is interesting that the supporters still acknowledge that we did have a world-class footballer in our midst.

However, Trevor Steven won the fans vote. True class always shines through and after taking time to settle at Goodison, 'Tricky Trev' became a fans favourite and also represented his country at the very highest level - playing for England in the 1986 World Cup. As with the defence, the central midfield area prompted a vast

number of combinations. Again though, two players with World Cup experience won the day.

Alan Ball is, quite simply, a footballing icon. He endeared himself to the nation in July 1966 when he ran his socks off at Wembley in the World Cup Final and earned himself a move to Everton shortly after. His subsequent all-action displays made him a Goodison Park idol and his departure to Arsenal in 1971 still hasn't sunk in with some fervent Evertonians! What a tigerish pair Bally and Reidy would make!

The Scouser came to Everton having recovered from some appalling injuries and he played himself into the 1986 England World Cup squad, picking up the PFA Player of the Year award en-route.

Other central midfielders to return high voting scores were Paul Bracewell, Howard Kendall, Colin Harvey and Tony Kay.

When it came to strikers, everyone voted for the greatest goalscorer that's ever played the game.

William Ralph 'Dixie' Dean scored 349 league goals in 399 league games for Everton and he was always going to be an automatic choice in any select eleven. But who would partner him? Bob Latchford, Tommy Lawton, Joe Royle, Gary Lineker and even Wayne Rooney all attracted interest but in the end the man who is second behind Dixie in the Everton all-time goalscoring list secured the position. Graeme Sharp scored 159 goals in all competitions and is a worthy partner for the great man.

Everton's Greatest Team, as voted for by the supporters in 2004, v Bolton 2003/04

Peter Reid, Howard Kendall and Bran Labone present Everton's donation

For over 25 years, Dr David France has been assembling what has been quoted as the most comprehensive collection of football memorabilia in the world...

A Collection of artifacts, letters and other ephemera, the David France Collection is a timeline of Everton history stemming from the very roots of the Club's existence to the present day.

Containing items that crystallised and created a nation of blue-blooded Evertonians, the Collection traces the Club's heritage back to 1878 when Everton's time first began. Further to this, the Collection is also of the utmost historical importance in illustrating and chronicling the formation of the oldest League system in the world. Featuring some of football's rarest artifacts, of the 10,000 collated items, many pre-date the formative years of the Football League.

Dating as far back as 1886, the Collection contains 6,065 programmes covering the Club's participation in league, cup competitions, friendly games and reserve team fixtures between 1886 - 2001. The programmes provided the starting block for David France's Collection when he first started assembling them as a young boy in 1953. Added to his first one are now all the away, home, and most of the away, programmes for every game in which Dixie Dean played for Everton, along with 30 home issues and one away edition from the pre-League era and many more since.

Added to the programmes, season tickets, ticket stubs, medals, photographs, contracts, cash books, handbooks, financial statements and other ephemera, every item amassed in the collection assists in mapping out the Club's distinguished past and it's unparalleled heritage. Other items include cigarette cards, postcards and international caps from the turn of the century.

Each piece of memorabilia is unique and special in its own right. Some pieces date back to the pioneering days at Stanley Park, Priory Road and Anfield with the Everton Ledgers shedding much light and insight into the Club's history from 1886 through to 1964, including diverse issues such as the choice of colours, selection of team line-ups and the acrimonious split which resulted in the formation of Liverpool Football Club.

With this in mind, the Collection not only documents the history and pedigree of Everton Football Club, but also the history of football in the city of Liverpool, Merseyside, and the world. It's contents provide an ideal tool to educate people in the history of the beautiful game and life in Liverpool itself, however it is also a box of memories opening a wealth of opportunity to look back and reminisce about the past and the glory of Everton Football Club. David France plans to sell his precious collection, with an intention for it to return home to the people of Merseyside, so that it can be enjoyed by Evertonians and football enthusiasts alike, preserving its integrity and historical significance.

The Collection has been valued at £1.2 million, but would fetch considerably more if broken up and sold as individual items. However, as a loyal Evertonian, David is passionate that it should remain in its entirety and has offered it to Evertonians for £800,000.

In order to acquire this outstanding Collection, a Charitable Trust has been established by Evertonians to raise the funds needed to bring it home.

Established by Trustees, Lord Grantchester (grandson of former Everton Chairman Sir John Moores), Keith Wyness (Chief Executive of Everton) and another True Blue Evertonian, Tony Tighe, The Everton Collection Charitable Trust aims to secure the Collection for future generations, maintaining and preserving each individual item to ensure the legacy of Everton and the history of football on Merseyside and the world, lives on.

Once acquired, the Collection will initially be on display periodically at Goodison Park. However, in order that it be openly accessible to all for purposes such as research, the advancement of education and public interest, the Everton Collection Charitable Trust is currently working in partnership with the City of Liverpool's Record Office and National Museums Liverpool, to ultimately house the Collection securely in a venue where the public may enjoy it in its full glory.

Everton Football Club itself has donated £250,000 to the Charitable Trust and a further £100,000 has been donated by Lord Grantchester. We launched the appeal last month with a bang but in order to reach our target we need your help.

This unparalleled Collection of Football memorabilia is Everton and Merseyside's heritage and should be put back in the hands of the supporters of the People's Club. We are asking those who recognise its worth and historical importance, including the people of Merseyside and loyal Evertonians, to help us achieve our goal, and in doing so implore you to consider making a donation to the Everton Collection Charitable Trust.

All it takes is a small donation to play your part in obtaining these valuable pieces of history for The People's Club and the people of Merseyside.

There are a number of ways to donate...
• Donate online by visiting evertonfc.com
• Call the donation hotline on 0871 789 6089
• Donate using a match-day collection envelope available on allocated match days.
• Complete a donation form found in special programmes.

Please make all cheques and postal orders payable to The Everton Collection Charitable Trust and send to:
FREEPOST
THE EVERTON
COLLECTION APPEAL

Moves to secure funding in a bid to obtain Dr David France's Everton Collection are announced, v Villarreal, 2005/06

1

Inside **Goodison**

● It was wholly in keeping with Duncan Ferguson's Roy of the Rovers relationship with Everton Football Club, that he should become a Magnificent Seventh signing of a frantic summer of transfer activity.

Ferguson signed a five-year contract last Thursday which could see him end his career with the club - which is apt because the player always said he never wanted to leave Goodison in the first place. Tonight he hopes to make his second home debut, almost six years after the first.

"Stepping out at Goodison again will be a high point of my career," he said after re-signing last week.

"I've never been back since I left, even though I always looked out for the results and kept in touch with what was happening. The reception I got when I came back to sign was incredible, really amazing. Ive been away nearly two years and they still remembered me which is great. Obviously I need to keep myself fit and available for selection as much as possible, but I think if I can do that everything will go well."

The reception Ferguson will receive tonight will leave him in no doubt as to Evertonian emotions regarding his homecoming. The player himself was equally passionate when asked about Evertonians at last Thursday's press conference.

"I wouldnt have left Newcastle for any other club but Everton," he declared.

"All the fans know how I feel about the club, and yes I still have my tatoo. There was never a doubt in my mind once Newcastle had decided they no longer required my services. I was delighted to come back to Everton.

"When I first came here the fans took to me right away. I dont know what it is, but you know Evertons in my blood and its always been there. This opportunity is just a fantastic one for myself. I had such a great rapport here with the club and the fans that you always have it in the back of your mind one day that you will go back. Im just delighted its happened.

"The Everton fans rate right at the top of all the fans I have played in front of. They are the best fans of all. Theres no question. I couldnt have imagined at the beginning of pre-season that I would be coming back here. I was happy at Newcastle, but when it became apparent that they were prepared to sell me there was only one club I wanted to join."

There are a number of attacking options now open to manager Walter Smith, especially when Kevin Campbell makes a full recovery from his knee injury. Competition for places will be intense, but Duncan believes admits that is good for the club.

"Every top club has three or four strikers competing for two places," he said.

"That is the way forward in modern football. I hope to stay fit and make sure I claim one of the places - and if I'm selected hopefully I can forge a good partnership with whoever I play with.

"Obviously there are good strikers here. There's Kevin Campbell, young Franny Jeffers, Mark Hughes, Joe-Max Moore and youngsters like Danny Cadamarteri and Phil Jevons.

"Ive just got to keep myself fit and hopefully I can get one of those places. I know I can do a job here again. I think if you asked Alan Shearer how he felt at playing alongside me I think it would speak for itself."

With Walter Smith having signed natural wide players like Niclas Alexandersson and Stephen Hughes, Ferguson is hoping for the kind of service centre-forwards crave this season.

"Every centre-forward screams for service," he added.

"It doesnt matter what club youre at. If youre at Newcastle you screaming for wide men and if you're at Everton youll be screaming for wide men. I see myself as a new player coming into a new team. Its an exciting time."

The Duncan Ferguson fairytale began when he scored his first

Everton goal in a Merseyside derby match - with the Blues rooted to the botom of the Premiership.

It continued with memorable goals - and celebrations - in the matches the fans hold dearest, against Manchester United and Liverpool. When he was appointed captain shortly after Christmas 1997, he celebrated with his first Everton hat-trick.

Tonight he will hope to add another chapter to his Goodison fairytale... with many more to follow.

Big Dunc is Back!

Rocky at Goodison today

3

SCREEN legend Sylvester Stallone will be at Goodison to cheer on David Moyes' side this afternoon.

A close friend of new Everton major shareholder, Robert Earl, the star of Rocky, Rambo and Escape To Victory will be taking the opportunity to attend Sunday's match before travelling to London for Tuesday's UK Premiere of Rocky Balboa, the sixth film in the famous boxing series.

There will be some special events planned before the game to mark Sly's arrival at Goodison. Chief Executive Keith Wyness said: "It is exciting news that Sylvester Stallone is coming across to Goodison.

"Robert Earl, the new investor, has been very kind to arrange for Rocky to come up to a game and it is going to be quite an occasion. I think of all the film stars around today, there are not many you can take onto the pitch at a sporting occasion and have some relevance. But Sylvester - and his part as Rocky - has a special place in the hearts of sports fans."

A POWERFUL MESSAGE

4

Everton's players wore specially-commissioned shirts in Saturday's game against Norwich City to support a campaign backed by main sponsor Chang to help victims of the recent floods in Thailand.

The players' shirts didn't feature the usual logo of Chang Beer, but that of the 'Power of Thai', a new relief fund to help those affected by the natural disaster which swept across mainland Thailand earlier this year.

Under the banner 'One Flag Unites Thailand', Chang and other likeminded Thai organisations have established the 'Power of Thai' fundraising appeal to help the hundreds of thousands of people hurt or who have lost everything. The specially commissioned appeal logo, which incorporates the national flag of Thailand and the English and Thai statement the 'Power of Thai', was given the royal seal of approval by the King of Thailand, King Bhumibol Adulyadej, who granted permission to use the national flag.

The match-worn shirts from Saturday's fixture will now be autographed and auctioned online, with 100 per cent of the winning bids donated to the 'Power of Thai'.

พลังน้ำใจไทย
Power of Thai

BLUE ACADEMY FA Youth Cup

MEET THE BOYS

Everton will be bidding to win the FA Youth Cup for the fourth time in the club's history when we take on Aston Villa next month in the two-legged final.

The Blues will meet Villa here at Goodison Park on Tuesday May 14th with a 8.05pm kick-off and then travel to Villa Park on Saturday May 18th for a 12-noon kick-off. It's Everton's second final appearance in four years and Academy Director, Ray Hall, introduces the squad of players hoping to emulate the successful 'Class of 98'.

ANDREW PETTINGER
"We signed him from Scunthorpe and he's the only player in the squad for whom we've paid what's called a Compensation Fee. He found it difficult to settle at first, being from a little village outside Scunthorpe but he's worked his way through it, he's had help from all the staff and he was in the first team squad last week."

MARTIN CROWDER
"He's a tidy player with a good left foot. Another boy who joined us from Liverpool, for whom he played up front, like a few players who eventually move back into the defence. He has the ability to go forward and has worked very hard on his defensive qualities, which have really improved."

BRIAN MOOGAN
"Brian's an Under-17s player who joined us from Liverpool when he was 13. He's a mad Evertonian with a burning desire to play for the first team. He's the type of boy you could play anywhere. He's reached a level of consistency now that can only bode well for the future."

STEPHEN SCHUMACHER
"He's the leader in the side and he's the type of lad that, if you looked around the dressing room, you'd be delighted to have on your side. He's captained England Under-18s and he can also play in midfield. He's suffered with injuries this season."

CRAIG GARSIDE
"Craig's played in many different positions and he got his chance to play centre-back when Robert Southern got injured. Another big Evertonian, he's been with us since he was 9 years old and was a season ticket holder before that. He knows what it means to be here and he's worked very hard - he's a Welsh international.

ROBERT SOUTHERN
"Robert's been unfortunate in picking up a knee injury that's kept him out for the second half of the season. He was making good progress before that. He's from Gateshead and as he's settled into his new environment his performances have improved. I hope he's fit enough to be in and around the squad because he deserves it."

FRANKLYN COLBECK
"A defender who came to us when he was 13 years old from Tranmere Rovers and has progressed steadily. I think there's more to come in a physical sense, he's still got some growing to do and when he does I'm sure his level of consistency will improve."

ALAN MOOGAN
"One of the first names on the teamsheet I would think. He has a terrific attitude and he's another that can play anywhere. Came to us from Liverpool when he was 14 and he's done very well. What I like about Alan is that he tackles his weight and the opposition know they're in a game."

STEVEN BECK
"Steven is a gifted player, technically and he's still improving. He has a fine array of passing skills and can unlock defences in and around the

2

goals this season and he also pops up with one or two of his own. He's another of our England internationals."

SCOTT BROWN
"Scottie's a real character who's been here since he was 9. Not the tallest player but anyone playing against him knows he's about. He's an Under 17s England player and he's technically very gifted. What I like about him though is that he's more interested in the team and in winning than he is about his own performance - and you don't often see that in such a young player."

DAVID CARNEY
"I go over to Australia and watch their Youth Championships where all the best young players play. I saw David playing for NSW and he had this laid back style and we brought him over for a trial and then signed him. Ironically, his family are from Scotland Road originally and they're all big Evertonians."

MICHAEL SYMES
"In my opinion the most improved player at the club. Michael has developed physically into a terrific athlete and he's getting better and better. You need two front players who will put in a work rate that will make it easier for the rest of the team to defend. He certainly did that in the 2nd leg of the semi-final against Tottenham."

WAYNE ROONEY
"Wayne's a special talent but we're all aware that it's not just about talent. It's about application and whether or not you live your life correctly. We're certain that Wayne's got the mental strength and desire to do whatever he wants."

"As far as the substitutes are concerned, they'll probably be an Under-16s mix - I just hope that Damon Martland stays on a bit longer than he did last time! He's a brave little character and he works tirelessly. Alex Cole did well for the Under 19s on Saturday when Andrew was at Southampton and that will encourage him. Jack Flood, James Potter, Joseph Jones and Anthony Gerrard may be involved and they've all been Under 17s regulars this season."

Ray Hall is insisting that the FA Youth Cup Final achievement is a credit to the entire Academy. "If you look at the boys who have come through the Academy into the first team the supporters enjoy the end product, but what they won't have seen is the work that has already gone in to make the young player arrive at that stage. When a boy breaks through it's looked upon as the beginning of a career but from an Academy point of view it's more like the 'end' of a career because we've fulfilled our aim to provide players for the first team - and from there it's up to other people. Some of these lads have been with us since they were 7,8 or 9 years of age and they've had many different coaches here who've helped with their development both on the field of play and also in the way they lead their lives. And now, of course, the icing on the cake is the opportunity to work with a coach like Colin Harvey."

Michael Symes

"I WOULDN'T HAVE LEFT NEWCASTLE FOR ANY OTHER CLUB BUT EVERTON"

1 **All change (v Charlton Athletic, 2000/01)**
With the departure of first-teamers Don Hutchison, John Collins and Nick Barmby, Evertonians needed a summer boost to appease the growing discontent over the departures. Overseas stars such as Thomas Gravesen, Alex Nyarko and Niclas Alexandersson had come in – but it was the seventh signing of the summer that was a reason to rejoice – the return of crowd favourite Duncan Ferguson. He celebrated in typical headline-grabbing style, coming off the bench to net twice in a 3-0 win.

2 **Stars of the future? (v Blackburn Rovers, 2001/02)**
Everton's run to the final of the FA Youth Cup grabbed national headlines in some quarters, in no small part thanks to some spectacular goals by a young prospect by the name of Wayne Rooney. In this programme spread ahead of the two-legged clash with Aston Villa, Academy director Ray Hall was asked to introduce the class of '02. On Wayne, he noted: "We're certain that Wayne's got the mental strength and desire to do whatever he wants."

3 **Rocky! (v Reading, 2006/07)**
The high-profile visit of Sylvester Stallone to Goodison in early 2007 coincided with the film star's promotion of his latest Rocky instalment, Rocky Balboa. A friend of major Everton shareholder Robert Earl, his appearance and reception brightened up what turned out to be a 1-1 draw. Although his current supporter credentials might be brought into question, his Everton scarf was also sported when he promoted the film in France the following day...

4 **Thai Support (v Arsenal, 2011/12)**
The club's main sponsor, Chang, was replaced on the home shirts against Norwich City by the legend 'The Power Of Thai', a relief fund set up to help people affected by the 2011 floods in Thailand. As well as raising awareness for the cause, the match shirts were also signed and auctioned to raise funds for the initiative.

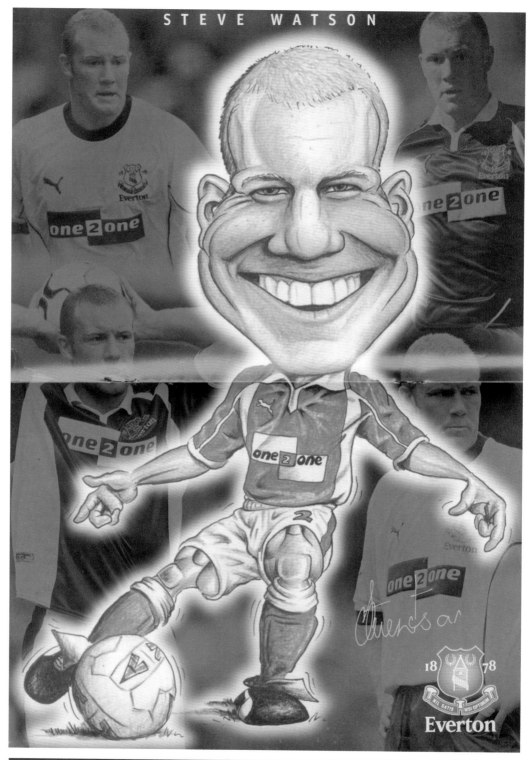

STEVE WATSON

Above: Steve Watson is the subject of this 2000/01 programme series of first-team players as 'cartoon figures'; opposite top: Rocky wows Goodison as players and management clamour for Sylvester Stallone's attention; opposite: how Everton's late show against Tottenham Hotspur was captured in 2012/13

Rocky at Goodison Park 14.01.07

PicturePower

A crazy couple of minutes...
Everton 2 – 1 Tottenham Hotspur

"I thought Seamus Coleman played great today but I'm not convinced he was trying to pick out Steven. But it's a ball that gave us a chance to score and Steven's header was terrific.

Jelavic's finish was great as well because he was alert and alive. He could have been still but he gambled on something maybe nicking through and to finish it first time was excellent."

- **DAVID MOYES**

"When we were making cross after cross and chance after chance I was thinking, 'someone please just score', so that's why in the end I was pleased I got my head up and picked out Pienaar."

- **SEAMUS COLEMAN**

"The last header I scored was in 2001 for Ajax! I'm quite pleased with it. The timing was perfect and to score in the last minute meant it was a special goal. To score against your former club is always nice. Nicky showed he is a striker who can score and his was a real poacher's goal."

- **STEVEN PIENAAR**

"What a result that was! Great performance from the lads!"

- **DARRON GIBSON**

"I didn't see Nikica's goal! All I saw was the celebration but the guys soon told me about it. I was happy I could help get the winner."

- **APOSTOLOS VELLIOS**

"Whether we are 1-0 down or 2-0 up, we play from the first second to the last second. We always believe we can win and we proved it again."

- **SYLVAIN DISTIN**

"It was almost inevitable for Steven to score but I don't think many would have bet on a header! Then it's a great ball into the box from Gibbo, and a superb finish from Jela. We were all absolutely delighted in the changing room."

- **PHIL JAGIELKA**

United

Bobby Robson aims to bring success to the new St James' Park...

Villa thriller. Georgios Samaras celebrates his double strike against Aston Villa last Saturday

...thing good has ...season

THE club shook to the foundations of the stands until Bobby Robson revived a team with one point ...the first six games last

played 24 matches in London without a win since beating Crystal Palace 2-1 in November 1997.

The most recent away game, at Charlton, completed a full set of defeats in the capital this season and apparently broke the patience of a normally unflappable manager. The words of Mr Robson echoed round The Valley: "Sorry for our supporters" ... "who have paid

good money and seen a dismal first-half performance"... "I apologise to them."

The bottom line is that Newcastle have two very different away records:

In London:
P	W	D	L	F	A	Pts
5	0	0	5	3	15	0

Elsewhere:
P	W	D	L	F	A	Pts
9	4	2	3	11	10	14

So, with top-six hopes dented by another defeat, at home to Manchester City, Mr Robson might be grateful that today is the start of a provincial travelling programme with assignments to come at Bradford, Ipswich, Sunderland and Liverpool. They have won at Coventry, Manchester City, Middlesbrough and Leeds (the latter result registering a double under a month over the Champions League contenders), and there were draws at Leicester and Aston Villa.

"Even the best-laid plans can somersault into a kick in the teeth - and that's probably how Newcastle felt about the injuries which sidelined a £22m strike force.

Everything was rosy in August when Carl Cort scored on his home debut against Derby, but the former Wimbledon raider was soon to spend months in the treatment room after only three starts for his new club.

This meant that Alan Shearer soldiered on as the main goal-scorer, though increasingly troubled by tendinitis in his right knee.

Manchester on our turf

City's travelling fans will be hoping they finally have something to cheer this afternoon.

For while there have been grounds for optimism so far as the form at the City of Manchester Stadium is concerned, there has been precious little on the road.

A trip to champions Chelsea was hardly the place where Stuart Pearce

would have wanted the season to start and City went down 3-0 at Stamford Bridge.

But following a home draw with high-flying Portsmouth, the fans were given a fillip when City saw off Arsenal at Eastlands the following weekend thanks to a Joey Barton penalty.

Yet the opportunity to build on that success slipped away as City lost back-to-back away matches at Reading and Blackburn in the space

of six days.

City were left rueing their luck at the Madejski Stadium, as Ivar Ingimarsson's header from a free kick midway through the first half proved the difference in a game which also saw summer signing Ousmane Dabo dismissed – a decision which was upheld despite a City appeal to have the red card rescinded.

Things didn't get any better at Ewood Park when manager Stuart Pearce left to reflect on a series of missed chances and defensive lapses

City went down 4-2.

And a miserable week was completed when City crashed out of the Carling Cup at League One side Chesterfield, going down 2-1 at Gartergate.

But Pearce's men showed their character by bouncing back to record a fine 2-0 home win over West Ham last Saturday with Greek International Georgios Samaras netting both goals.

The City boss was delighted with the performance, saying: "The players have been under the microscope and it would have been easy for them to have gone under.

"I was pleased with the performance and effort. They were only 21 and learning the game. He's an uncut diamond."

Frenchman Dabo is one of several new faces in the City squad this season. Dietmar Hamann and DaMarcus Beasley add to the competition for places in midfield, while striker Bernard Corradi has bolstered the attack along with the returning Paul Dickov. Swedish international goalkeeper Andreas Isaksson is another new arrival while Tunisian full-back Hatem Trabelsi joined from Ajax on deadline day.

Summer signing:
Bernard Corradi

AUG
19 Chelsea
23 Portsmouth
26 ARSENAL
Barton

SEP
11 Reading
17 Blackburn
Barton, Ooijer (og)
23 WEST HAM
Samaras 2

MANCHESTER UNITED
Position: Midfielder

Age: 23
Birthplace: Madeira
Portugal caps: 59
United Apps: 247
United Goals: 95

ONE of the most exciting talents in world football, Ronaldo has exhausted just about every superlative in the book since arriving in the Premier League.

The Portuguese winger has exceeded expectations since joining from Sporting Lisbon in a £12.24m deal in 2003, maturing into a consistent performer.

Named the Sir Matt Busby Player of the Year for 2003/04 in his first year at Old Trafford, a quieter second season followed before 2005/06 saw him return to something approaching his best.

In 2006/07, Ronaldo bounced back from a controversial World Cup to hit new heights as he scooped both the PFA Player of the Year and Young Player of the Year awards.

...last season,

after start...

A product of the ...
Rooney played for England as an ...year-old at Euro 2004, and although it seems he has been around for years, he only celebrated his 23rd birthday yesterday. He became the world's most expensive teenager after that tournament, moving to Old Trafford for an initial fee of £23 million. The pressure did little to faze him, and he hit a hat-trick against Fenerbahce in his first game at Old Trafford. At the end of the 2004/05 campaign, he was named PFA Young Player of the Year.

Rooney's second season at Old Trafford brought further progress, as he scored 19 goals and retained the PFA Young Player of the Year award. He improved his goals tally in 2006/07 and 23 goals to bounce back from a difficult World Cup campaign with England the previous summer.

Last season produced 18 more goals as United claimed a Premier League and Champions League double.

MANCHESTER UNITED
Position: Striker

Age: 27
Birthplace: Blagoevgrad
Bulgaria caps: 64
United Apps: 7
United Goals: 5

BULGARIAN striker who completed a deadline day move to United from Spurs for a fee of £30 million on 1 September.

At the age of just 17, Berbatov moved to CSKA Sofia, following in the footsteps of his father, Ivan, who also played for the club. He played for CSKA between 1998 and January 2001 before moving to Bayer Leverkusen. In his first full season in Germany, he helped the club to the Champions League final - making an appearance as a second-half substitute in the final against Real Madrid.

After more than five successful years in Germany with Leverkusen, Spurs swooped to sign him in May 2006 for a fee of £10.9 million, making him the most expensive Bulgarian player in history.

He was an immediate success at White Hart Lane with his clever style, deft touches and eye for goal helping...

MANCHESTER UNITED
Position: Defender

Age: 29
Birthplace: Peckham
England caps: 72
United Apps: 278

A ROCK at the heart of the United defence, he has forged a fine partnership with Ferdinand, and their axis has been the foundation of the team's recent successes.

...
remain his reading of the game and leadership in defence - qualities that have made him a solid foundation for both United and England, and have brought him the captaincy for club and country on numerous occasions.

He signed a new five-year contract with United in May, and just six days later went on to captain United to Champions League glory in Moscow. He had earlier won his third Premier League title with the club.

...experienced, Ferdinand's ...

Birth...
England caps...
United Apps: 109
United Goals: 6

A graduate of Red Star Belgrade's youth system, his senior career started with a season-long loan deal at Spartak Subotica in 2000. He moved back to Red Star and won the 2001/02 Yugoslav Cup. Vidic went on to become captain, leading the club for three seasons and signing off on a high by winning a domestic double in his final season.

In July 2004, he joined Russian Premier League side Spartak Moscow and another successful couple of years there led to his move to United in January 2006 for a reported fee of around £7 million.

In his first full season, he won a Premier League medal and added another to his collection last season, alongside the coveted UEFA Champions...

Among his most historic treble season of 1998/99, while last season's double of Champions League and Premier League also ranks highly.

OPPOSITION NOTES...

Four-six page sections on the away team became standard form in the matchday programme, content ranging from player overviews, in-depth 'One To Watch' style write-ups and a look at previous meetings between the sides.

The late 2000s saw some more quirkier elements, including 'worst kit' and celebrity fan features – the late darts commentating legend Sid Waddell being a particular highlight.

Latterly standard form has included current progress, manager, player profiles and often interviews with players who have played for both sides.

MATCHSTATISTICS 04/05

Date	Fixture	V	Res	Att	Pts	Pos	FIRST TEAM				KEY: GOALSCORERS
Sat Aug 14	Arsenal	H	1-4	35,521	-	-	Martyn	Naysmith	Yobo	Stubbs	Pist
Sat Aug 21	Crystal Palace	A	3-1	23,666	3	8	Martyn	Hibbert	Yobo	Stubbs	Nay
Sat Aug 28	West Bromwich Albion	H	2-1	34,510	6	7	Martyn	Hibbert	Yobo	Stubbs	Pist
Mon Aug 30	Manchester United	A	0-0	67,803	7	7	Martyn	Hibbert	Weir	Stubbs	Pist
Sat Sep 11	Manchester City	A	1-0	47,006	10	5	Martyn	Hibbert	Weir	Stubbs	Pist
Sun Sep 19	Middlesbrough	H	1-0	34,078	13	3	Martyn	Hibbert	Weir	Stubbs	Pist
Wed Sep 22	Bristol City (CC2)	A	2-2	15,264	Won 4-3 Pens		Wright	Hibbert	Yobo■	Stubbs	Nay
Sun Sep 26	Portsmouth	A	1-0	20,125	16	3	Martyn	Hibbert	Weir	Stubbs■	Pist
Sat Oct 2	Tottenham Hotspur	H	0-1	38,264	16	3	Martyn	Hibbert	Weir	Stubbs	Pis
Sat Oct 16	Southampton	H	1-0	35,256	19	3	Martyn	Hibbert	Weir	Stubbs	Pis
Sat Oct 23	Norwich City	A	3-2	23,871	22	3	Martyn	Hibbert	Weir■	Stubbs	Pist
Wed Oct 27	Preston North End (CC3)	H	2-0	33,922	-	-	Wright	Hibbert	Weir	Yobo	Pist
Sat Oct 30	Aston Villa	H	1-1	37,816	23	3	Martyn	Hibbert	Weir	Stubbs	Pis
Sat Nov 6	Chelsea	A	0-1	41,965	23	3	Martyn	Hibbert	Weir	Stubbs	Pis
Tue Nov 9	Arsenal (CC4)	A	1-3	27,791	-	-	Wright	Hibbert	Yobo	Stubbs	Pis
Sat Nov 13	Birmingham City	A	1-0	28,388	26	3	Martyn	Hibbert	Weir	Stubbs	Pis
Sat Nov 20	Fulham	H	1-0	34,763	29	3	Martyn	Hibbert	Weir	Stubbs	Pis
Sun Nov 28	Newcastle United	A	1-1	51,247	30	3	Martyn	Hibbert■	Weir	Stubbs	Pis
Sat Dec 4	Bolton Wanderers	H	3-2+	35,929	33	3	Martyn	Hibbert	Weir	Stubbs	Pis
Sat Dec 11	Liverpool	H	1-0	40,552	36	2	Martyn	Hibbert■	Weir	Stubbs	Pis
Sat Dec 18	Blackburn Rovers	A	0-0	25,191	37	3	Martyn	Hibbert■	Weir	Stubbs	Pis
Sun Dec 26	Manchester City	H	2-1	40,530	40	3	Martyn	Hibbert	Weir	Stubbs	Pis
Tue Dec 28	Charlton Athletic	A	0-2	27,001	40	4	Martyn■	Hibbert	Weir	Stubbs	Pis
Sat Jan 1	Tottenham Hotspur	A	2-5	36,102	40	4	Wright	Hibbert	Weir	Yobo	Pis
Tue Jan 4	Portsmouth	H	2-1	35,480	43	4	Wright	Hibbert	Yobo	**Stubbs**	Na
Sat Jan 8	Plymouth Argyle (FAC3)	A	3-1	20,112	-	-	Wright	Naysmith	Yobo	Stubbs	Pis
Sun Jan 16	Middlesbrough	A	1-1	31,794	44	4	Wright	Hibbert	Weir	Stubbs	Pis
Sat Jan 22	Charlton Athletic	H	0-1	36,041	44	4	Wright	Hibbert	Weir	Stubbs	Pis
Sat Jan 29	Sunderland (FAC4)	H	3-0	33,186	-	-	Wright	Naysmith■	Yobo	Stubbs■	Pis
Wed Feb 2	Norwich City	H	1-0+	37,486	47	4	Martyn	Hibbert■	Weir■	Stubbs	Pis
Sun Feb 6	Southampton	A	2-2	31,509	48	4	Martyn	Hibbert■	Weir	Stubbs■	Pi
Sat Feb 12	Chelsea	H	0-1	40,270	48	4	Martyn	Naysmith■	Weir	Stubbs	Pi
Sat Feb 19	Manchester Utd (FAC5)	H	0-2	38,664	-	-	Martyn	Hibbert	Yobo	Stubbs	Na
Sat Feb 26	Aston Villa	A	3-1	40,248	51	4	Martyn	Hibbert	Weir	Yobo	Pi
Sun Mar 6	Blackburn Rovers	H	0-1	32,406	51	4	Martyn	Hibbert	Weir■	Yobo	Pi
Sun Mar 20	Liverpool	A	1-2	44,224	51	4	Martyn	Hibbert■	Weir■	Stubbs	Pi
Sat Apr 2	West Bromwich Albion	A	0-1	26,805	51	4	Martyn	Hibbert	Weir	Stubbs■	Pi
Sun Apr 10	Crystal Palace	H	4-0	36,519	54	4	Martyn	Hibbert	Weir	Stubbs■	N
Wed Apr 20	Manchester United	H	1-0	37,160	57	4	Martyn	Hibbert■	Weir	Yobo	W
Sat Apr 23	Birmingham City	H	1-1	36,828	58	4	Martyn	Hibbert	Weir	Yobo	P
Sat Apr 30	Fulham	A	0-2	21,881	58	4	Martyn	Watson	Weir	Yobo	P
Sat May 7	Newcastle United	H	2-0	40,438	61	4	Martyn	Hibbert	**Weir**	Yobo	W
Wed May 11	Arsenal	A	0-7	38,073	61	4	Wright	Hibbert	Weir	Yobo	P
Sat May 14	Bolton Wanderers	A	2-3	27,701	61	4	Wright	Hibbert■	Weir	Yobo	W

[FIRST] SUB ■ SECOND SUB ■ THIRD SUB ■ YELLOW CARD ■ RED CARD +OWN GOAL SUBSTITUTES

						Wright	Watson	Bent■	Ferguson■	Hibbert■
bell	Gravesen	**Carsley**■	Kilbane	Osman■	McFadden■	Wright	Watson	Bent■	Ferguson■	Hibbert■
bell■	**Gravesen 2**	Carsley	Kilbane	Osman■	**Bent**■	Wright	Watson■	Pistone■	Ferguson■	McFadden
bell■	Gravesen	Carsley	Kilbane	**Osman 2**	Bent	Wright	Watson	Weir	Ferguson■	McFadden
■	Watson	Carsley	Kilbane	Osman■	Bent■	Wright	Campbell	Naysmith■	Ferguson■	McFadden
■	Watson	Carsley	Kilbane■	Osman■	Bent■	Wright	Gravesen■	Naysmith■	Ferguson■	McFadden
on■	Gravesen	Carsley	Kilbane■	Osman	**Bent**■	Wright	Yobo	Naysmith	Ferguson■	McFadden■
	Watson	Carsley	McFadden	Osman■	**Ferguson**■	Turner	Campbell■	Weir	Pistone■	**Chadwick**■
	Gravesen	Carsley	Kilbane	Watson■	Bent	Wright	Campbell	Yobo■	Ferguson■	McFadden
	Gravesen	Carsley■	Kilbane	Osman	Bent	Wright	Watson■	Yobo	Ferguson■	McFadden■
	Gravesen	Carsley	Kilbane■	**Osman**	Bent■	Wright	Watson■	Yobo	Ferguson■	McFadden■
	Gravesen	Carsley■	**Kilbane**	Osman■	**Bent**■	Wright	Watson■	Yobo■	**Ferguson**■	McFadden
dden■	Watson	**Carsley**■	Kilbane	Osman	Ferguson■	Turner	Campbell	Gravesen	**Bent**■	Cahill■
	Gravesen	Watson■	Kilbane	Osman■	**Bent**	Wright	Campbell	Fox	Ferguson■	McFadden
	Gravesen	Watson■	Kilbane■	Osman■	Bent■	Turner	Campbell■	Yobo	Chadwick■	McFadden■
	Gravesen	Watson■	Kilbane	McFadden	Bent■	Turner	Weir	Naysmith	Chadwick■	Osman■
	Gravesen	Carsley	Kilbane■	Osman	Bent	Wright	Watson■	Naysmith	Ferguson■	McFadden
	Gravesen■	Carsley	Kilbane	Osman■	Bent■	Wright	Watson■	Yobo	**Ferguson**■	McFadden■
■	Gravesen■	**Carsley**	Kilbane	Osman	Bent■	Wright	Watson■	Yobo■	Ferguson■	McFadden
	Gravesen	Carsley .	Kilbane■	**Ferguson**■	Bent	Wright	Watson	Yobo■	Osman■	McFadden■
	Gravesen■	**Carsley** .	Kilbane	Osman■	Bent■■	Wright	Watson■	Yobo■	McFadden	Ferguson■
	Gravesen	Carsley■	Kilbane	Osman■	Bent■	Wright	Watson■	Yobo	McFadden■	Ferguson■
■	Gravesen■■	Carsley	Kilbane	Watson■	**Bent**■	Wright	Naysmith	Yobo■	Ferguson■	McFadden■
	Gravesen	Carsley	Kilbane	Yobo■	Bent■	Wright■	Naysmith	Ferguson■■	Campbell	McFadden■
	Gravesen	Carsley	McFadden■	**Osman**	Campbell■	Turner	Naysmith■	Osman■	Campbell	Chadwick
dden■	**Osman**	Carsley	Kilbane	Beattie■■	Bent■	Turner	Weir	Pistone	Bent■	Kilbane■
■	Yobo■	Carsley	Kilbane	Beattie■■	Bent	Turner	Weir	Gravesen■	Cahill■■	**Chadwick**■
	Beattie	Carsley	Kilbane■	Osman	Bent■	Turner	Naysmith■	Chadwick	Ferguson■	McFadden■
■	Osman	Carsley	Kilbane■	**Beattie**■	**McFadden**■	Turner	Naysmith	Yobo■	Ferguson■	McFadden■
■	Yobo	Carsley	Kilbane■	Beattie■	McFadden■	Martyn	Hibbert	Weir■	Bent■	Chadwick■
■	Yobo	Carsley■	Kilbane■	**Beattie**	McFadden	Wright	Naysmith■	Chadwick	Bent■	Ferguson■
■	Yobo	Carsley■	Kilbane	Beattie■	Bent	Wright	Naysmith	Arteta■	**Bent**■	Ferguson■
a■	Osman	Carsley	Kilbane	McFadden■	Bent	Wright	Plessis	Arteta■	Gerrard	Ferguson■
■	Arteta	Carsley	Kilbane	**Osman 2**	Bent■	Wright	Plessis	Vaughan	Weir■■	Pistone■
■	Arteta■	Carsley■	Kilbane	Osman■	Bent	Wright	Plessis	Vaughan	Naysmith■	Ferguson■
■	Yobo■■■	Carsley	Kilbane	Osman■	Bent■	Wright	Stubbs	Plessis	Ferguson■	McFadden■
■	Arteta■	Carsley■	Kilbane	Osman	Bent	Wright	Watson■	Naysmith	Beattie■	Ferguson■
■ 2	**Arteta**	Ferguson	Kilbane	Osman	Bent■	Wright	Watson■	Yobo■	Plessis	Ferguson■■
■	Arteta■	Carsley	Kilbane	**Ferguson**■■	Bent	Wright	Watson■	**Vaughan**■	Carsley■	McFadden
	Arteta	Carsley■	Kilbane	Osman	Beattie■	Wright	Osman■	Vaughan	Beattie■	McFadden■
■	Arteta■■	Carsley	Kilbane	Ferguson	Bent■	Wright	Watson■■	Bent■	**Ferguson**■	Mcfadden
■■	Arteta■	Carsley■	Kilbane	Ferguson■	Bent■	Wright	Osman■	Plessis	Beattie■	McFadden■■
on	Arteta■	Carsley	Kilbane	Beattie■	McFadden	Wright	Stubbs■	Pistone	Beattie■	McFadden■
■■	Arteta■	**Carsley**	Kilbane	Ferguson	McFadden	Turner	Stubbs	Plessis	Bent■	Ferguson■
						Martyn	Stubbs■	Pistone	Vaughan■	Osman■

Blues Stats
Everton Statistics 2000-2001 Season

EVERTON ROLL CALL 00-01

Player	2000-2001 Apps	Gls	Everton Career Apps	Gls	Other Career Apps	Gls
1 Paul GERRARD — Heywood, 22.1.73	22	-	64(1)	-	135	-
	2	-	8	-	17	-
2 Steve WATSON — North Shields, 1.4.74	25	-	25	-	249	12
	4	1	4	1	66	3
3 Alessandro PISTONE — Milan, 27.7.75	2	-	2	-	46	1
	1	-	1	-	17	-
4 Richard GOUGH — Stockholm, 5.4.62	6	-	35	1	539	51
	-(1)	-	3(1)	-	211	22
5 David WEIR — Falkirk, 10.5.70	27	-	73(3)	2	225	16
	2	-	10	-	41	4
6 David UNSWORTH — Chorley, 16.10.73	10(10)	1	183(20)	19	32	2
	3	-	31(2)	5	9	-
7 Niclas ALEXANDERSSON — Halmstad, 29.12.71	10(1)	-	10(1)	-	75	8
	3	-	3	-	12	4
8 Alex NYARKO — Accra, 15.10.73	15(2)	1	15(2)	1	-	-
	2	-	2	-	-	-
9 Kevin CAMPBELL — Lambeth, 4.2.70	19(2)	7	53(2)	28	273	92
	2(1)	1	7(3)	1	77	17
10 Stephen HUGHES — Workington, 18.9.76	16(2)	-	27(2)	1	52	4
	3(1)	1	3(1)	1	28	3
11 Mark PEMBRIDGE — Merthyr Tydfil, 29.11.70	14	-	43(2)	2	263	45
	2	-	7	-	53	10
12 Michael BALL — Liverpool, 2.10.79	19	1	92(19)	6	-	-
	3(1)	-	14(4)	-	-	-
13 Steve SIMONSEN — South Shields, 3.4.79	-(1)	-	-(2)	-	35	-
	-	-	2	-	7	-
14 Francis JEFFERS — Liverpool, 25.1.81	9	6	36(10)	18	-	-
	2	1	8(3)	2	-	-
15 Gary NAYSMITH — Edinburgh, 16.11.78	15(2)	2	15(2)	2	97	3
	1	-	1	-	23	1
16 Thomas GRAVESEN — Vejle, 11.3.76	23(1)	2	23(1)	2	-	-
	3	-	3	-	-	-
17 Scot GEMMILL — Paisley, 2.1.71	15(3)	2	28(11)	4	245	21
	1(1)	-	3(2)	-	66	8
18 Paul GASCOIGNE — Gateshead, 27.5.67	10(2)	-	10(2)	-	299	74
	-(1)	-	-(1)	-	70	27
19 Joe-Max MOORE — USA, 23.2.71	7(11)	-	18(15)	6	-	-
	1(3)	-	2(5)	2	-	-
20 Alec CLELAND — Glasgow, 10.12.70	2(3)	-	21(11)	-	246	12
	1(1)	-	7(2)	-	68	5
21 Danny CADAMARTERI — Bradford, 12.10.79	7(8)	4	36(52)	13	5	1
	2	-	12(6)	2	-	-
22 Dave WATSON — Liverpool, 20.11.61	-	-	419(4)	23	212	11
	-	-	104(2)	15	44	4
24 Duncan FERGUSON — Stirling, 27.12.71	4(3)	3	114(9)	40	121	38
	1	-	17(1)	5	33	15
26 Phillip JEVONS — Liverpool, 1.8.79	-(3)	-	2(5)	-	-	-
	-	-	1	-	-	-
27 Jamie MILLIGAN — Blackpool, 3.1.80	-	-	-(4)	-	-	-
	-	-	-	-	-	-
28 Abel XAVIER — Mozambique, 30.11.72	6(1)	-	24(3)	-	-	-
	1	-	4	-	-	-
29 Kevin McLEOD — Liverpool, 12.9.80	-(4)	-	-(4)	-	-	-
	-	-	-	-	-	-
30 Peter CLARKE — Southport, 3.1.82	-(1)	-	-(1)	-	-	-
	-	-	-	-	-	-
33 Idan TAL — Israel, 13.9.75	10(6)	1	10(6)	1	-	-
	-(2)	-	-(2)	-	-	-
35 Thomas MYHRE — Sarpsborg, 16.10.73	6	-	70	-	13	-
	2	-	12	-	6	-

Also played: Richard Dunne (to Manchester City) 3 lge, 1 Cup;
Mark Hughes (to Blackburn Rovers) 6(3) lge, 1 Cup

Everton Roll Call Info: 1st Line: Premiership and Football League games. 2nd Line: Cup games. Other career figures include the above competitions as well as Scottish League and Cup appearances and games while on loan from Everton, but appearances for foreign clubs are not included. Up to and including Saturday 24 February 2001.

Key to symbols and abbreviations
- ① Goals Scored
- ⑬ Substitute/Goal and Player Replaced
- Booked
- Booked & sent off
- Sent off

	Date	Opponents	V	Res	Att	Pts
Sat	Aug 19	Leeds United	A	0-2	40,010	-
Wed	Aug 23	Charlton Athletic	H	3-0	36,300	3
Sat	Aug 26	Derby County	H	2-2	34,840	4
Tue	Sep 5	Tottenham Hotspur	A	2-3	35,316	4
Sat	Sep 9	Middlesbrough	A	2-1	30,885	7
Sat	Sep 16	Manchester United	H	1-3	38,541	7
Sun	Sep 24	Leicester City	A	1-1	18,084	8
Sat	Sep 30	Ipswich Town	H	0-3	32,597	8
Sat	Oct 14	Southampton	H	1-1	29,491	9
Sat	Oct 21	Newcastle United	A	1-0	51,625	12
Sun	Oct 29	Liverpool	A	1-3	44,718	12
Sun	Nov 5	Aston Villa	H	0-1	27,670	12
Sat	Nov 11	Bradford City	A	1-0	17,276	15
Sat	Nov 18	Arsenal	H	2-0	33,106	18
Sat	Nov 25	Chelsea	A	2-1	33,515	21
Mon	Dec 4	Sunderland	A	0-2	46,372	21
Sat	Dec 9	Manchester City	A	0-5	34,516	21
Sat	Dec 16	West Ham United	H	1-1	31,260	22
Sat	Dec 23	Charlton Athletic	A	0-1	20,043	22
Tue	Dec 26	Coventry City	H	1-2	35,704	22
Mon	Jan 1	Derby County	A	0-1	27,358	22
Sat	Jan 13	Tottenham Hotspur	H	0-0	32,290	23
Sat	Jan 20	Coventry City	A	3-1	19,174	26
Wed	Jan 31	Middlesbrough	H	2-2	34,244	27
Sat	Feb 3	Manchester City	H	0-1	67,528	27
Wed	Feb 7	Leeds United	H	2-2	34,224	28
Sat	Feb 10	Leicester City	H	2-1	30,409	31
Sat	Feb 24	Ipswich Town	A	0-2	22,220	31
Sat	Mar 3	Newcastle United	H				
Sat	Mar 17	Southampton	A				
Sat	Mar 31	West Ham United	A				
Sun	Apr 8	Manchester City	H				
Sat	Apr 14	Aston Villa	A				
Mon	Apr 16	Liverpool	H				
Sat	Apr 21	Arsenal	H				
Sat	Apr 28	Bradford City	H				
Sat	May 5	Chelsea	H				
Sat	May 19	Sunderland	A				

WORTHINGTON CUP
Wed	Sep 20	Bristol Rovers 2(1)	H	1-1	25,564	-
Wed	Sep 27	Bristol Rovers 2 (2)	A	1-1	11,046	(lost 2-4...)

FA CUP
Sat	Jan 6	Watford (Rd 3)	A	2-1	15,635	-
Sat	Jan 27	Tranmere R (Rd 4)	H	0-3	39,207	-

OFFICIAL EVERTON FC MATCHDAY PROGRAMME
Designed & Produced by TOBINDESIGN
Editorial by Mike Beddow & George Orr
Photography by Sportsphoto, Alan Whyte, Northpix and Liverpool Daily Post & Echo.
Printed by Colourplan

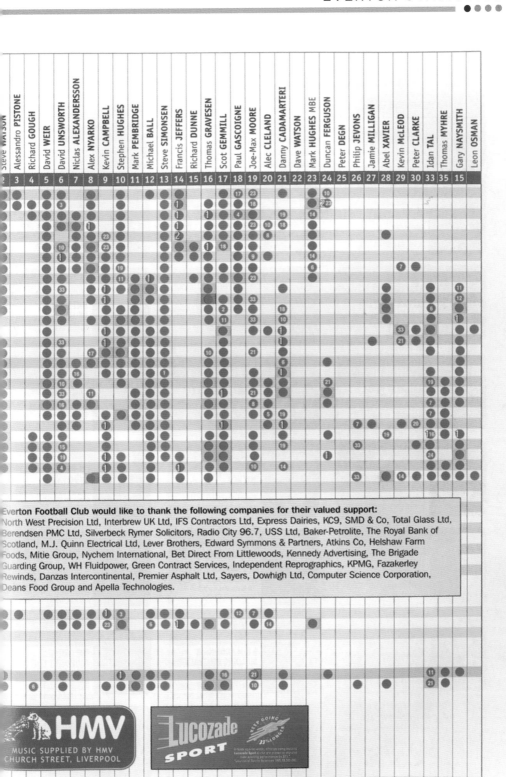

"OH COME LET US ADORE THEM - EVERTON "

The occasion of Everton's 100th year in the top flight of English football was enough cause for celebration at Goodison.

As well as a range of events and an official logo, sported on the team's strips during the 2002/03 campaign, the club released two new songs – 'No Other Team' and 'The Everton Anthem'.

Supporters were encouraged to sing along ahead of the opening game against Tottenham Hotspur, the latter written to the tune of 'Come all ye faithful'.

The turn of the 21st century signalled the death-knell for pen pal requests for Everton in the club programme – although one message did catch the eye (below), presumably related to a summer holiday meeting...

To Christmas 2003, and the club's official Merry Christmas greeting. A number of players, plus coaching staff, were asked to recall presents they had received in their childhood

● A message to Joely. Pete, who you met in Gran Canaria, is still thinking about you and would still like to get in touch. If you no longer have my details, please contact the Communications Department and they can pass them on.

SINGING THE BLUES

The brand new Everton songs, now available to purchase from all good record stores, will be sung with gusto before the kick-off at Goodison Park this afternoon! To help you along, and to make sure we're all in tune together, here are the words to 'No Other Team' and 'The Everton Anthem'.

NO OTHER TEAM

St Domingo's FC, was what we used to be
Our first match - eighteen seventy nine
Yeah we won that game
And though we changed our name
Our skill's not diminished with time.

No, no other team
Have for one hundred years reigned supreme
We're the first in the game,
To have that claim to fame
No there really is no other team.

Stanley Park was the ground
Where our birthplace is found
Priory Road, where we first made our mark
Then to Old Mere Green field
where our future was sealed
'Cos today it's called Goodison Park.

No, no other team
Have for one hundred years reigned supreme
We're the first club you see,
To make one century
And there really is no other team.

In five FA Cups we have triumphed
Nine times League Championships won
The Blue and White Army are on the march
Come on now you Everton.

No, no other team
Has legends like Lawton and Dean
Harvey, Kendall and Ball
Alex Young and yes all
Of the greats that have come in between
There really is no other team.

THE EVERTON ANTHEM

Come all ye faithful
Joyful and triumphant
For we are the People's Club on Merseyside
Come and support them
On their way to glory

Come let us adore them
Oh come let us adore them
Oh come let us adore them - Everton

Come all ye people
We are Moyses' Army
Oh come ye, oh come ye to Goodison
Come and support them
On their way to glory

Come let us adore them
Oh come let us adore them
Oh come let us adore them - Everton

Come let us adore them
Oh come let us adore them
Oh come let us adore them - Everton

Merry Christmas from Everton Football Club

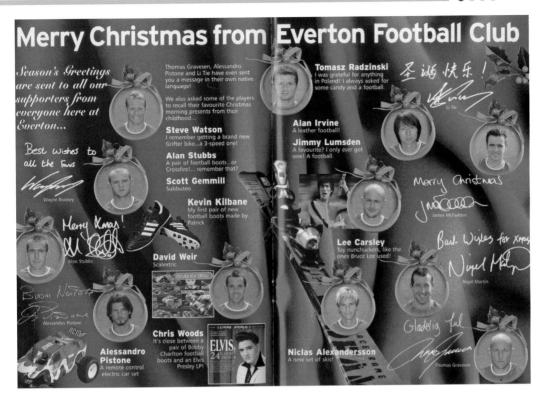

Season's Greetings are sent to all our supporters from everyone here at Everton...

Thomas Gravesen, Alessandro Pistone and Li Tie have even sent you a message in their own native language!

We also asked some of the players to recall their favourite Christmas morning presents from their childhood...

Steve Watson
I remember getting a brand new Grifter bike...a 3-speed one!

Alan Stubbs
A pair of football boots...or Crossfire!... remember that?

Scott Gemmill
Subbuteo

Kevin Kilbane
My first pair of new football boots made by Patrick

David Weir
Scalextric

Chris Woods
It's close between a pair of Bobby Charlton football boots and an Elvis Presley LP!

Alessandro Pistone
A remote control electric car set

Best wishes to all the Fans
Wayne Rooney

Alan Stubbs

Alessandro Pistone

Tomasz Radzinski
I was grateful for anything in Poland! I always asked for some candy and a football.

Alan Irvine
A leather football!

Jimmy Lumsden
A favourite? I only ever got one! A football.

Lee Carsley
Toy nunchuckers, like the ones Bruce Lee used!

Niclas Alexandersson
A new set of skis!

Li Tie

Merry Christmas
James McFadden

Nigel Martin

Thomas Gravesen

Bill Kenwright, Sir Philip Carter and Charlton Athletic Chairman, Richard Murray, celebrate the New Year by taking a sip from the Loving Cup. This wonderful piece of china was presented to every founder member of the Football League and it is the tradition at Everton to take a sip from it prior to the first home fixture of each New Year.

evertonnews

EVERTON NEWS

MOYES WINS MANAGER OF THE MONTH

David Moyes has been named the Barclays Premier League Manager of the Month for January.

The Everton boss received his award at Finch Farm on Friday after steering his side to three wins and a draw in the league.

Moyes, who last won the award in February 2009, said: "I would like to thank Barclays and the Premier League for this award but it is for the players really because they have done really well throughout the month of January."

SAHA SIGNS NEW DEAL

Striker Louis Saha has put pen to paper on a two-year contract extension.

The Frenchman's existing deal was due to expire in the summer but he will now remain with the Club until the end of the 2011/12 campaign.

"It was an easy decision," said Saha in an exclusive interview with evertonfc.com. "You always think carefully but it didn't take me long to know I wanted to stay. I have enjoyed my time here and I want to be part of the future of Everton.

"It is a pleasure and an honour to stay here. At certain stages in your career you look at where you are going and by staying at Everton I feel I am going up in my career."

HAVE YOU GOT THE GOLDEN TICKET?

Will you be one of the lucky supporters who will win hospitality for two at next Tuesday's game against Sporting Lisbon?

If you find a golden ticket inside this evening's programme, you could be watching us take on our Portuguese Europa League opponents in style.

"We had a fabulous night," said our last Golden Ticket winner, Sue Judge. "We had a great time and enjoyed every minute. It was truly a night to remember. The hospitality we received from the staff in the lounge was brilliant. We wanted to say a special thank you for making our night - meeting David Moyes and presenting the Man of the Match award to Sylvain Distin was amazing!"

Look out for a golden ticket somewhere inside this programme.

10 efc

- with, among the football-related gifts, other notable responses coming from Niclas Alexandersson ("skis"), Lee Carlsey ("toy nunchuckers") and Tomasz Radzinski ("I was grateful for anything in Poland!").

Charlton Athletic officials were beneficiaries in the first home game of 2006, with tradition dictating they take a sip from the 'Loving Cup', a piece of china presented to every founder member of the Football League.

While in February 2010 the Everton news page was dominated by David Moyes' manager of the month award and the fact that Louis Saha had signed a new contract.

'Who's the greatest of them all? Little, curly Alan Ball'

Evertonians had two last opportunities to hear Alan Ball in recent weeks. He addressed the annual Hall of Fame dinner at the Adelphi Hotel in mid-March, where he spoke passionately – unscripted as always – about his love for the club.

The following week, he was at the Crowne Plaza, speaking in his role as honorary president of the Everton Collection Charitable Trust at the eve-of-match dinner ahead of the fundraising game between Everton Former Players and Barcelona Veterans.

The reception he received at both events spoke volumes for the esteem in which he was held by Evertonians.

Quite simply, he was idolised. Ball's passionate, firebrand approach epitomised and galvanised Everton; a diminutive dynamo driving them on to new heights.

His promise was evident at an early age and he had trials with Wolves and Bolton before establishing himself at Blackpool after turning professional in May 1962.

Such was his progress, he became the youngest member of Alf Ramsey's 1966 World Cup squad, proving an inspiration in the strength-sapping period of extra-time in the gruelling final. Many of his England team-mates saw him as the man of the match.

The Blues signed him for a British record transfer fee of £110,000 just weeks later, prompting his good friend and team-mate Howard Kendall to quip: 'Everton's scouting network was legendary. They spotted Alan Ball in the World Cup final!'

After scoring on his debut – the Blues' last win at Fulham, he wrote himself into Goodison folklore with a double on his derby debut as Everton defeated Liverpool in front of a crowd of 64,318 mostly ecstatic fans.

He grabbed 17 goals in his first season with the Blues, netted 20 league goals the following season and another 16 the season after.

In 1969-70, with his midfield partnership with Howard Kendall and Colin Harvey working fluidly, he played a key role in the Blues' championship success.

In September 1970, he made Everton history by becoming the first player in the club's history to score a European Cup hat-trick as Icelandic side IB Keflavik were beaten 6-2.

Harry Catterick always said he would never sell Ball but in 1971 he did just that, accepting a new British record fee of £220,000 on the grounds that the player was losing his pace and could no longer be the goalscoring midfielder of yore.

If that was the case, Ball disguised it well, remaining a regular in the England team while starring for the Gunners and, later, Southampton.

Ironically it was against Everton that he played his last game for the Saints in October 1982.

It was a major surprise that Ball did not go on to become a successful manager. One explanation was he felt frustrated that his teams failed to match the levels of desire he showed in his own playing days.

His managerial career took in spells at clubs as varied as Philadelphia Fury and Portsmouth, also including Blackpool, Southampton, Exeter City and Manchester City.

He left Pompey after his second spell in charge in December 1999 and the following year he and four other members of the World Cup winning team were awarded the MBE for services to football. It was an award long overdue in the eyes of many.

In 2000, Everton paid their own tribute when he was named as one of the club's Millennium Giants. At the start of the 2003-04 season, to commemorate the club's 125th Anniversary, supporters were invited to compile the definitive 'Greatest Ever Everton Team' and Ball was duly selected in midfield.

In 2003 he was inducted into the English Football Hall of Fame. He won 72 England caps and the Football Association has announced that black armbands will be worn in his honour when England play Brazil in the first senior international at the new Wembley on June 1.

Away from football, he faced adversity in his personal life.

He lost his father – the biggest influence on his footballing career – when Alan senior died after a car crash in Cyprus in 1982. Into the new millennium, his wife and daughter were diagnosed with cancer within six weeks of each other.

The death of childhood sweetheart Lesley, in May 2004, after a three-year battle against ovarian cancer, hit him hard. But speaking recently he admitted to coming to terms with his losses.

Through it all, the passion for the Blues never dimmed.

Earlier this year he commented that: "Although I left Everton, Everton never left me".

As the supporters used to sing: "Who's the greatest of them all? Little, curly, Alan Ball."

Alan Ball, 2005-07

The occasion of Everton's 2000th home game in the top division, against West Ham United in 2005/06, was reason enough for a special edition programme.

It also seemed an appropriate occasion to look at the club's records during that period – many of which are likely to be beaten any time soon...

The loss of Alan Ball in April 2007 was a loss deeply felt around the football world – and Everton paid their own tribute to the World Cup winner. Arguably the club's finest post-War player, tributes were plentiful and generous – while the Manchester United programme of 2006/07 remains a sought-after edition.

STUCK ON YOU

Paul Wilkinson
His brief career has two memorable contexts. The one that the 22 year old Louth-born striker cherishes is the last minute Milk Cup winner at Goodison Park – against Everton, for Grimsby. The other memory is of scoring the winner in his first Murcey derby. Paul has already won England Under 21 caps.

THE *Daily Mirror* sticker album from 1986/87 provides a permanent reminder of Paul Wilkinson's improbable hairstyle, if you'll forgive the pun.

caught on camera >>>

It's the 1985 FA Cup final between Everton and Manchester United. While his identity might be protected, his modesty barely is. We also enjoyed the variety of headwear amongst the fans, particularly the bobble hats

EFC Autobiography

The Official Everton Autobiography is available to purchase in the Everton One and Everton Two stores, or online from evertonfc.com/publications.

The definitive story of the world's greatest football club is told by the people who contributed to its development – it's the story of Everton as seen through Royal Blue eyes, with news, reports and reaction taken from the local and national Press, from 1892 onwards.

Here we include excerpts, some which failed to make the final cut – including how Tommy Wright missed out on a cap at Swansea, and news on former Blues and Swans striker Bob Latchford.

The Official Autobiography

AUGUST 1979
GRAY FOR LATCHFORD THE NEXT MOVE?
By Charles Lambert (Liverpool Daily Post)

Bob Latchford in a swap for Andy Gray - that could be Everton manager Gordon Lee's answer to the club's goals shortage.

With Aston Villa striker Gray demanding a move, I believe Mr Lee will be among the first managers to make inquiries. And he could offer Latchford, the current England number nine, in a dramatic exchange package.

And whether that deal comes off or not, the Goodison careers of Latchford and team-mates Mike Pejic and Dave Thomas are likely to end in the near future.

All three players are believed to want away from Everton, although Mr Lee last night denied reports that they have submitted transfer requests.

Meanwhile, Everton have withdrawn from the hunt for Chelsea's Ray Wilkins. Mr Lee had talks with Wilkins yesterday, and was unable to persuade the England midfielder to move to Goodison.

"He is grateful we were interested in him, but he wants to stay with Chelsea for the time being," said Mr Lee. "It is another setback and I am very disappointed."

FEBRUARY 1974
£350,000 RECORD BUSTER
By Dave Horridge (Daily Mirror)

Everton will hoist the British record transfer fee to a staggering £350,000 today when they buy Birmingham striker Bob Latchford.

In return for the player Birmingham will get Everton midfield man Howard Kendall and left-back Archie Styles, plus £80,000 cash.

With Kendall valued at £180,000 and Styles at £90,000, the deal smashes the previous record by £100,000. That was set up 18 months ago, when Derby bought left-back David Nish from Leicester.

The 22-year-old Latchford will collect £17,500 as his share of the fee. The deal was set up a few days ago, and the parties met at a secret rendezvous near Manchester yesterday afternoon.

I understand the three players involved have agreed terms and the deal will go through today. Birmingham supporters will be shocked at the departure of a player they regard as vital to their hopes of avoiding relegation from the First Division.

In November, Latchford hit two hat-tricks in four days. Shortly afterwards Goodwin claimed he would rather be sacked than sell him.

OCTOBER 1967
FOOTBRAWL –
NOW EVERTON STAR MISSES A CAP
By Michael Charters (Liverpool Echo)

Tommy Wright, one of nine Everton players injured during Saturday's soccer brawl at Newcastle, will miss an international cap as a result.

Everton manager Harry Catterick said yesterday that Wright, who received a bad ankle knock, will be unfit to play for England's Under-23 team against Wales at Swansea on Wednesday.

Wing-half Colin Harvey, who was on reserve for England, will be unable to travel, and Howard Kendall and John Hurst – also in the England side – will have to receive treatment.

The manager added that other casualties were Morrissey, who left the field after 40 minutes; Wilson, Ball, Hunt and Young. But Mr Catterick refused to comment on the sending off of goalkeeper Gordon West, as did Everton chairman Jack Sharp.

Newcastle full-back Burton was also sent off in a rough game which Everton lost by a twice-taken penalty in the closing minutes.

Golden Vision,
EFC Autobiography, 2008-13

A regular programme feature from 2006 to 2009, the 'Golden Vision' was a fans-related section looking at cult heroes, unique photography and the increasing influence of social networking. 'YourEverton' took a look at various fans' groups - with Leon Osman the subject of this particular edition...

The EFC Autobiography, released in 2012, looked at how the history of the club was formed and reported through the years. Reports, news and articles were duly noted chronologically, and many of the subjects gave rise to rich material involving Everton's opponents on a particular matchday.

The 2012/13 Swansea City game retained a Welsh theme, with subjects including Tommy Wright's absence from a Wales v England U23 clash, plus news related to then future Swans striker Bob Latchford.

Stop Press

The big games, the European nights, the friendlies, the Zenith Data Systems Cup – a small selection of 'classic' covers and content from more unusual games

Much sought-after FA Cup final programmes from the 19th and early 20th centuries differed little from those offered by Everton and Liverpool. Littered with adverts for alcohol, tobacco, ailments and national newspapers, the 'working man' was well served ahead of 'his' glimpse of royalty.

Indeed, our 1933 cover (opposite, top left) even trumpeted the 'expert criticism' of former Sunderland legend and influential journalist Charles Buchan, set to come the way of finalists Everton and Manchester City the following Monday in the *News Chronicle*. What was apparent in the early years was the investment in colour, the extra cover price presumably absorbing the cost.

As the seasons progressed – standard for the football programme industry as a whole – publications became glossier, more substantial and more expensive than usual league and cup fixtures. Domestic cup semi-finals, held at neutral venues, also provided collectors with unique publications, often produced and designed by the host club's editorial and design teams.

The extra games caused by replays often resulted in some programmes having a 'cobbled together' feel (see Manchester City second replay programme overleaf), although some final programmes have gone down in Everton folklore – with Fred Pickering being included in the official team list ahead of the 1966 final...

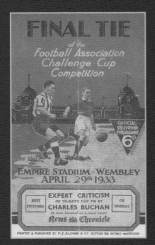

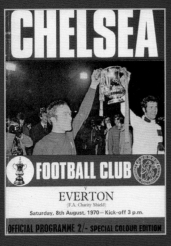

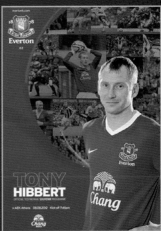

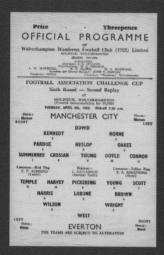

Selected covers from key games, testimonials and youth-team matches. Clockwise from above: v Manchester City (FA Cup Q-F, second replay), 1965/66; v Manchester United (FA Cup S-F), 1965/66; v West Bromwich Abion (FA Cup final), 1967/68; v Aston Villa (League Cup final), 1976/77; Aston Villa (League Cup final replay), 1976/77; v West Ham United (FA Cup S-F), 1979/80; Everton Youth v England Youth, 1977/78

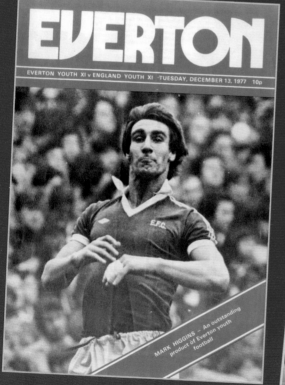

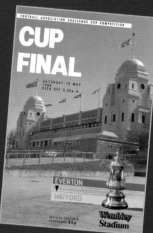

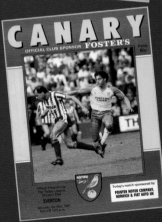

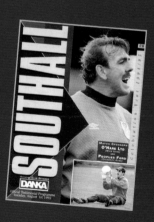

Selected covers from key games, testimonials and youth-team matches. Top row, left to right: v Watford (FA Cup final), 1983/84; v Rapid Vienna (European Cup Winners' Cup final), 1984/85; v Liverpool (FA Charity Shield), 1984/85; middle row, left to right: v Norwich City (First Division), 1986/87; v Tottenham Hotspur (FA Cup semi-final), 1994/95; v Manchester United (FA Cup final), 1994/95; bottom row, left to right: v Celtic (Neville Southall testimonial), 1995/96; v Chelsea (FA Cup final), 2008/09; v Real Betis (friendly), 2013/14

Crystal Palace, Easter Monday, Great Football Match, Notts Forest v. Dundee. Professional Cycle Races.

CRYSTAL PALACE.

Saturday, April 10th, 1897.

FINAL TIE
FOR THE
CHALLENGE CUP of the FOOTBALL ASSOCIATION.

LEFT. RIGHT.

ASTON VILLA.
Colours—Claret and Light Blue Shirts, White Knickers.

Goal.
x WHITEHOUSE.

Backs.
x SPENCER.   x EVANS.

Half-Backs.
x REYNOLDS.   x JAMES COWAN.   x CRABTREE.

Forwards.
x ATHERSMITH.   x DEVEY.   x CAMPBELL.   x WHELDON.   x JOHN COWAN.

(O)

Forwards.
x MILWARD.   x CHADWICK.   x HARTLEY.   x BELL.   x TAYLOR.

Half-Backs.
x STEWART.   x HOLT.   x BOYLE.

Backs.
x STORRIER.   x MENHAM.

Goal.
x MENHAM.

Colours—Blue Shirts, White Knickers.
EVERTON.

RIGHT. LEFT.

Referee—J. LEWIS (Lancashire). Linesmen—J. HOWCROFT (Redcar). A. SCRAGG (Crewe).
Official Programme. ONE PENNY.

Photo Prints of the Aston Villa Team, price One Penny, on Sale at the Palace this day.

SHEFFIELD WEDNESDAY

(*Colours: White Shirts, White Shorts*
White Stockings)

1. R. SPRINGETT (*Goalkeeper*)
2. W. SMITH (*Right Back*)
3. D. MEGSON (*Left Back*) Captain
4. P. EUSTACE (*Right Half*)
5. V. MOBLEY (*Centre Half*)
6. G. YOUNG (*Left Half*)
7. G. PUGH (*Outside Right*)
8. J. FANTHAM (*Inside Right*)
9. J. McCALLIOG (*Centre Forward*)
10. D. FORD (*Inside Left*)
11. J. QUINN (*Outside Left*)

EVERTON

(*Colours: Blue Shirts, White Shorts*
Blue and White Stockings)

1. G. WEST (*Goalkeeper*)
2. A. BROWN (*Right Back*)
3. R. WILSON (*Left Back*)
4. J. GABRIEL (*Right Half*)
5. B. LABONE (*Centre Half*) Captain
6. B. HARRIS (*Left Half*)
7. A. SCOTT (*Outside Right*)
8. A. YOUNG (*Inside Right*)
9. F. PICKERING (*Centre Forward*)
10. C. HARVEY (*Inside Left*)
11. D. TEMPLE (*Outside Left*)

TODAY'S OFFICIALS

REFEREE
J. K. TAYLOR
(*Wolverhampton*)

LINESMEN
W. Morris
(*Kettering, Flame Flag*)
E. D. Wallace
(*Swindon, Orange Flag*)

THE PATH TO THE FINAL

SHEFFIELD WEDNESDAY

THIRD ROUND	Reading (Away) ... ... 3–2 (Fantham 2, McCalliog)	
FOURTH ROUND	Newcastle United (Away) ... 2–1 (Dobson, McGrath o.g.)	
FIFTH ROUND	Huddersfield Town (Away) ... 2–1 (Ford, Usher)	
SIXTH ROUND	Blackburn Rovers (Away) ... 2–1 (Ford 2)	
SEMI-FINAL	Chelsea (Villa Park, Birmingham) ... 2–0 (Pugh, McCalliog)	

EVERTON

THIRD ROUND	Sunderland (Home) ... ... 3–0 (Temple, Young, Pickering)	
FOURTH ROUND	Bedford Town (Away) ... ... 3–0 (Temple 2, Pickering)	
FIFTH ROUND	Coventry (Home) ... ... 3–0 (Young, Temple, Pickering)	
SIXTH ROUND	Manchester City (Away) 0–0	
(REPLAY)	Manchester City (Home) 0–0	
(SECOND REPLAY)	Manchester City (at Wolverhampton) ... 2–0 (Temple, Pickering)	
SEMI-FINAL	Manchester United (Burnden Park, Bolton) ... 1–0 (Harvey)	

WONDERFUL PRIZES

Just a few of the fantastic prizes offered in connection with our weekly Bingo and Football competitions.

In addition to these super gifts over £1,000 in cash has to be won each week!

Why not enrol as an agent and be sure of a "dividend" every week.

● Generous Expense Allowance ● Agents Prize Scheme ● Season Ticket rebates ● Free trips to away matches.

Don't miss out – send for details today.

I am interested in becoming an agent for your *Bingo/Football tickets.
* *Delete as appropriate.*

Name ....

Address ....

Send to: Everton Promotions, Goodison Park, Liverpool 4.

Two spots from 1970s pre-season friendlies – above: 'Wonderful Prizes' on offer with Everton's weekly Bingo and Football competitions, v Nathanya Maccabi, 1971/72; opposite page: cartoon and news surrounding Bob Latchford's £10,000 goal, after reaching the magic 30 at the end of the previous season against Chelsea, v Roda JC, 1978/79

A new-look Bob Latchford receives a surprise present at the club's pre-season photo-call: an album containing pictures of all 30 goals he scored last season to win the £10,000 prize offered by the Daily Express.

The album was produced for Bob by the Everton programme team — Brian West (manager), Mike Beddow (editor) and Terry Mealey (photographer) — and handed over by Brian. All the pictures in the album were taken by Terry, who will again be on duty this season to capture match highlights for the programme.

On the left we look back to Goal No. 30 — a penalty against Chelsea in the last match of the season — and on the opposite page Everton supporter Gerard Brennan pays tribute to Bob's achievement in a splendid cartoon. Gerard, who became a season ticket holder last season, has just completed a two-year course in design, exhibition and display at the Hugh Baird College, Bootle. He lives at 166 Bedford Road, Bootle.

**THE OFFICIAL
MATCHDAY PROGRAMME BOOK**